T0257664

IET PROFESSIONAL APPLICATIONS OF COMPUTING SERIES 24

Ultrascale Computing Systems

Other volumes in this series:

Ultrascale Computing Systems

Edited by
Jesus Carretero, Emmanuel Jeannot and Albert Y. Zomaya

The Institution of Engineering and Technology

Published by The Institution of Engineering and Technology, London, United Kingdom

The Institution of Engineering and Technology is registered as a Charity in England & Wales (no. 211014) and Scotland (no. SC038698).

The Institution of Engineering and Technology
Michael Faraday House
Six Hills Way, Stevenage
Herts, SG1 2AY, United Kingdom

www.theiet.org

British Library Cataloguing in Publication Data
A catalogue record for this product is available from the British Library

ISBN 978-1-78561-833-8 (hardback)
ISBN 978-1-78561-834-5 (PDF)

Typeset in India by MPS Limited
Printed in the UK by CPI Group (UK) Ltd, Croydon

Contents

*Ariel Oleksiak, Laurent Lefevre, Pedro Alonso, Georges Da Costa,
Vincenzo De Maio, Neki Frasheri, Victor M. Garcia, Joel Guerrero,
Sebastien Lafond, Alexey Lastovetsky, Ravi Reddy Manumachu,
Benson Muite, Anne-Cecile Orgerie, Wojciech Piatek,
Jean-Marc Pierson, Radu Prodan, Patricia Stolf, Enida Sheme,
and Sebastien Varrette*

List of figures

List of tables

About the editors

Jesus Carretero is a Full Professor of Computer Architecture and Technology at Universidad Carlos III de Madrid (Spain) since 2000. In 1997 and 1998 he was a visiting scholar at the NorthWestern University of Chicago (IL, USA). His research activity is centered on high-performance computing systems, large-scale distributed systems, data-intensive computing, IoT, and real-time systems. He has participated and led several national and international research projects in these areas, founded by Madrid Regional Government, Spanish Education Ministry, and the European Union. He was Action Chair of the IC1305 COST Action "Network for Sustainable Ultrascale Computing Systems (NESUS)." He has published more than 250 papers in journals and international conferences, is an editor of several books of proceedings, and is guest editor for special issues of journals such as *International Journal of Parallel Processing*, *Cluster Computing*, and *Future Generation Computing Systems*. He has participated in many conference organization committees, and he has been General Chair of CCGRID 2017, ISPAS2016, HPCC 2011, and MUE 2012. He is a senior member of the IEEE Computer Society and a member of the ACM.

Emmanuel Jeannot is a Senior Research Scientist at INRIA Bordeaux Sud-Ouest and at the LaBRI laboratory (University of Bordeaux), France. He is the vice-chair of the NESUS COST action. From 2005 to 2006, he was a researcher at INRIA Nancy Grand-Est. In 2006, he was a visiting researcher at the University of Tennessee, ICL laboratory. From 2000 to 2005, he was an assistant professor at the Université Henry Poincaré. During the period from 2000 to 2009, he did his research at the LORIA laboratory. He got his Ph.D. and Master degree in computer science (resp. in 1996 and 1999) both from Ecole Normale Supérieur de Lyon at the LIP laboratory. His main research interests lie in parallel and high-performance computing and more precisely: process placement, topology-aware algorithms, scheduling for heterogeneous environments, data redistribution, algorithms and models for parallel machines, distributed computing software, adaptive online compression, and programming models.

Albert Y. Zomaya is the Chair Professor of High Performance Computing & Networking in the School of Information Technologies, University of Sydney, and he also serves as the Director of the Centre for Distributed and High Performance Computing. He published *more than* 600 scientific papers and articles and is author, co-author, or editor of *more than 20 books*. He is the Founding Editor in Chief of the *IEEE Transactions on Sustainable Computing* and serves as an associate editor for more than 20 leading journals. He served as an Editor-in-Chief for the *IEEE Transactions on Computers* (2011–2014). He is the recipient of the IEEE Technical Committee on Parallel Processing Outstanding Service Award (2011), the IEEE Technical Committee on Scalable Computing Medal for Excellence in Scalable Computing (2011), the IEEE Computer Society Technical Achievement Award (2014), and the ACM MSWIM Reginald A. Fessenden Award (2017). He is a Chartered Engineer, a Fellow of AAAS, IEEE, and IET. His interests are in the areas of parallel and distributed computing and complex systems.

List of authors

Francisco Almeida	Universidad de La Laguna, Spain
Pedro Alonso	Universitat Politecnica de Valencia, Spain
Emanouil Atanassov	Bulgarian Academy of Sciences, Bulgaria
Jorge G. Barbosa	Faculdade de Engenharia da Universidade do Porto, Portugal
Vicente Blanco	Universidad de La Laguna, Spain
Xavier Besseron	University of Luxembourg, Luxembourg
Angelos Bilas	Institute of Computer Science, FORTH (ICS), Greece
Pascal Bouvry	University of Luxembourg,Luxembourg
Alberto Cabrera	Universidad de La Laguna, Spain
Jesus Carretero	University Carlos III, Madrid, Spain
Raimondas Čiegis	Vilnius Gediminas Technical University, Lithuania
Toni Cortes	BSC and Universitat Politecnica de Catalunya, Spain
Georges Da Costa	University of Toulouse, France
Vincenzo De Maio	Vienna University of Technology, Austria
Juan C. Díaz-Martín	University of Extremadura, School of Technology, Spain
Neki Frashëri	Polytechnic University of Tirana, Albania
Victor M. Garcia	Universitat Politecnica de Valencia, Spain
Javier Garcia-Blas	University Carlos III of Madrid, Spain
Juan L. García-Zapata	University of Extremadura, Spain
Pilar González-Férez	University of Murcia, Spain
Stanislav Harizanov	Vilnius University, Lithuania
Abdallah A.Z.A. Ibrahim	University of Luxembourg, Luxembourg
Matthias Janetschek	University of Innsbruck, Austria
Emmanuel Jeannot	INRIA, Université de Bourdeaux, France
Rima Kriauzien	Vilnius University, Lithuania
Pierre Kuonen	University of Applied Sciences of Western Switzerland, Switzerland
Sebastien Lafond	Åbo Akademi University, Finland
Alexey L. Lastovetsky	University College Dublin, Ireland
João Leitão	Universidade Nova de Lisboa, Portugal
Ravi Reddy Manumachu	University College of Dublin, Ireland
Svetozar Margenov	Bulgarian Academy of Sciences, Bulgaria
Fabrizio Marozzo	DIMES, University of Calabria, Rende, Italy

Anne-Cécile Orgerie	Univ. Rennes, INRIA, CNRS, IRISA, France
Anastasios Papagiannis	Institute of Computer Science, FORTH (ICS), Greece
Jean-Marc Pierson	University of Toulouse, France
Radu Prodan	University of Klagenfurt, Austria
Anna Queralt	Barcelona Supercomputing Center (BSC), Spain
Thomas Rauber	University Bayreuth, Germany
Juan A. Rico-Gallego	University of Extremadura, Spain
Gudula Rünger	Chemnitz University of Technology, Germany
Giorgos Saloustros	Institute of Computer Science, FORTH (ICS), Greece
Pablo San Segundo	Universidad Politecnica de Madrid, Spain
Enida Sheme	Polytechnic University of Tirana, Albania
Ali Shoker	HASLab, INESC TEC and University of Minho, Portugal
Leonel Sousa	INESC-ID, Universidade de Lisboa, Portugal.
Adimas Starikovičius	Bulgarian Academy of Sciences, Bulgaria
Patricia Stolf	University of Toulouse, France
Sandor Szabo	University of Pecs, Hungary
Domenico Talia	DIMES, University of Calabria, Rende, Italy
Tuan Anh Trinh	Corvinus University of Budapest, Hungary
Paolo Trunfio	DIMES, University of Calabria, Rende, Italy
Muhammad Umer Wasim	University of Luxembourg, Luxembourg
Albert van der Linde	Universidade Nova de Lisboa, Portugal
Peter Van Roy	Université Catholique de Louvain, Belgium
Sebastien Varrette	University of Luxembourg, Luxembourg
Bogdan Zavalnij	University of Pecs, Hungary

Preface

The ever-increasing presence of digital data and computers requires pushing for new levels of scalability and sustainability of computing systems in order to address the huge data and processing requirements of the near future. Ultrascale computing systems (UCSs) are a solution. Envisioned as large-scale complex systems joining parallel and distributed computing systems, which can be located at multiple sites and cooperate to provide the required resources and performance to the users, they could extend individual systems to provide the resources needed. UCSs are expected to be two to three orders of magnitude larger than today systems, including systems with unprecedented amounts of heterogeneous hardware, lines of source code, numbers of users, and volumes of data.

The goal of this book is to present important research aspects to advance toward UCSs, following the results of the research work in the COST Action IC 1305 Network for Sustainable Ultrascale Computing (NESUS), held from 2014 to 2018. NESUS COST Action brought together scientists and teams from more than 75 research institutions, belonging to 35 EU countries, and 10 non-EU countries, including leading European researchers on the software stack for high-performance computing and distributed systems. NESUS Action followed on a cross-community approach of exploring system software and applications for enabling a sustainable development of future high-scale computing platforms.

The book is composed of seven chapters covering aspects related to programming models, runtimes, resilience, data management, energy efficiency, and applications. Globally, the book shows that UCS development requires research and development of novel domain-specific, but interoperable tools to enable high productivity of human-computer interaction, leading toward robust solutions through multi-domain cooperative approaches using energy efficient hardware–software co-design principles.

The book is oriented toward those professionals and researchers interested in the large-scale parallel and distributed systems area, especially to those interested in the software stack. It could be used as an introduction to the area, as it covers the most important areas, presenting applied research works. The book identifies and shows mid-term research challenges that are still to be solved. Thus, it could be used also by researchers starting their work in the area.

Jesus Carretero
Department of Computer Science and Engineering,
University Carlos III of Madrid, Madrid, Spain
Emmanuel Jeannot
INRIA Bordeaux Sud-Ouest, France
Albert Zomaya
School of Information Technologies, University of Sydney, Australia

Acknowledgments

This publication is based upon work from COST Action IC1305 "Network for Sustainable Ultrascale Computing" (NESUS), supported by COST (European Cooperation in Science and Technology).

COST (European Cooperation in Science and Technology) is a funding agency for research and innovation networks. COST Actions help to connect research initiatives across Europe and enable scientists to grow their ideas by sharing them with their peers. This boosts their research, career, and innovation.

More information can be found at www.cost.eu.

EUROPEAN COOPERATION
IN SCIENCE & TECHNOLOGY

Funded by the Horizon 2020 Framework Programme
of the European Union

List of acronyms

ABFT	Algorithm-based fault tolerance
AC	Alternate current
AEA	Agent-based evolutionary algorithm
AES	Advance encryption standard
AIK	Attestation identity key
AJAX	Asynchronous JavaScript and XML
ALU	Arithmetic logic unit
AMI	Amazon machine image
ANTLR	ANother tool for language recognition
API	Application programming interface
AST	Abstract syntax tree
BA	Byzantine Agreement
BFT	Byzantine fault tolerance
BGP	Byzantine generals' problem
BNF	Backus-Naur form
BSP	Bulk-synchronous parallel model
CA	Certificate authority
CAP	Consistency, availability, and partition
CBC	Cipher block chaining
CC	Cloud computing
CEA	Cellular evolutionary algorithm
CFB	Cipher feedback
CFG	Context-free grammar
CFL	Context-free language
CLAtse	Constraint-logic-based attack searcher
COST	European Cooperation in Science & Technology
CPU	Central process unit
CRC	Cyclic redundancy check
CRDT	Conflict-free replicated data types
CRTM	Core root of trust for measurement
CSC	Computer science and communications
CTR	CounTeR
DAG	Direct acyclic graph
DDoS	Distributed denial of service
DIW	Data-intensive workflows

DES	Data encryption standard
dBFT	delegated Byzantine fault tolerance
DCI	Distributed computing infrastructure
DFA	Deterministic finite automata
DFT	Discrete Fourier transform
DLT	Distributed ledger technologies
DMCF	Data mining Cloud framework
DOE	U.S Department of Energy
DoS	Denial of service
DPoS	Delegated proof-of-stake
DSL	Domain-specific language
DGVCS	Desktop grid and volunteer computing system
DVFS	Dynamic voltage and frequency scaling
EA	Evolutionary algorithm
EBNF	Extended BNF
EBS	Elastic bloc store
EC	Eventual consistency
ECB	Electronic codeBook
ECMA	European Computer Manufacturer's Association
EC	Elliptic curve
ECU	Energy communication unit
EK	Endorsement key
ET	Expression tree
FAI	Fully automatic installation
FBA	Federated Byzantine Agreement
FC	Fiber channel
FS	File system
FPGA	Field programmable gate array
FTE	Full-time equivalent
GA	Genetic algorithm
GC	Grid computing
GEP	Gene expression programming
GP	Genetic programming
GPU	Graphics processing unit
GRUB	GRand unified bootloader
HaaS	Hardware as a service
HDD	Hard disk drive
HLPSL	High-level protocols specification language
HMAC	Hash message authentication code
HPC	High-performance computing
HPCC	HPC challenge
HPL	High-performance linpack
HPVZ	High-performance virtual zone
HT	Hyper-threading

IB	InfiniBand
IaaS	Infrastructure-as-a-service
ICT	Information and communications technology
ICTs	Information and communications technologies
IDS	Intrusion detection system
IF	Intermediate format
IRP	Integrity reporting protocol
ISP	Internet service provider
KV	Key-value
KVM	Kernel-based virtual machine
LAN	Local area network
LCSB	Luxembourg Centre for Systems Biomedicine
LFSR	Linear feedback shift register
LUN	Logical unit number
LVM	Logical volume manager
MAS	Multi-agent system
MBF	Mean best fitness
MBR	Master boot record
MCT	Minimum completion time
MD5	Message-digest algorithm 5
MDS	Meta-data server
MIC	Many integrated core architecture
MITM	Man in the middle
MKL	Intel® Math Kernel Library
MOEA	Multi-objective evolutionary algorithm
MPI	Message passing interface
MPP	Massively parallel processor
MPS	Minimum percentage supply
MPSS	Massively parallel signature sequencing
MWRE	Manycore workflow runtime engine
NESUS	Network for sustainable ultrascale computing systems
NFA	Non-deterministic finite automata
NFS	Network file system
NIST	National Institute of Standards and Technology
NNSA	National Nuclear Security Administration
NSA	National Security Agency
NSF	National Science Foundation
NUMA	Non-uniform memory access
OCCI	Open cloud computing interface
OFB	Output feedBack
OFMC	On-the-fly model-checker
OO	Object oriented
OS	Operating system
OSS	Object storage servers

OST	Object storage target
P2P	Peer-to-peer
PaaS	Platform-as-a-service
PAPI	Performance application programming interface
PBFT	Practical Byzantine Fault Tolerance
PCC	Proof carrying code
PCR	Platform configuration register
PDE	Partial differential equations
PDU	Power distribution unit
PFA	Principal factor analysis
PGP	Pretty good privacy
PI	Principal investigator
PIPS	Automatic parallelizer and code transformation framework
PKI	Public-key infrastructure
PM	Physical machine
PoA	Proof-of-authority
PoC	Proof-of-cooperation
PoH	Proof-of-hold
PoI	Proof-of-importance
PoMAS	Proof-of-minimum aged stake
PoR	Proof-of-retrievability
PoS	Proof-of-stake
PoST	Proof-of-stake/time
PoSV	Proof-of-stake velocity
PoU	Proof-of-use
PoW	Proof-of-work
PoWeight	Proof-of-weight
PRAM	Parallel random access machine
PRNG	Pseudo-random number generator
PUE	Power usage efficiency
QoS	Quality of service
RAID	Redundant array of independent disks
RAM	Random access memory
RBAC	Role-based access control
RSA	Rivest Shamir Adleman
RTM	Root of trust for measurement
RTR	Root of trust for reporting
RTS	Root of trust for storage
SEM	Structural equation modeling
Sec-aaS	Security as a service
SHA	Secure hash algorithm
SLA	Service level agreement
SRK	Storage root key
SaaS	Software-as-a-service

SPSS	Statistical Analysis Software Package
SVM	Support vector machine
TA4SP	Tree automata-based automatic approximations for the analysis of security protocols
TBB	Trusted building blocks
TCCP	Trusted cloud computing platform
TCG	Trusted computing group
TCRR	TPM-based certification of a remote resource
TC	Trusted computing
TCO	Total cost of ownership
TOCTOU	Time of check time of use
TPM	Trusted platform module
UCS	Ultrascale computing system
UL	University of Luxembourg
VLAN	Virtual local area network
VMI	Virtual machine image
VMM	Virtual machine manager
VM	Virtual machine
WEP	Workflow execution plan

Chapter 1

Introduction

Jesus Carretero[1], Pierre Kuonen[2], Radu Prodan[3], and Leonel Sousa[4]

With the spread of the Internet, applications and web-based services, distributed computing infrastructures, local parallel systems, and the availability of huge amounts of dispersed data, software-dependent systems will be more and more connected, more and more networked, leading to the creation of supersystems. The phrase ultrascale computing systems (UCSs) refers to this type of IT supersystems. UCSs are complex large-scale ecosystems aggregating high-performance parallel and distributed computing infrastructures. These systems provide to the end user intrinsically heterogeneous solutions, located at multiple sites and capable of delivering tremendous performance boosts. They are indispensable to applications offering several orders of magnitude increase in the size of data and in the computing power relative to today's existing conventional technologies. However, to really speak of UCS, we must consider several orders of magnitude increase in the size of data, in the computing power and in the network complexity relative to what is existing now.

By making explicit the characteristics of UCS, we better understand to which extent these systems are different from what exists today. The challenges that sustainable UCS posed require a change in perspective. We need to replace the satisfaction of requirements using traditional approaches based on rational top-down engineering by the orchestration of complex, decentralized systems. Moreover, building sustainable UCSs requires researching the entire stack from a holistic perspective to support them. Hardware, software, and middleware layers need to be jointly investigated to provide these large-scale distributed computing infrastructures with an ever-higher number of networked local parallel systems for efficient handling of the huge amounts of dispersed data.

This book is a result of the scientific cooperation held in a European Concerted Research Action, designated as COST Action IC1305: Network for Sustainable Ultrascale Computing (NESUS) [5]. The framework and the action are briefly described below.

[1] Department of Computer Science and Engineering, University Carlos III of Madrid, Spain
[2] University of Applied Sciences of Western Switzerland, Switzerland
[3] Institut für Informationstechnologie, Alpen-Adria Universitat Klagenfurt, Austria
[4] INESC-ID and Instituto Superior Técnico (IST), Universidade de Lisboa, Portugal

1.1   European COST program

COST—European Cooperation in Science and Technology— is an intergovernmental framework aimed at facilitating the collaboration and networking of scientists and researchers at the European level. It was established in 1971 by 19 member countries and currently includes 35 member countries across Europe, and Israel as a cooperating state.

COST funds pan-European, bottom-up networks of scientists and researchers across all science and technology fields. These networks, called "COST Actions," promote international coordination of nationally funded research.

By fostering the networking of researchers at an international level, COST enables break-through scientific developments leading to new concepts and products, thereby contributing to strengthening Europe's research and innovation capacities.

COST's mission focuses in particular on:

- Building capacity by connecting high-quality scientific communities throughout Europe and worldwide;
- Providing networking opportunities for early career investigators;
- Increasing the impact of research on policy makers, regulatory bodies, and national decision makers as well as the private sector.

Through its inclusiveness, COST supports the integration of research communities, leverages national research investments, and addresses issues of global relevance.

Every year thousands of European scientists benefit from being involved in COST Actions, allowing the pooling of national research funding to achieve common goals.

As a precursor of advanced multidisciplinary research, COST anticipates and complements the activities of European Union (EU) Framework Programs, constituting a "bridge" toward the scientific communities of emerging countries. In particular, COST Actions are also open to participation by non-European scientists coming from neighbor countries (for example, Albania, Algeria, Armenia, Azerbaijan, Belarus, Egypt, Georgia, Jordan, Lebanon, Libya, Moldova, Montenegro, Morocco, the Palestinian Authority, Russia, Syria, Tunisia, and Ukraine) and from a number of international partner countries.

COST's budget for networking activities has traditionally been provided by successive EU RTD Framework Programs. COST is currently executed by the European Science Foundation (ESF) through the COST Office on a mandate by the European Commission, and the framework is governed by a Committee of Senior Officials (CSO) representing all its 35 member countries.

More information about COST is available at www.cost.eu. In particular, the COST Vademecum provides all the administrative and financial rules with respect to the management and implementation of COST Actions and associated activities. The COST Vademecum is a legally binding document approved by the ESF and follows the rules established by the CSO.

1.2 COST Action IC1305—Network for sustainable ultrascale systems (NESUS)

NESUS ran for the past four years, starting in 2014. Its main objective was to collaboratively rethink the development of current system software toward scalable computing systems to contribute to a future sustainable growth and to improve coordination of efforts between complementary communities. While the scientific community supports the emergence of Exascale systems, companies and researchers are engaged in efforts of scaling data centers and system software to meet the requirements of cloud applications and services. There is already some level of cross-domain interaction, for example, in high-performance computing (HPC) in clouds or on the adoption of distributed programming paradigms such as Map-Reduce for scientific applications. However, a stronger cooperation between HPC and distributed systems communities for the construction of ultrascale systems is of utmost importance.

Thus, NESUS Action followed on a cross-community approach of exploring system software and applications for enabling a sustainable development of future high-scale computing platforms. In detail, the Action work was focused in the following scientific tasks:

- First, the current state of the art on sustainability in large-scale systems has been studied. The Action strives for continuous learning by looking for synergies among HPC, distributed systems, and big data communities in cross cutting aspects such as programmability, scalability, resilience, energy efficiency, and data management.
- Second, the Action explores new programming paradigms, runtimes, and middleware to increase the productivity, scalability, and reliability of parallel and distributed programming.
- Third, as failures will be more frequent in ultrascale systems, the Action looks for new approaches of continuous running in the presence of failures, trying to find synergies between resilient schedulers that handle errors reactively or proactively, monitoring and assessment of failures, and malleable applications that can adapt their resource usage at runtime.
- Fourth, future scalable systems will require sustainable data management for addressing the predicted exponential growth of digital information. The Action explores synergistic approaches from traditionally separated communities to reform the handling of the whole data life cycle, in particular, restructure the Input/Output (I/O) stack, advance predictive and adaptive data management, and improve data locality.
- Fifth, as energy is a major limitation for the design of ultrascale infrastructures, the Action has addressed energy efficiency of ultrascale systems by investigating and promoting novel metrics for energy monitoring, profiling, and modeling in ultrascale components and applications, energy-aware resource management, and hardware/software co-design.
- Finally, the Action has identified applications, high-level algorithms, and services amenable to ultrascale systems and investigated the redesign and reprogramming

efforts needed for applications to efficiently exploit ultrascale platforms, while providing sustainability.

NESUS COST action brought together scientists and teams from more than 75 research institutions, belonging to 35 EU countries and 10 non-EU countries, including leading European researchers on the software stack for high-performance computing and distributed systems. All these people have worked intensively together to achieve the main objectives defined in the initial proposal. The work was organized and carried out in six main working groups (WGs), encompassing the main scientific areas of the action.

WG1 was devoted to the state-of-the-art and continuous learning with a predominant focus on hardware platforms and software stack for very large-scale systems. It gathered experience and knowledge about the software stack of large-scale systems and delivered the roadmap to achieve sustainable UCSs [6]. The activity of WG1 and the produced results were useful and used as input by all other WGs.

WG2, devoted to programming models and runtimes, promoted new sustainable programming and execution models, exploring synergies among emerging programming models and runtime environments for HPC, distributed systems, and big data management.

WG3 targeted performance of modern continuously evolving platforms, while providing resilience and fault-tolerant mechanisms to tackle the increasing probability of failures throughout the entire software stack.

WG4 studied the data management lifecycle on scalable architectures combining HPC and distributed computing. This is crucial for these systems to cope with the exponential growth and complexity of digital information. These include challenges such as scaling I/O stack, exposure and exploitation of data locality, energy efficient data management, and scalability of big data applications and analytics.

WG5 addressed the issue of energy efficiency as the main limiting factor in the design of ultrascale systems. New metrics, programming methods, analysis techniques, frameworks, and tools have been explored by considering energy as a primary non-functional parameter alongside performance, resilience, and quality of service (QoS).

WG6 identified, designed, and adapted algorithms and applications that require and can benefit from such complex ultrascale systems and services. This has been done for various domains, including earth sciences, astrophysics, physics and chemistry, material sciences, biology and life sciences, health science, high-energy physics, fluid dynamics, as well as social, financial, and industrial sciences.

1.3 Contents of the book

This book on sustainable ultrascale computing encompasses and gathers the experience and results achieved by NESUS COST Action and delivered by several individual research teams across various WGs. The topics covered in this book are organized into seven chapters. After this first introductory chapter and an overview of the book, the next five chapters follow the organization of the WGs, while the last chapter draws the conclusions.

Chapter 2 focuses on programming models and execution environments. The objective is not only to facilitate scaling and performance extraction on evolving ultra-scale platforms, but also to provide resilience and fault-tolerance mechanisms to cope with increasing probability of failures across the entire software stack. This chapter shows that the current wall between runtime and application models leads to most of the problems faced in UCSs. The chapter has five sections. Section 2.1 describes methods, facilities, and tools for building performance and energy models, with the goal of aiding in the design, development, and tuning of data-parallel and task-parallel applications running on complex heterogeneous parallel platforms. Section 2.2 presents a compiler and runtime environment for executing scientific workflows, originally designed for loosely coupled distributed computing infrastructures (such as Grids and Clouds) on tightly coupled shared memory many-core architectures. Section 2.3 introduces recent advances in edge computing that makes the coordination of edge networks synchronization-free and convergent, addressing the main application challenges in data management and communication aspects. The section also provides convenient runtime environments for different categories of edge computing scenarios. Section 2.4 presents a specific work on spectral graph partitioning for process placement on heterogeneous platforms extended in two directions. The chapter concludes with Section 2.5 highlighting several research directions, topics, and challenges that need to be pursued by the community to deal with the programming and runtime complexity of UCSs.

Chapter 3 tackles the challenge of resilience and fault tolerance in UCSs, considering both technical and legal aspects. This chapter reviews the general concepts of faults, fault tolerance, and robustness and details the main approaches suitable for large-scale HPC systems. It highlights opportunities and challenges, particularly in terms of hardware, network, and message transmission resilience. It presents new data structures based on distributed general ledger technology as a new field worth further investigations for large-scale experiments and validations. The chapter contains three sections. Section 3.1 reviews the basic notions of faults, fault tolerance, and robustness. It proposes applications and implementations for UCSs and highlights novel challenges and opportunities linked to the development of modern distributed-ledger technologies. Section 3.2 covers regulation compliance aspects to ensure the desired level of reliability, expected to be of paramount importance in large-scale computing platforms such as UCSs. Finally, Section 3.3 concludes the chapter and provides important future directions and perspectives related to resilience and fault tolerance in UCSs.

Chapter 4 starts by highlighting why data storage and management are key challenges for ultrascale computing, exemplified further through three techniques. Section 4.1 presents Tucana, a novel key-value store designed to work with fast storage devices such as Solid State Drives (SSDs), advancing the idea that ultrascale computing requires new abstractions to store data. Section 4.2 presents Hercules and its benefits of integrating a data mining cloud framework as an alternative to a classical parallel file system, enabling the execution of data-intensive applications in cloud environments. Finally, Section 4.3 elaborates on the idea of conflict-free replicated data types as a methodology that helps implementing basic types, replicated without the overhead of synchronization on the critical path of data update. Section 4.4 summarizes the chapter and concludes with an outlook to future challenges in data management techniques for ultrascale systems.

Chapter 5 addresses the issue of energy efficiency as a primary metric for designing UCSs, exploring the establishment and research of new metrics, analysis methodologies, frameworks, and tools in this direction. The chapter puts emphasis to the idea of "energy complexity," reflecting the synergies between energy efficiency and QoS, resilience, and performance. In doing so, it analyzes the computation power, the communication and data sharing power, the data access power, and algorithms for reducing the energy consumption. The chapter is organized into six sections. Section 5.1 focuses first on modeling energy consumption of physical data center nodes providing models for the component with the highest power draw such as CPU, RAM, I/O, network, and cooling systems. Afterward, it focuses on modeling the parameters affecting the data center runtime, such as workload and computational resource management. Section 5.2 reviews important examples of renewable energy modeling, such as solar power model, wind power model, and renewable quantity model, and presents an algorithm to schedule tasks in this context. Section 5.3 represents an introduction to data center cooling and introduces the main technologies and problems to be overcome it in future UCSs. Section 5.4 provides an analysis of the total cost of ownership of a medium-sized internal HPC university facility operated at the University of Luxembourg since 2007. This cost is then compared to the investment to run the same platform (and workload) on a competitive cloud infrastructure provider. Section 5.5 presents an experimental case study of performance and energy analysis (including a functional prediction model). This study was performed on a matrix multiplication algorithm running on a heterogeneous server with three different devices: a multi-core processor, an NVIDIA Tesla GPU, and an Intel Xeon Phi coprocessor. Section 5.6 represents a summary for future challenges in the area of energy consumption and efficiency for ultrascale systems.

Chapter 6 identifies and presents applications in need of ultrascale computing. This is the case, for example, for scientific simulations of larger problems in a reasonable time. It discusses how to rewrite or adapt them to make usage of this new platform, integrating the techniques and methods developed in the previous chapters. Inversion of geophysical anomalies and massive parallelization of the maximum clique problem are examples of applications considered in this chapter, taking advantage of the UCSs. The chapter is organized into six sections. Section 6.1 section presents analytical models that capture the power and energy behavior of different application classes and proposes novel metrics such as energy-delay product that captures their energy efficiency, such as the energy-delay product. Section 6.2 presents five different parallel numerical algorithms for the numerical solution of problems with fractional powers of elliptic operators. The first four of them relying on transformations of the original non-local problem into well-known local partial differential equation problems introducing an additional space dimension. Section 6.3 describes scalability results for a modified and simple relaxation algorithm for the three-dimensional inversion of gravity anomalies on an HPC of the Bulgarian Academy of Sciences. The need of ultrascale computing to realize high-resolution inversions for engineering works has been confirmed by this study. Section 6.4 describes k-clique problem as a representative combinatorial optimization problem, analyzing the possibility of using different sub-chromatic methods to divide it into sub-problems appropriate for massive parallelization in ultrascale systems. Section 6.5 concludes the chapter with an outlook into future challenges related to application design and engineering for ultrascale systems.

Finally, Chapter 7 draws the conclusions of the work developed in the NESUS COST Action and reported in this book, highlighting the need of supporting the evolution of ultrascale systems toward on-demand computing across highly diverse environments. This requires research and development of novel domain-specific but interoperable tools to enable high productivity of human–computer interaction, leading toward robust solutions through multi-domain cooperative approaches using energy-efficient hardware–software co-design principles.

Chapter 2

Programming models and runtimes

Georges Da Costa[1], Alexey L. Lastovetsky[2], Jorge G. Barbosa[3], Juan C. Díaz-Martín[4], Juan L. García-Zapata[4], Matthias Janetschek[5], Emmanuel Jeannot[6], João Leitão[7], Ravi Reddy Manumachu[2], Radu Prodan[8], Juan A. Rico-Gallego[4], Peter Van Roy[9], Ali Shoker[10], and Albert van der Linde[7]

Several millions of execution flows will be executed in ultrascale computing systems (UCS), and the task for the programmer to understand their coherency and for the runtime to coordinate them is unfathomable. Moreover, related to UCS large scale and their impact on reliability, the current static point of view is not more sufficient. A runtime cannot consider to restart an application because of the failure of a single node as statically several nodes will fail every day. Classical management of these failures by the programmers using checkpoint restart is also too limited due to the overhead at such a scale.

Emerging programming models that facilitate the task of scaling and extracting performance on continuous evolving platforms while providing resilience and fault-tolerant mechanisms to tackle the increasing probability of failures throughout the whole software stack are needed to achieve scale handling (optimal usage of resources, faults), improve programmability, adaptation to rapidly changing underlying computing architecture, data-centric programming models, resilience, and energy efficiency.

One key element on the ultrascale front is the necessity of new sustainable programming and execution models in the context of rapid underlying computing

[1] IRIT, University Paul Sabatier Toulouse, France
[2] University College Dublin, Ireland
[3] Faculdade de Engenharia da Universidade do Porto, Portugal
[4] School of Technology, University of Extremadura, Spain
[5] Institute of Computer Science, University of Innsbruck, Austria
[6] INRIA Bourdeaux Sud-Ouest, LaBRI, Université de Bourdeaux, France
[7] Universidade Nova de Lisboa, Portugal
[8] Institute of Information Technology, University of Klagenfurt, Austria
[9] Université Catholique de Louvain, Belgium
[10] HASLab, INESC TEC and University of Minho, Portugal

architecture changing. There is a need to explore synergies among emerging programming models and runtimes from high-performance computing (HPC), distributed systems, and big data management communities. To improve the programmability of future systems, the main changing factor will be the substantially higher levels of concurrency, asynchrony, failures, and heterogeneous architectures.

UCS need new sustainable programming and execution models, suitable in the context of rapidly changing underlying computing architecture, as described in [7]. Advances are to be expected at three levels: innovative programming models with a higher level abstraction of the hardware; breakthrough for more efficient runtimes at large scale; and cooperation between the programming models and runtime levels.

Furthermore, all the programming ecosystem must evolve. A large number of scientific applications are built on the message passing paradigm which needs a global point of view during the programming phase and usually requires global synchronization during execution. But even at lower granularity, classical libraries must evolve. As an example, a large number of scientists use the linear algebra Basic Linear Algebra Subprograms (BLAS) libraries for their optimized behavior on current supercomputers. Improving the performance of this library on UCS would prove largely beneficial.

This chapter explores programming models and runtimes required to facilitate the task of scaling and extracting performance on continuously evolving platforms, while providing resilience and fault-tolerant mechanisms to tackle the increasing probability of failures throughout the whole software stack. However, currently no programming solution exists that satisfies all these requirements. Therefore, new programming models and languages are required toward this direction. The whole point of view on application will have to change. As we will show, the current wall between runtime and application models leads to most of these problems. Programmers will need new tools but also a new way to assess their programs. Also, data will be a key concept around which failure-tolerant high number of micro-threads will be generated using high-level information by adaptive runtime. One complex element comes from the difficulty to test these approaches as UCS systems are not yet available. Most of the following explorations are extrapolated to the UCS scale but only actually proven a currently existing infrastructure.

The complexity of UCS computing architecture integrating in a hierarchical heterogeneous way multicore CPUs and various accelerators makes many traditional approaches to the development of performance and energy-efficient applications ineffective. New sustainable approaches based on accurate and sustainable application-level performance and energy models have a great potential to improve the performance and energy efficiency of applications and create a solid basis for the emerging UCS programming tools and runtimes. Section 2.1 covers this topic by describing accurate models of the hardware and software usable during the design phase, but also means of reasoning on these models. With these tools, it becomes possible to adapt and finely tune applications during the design phase to run efficiently on large-scale heterogeneous platforms.

Optimizing UCS usage is difficult due to a large number of possible use-cases. In particular ones such as Scientific workflow, it becomes possible to use a dedicated abstraction. As scientific workflow scheduling for UCS is a major challenge, the impact of proposing a particular abstraction along with dedicated runtime harnessing the particularities of this abstraction leads to a high improvement of the efficiency of using a UCS. The approaches to solve this challenge are covered in Section 2.2. In this section, both the *Abstract part* (linked with the design and programming of the workflow) and the *Concrete part* (linked with its actual scheduling and execution) are described. This specific high-level abstraction shows that link between programming models and runtime helps to simplify the task of programmers to harness the power of the underlying large-scale heterogeneous systems.

With the emergence of UCS, a new computing revolution is coming: edge computing. Instead of harnessing computing power directly from large-scale data centers, a new proposal comes from the possibility to interconnect and coordinate a large number of distributed computing nodes. Due to the explosion of Internet of Things (IoT) applications, the aggregated edge computing power is increasing extremely fast. These two systems (Edge and UCS) share the difficulty to manage a large number of distributed execution flows in a dynamic and heterogeneous environment. These similarities are explored in Section 2.3 where key elements of programming models and runtime for large-scale edge computing are explored.

Due to the scale of UCS, even classical management operation of the platform becomes complex. As an example, Section 2.5 shows how a simple operation such as graph partitioning becomes complex at a large scale. This operation is central in the management of a platform as it is needed to minimize communication between nodes when used for placing the tasks. In this section, several challenges are addressed such as the scale but also the heterogeneity of tasks, computing nodes and networking infrastructure.

This chapter concludes with a description of the main global challenges linked to programming models, runtimes and the link between these two as described in the NESUS roadmap [6].

2.1 Using performance and energy models for ultrascale computing applications

Ultrascale systems, including HPC, distributed computing and big data management platforms, will demand a huge investment in heterogeneous computing and communication equipment. Ensuring the availability of current and future social, enterprise and scientific applications with efficient and reliable execution on these platforms remains nowadays an outstanding challenge. Indeed, reducing their power footprint while still achieving high-performance has been identified as a leading constraint in this goal. Model-driven design and development of optimal software solutions should play a critical role in that respect.

Energy consumption is one of the main limiting factors for designing and deploying ultrascale systems.

Using monitoring and measurement data, performance and energy models contribute to quantify and gain insights into the performance and power consumption effects of system components and their interactions, including both hardware and the full software stack. Analysis of the information provided by the models is then used for running applications and predicting its behavior under different conditions, mainly at a large scale.

This chapter describes methods, facilities, and tools for building performance and energy models, with the goal of aiding in the design, development, and tuning of data-parallel and task-parallel applications running on complex heterogeneous parallel platforms.

2.1.1 Terminology

In this section, we describe the various terms related to power and energy predictive models used in this work.

There are two types of power consumptions in a component: dynamic power and static power. Dynamic power consumption is caused by the switching activity in the component's circuits. Static power is the power consumed when the component is not active or doing work. Static power is also known as idle power or base power. From an application point of view, we define dynamic and static power consumption as the power consumption of the whole system with and without the given application execution, respectively. From the component point of view, we define dynamic and static power consumption of the component as the power consumption of the component with and without the given application utilizing the component during its execution, respectively.

There are two types of energy consumptions, static energy and dynamic energy. We define the static energy consumption as the energy consumption of the platform without the given application execution. Dynamic energy consumption is calculated by subtracting this static energy consumption from the total energy consumption of the platform during the given application execution. That is, if P_S is the static power consumption of the platform, E_T is the total energy consumption of the platform during the execution of an application, which takes T_E seconds, then the dynamic energy E_D can be calculated as

$$E_D = E_T - (P_S \times T_E) \tag{2.1}$$

2.1.2 Performance models of computation

In this section, we survey prominent models used for prediction of the cost of computations in the execution of ultrascale computing applications.

The seminal models are the parallel random access machine (PRAM) [8], the bulk-synchronous parallel (BSP) model [9], and the LogP model [10]. All these models assume a parallel computer to be a homogeneous multiprocessor.

The PRAM is the most simplistic parallel computational model . It consists of p sequential processors sharing a global memory. It assumes that synchronization and communication is essentially cost free. However, these overheads can significantly affect algorithm performance. Many modifications to the PRAM have been proposed that attempt to bring it closer to practical parallel computers.

The BSP model is a bridging model that consists of p parallel/memory modules, a communication network, and a mechanism for efficient barrier synchronization of all the processors. A computation consists of a sequence of supersteps. During a superstep, each processor performs synchronously some combination of local computation, message transmissions, and message arrivals.

Finally, LogP (covered later in much detail) abstracts the performance of a system with four parameters, L, o, g, and P, which stand for network delay, overhead or cycles that a CPU devotes to sending the message, gap per message or minimum time interval between two consecutive injections to the network, and, finally, the number of processes. It has been successfully used for developing fast and portable parallel algorithms for (homogeneous) supercomputers and has become a foundation for numerous subsequent models.

A dominant class models parallel computation by directed acyclic graph (DAG) where the nodes represent local computation and the edges signify the data dependencies. This model forms the fundamental building block of runtime schedulers in KAAPI [11], StarPU [12], and DAGuE [13].

Graphical models are commonly used to structure mesh-based scientific computations. The objective of a graph partitioning problem is then to divide the vertices of the graph into approximately equal-weight partitions (balance computations) and minimize the number of cut edges between partitions (minimize total runtime communication) [14–17].

We will now review performance models of computation for heterogeneous platforms where they are even more paramount.

Performance models of computation for heterogeneous HPC platforms

Realistic and accurate performance models of computation are the fundamental building blocks of data partitioning algorithms. Over the years, load balancing algorithms developed for performance optimization on parallel platforms have attempted to take into consideration the real-life behavior of applications executing on these platforms. This can be discerned from the evolution of performance models for computation used in these algorithms.

The simplest models used positive constant numbers and different notions such as normalized processor speed, normalized cycle time, task computation time, average execution time, etc. to characterize the speed of an application [18–20]. A common crucial feature of these efforts is that the performance of a processor is assumed to have no dependence on the size of the workload.

The most advanced load balancing algorithms use functional performance models (FPMs), which are application-specific and represent the speed of a processor by a continuous function of problem size but satisfying some assumptions on its shape [21–24]. These FPMs capture accurately the real-life behavior of applications executing on nodes consisting of uniprocessors (single-core CPUs).

Modern multicore platforms have complex nodal architectures with highly hierarchical arrangement and tight integration of processors where resource contention and non-uniform memory access (NUMA) are inherent complexities. On these platforms, load balancing algorithms based on the traditional and state-of-the-art performance models (FPMs) will return sub-optimal solutions due to the complex nature of the performance models. Therefore, there is a need for novel performance models of computation that take into account these inherent complexities.

Lastovetsky *et al.* [25,26] present an advanced performance model of computation (FPMs) that contains severe variations reflecting the resource contention and NUMA inherent in the modern multicore platforms. These models (or performance profiles) have complex shapes (non-linear, non-convex), which do not satisfy the assumptions on shape that allow load balancing algorithms based on smooth FPMs to return optimal workload distribution. The authors then propose data partitioning algorithms that use these advanced FPMs as building blocks to minimize the computation time of the parallel application.

2.1.3 Performance models of communications

This section fairly describes the issue of optimizing communication using analytical representations of the transmissions departing from a given workload balance of the computation between the processes of an application. We also introduce foundational analytical communication performance models and we apply one of the models to an example of a real-world kernel.

Ultrascale computer systems are composed of heterogeneous multicore processors and accelerators, connected by a hierarchy of communication channels. Such heterogeneity is partially due to the necessity of increasing the system performance keeping the energy cost at a reasonable level. Scientific applications executing on UCS platforms are composed of *kernels*, which are computationally intensive tasks conceived for being executed by a set of heterogeneous processors. Usually, every processor runs the same code on a different *data region* of a global data space. UCS applications face the challenge of obtaining as much performance as possible from the specific platform.

During the execution of a kernel, each of the processes needs data from other processes to compute its own values. Therefore, the necessity of communication appears periodically during its execution. The challenge is not only to balance the overall computational load of the kernel among the available computing resources but also to optimize the completion time of its communications.

The current approach is based on design and implement evaluation tests, executes them in the target platform, hence consuming computational resources along a significant amount of time, and extrapolates estimations obtained from the whole application. A model-based methodology replaces the previous test-based approach with a fully analytical modeling of the behavior of the application. Optimization of computation and communication in data parallel applications is usually addressed separately. First, the computational load is distributed between processors according to their capabilities, following different approaches (see Section 2.1.2). Then, communication optimization is addressed by building communication performance models and applying them for searching a distribution of the data space to the processes that reduces the communication cost.

A communication performance model provides with an analytic framework that represents communications as a parameterized formal expression. The evaluation of this expression determines the cost of the communication in terms of time, as a function of system parameters. Many models have been proposed, covering different aspects of the communication. They can be generally classified into two types: *hardware models* and *software models*. Following, we introduce some of the representative models of each type.

Hardware models use hardware-related parameters to build the analytical expression representing the cost of communications. LogP [10] is a foundational model representing the cost of a communication by four parameters: L is the *network delay* and represents the latency of the network, o is the *overhead* or cycles that a CPU devotes to send the message, g is the *gap per message* and represents the minimum time interval between two consecutive injections to the network, and, finally, P is the number of processes. The LogP model was improved by LogGP [27], which includes a new parameter G (gap per message) allowing one to represent the influence of the network bandwidth in the transmission of large messages. In LogGP, the cost of a point-to-point transmission of a message of size m is represented as $T_{p2p}(m) = 2o + L + (m - 1)G$. More advanced models have been proposed, as PLogP [28], that considers parameters gap per message and overhead linear functions of the message size, achieving higher accuracy. Derived models have been proposed to represent communication costs in heterogeneous platforms, by extending previous purely homogeneous models with additional parameters representing specific features of the platform, such as HLogGP [29] and LMO [30].

Software models address the modeling of the *middleware* costs of a communication. They abstract from hardware and use middleware-related parameters to build analytical expressions representing the costs associated to data movement. log_nP [31] considers a point-to-point transmission as a sequence of *transfers* (copies) through intermediate buffers between the endpoints of a homogeneous platform. The aggregation of the costs of the individual transfers yields the cost of the transmission in an expression as $T(m) = \sum_{i=0}^{n-1}(o_i + l_i)$, where o (*overhead*) is the per transfer time dedicated by the CPU to a contiguous message, and the *latency l* is the additional cost if the message is non-contiguous in memory. The τ-*Lop* model [32,33] addresses the challenge of accurately modeling MPI communications on heterogeneous ultrascale platforms. It relies on the concept of *Concurrent Transfers* of data and uses this concept as a building block to represent the communications on hierarchical communication channels, capturing the impact of contention and process mapping. The cost of a point-to-point message transmission is modeled using two parameters: the *overhead $o^c(m)$* represents the time needed to start the injection of data in the communication channel c from the invocation of the operation, and the *transfer time $L^c(m, \tau)$* is the time invested in each one of the data movements composing the transmission and depends on the message size and the number of concurrent transfers progressing through the channel c. The parameter τ allows the model to represent the cost derived from contention, and hence the channel bandwidth sharing, appearing naturally in collective and kernel communications. The τ-*Lop* expression describing the cost of a message transmission in n equal transfers is $T^c(m) = o^c(m) + n \times L^c(m, 1)$. To represent the cost in complex heterogeneous platforms, τ-*Lop* adopts a compositional approach for representing the concurrency of full point-to-point transmissions, by using the concurrency operator $||$. As an example, the cost of the pair of concurrent transmissions is represented as $T^c(m)||T^c(m) = 2||T^c(m) = o^c(m) + n \times L^c(m, 2)$. Note how the amount of concurrent transmissions represented using the concurrency operator is propagated to the τ parameter of the transfers.

Using analytical models to optimize the performance of complex heterogeneous kernels requires a high level of accuracy in the predictions and enough representation capabilities for the high amount of convoluted communications of the processes. Accuracy has to do with the representation of the cost but also with the parameter measurement in the specific platform. A methodology for measuring the parameter values that captures the parameter meaning is essential for achieving accurate predictions of the communication cost.

Following, we develop an example of a simple communication optimization for a real data parallel kernel. The kernel (named *Wave2D*) uses the technique of finite differences to numerically solve the following wave equation in an $N \times N$ data space:

$$\frac{\partial^2 u}{\partial t^2} = c^2 \left(\frac{\partial^2 u}{\partial x^2} + \frac{\partial^2 u}{\partial y^2} \right) \tag{2.2}$$

Along time t, $u(x,y,t+1)$ is generated from its previous instances $u(x,y,t)$ and $u(x,y,t-1)$. The left side of Figure 2.1 shows this matrix at a given step of the algorithm.

The communication optimization procedure departs from a previously established process distribution to the resources of the platform, involving multicore CPUs and accelerators. The first step is to balance the computational load between the processors. In a heterogeneous platform, the processors have different computing capabilities, therefore, this step involves the characterization of the speeds of the processes by a vector $s = \{s_0, \ldots, s_{P-1}\}$, and the assignation to p_i of an amount of data proportional to its speed s_i. Usually, such speed characterization is done through benchmarking that outputs a speed number per process, or a function describing the speed as a function of the task size (see Section 2.1.2).

Regions of data distributed to the processes must tile the entire data space. Partitioning and distributing the data space in P regions of sizes proportional to s is subject to multiple variations, called *data mappings*. Alternative data mappings can be evaluated to choose which minimizes the communication cost. Note that, for the set of possible data mappings, every process performs the same amount of computational work on a different set of data points, and hence, the workload balance does not change, but does the communication cost. An example of a data mapping is shown in the right part of Figure 2.1. It represents the kernel running in an experimental platform composed of two nodes identified by a background color. The $P = 8$ processes communicate through shared memory or network depending on their location. Inside each node, each process may run on a set of assigned resources of different types. The *FuPerMod* tool [34] was used to provide a load-balanced partition following a

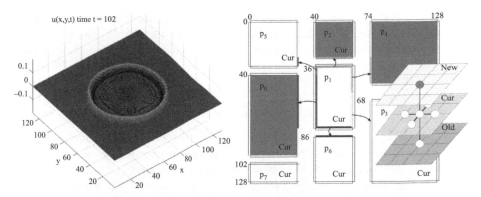

Figure 2.1   *Left: visualization of discrete solution $u(x, y, t)$ of a wave equation in an $N \times N$ data mesh with $N = 128$, at time $t = 102$, for particular initial and boundary conditions. Right: an example data space partition and distribution to $P = 8$ processes with different computational capabilities running in two nodes*

column-based approach [35]. Partitioning algorithms do not take into account the communication cost of the kernel, but only the relative speed of the processes. In this example, we use τ-*Lop* analytical framework to find a more efficient data mapping in terms of its communication costs.

In homogeneous systems, models of point-to-point and collective operations basically contain expressions in the forms $n||T^c(m)$ representing the cost of n concurrent transmissions of a message of size m through a communication channel c, and $T^c(m_1)||T^c(m_2)$, representing the cost of a sequence of two transmissions of different message sizes through the same communication channel. Communication models in heterogeneous systems become more complex. τ-*Lop* provides with extensions to evaluate these types of complex expressions [33] which shuffle concurrent and sequential transmissions of different message lengths progressing through the same or different communication channel, e.g., $T^{c_1}(m_1)||T^{c_2}(m_2)$. Anyway, expressions of actual kernels rapidly become complex enough to require an automatic evaluation. The τ-*Lop* toolbox[1] is a package that provides with a C++ function interface to describe and automatically evaluate the communication cost expressions of a data parallel kernel. Their inputs are the τ-*Lop* parameters built for the platform and a description of the data mapping and the kernel communications, both point-to-point and collectives. The toolbox provides with facilities to provide such description and to efficiently evaluate its communication cost. It allows one to evaluate efficiently a set of partitions, leading to an optimal election.

As shown in the right part of Figure 2.1, at each time $t + 1$, every data point in matrix *New* is calculated as a combination of the neighbor points in matrix *Cur*, which requires a previous communication stage of the needed data from neighbor processes at step t. Such communications are represented in the figure for process p_1.

---

[1] http://hpc.unex.es/taulop

As the computation is (unevenly) load balanced, all processes come into the communication phase at the same time. Hence, all processes interchange their boundaries simultaneously. From this assumption, we can derive a communication cost expression of the kernel:

$$\Theta = t \times \left[\mathop{\|}_{p=0}^{P-1} \Theta_p \right], \quad \text{with } \Theta_p = \sum_{i \in \eta_p} T^{c(i)}(m(i)). \tag{2.3}$$

All of the processes communicate concurrently, so the total cost Θ is calculated using the concurrency operator $\|$ for every process communication over t steps. A process p transmits its boundary data to its neighbor processes (the set η_p) using the channel $c(i)$ for transmitting the message of size $m(i)$ to the neighbor i. The transmissions of a process to its neighbors are accomplished sequentially, hence the sum.

Extending previous cost expression to every individual cost transmission is indeed complex enough to require evaluation using an automatic tool. Code 1 uses the τ-*Lop* toolbox to describe and evaluate the previous cost model representing the communications and data mapping of the kernel. Array node represents the mapping of processes to nodes, numbered 0 and 1. Following, an array of processes is created, with the rank number and mapping node of each Process. Then, Neighbors() function is used to create the neighbor set of each process (η_p). Neighbor sets are specific for a given arrangement of the rectangles in the data space (data mapping) and determine the destination and amount of data transmitted through different communication

---

Algorithm 1: Code for evaluating the communication cost of the Wave2D kernel in a heterogeneous platform

---

```
int P = 8;
int nodes = {0, 1, 0, 1, 0, 1, 1, 1}; // Node mapping
Process *p[P];
int *η[P];
for rank in {0, P-1}:
p[rank] = new Process (rank, nodes[rank]);
for rank in {0, P-1}:
η[rank] = new Neighbors (p);
TauLopConcurrent *conc = new TauLopConcurrent ();
for rank in {0, P-1}:
TauLopSequence *seq = new TauLopSequence ();
for dst in {η[rank]}:
m = getMsgSize (p, dst) * sizeof(double);
seq→add (new Transmission (p[rank], p[dst], m));
conc→add(seq);
TauLopCost *tc = new TauLopCost ();
conc→evaluate (tc);
double t = tc→getTime ();
```

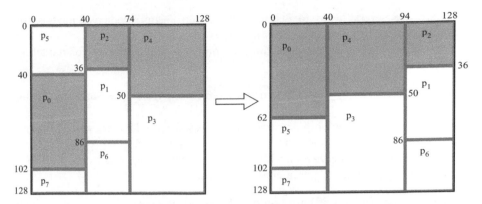

Figure 2.2   Rearranging the data regions assigned to processes in the 2D mesh data space in such a way that network transmissions have been minimized

channels, and, as a consequence, the final cost. As an example, Figure 2.2 shows two partitions with different communication costs. In the left figure, the number of data points in process p_5 boundaries for transmitting through the network to processes in $\eta_5 = \{0, 1, 2\}$ is 76, while in the right figure, with $\eta'_5 = \{0, 3, 7\}$, the number is 40, reducing the transmissions through the slower network communication channel, and hence, the cost. The rest of the code composes and evaluates the cost for the specific partition. The cost expression is composed using the `TauLopConcurrent` and `TauLopSequence` objects. All transmissions added to a `TauLopSequence` object will be evaluated under the assumption that they progress sequentially. Then, `TauLopSequence` objects added to a `TauLopConcurrent` object will be evaluated under the assumption that they progress concurrently, applying the transfer time parameter values for specific m and τ. The communication channel used for each transmission is internally figured out from the node location obtained from the processes. Finally, `TauLopCost` object evaluates the cost expression and returns a time in seconds.

By executing the algorithm using all possible data mappings, the optimum arrangement is obtained. Actually, this procedure is unfeasible when the number of processes grows, because the number of combinations grows exponentially. In practice, only a reduced set of possible data mappings is evaluated. A straightforward heuristic-based optimization decision for Wave2D, proposed by Malik *et al.* [36], is based on the rearrangement of the regions assigned to processes running on the same node to be as close as possible, which decreases the network communication, more expensive in terms of time.

2.1.4   Power and energy models of computation

In this section, we will survey research works that have proposed power and energy predictive models for optimization of applications for energy on ultrascale systems.

There are several ways to classify power and energy predictive models for ultrascale computing systems and applications.

First classification is based on three dominant approaches used for modeling power and energy consumption.

- *System-level*: The approach is to use system-level physical measurements using power meters.
- *On-chip sensors*: On-chip sensors supplied by the vendors and their APIs are used for obtaining the power and energy consumptions.
- *Performance monitoring events (PMCs)*: This dominant approach uses the PMCs provided by a vendor as parameters for the models.

Second classification is based on the characteristic *Level of abstraction*, which specifies how the model captures the inherent hierarchical and heterogeneous nature of modern processor architectures.

- *Linear Independence*—All the components of a node are modeled independently. The model for a node is a linear combination of the models of its components.
- *Linear Dependence*—The components of a node are modeled taking into account the dependencies (shared structures) between them and expressing these dependencies linearly. For example:
  - The models for CPUs are constructed taking into account the shared resources (last level cache (LLC)) between them.
  - For an application employing both CPUs and accelerators, the models for CPUs and the accelerators are constructed taking into account the shared resources (LLC) between the CPUs and the communication link (PCIe) connecting the CPUs and the accelerators.
- *Non-linear Independence* —All the components of a node are modeled independently. However, the model for a node is a non-linear combination of the models of its components.
- *Non-linear Dependence* —This is the most complex model. The components and dependencies between them (shared resources, communication links) are modeled non-linearly by taking into account their inherent hierarchical and heterogeneous nature.

From our survey, almost all the models fall into the category of *linear independence*.

However, we divide our survey into categories using the following more readable classification: (a) models for CPUs, (b) models for GPUs, (c) models for Xeon Phis and field programmable gate arrays (FPGAs), (d) application-specific models, and (e) critiques of PMC-based models.

Due to length constraints, we will look at only the most prominent works in each category.

Power and energy models for CPUs. The first notable model in this category is [37], which is based on events such as integer operations, floating-point operations, memory requests due to cache misses, etc. that the authors believed to strongly correlate with power consumption. Icsi *et al.* [38] propose a methodology to determine unit-level power estimates based on hardware performance counters. They select 22 strictly collocated physical units based on an annotated P4 die photo. The total power consumption is then estimated as the sum of the power consumptions of the 22 physical units plus the base power. The power estimate for each unit is a linear function of the access rate of it, with the exception of few issue logic units where an extra parameter is introduced to model the non-linear behavior.

Several models are employed as predictor variables utilization metrics of the key components such as CPU, memory, disk, and network. The most comprehensive model in this group is proposed in [39] that used as parameters, the utilization metrics of CPU, disk, and network components and hardware performance counters for memory. Here, the general model can be described as follows:

$$P = C_{base} + C_1 \times U_{CPU} + C_2 \times U_{Mem} + C_3 \times U_{Disk} + C_4 \times U_{Net} \tag{2.4}$$

where C_{base} is the base power consumption of a node and U_{CPU}, U_{Mem}, U_{Disk}, and U_{Net} are the CPU, memory, disk, and network utilizations, respectively.

Basmadjian *et al.* [40] construct a power model of a server as a summation of power models of its components, the processor (CPU), memory (RAM), fans, and disk (HDD). Bircher *et al.* [41] propose a non-linear model to predict power using PMCs. They use PMCs that trickle down from the processor to other subsystems such as CPU, disk, and GPU and PMCs that flow inward into the processor such as direct memory access and I/O interrupts.

Power and energy models for GPUs. GPUs are now an integral part of high-performance computing systems due to their enormous computational powers and energy efficiency (performance/watt). In a node, the GPU is used as a coprocessor and is connected to a CPU through a PCI-Express (PCIe) bus. Work is offloaded from a CPU to the GPU.

The first comprehensive model developed for GPUs was by [42]. The GPU power consumption in their prediction model is modeled similar to the PMC-based unit power prediction approach of [38]. In their model, the power consumption is calculated as sum of power consumptions of all the components composing the streaming multiprocessor and graphics double data rate (GDDR) memory.

The majority of other models employ machine learning methods. Sunpy and Kim [43] propose power and energy prediction models that employ a configurable, back-propagation, artificial neural network (BP-ANN). The parameters of the BP-ANN model are ten carefully selected PMCs of a GPU. The values of these PMCs are obtained using the CUDA Profiling Tools Interface [44] during the application execution. Wang and Cao [45] use the technique of program slicing to model GPU power consumption. The source code of an application is decomposed into slices and these slices are used as basic units to train a power model based on fuzzy wavelet artificial neural networks. So, unlike earlier research efforts which use PMCs, slicing features are extracted from the programs and used in their model.

Power and energy models for Xeon Phis and FPGAs. In this category, we cover the other accelerators that are used in high-performance computing systems.

There is an abysmal shortage of power and energy prediction models for Xeon Phis. We found just one for Xeon Phis even though this accelerator enjoys a noticeable space in the Top500 [46] supercomputers. Shao and Brooks [47] construct an instruction-level energy model of a Xeon Phi processor and report an accuracy between 1% and 5% for real-world applications.

To the best of our knowledge, there are no linear regression models using PMCs because PMCs are not yet offered by FPGAs. Ou and Prasanna [48] construct a linear energy prediction model based on instruction level energy profiling. Wang *et al.* [49] propose a linear component-based model to predict energy consumption of a reconfigurable multiprocessors-on-a-programmable-chips implemented on Xilinx FPGAs. Al-Khatib and Abdi [50] propose a linear instruction-level model to predict dynamic energy consumption for soft processors in FPGA. The model considers both inter-instruction effects and the operand values of the instructions.

Application-specific models. Here, we present studies for saving power and energy in HPC applications. Previous sections dwelt on power and energy models for dominant components in a node that predicted power and energy consumptions for all kinds of applications executing on these components. Our focus in this category is application-specific.

Lively *et al.* [51] propose application-centric predictive models for power consumption. For each kernel in an application, multivariate linear regression models for system power, CPU power, and memory power are constructed using PAPI performance events [52] as predictors.

Bosilca *et al.* [53] compare the power consumptions of two high-performance dense linear algebra libraries, i.e., LAPACK and PLASMA. Their results show that PLASMA outperforms LAPACK both in performance and energy efficiency.

Witkowski *et al.* [54] and Jarus *et al.* [55] propose system-wide power prediction models for HPC servers based on performance counters. They cluster real-life HPC applications into groups and create specialized power models for them. They then use decision trees to select an appropriate model for the current system load.

Lastovetsky *et al.* [56] present an application-level energy model where the dynamic energy consumption of a processor is represented by a function of problem size. Unlike PMC-based models that contain hardware-related PMCs and do not consider problem size as a parameter, this model takes into account highly non-linear and non-convex nature of the relationship between energy consumption and problem size for solving optimization problems of data-parallel applications on homogeneous multicore clusters for energy.

Critiques of PMC-based models. In this category, we review attempts that have critically examined and highlighted the poor prediction accuracy of PMCs for energy predictive modeling.

Economou *et al.* [39] highlight the fundamental limitation, which is the inability to obtain all the PMCs simultaneously or in one application run. They also mention the lack of PMCs to model energy consumption of disk I/O and network I/O. McCullough *et al.* [57] evaluate the competence of predictive power models for modern node architectures and show that linear regression models show prediction errors as high as 150%. They suggest that direct physical measurement of power consumption should be the preferred approach to tackle the inherent complexities posed by modern node architectures. Hackenberg *et al.* [58] present a study of various power measurement strategies, which includes *Intel RAPL* [59]. They report that the accuracy of *RAPL* depends on the type of workload and is quite poor for workloads that use the hyper-threading feature. They also report that the accuracy is poor for applications with small execution times and becomes better only for applications with longer execution times since the predictions are energy averages.

O'Brien *et al.* [60] survey predictive power and energy models focusing on the highly heterogeneous and hierarchical node architecture in modern HPC computing platforms. Using a case study of PMCs, they highlight the poor prediction accuracy and ineffectiveness of models to accurately predict the dynamic power consumption of modern nodes due to the inherent complexities (contention for shared resources such as LLC, NUMA, and dynamic power management). Arsalan *et al.* [61] propose a novel selection criterion for PMCs called *additivity*, which can be used to determine the subset of PMCs that can potentially be considered for reliable energy predictive modeling. They study the *additivity* of PMCs offered by two popular tools, *Likwid* [62] and *PAPI* [52], using a detailed statistical experimental methodology on a modern Intel Haswell multicore server CPU. They show that many PMCs in *Likwid* and *PAPI* are *non-additive* and that some of these PMCs are key predictor variables in energy predictive models thereby bringing into question the reliability and reported prediction accuracy of these models.

Prominent surveys on power and energy predictive models

In this category, we present recent surveys summarizing the power and energy efficiency techniques employed in high-performance computing systems and applications.

Mobius *et al.* [63] present a survey of power consumption models for single-core and multicore processors, virtual machines, and servers. They conclude that regression-based approaches dominate and that one prominent shortcoming of these models is that they use static instead of variable workloads for training the models.

Inacio *et al.* [64] present a literature survey of works using workload character-ization for performance and energy efficiency improvement in HPC, cloud, and big data environments. They report a remarkable increase in research papers proposing energy modeling and energy efficiency techniques from 2009 to 2013, thereby sug-gesting an increasing importance of energy saving techniques in the HPC, cloud, and big data environments.

Tan *et al.* [65] survey the research on saving power and energy for HPC linear algebra applications. They separate the surveyed efforts into two categories: (1) power management in HPC systems and (2) power and energy-efficient HPC applications (Cholesky, LU, and QR). They construct a linear model of an HPC system as a sum-mation of power consumptions of all the nodes in the system. The power consumption of a node is modeled as the sum of all the major components (CPU, GPU, and RAM) of a node.

Dayarathna *et al.* [66] present an in-depth and voluminous survey on data center power modeling.

O'Brien *et al.* [60] survey the state-of-the-art energy predictive models in HPC and present a case study demonstrating the ineffectiveness of the dominant PMC-based modeling approach for accurate energy predictions.

2.1.5   Holistic approaches to optimization for performance and energy

In this section, we will review research that has proposed solutions for optimization of scientific applications on ultrascale platforms for both performance and energy. We believe that realistic and accurate performance and energy models of computations and communications are fundamental to the effectiveness of these solution approaches.

The methods solving the bi-objective optimization problem for performance and energy (*BOPPE*) can be broadly classified as follows:

- *System-level*: Methods that aim to optimize several objectives of the system or the environment (for example, clouds, data centers, etc.) where the applications are executed. The leading objectives are performance, energy consumption, cost, and reliability. A core characteristic of the methods is the use of application-agnostic models for predicting the performance of applications and energy consumption of resources in the system.
- *Application-level*: Methods focusing mainly on the optimization of applications for performance and energy. These methods use application-level models for predicting the performance and energy consumption of applications. This category can be further sub-classified into methods that target intra-node optimization and methods that target both intra-node and inter-node optimization.

System-level: Mezmaz *et al.* [67] propose a parallel bi-objective genetic algorithm to maximize the performance and minimize the energy consumption in cloud computing infrastructures. Fard *et al.* [68] present a four-objective case study comprising performance, economic cost, energy consumption, and reliability for optimization of scientific workflows in heterogeneous computing environments. Beloglazov *et al.* [69] propose heuristics that consider twin objectives of energy efficiency and quality of service (QoS) for provisioning data center resources. Kessaci *et al.* [70] present a multi-objective genetic algorithm that minimizes the energy consumption, CO_2 emissions, and maximizes the generated profit of a cloud computing infrastructure. Durillo *et al.* [71] propose a multi-objective workflow scheduling algorithm that maximizes performance and minimizes energy consumption of applications executing in heterogeneous high-performance parallel and distributed computing systems.

Application-level: Freeh *et al.* [72] propose an intra-node optimization approach that analyzes the performance-energy trade-offs of serial and parallel applications on a cluster of DVFS-capable AMD nodes. In their study, they consider three intra-node parameters to characterize the performance and energy of serial and parallel applications. Ishfaq *et al.* [73] formulate a bi-objective optimization problem for power-aware scheduling of tasks onto heterogeneous and homogeneous multicore processor architectures. Their solution method targets intra-node optimization. They consider intra-node parameters such as DVFS, computational cycles, and core architecture type. Balaprakash *et al.* [74] is an intra-node optimization approach that explores trade-offs among power, energy, and performance using various application-level tuning parameters such as number of threads and hardware parameters such as DVFS.

Drozdowski *et al.* [75] propose a concept called an iso-energy map, which represents points of equal energy consumption in a multi-dimensional space of system and application parameters. They study three analytical models, two intra-node and one inter-node. For the inter-node model, they consider eight parameters. From all the possible combinations of these parameters, they study 28 combinations and their corresponding iso-energy maps. However, one of the key assumptions in their model is that the energy consumption is constant and independent of problem size. Marszakowski *et al.* [76] analyze the impact of memory hierarchies on performance-energy trade-off in parallel computations. They study the effects of 12 intra-node and inter-node parameters on performance and energy. In their problem formulations, they represent performance and energy by two linear functions of problem size, one for in-core computations and the other for out-of-core computations.

Reddy *et al.* [77] study the bi-objective optimization problem for performance and energy (*BOPPE*) for data-parallel applications on homogeneous clusters of modern multicore CPUs, which is based on only one but heretofore unstudied decision variable, the problem size. They present an efficient and exact global optimization algorithm that solved the *BOPPE*. It takes functions of performance and dynamic energy consumption against problem size as inputs, and outputs the globally Pareto-optimal set of solutions. These solutions are the workload distributions, which achieve inter-node optimization of data-parallel applications for performance and energy.

2.2 Impact of workflow enactment modes on scheduling and workflow performance

In the past decade, computer architectures have experienced an important paradigm shift. From a single processor containing a few homogeneous cores, computers have evolved to complex dynamic systems containing tens or hundreds of heterogeneous computing resources, the so-called *manycore* computers. Despite these trends, the majority of popular parallel programming languages, development tools, and compilers remain to be based on the old symmetric multi-processing paradigm. Past efforts to make parallel computers more accessible for programmers resulted in a multitude of different and often incompatible programming libraries and language extensions, including successful standards such as OpenMP, OpenCL, and MPI.

On distributed computing infrastructures (DCIs), *scientific workflows* emerged in industry, business, and science as an easy way to develop large-scale applications as a composition of smaller loosely coupled components [78]. Existing DCI workflow engines are currently mature and come with rich ecosystems which support the user in all aspects of a workflow lifecycle from creating to execution, monitoring and results retrieval, interfaced toward the domain scientists and ease of use rather than the computer science underneath [79–84]. Because of the similarity in terms of scale and heterogeneity, workflow systems represent today a promising alternative for development and execution of scientific applications on shared memory heterogeneous manycore architectures. However, existing workflow engines targeted at DCIs are prone to high overheads and latencies [1]. While such overheads are acceptable on DCIs, tightly coupled manycore computers are much more sensitive to latencies and other forms of overheads.

To overcome these problems, Janetschek *et al.* [1] presented a *Manycore Workflow Runtime Engine (MWRE)* that efficiently exploits the low latency characteristics of heterogeneous manycore computers and which performs significantly better than traditional workflow engines on manycore computers.

There are two different strategies for enacting a workflow determining how and when the workflow engine evaluates a workflow execution plan: *early* and *late evaluation mode*. In theory, early enactment mode produces a better workflow schedule, while also having more enactment overhead. Late enactment mode theoretically produces a worse workflow schedule, while having less enactment overhead. The practical implications of early and late enactment modes on scheduling performance are still unclear, therefore, in this work, we simulated the execution of a large number and variety of random MWRE workflows with both early and late evaluation mode to gain more insights on how much early evaluation mode improves scheduling performance and to be able to deduct some guidelines on when to use early evaluation mode and when to use late evaluation mode.

Next, the following topics are addressed. Section 2.2.1 introduces the scientific workflow model, followed by an introduction to workflow enactment in Section 2.2.2 and to workflow scheduling in Section 2.2.3. Section 2.2.4 explains the MWRE workflow engine for manycores. Section 2.2.5 discusses the theoretical implications of an incomplete workflow execution plan on scheduling, followed by an explanation of the methodology used to conduct the experiments presented in Section 2.2.6. Section 2.2.7 discusses experimental results, and Section 2.2.8 presents conclusions.

2.2.1 Scientific workflow model

A workflow consists of two parts: an *abstract* part and a *concrete* part. A short overview of these two parts is presented next.

Workflow abstract part

The abstract part (see Figure 2.3) of a scientific workflow comprises a hardware and middleware agnostic (and therefore portable) description of its structure, the activities involved (identified by a unique name and a type), and the data and control-flow dependencies between the activities. The individual activities are treated as black boxes where only the input and output signatures are known.

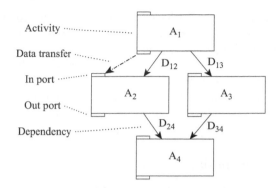

Figure 2.3   Abstract part of a scientific workflow

There are usually two different types of workflow activities:

1. *Atomic activities* are basic indivisible units of computation;
2. *Composite activities* combine several fine granular activities, including atomic and other composite activities, to form coarse-grained activities and impose a control flow on the contained inner activities.

Typical composite activities are sequential and parallel loops, conditional activities and sub-workflows.

Workflow concrete part

The concrete part of a workflow contains the hardware- and middleware-dependent implementations of the atomic activities and their accompanying meta-information. This part is often highly specific to each individual workflow system and the underlying computing infrastructure. It usually contains information about the available activity implementations, locations where they are installed, how they can be executed, and any other further information intended to help the workflow engine in selecting the most appropriate activity implementation.

2.2.2   Workflow enactment

A workflow engine executes a workflow instance (operation usually called *workflow enactment*) by traversing the DAG representing the workflow structure, determining the state of the individual activities, transferring data from finished activities to their successors in the dependency graph, unrolling composite activities and replacing them with the resulting subgraph, and delegating the actual execution of atomic activities to the scheduling and execution subsystems. We call the resulting DAG, where composite activities have been replaced with their contained subgraphs and enriched with additional state information, a *workflow execution plan (WEP)*.

We distinguish between two types of workflow enactment modes [1]:

1. *Early enactment mode*, where the engine reevaluates the WEP as soon as there are activity state changes and completes it as early as possible. This mode usually

comes with a much higher overhead but results in a more complete WEP comprising more information, which allows the scheduler to better plan the workflow execution on the underlying resources.

2. *Late enactment mode* (also called lazy evaluation mode), where the engine only partially reevaluates and completes the WEP when it is absolutely necessary for further workflow enactment. This mode has less overhead but also results in a less complete WEP with less information available for the scheduler to plan the workflow execution.

2.2.3 *Workflow scheduling*

Workflow scheduling describes the process of mapping atomic activities to available computing resources where they are executed. The resulting mapping of activities to computing resources is called *workflow schedule*. The scheduler optimizes the workflow schedule by maximizing or minimizing a given utility function, typically the overall execution time. Some scheduler implementations take more than one objective into account, some of which being in conflict with each other and requiring *multi-objective optimization* [85], or by considering one variable as a constraint [86] while optimizing the other.

Generating a full-ahead schedule is an NP-hard problem [87], and therefore, most existing full-ahead scheduling methods are approximate heuristic algorithms [88]. Existing scheduling heuristics can be broadly divided into the two following categories [89]:

1. *Just-in-time scheduling algorithms*: only consider the next activities to be scheduled when deciding on a mapping and ignore the rest of the WEP. They are usually linear in complexity with the number of activities (i.e., $O(N)$) and have a low overhead, but as a consequence produce poorer schedules;
2. *Full-ahead scheduling algorithms*: use the entire WEP when deciding on a mapping. They usually present a higher overhead, but consider more workflow information and therefore produce in general better results.

2.2.4 *Manycore workflow runtime engine*

We designed and developed a workflow engine called *Manycore Workflow Runtime Engine* (MWRE) [1], specifically tuned for shared-memory heterogeneous manycore parallel computers. Our motivation is to exploit the workflow paradigm, highly successful for programming DCIs (like Clouds), for programming heterogeneous manycore architectures, while supporting and integrating existing established parallel programming paradigms, such as OpenMP. Traditional workflow applications in DCIs usually have a rather simple structure, feature a coarse-grained parallelism with relatively few long-running parallel tasks, and exhibit large task submission and data transfer overheads. In contrast, shared memory manycore applications usually have a much more complex structure, feature a more fine-grained parallelism with a lot of short running parallel tasks, and hardly have any task submission and data transfer overheads.

The defining feature of our engine is compiling workflows into semantically equivalent C++ programs using a source-to-source compiler (and not interpreting workflows like most traditional engines for DCIs). The workflow engine is linked to the C++ program in the form of a shared library that uses a novel callback-driven enactment mechanism, where the engine is only responsible for maintaining and traversing the WEP. Dependency resolution and data transfers are implemented in callback functions, specifically tailored to the concrete workflow and are part of the workflow specification. This keeps the engine clean and minimizes the enactment overhead.

2.2.5   Impact of incomplete WEP on full-ahead scheduling

When using a full-ahead scheduling algorithm, the workflow enactment mode can theoretically have a huge influence on the scheduling performance. Full-ahead scheduling considers the entire WEP when calculating a schedule; therefore, an incomplete WEP may lead to a comparatively worse workflow schedule.

For example, let us assume the workflow in Figure 2.4a executed on a heterogeneous system consisting of two different computing resources: resource $R1$ and resource $R2$. Resource $R1$ has a fast CPU, and resource $R2$ has a twice as slow CPU. The example workflow consists of two parallel atomic activities A and B, and a sequential `for` loop with a data dependency on activity B containing a single atomic activity C. The number of iterations of the `for` loop is known from the beginning and assumed here as two. The number in brackets represents the activity execution times on resources $R1$ and $R2$, respectively.

Most full-ahead scheduling algorithms try to prioritize the atomic activities lying on the workflow's *critical path*, defined as the longest path from the start to the end of the workflow, and the *length* of the critical path is defined as the sum of the activity execution times on the critical path. The activities on the critical path have the

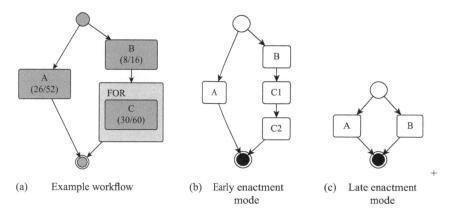

(a)   Example workflow   (b)   Early enactment   (c)   Late enactment
                                         mode   mode

Figure 2.4   WEPs in early and late enactment modes at workflow execution start
for an example workflow, where the numbers in brackets represent the
execution times on resources R1 and R2

most influence on performance, and any delay on the critical path delays the entire workflow.

The critical path of our example workflow consists of activities B, $C1$, and $C2$ (where $C1$ refers to the instance of C in the first loop iteration, and $C2$ to the instance of C in the second loop iteration), and the minimum length of the critical path is 68. Therefore, an optimal workflow schedule maps activity A to resource $R2$, and activities B, $C1$, and $C2$ to resource $R1$ to achieve a workflow makespan of 68.

When using early enactment mode, the `for` loop is immediately evaluated and the resulting WEP (see Figure 2.4b) contains all the necessary information to find the correct critical path. Therefore, a full-ahead scheduling algorithm can calculate an optimal workflow schedule as depicted above.

In late enactment mode, the evaluation of the `for` loop is deferred until activity B has finished its execution. Therefore, the resulting WEP (see Figure 2.4c) initially misses the activities $C1$ and $C2$, and a full-ahead scheduler would base its calculation of a workflow schedule on incomplete information. It may be deducted from the WEP that the critical path only consists of activity A and map it onto the fastest resource $R1$, while activity B is mapped onto the slower resource $R2$. The `for` loop will be evaluated only after activity B has finished and the WEP will look like Figure 2.4b. At this time, the critical path activity B has already been executed by the slower resource, and resource $R1$ is still occupied executing activity A. Therefore, the scheduler can only map activity $C1$ onto the slower resource, $C2$ is the only critical path activity mapped to the fastest resource. The workflow makespan in this scenario is 106, which is about 56% larger than the optimal makespan.

Based on this observations, one may conclude that early enactment mode should always be preferred to late enactment mode. However, our experience with MWRE has shown that depending on the particular workflow to be executed, early enactment mode can exhibit drastic performance losses and a limited scalability compared to late enactment mode. For example, Figure 2.5 (taken from [1]) shows the enactment overhead of the Montage workflow executed with MWRE, referring to the time spend in the engine not including the execution times of the atomic activities. In this experiment, we executed the Montage workflow several times with a different number of atomic activities. The enactment time in late enactment mode stays close to the enactment time of an equivalent OpenMP program for the whole experiment. In contrast, the enactment time of early enactment mode is also close to the enactment time of the OpenMP version in the beginning but significantly increases beyond 600 activities.

2.2.6 Methodology

To evaluate the impact of early and late evaluation mode on scheduling performance, we simulated the execution of a large number and variety of workflows on manycore architectures. Due to the lack of a sufficient number of complex real-world workflows, we used an algorithm to generate a large number of random workflows with varying parameters.

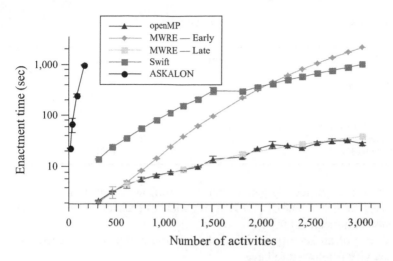

Figure 2.5   Enactment times of the Montage workflow [1]

Algorithm 2: Random hierarchical workflow generation

 1: **procedure** GENRANDOMWORKFLOW($v, \alpha, o, w, \beta, l$)
 2:      $W \leftarrow$ ORIGGENRANDOMWORKFLOW(v, α, o, w, β)
 3:      **if** $l > 1$ **then**
 4:          $s \leftarrow$ SELECTRANDOMACTIVITY(W)
 5:          $t \leftarrow$ SELECTRANDOMCOMPOSITETYPE(if, parallel for)
 6:          $SW[0] \leftarrow$ GENRANDOMWORKFLOW($v, \alpha, o, w, \beta, l - 1$)
 7:          **if** $t =$ if **then**
 8:              $SW[1] \leftarrow$ GENRANDOMWORKFLOW($v, \alpha, o, w, \beta, l - 1$)
 9:          **end if**
10:          CONVERTATOMICTOCOMPOSITE(s, t, SW)
11:          $p \leftarrow$ SELECTRANDOMPREDECESSOR(s)
12:          $h \leftarrow$ CREATEHELPERNODE(t)
13:          INSERTNODE(h, p, s)
14:      **end if**
15:      **return** W
16: **end procedure**

2.2.6.1   Random workflow generation

For generating random workflows, we used an existing algorithm [88] that creates workflows consisting of solely atomic activities, extended to cover composite ones, as shown in Algorithm 2. The algorithm considers the following parameters as input to influence the shape and structure of the generated workflows:

- *Average number of activities v* in the workflow;

Table 2.1   Random workflow generation parameters

Parameter	Symbol	Value set
Average number of activities	v	10
Workflow shape	α	$\{0.1, 0.5, 1.0, 1.5, 2.0\}$
Activity output degree	o	$\{1, 3, 20\}$
Activity average execution time	w	3 s
Computational heterogeneity	β	3.0
Maximum nesting level	l	$\{1, 2\}$

- *Workflow shape* α by randomly generating the workflow height from a uniform distribution with a mean value of $\sqrt{v}/\alpha$ and the width of each level from a uniform distribution with a mean value of $\sqrt{v} \cdot \alpha$;
- *Output degree* o of an activity, which is the maximum number of successors a workflow activity is allowed to have;
- *Average execution time* w of an atomic activity;
- *Computational heterogeneity* β by randomly selecting the execution time of an activity on a specific resource from the interval $(w \cdot (1 - \beta/2), w \cdot (1 + \beta/2))$;
- *Maximum nesting level* l of the composite activity.

At first, a workflow is generated using the original algorithm (line 2). As long as the maximum nesting level has not been reached, a random activity is selected (line 4), a random composite activity type is chosen (line 5), one or two sub-workflows representing the body of the composite activity are created by recursively calling the algorithm (lines 6–9), and finally, the selected activity is converted into the corresponding composite activity (line 10). Next, we select a random predecessor (line 11) of the composite activity, which supplies it with specific input data, such as conditional argument for if activities and loop counter boundaries for *parallel for* activities. To ease implementation of the algorithm composite activity-specific data is supplied by a helper activity inserted between the selected predecessor and the composite activity (lines 12 and 13). The helper activity randomly chooses for if activities whether the supplied condition is true or false, and the loop iteration count between 2 and 10 for parallel for activities.

2.2.6.2 Experimental setup

We conducted our experiments by generating five different workflows for each parameter combination (see Table 2.1) and then simulated the execution of each workflow five times for both evaluation modes on three heterogeneous hardware configurations (see Table 2.2) using seven different schedulers.

The workflow generation parameters were chosen to best represent the characteristics of manycore workflow applications, characterized by a relatively high number of short running activities. The generated workflows consist of 20–110 unique activities, each having a different randomly chosen execution time of 0.1–6 s for each resource type. The workflows have highly different shapes, ranging from nearly sequential to workflows with a high degree of parallelism and from workflows with very few

Table 2.2   Simulated hardware configurations

Configuration	Description
Configuration 1	Four different single-core CPUs
Configuration 2	Eight different 10-core CPUs
Configuration 3	One 4-core CPU and 2 different GPUs

dependencies between activities to nearly fully connected ones. Larger workflows were not created, as MWRE early evaluation mode leads from our experience to a significant increase in enactment overhead (e.g., see Figure 2.5) beyond a few hundred workflow activities. For the experiments, we aimed to have early and late evaluation modes with roughly the same enactment overhead to not bias the results.

To get meaningful results independent from a specific scheduler, the following schedulers implemented in MWRE were used:

- *Minimum completion time* (MCT) [90] is a just-in-time algorithm that assigns ready-to-execute tasks in no particular order to the resource with the minimum completion time.
- *Heterogeneous earliest finish time* (HEFT) [88] is a list based heuristic consisting of two phases. In the ranking phase, all tasks are assigned a rank representing the longest path from the task to the exit node. In the processor selection phase, the tasks are assigned to a free processor with the earliest finish time in the order of their ranks.
- *Predict earliest finish time* (PEFT) [91] is also a list-based heuristic similar to HEFT, which uses the average path from the task to the exit node for assigning a rank.
- The *Lookahead* [92] algorithm is another variant of HEFT also taking the children of a task into account in the processor selection phase.
- The *Min–Min* [90] is a batch mode heuristic consisting of two phases. In the first phase, the minimum expected completion time is calculated for each task, and in the second phase, the tasks are assigned to processors according to their minimum expected completion time in the order of the overall minimum expected completion time.
- The *Max–Min* [90] scheduling algorithm is very similar to Min–Min except that the second phase takes the maximum expected completion time into account.
- The *Sufferage* [90] scheduling algorithm assigns tasks to processors according to how much the task would "suffer" in terms of expected completion time if it is not assigned to that processor.

For each workflow, the average makespan, hardware configuration, scheduler, and evaluation mode combination are registered. The results are grouped according to the scheduler, hardware configuration, workflow shape, activity output degree, and composite activity nesting level, and the relative time difference $\Delta T_{rel} = \frac{T_{late} - T_{early}}{T_{late}}$ of the makespan of early evaluation mode T_{early} compared to the makespan

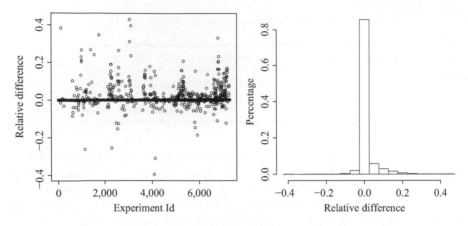

Figure 2.6   Result overview of all experiments

of late evaluation mode T_{late} is calculated. If the relative time difference is less than $\pm 2.5\%$, it is assumed that there is no significant difference. The relative number of experiments showing no significant performance improvement, the relative number of experiments showing a significant performance improvement with early evaluation mode, and the relative number of experiments showing a significant performance degradation are determined.

Simulations are run on an Intel Core i7-2600K running at 3.40 GHz with 16 GB RAM.

2.2.7   Experimental results

The results of all experiments are shown in Figure 2.6. For 85.7% of the experiments, the workflow makespan in early evaluation mode is nearly the same as the makespan in late evaluation mode. For 11.6% of all experiments, the early evaluation mode is faster, while for 2.7%, it is slower than the late evaluation mode. In the best case, early evaluation mode is 43% faster, and in the worst case, early evaluation mode is 39.6% slower. The experiments for which early evaluation mode is faster show an average performance improvement of 9.4%, and the experiments for which is slower show an average performance degradation of -7.3%.

These results indicate that for the majority of workflows, using early or late evaluation mode has practically no significant impact on scheduling performance. Only for a minority of 10%, the executed workflows in early enactment mode caused a performance improvement of 10%. It is also observed that 3% of the workflows executed in early enactment mode led to worse performance. The reason for this result is that the schedulers are suboptimal heuristics and that more but still incomplete information can still cause the scheduler to misjudge the critical path (see Section 2.2.5), while with less information the scheduler may correctly guess the critical path.

Table 2.3 and Figure 2.7 show the experimental results by scheduler type. MCT schedules activities to the fastest available machine as they are passed to the scheduler

Table 2.3   Results by scheduler type

Scheduler	No change (%)	Early better (%)	Late better (%)	Average improvement (%)	Average degradation (%)
MCT	74.5	15.9	9.5	8.2	−6.7
HEFT	89.3	10.1	0.5	10.9	−5.6
PEFT	84.5	12.2	3.3	10.2	−5.8
Lookahead	84.9	12.6	2.5	8.8	−5.1
Min-Min	89.6	9.3	1.1	10.7	−5.6
Max-Min	87.9	10.7	1.4	8.6	−18.2
Sufferage	89.3	10.2	5.5	9.2	−11.4

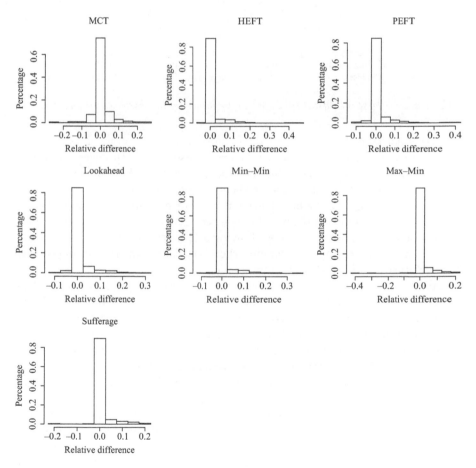

Figure 2.7   Histograms of relative performance by scheduler type

Table 2.4   Results by hardware configuration

Hardware config	No change (%)	Early better (%)	Late better (%)	Average improvement (%)	Average degradation (%)
Config 1	84.2	12.1	3.7	9.3	−7.8
Config 2	84.3	12.1	3.6	9.5	−7.5
Config 3	84.2	12.6	3.2	9.2	−7

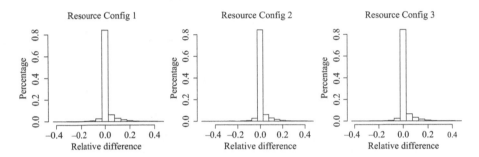

Figure 2.8   Histograms of relative performance by hardware configuration

and it does not take the rest of the WEP into account. Therefore, it is the least stable, and its results roughly follow a Gaussian distribution. However, MCT still shows a slight bias toward early evaluation mode, 6% more workflows showing better performance. The full-ahead scheduler shows rather stable performance with 80–90% of the workflows having no significant performance difference between early and late evaluation mode. For the workflows where there is a significant performance difference, it is early evaluation mode showing a better performance in the majority of cases. The only exception is Sufferage, where only twice as many workflows show better performance with early evaluation mode.

Table 2.4 and Figure 2.8 show the experimental results by the hardware configuration. There is no significant difference in the results for the different hardware configurations. For all hardware configurations, 84% of all experiments show no significant difference between early and late evaluation mode, 12% show 9% better performance with early evaluation mode, and 4% show 7% of worse performance.

Table 2.5 and Figure 2.9 show the experimental results by workflow shape α. Also here, there is hardly any difference between different workflow shapes. For all workflow shapes, 84% of the experiments show no significant difference between early and late evaluation mode, 12% show 9% better performance with early evaluation mode, and 3% show 7% of worse performance. The only difference is $\alpha = 1.0$, which shows an average performance improvement of 13.2% instead of 9%, and an average performance degradation of −3.1% instead of −7%. For $\alpha = 1.0$, the workflow height and width is the same, which means that all activities are equally distributed. This gives the scheduler the most opportunities for improving the mapping.

Table 2.5 Results by workflow shape α

Workflow shape (%)	No change (%)	Early better (%)	Late better (%)	Average improvement (%)	Average degradation (%)
0.1	85.8	11.4	2.8	9.3	−7.1
0.5	86.2	10.8	3	9.3	−7.4
1.0	83.7	13.2	3.1	13.2	−3.1
1.5	83.9	12.5	3.6	9.2	−7.4
2.0	84.4	12.1	3.5	9.2	−7.9

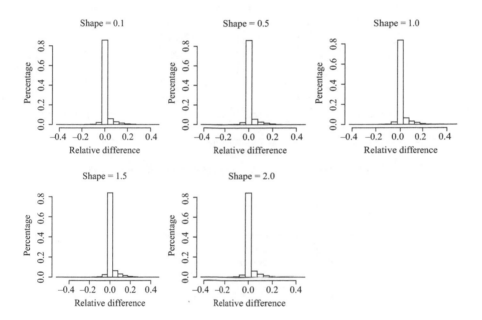

Figure 2.9 Histograms of relative performance by workflow shape α

Table 2.6 and Figure 2.10 show the experimental results concerning the output degree of workflow activities. Also here, there is hardly any difference between different output degrees. For 84% of the experiments, there is no significant difference between early and late enactment mode; for 12% of the experiments, early enactment mode causes 9% of better performance; and for 3% of the experiments, the early enactment mode causes 7% of worse performance.

Table 2.6 and Figure 2.10 show the experimental results considering whether there is nested composite activities in the workflow. Also here, there is hardly any difference, 84% showing the same performance, 12% showing better performance with early enactment mode with a performance improvement of 9% and 3% show 7% of worse performance.

Table 2.6   Results by outdegree

Outdegree	No change (%)	Early better (%)	Late better (%)	Average improvement (%)	Average degradation (%)
1	84.4	11.8	3.8	9.1	−6.9
3	83.8	12.8	3.4	9.5	−7.4
20	84.6	12.1	3.3	9.3	−8.2

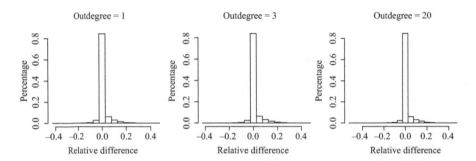

Figure 2.10   Histograms of relative performance by outdegree

Table 2.7   Results by composite nesting level

Nested	No change (%)	Early better (%)	Late better (%)	Average improvement (%)	Average degradation (%)
No	83.7	12.4	3.9	9.3	−7.9
Yes	83.6	12.7	3.7	9.3	−7

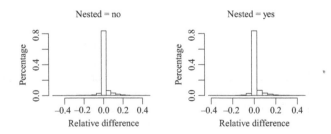

Figure 2.11   Histograms of relative performance by composite nesting level

2.2.8   Conclusion

The impact of early and late enactment modes on workflow execution performance were evaluated. Early evaluation mode provides more information to the scheduler, which can calculate a potentially better schedule, improving the workflow performance. On the other hand, early evaluation mode causes a significant increase in workflow enactment overhead degrading workflow execution performance and limiting scalability. In order to find guidelines to when early evaluation mode significantly improves workflow performance, results were broken down according to several parameters defining workflow shape and structure.

The first relevant result is that for 85.7% of the experiments we could not find a significant difference in workflow performance between early and late execution mode. We conclude that it is safe to use late evaluation mode for most workflows to get better scalability and less enactment overhead without the fear of losing performance because of a suboptimal workflow schedule. Only for 11.6% of the experiments we observed a significantly better performance with early enactment mode with an average improvement of 11.6% and a maximum improvement of 43%. For 2.7% of the experiments, we observed a significantly worse performance with early evaluation mode with an average performance degradation of 7.3% and a maximum performance degradation of 39.6%.

The second relevant result is that for 14.3% of the experiments, while there is a significant difference in performance between early and late enactment mode, no decisive guidelines were identified when a workflow performs better. The best enactment mode is highly individual for each workflow and no correspondence can be made to a specific parameter defining workflow shape or structure. The only way to determine whether early or late enactment will cause a better performance is to execute the workflow using both modes and compare the results.

Based on these results, the late enactment mode was selected as the default mode in MWRE. According to the experiments, the potential performance improvement of early enactment mode due to a better scheduling is too insignificant compared to the downsides of a higher enactment overhead and worse scalability.

MWRE is a workflow engine for shared-memory heterogeneous manycore computers, and thus, MWRE workflows have different characteristics than DCI (Cloud) workflows. More precisely, they feature a more complex workflow structure with a higher number of shorter running activities. The experimental results reflect this and, therefore, only have limited validity for common DCI environments. Because DCI workflows have a simpler structure with a lower number of longer running activities, the early evaluation mode here has less impact on scheduling performance.

2.3   Toward general-purpose computations at the edge

Originally designed to exploit the power of multicore processors through virtualization, Cloud Computing [93] has changed over the past decade to support ultrascale computations. The new paradigm, often called *aggregation*, collects a large number of resources in a pool to form a single service with huge storage and computation capacities. Unfortunately, with the huge amounts of data generated via modern applications, the cloud center has become a bottleneck and a single point of failure. This advocated an extended paradigm, called *edge computing*, that brings part of the data storage and computation closer to the user. The benefits are plenty: reduced delays, high availability, low bandwidth usage, improved data privacy, etc. In this section, we introduce recent advances in edge computing that makes the coordination of edge networks synchronization-free and convergent. We address the main challenges facing applications on the data management and communication aspects. The section also provides convenient runtime environments for different categories of edge computing scenarios.[2]

2.3.1   Motivation

Edge computing offers the opportunity to build new and existing ultrascale applications that take advantage of a large and heterogeneous assortment of edge devices and environments. Fully realizing the opportunities that are created by edge computing requires dealing with a set of key challenges related with the high number of different components that compose such systems and the interactions among them. In this work, the main challenges on the communication and data management levels were addressed allowing for robust communication and available data access.

On the communication frontend, the fact that applications are composed of components running in heterogeneous environments requires robust and efficient solutions for tracking these components. This implies the development of highly robust and adaptive membership services and mechanisms that allow efficient communication among these components. Among the promising class of gossip-based communication protocols are those "hybrid" ones [94,95], in which payloads are propagated though an elected logical *spanning tree*, supported by lightweight meta-data across the graph for recovery (reconstructing another logical tree) under failures.

The consequences of such hostile environments are also present on the data management level. Since application components run on different administrative domains scattered across heterogeneous environments, communication links between these components can be disrupted by external factors (i.e., network partitions) frequently. This implies that the progress of computations executed across different application components cannot depend on continuous communication with other components, or in other words, cannot depend on synchronous interactions. This advocates the use of synchronization-free (i.e., sync-free) programming abstractions backed by sync-free data propagation and replication techniques. An interesting approach is to make use of conflict-free replicated data types (CRDTs) [96–98] that are proven abstractions designed to achieve convergence under such conditions (this is explained later in more details).

[2] Credits go to all team members contributed to the success of this work within the EU FP7 Syncfree project and EU H2020 LightKone project. The research leading to these results has received funding from the European Union's Horizon 2020—The EU Framework Program for Research and Innovation 2014–2020, under grant agreement No, 732505, LightKone project.

Finally, heterogeneity is the norm in ultrascale edge applications, and it exists at various layers: execution environments, communication media, data sources, operating systems, programming languages, etc. Addressing this heterogeneity can be achieved by leveraging on different run-time supports and frameworks that provide a more unified vision of resources to application developers. These different run-time and frameworks will have to inter-operate through the use of standard protocols and common data representation models.

In the following, we refine the challenges associated with tapping on edge computing to design ultrascale applications, discuss enabling technology that paves the way to tackle these challenges, and finally discuss a set of run-time and framework support that can simplify the design of such applications.

2.3.2 Edge computing opportunities

Edge environments. To the contrary of cloud computing where the data and computation is centralized at the cloud data centers, the edge computing paradigm encompasses a large number of highly distinct execution environments that are defined by the network topology, connectivity, locality, and the storage and computation capacities of the devices used. In particular, we identify the following interesting edge environments:

- Fog computing: a variant of cloud computing where the cloud is divided into smaller cloud infrastructures located in the user vicinity. In such environments, each fog cloud often serves as an individual cloud, although the data can eventually be incorporated with other fog [99,100].
- Mobile Cloudlets: small cloud data centers that are located at the edge and are tailored to support mobile applications with powerful computations and low response times, e.g., in ISP gateways or 5G towers [101–103].
- Hardware-based clouds: self-contained devices, such as routers, gateways, or set-up boxes, that are enriched with additional computational and storage capabilities like [104,105].
- Peer-to-peer (P2P) clouds: these environments try to leverage existing devices, e.g., user mobiles, laptops, and computers in volunteer networks, aiming to cooperate toward achieving a common goal [94,106,107].
- Things and sensor network clouds: resource constrained devices, e.g., IoT devices, sensors, and actuators, capable of performing some computations on data without accessing or delegating to the (possibly unreachable) cloud center [108].

All of these different scenarios are characterized by having highly heterogeneous devices in terms of processing power and memory, but also regarding their connectivity to the backbone of the Internet or even their up-times (being continually running or being operating for only small periods of time). These different devices naturally run different operating systems from general-purpose Linux-based operating systems in the case of servers in cloud and private infrastructures, to proprietary operating systems in the case of set-up boxes, mobile operating systems, general-purpose multi-user operating system or even single process operating systems in the case of small sensors and actuators. Gathering the capacity of devices with very different properties is highly challenging, and devising solutions that can exploit devices located in different edge devices brings additional challenges. Next, we will discuss some of the key high-level challenges in tapping the potential of the edge.

Challenges at the edge. Despite the diversity of edge computing environments, components, and properties, the major challenges are common to most of the scenarios. In particular, we recognize the following four challenges:

Scalability. One of the reasons to move the data and computation off the cloud data center to the edge is to reduce the I/O overload on the cloud and avoid bottlenecks related with the limited network capability connecting clients to the cloud infrastructures. Nevertheless, this raises another challenges on handling the data and computation in a distributed way especially in ultrascale systems composed of, potentially, many data centers and thousands of edge devices. This scale requires special techniques across the data, computation, and communication planes. As captured by the CAP theorem [109], and because scaling out will increase the potential for network portions, link failures, and arbitrary communication delays, ensuring availability—as an essential requirement for most applications including novel edge applications—requires relaxing the consistency model employed in the design and implementation of these solutions. Consequently, the computation should also be decentralized and coordinated to achieve the common goals of the entire system. Finally, the communication middlewares should also scale to afford a high number of nodes, e.g., through asynchronous, P2P, or gossip protocols.

Interoperability. Considering the edge categories discussed above, one can notice the notable diversity level of the devices and platforms used within the same or across edge clouds. This brings interoperability challenges if all components shall communicate with each other, thus requiring well-studied interfaces and possibly introducing a common layer that all components can understand without compromising the characteristics deemed essential.

Resilience. While cloud data centers use high-quality equipment for the network and devices, edge computing often use commodity equipment that are far from perfect regarding failures. The problem is extrapolated with edge network problems that are likely to be loosely connected, mobile, and hostile. This threatens the QoS and makes the data and communication components even more complex. That said, one must consider the performance as well as the cost trade-offs (being a major factor due to the constrained resources).

Security and privacy. Given the heterogeneity of the edge applications, security and privacy measures must be analyzed and tackled individually. However, in general, it is desired to find a common security layer or security measures that govern a wide range of applications. Security and privacy on the edge need to be addressed on the infrastructure and data levels. The former can be deployed at the communication or network layer, ranging from establishing secure connections to enforcing secure group dynamics, and cover several dimensions including data integrity, data privacy, or resilience to DoS attacks. On the other hand, edge applications often deal with sensitive data which likely requires lightweight encryption and data sanitization techniques to control the disclosure of such data. These may also include secret-sharing, anonymization, noise addition or partitioning, etc., depending on the specific security and functional requirements of the implementations.

Use cases. As discussed in the edge environments, edge computing supports a plenty of applications and use-cases. In this section, we focus on three categories in which most of the use-cases lie:

- *Time series applications.* This category spans a multitude of applications with the popularity of IoT. The scenario is often a type of time series where data is generated by the IoT devices, e.g., sensors, and pushed to the edge devices to get stored, aggregated, and partially computed. The aggregated data is then pushed to the center of the cloud for further handling. The data-flow can sometimes be in the opposite sense if actuator devices exist; in this case, the processed data in the cloud is pushed back to the actuators to do some action. Consequently, this scenario represents a hybrid model of light and heavy devices, different types of networks (e.g., Zig-bee, WIFI, WAN, etc.), as well as data-flow direction.
- *Mobile edge applications.* This category covers all the applications in which devices are mobile and public. This makes the model very hostile as link failure and delays are expected, and the availability of nodes cannot be guaranteed (e.g., a mobile device can be switched off). The communication in such use cases does not follow a particular data-flow pattern, but it is often P2P or gossip-based due to the dominant dynamic graph-like network of nodes. In such applications, devices have moderate storage and computation resources that makes the interaction symmetric. Obviously, the main challenges in such use-cases are resilience and availability. In some cases, access points, towers, or routers with more capacities can assist in storage, computation, and communication, which can be used as third party authority when needed.
- *Highly available databases.* This category is a natural evolution of scalable databases in cloud and cluster systems. The intuition is to replicate the database geographically, brining replicas or cache servers closer to the user. In this scenario, devices are at least commodity computers or servers with non-scarce capacities, and then network is often the Internet. In addition to availability, the challenge in such use-cases is to tolerate network partitions and optimize data locality (especially when partial replication is used). These scenarios are close to Fog Computing and Cloudlets with the difference that all node must work as a single (often loosely) coordinated system.

2.3.3 Enabling technologies for the edge

Synchronization-free computing. Edge devices and edge networks are both unreliable. This follows both from their design, e.g., they are low-power systems that are often offline, and from the nature of the edge itself, e.g., it is directly involved with real world activities, such as in IoT. Despite this unreliability, we would like to perform computations directly on the edge.

To perform computations directly on the edge, we need distributed data structures and operations that tolerate the unreliability of the edge. Synchronization-free computing fits the bill because of its very weak synchronization requirement. A prominent example is CRDT, which is a replicated data type that is designed to support temporary divergence at each replica, while guaranteeing that when all updates are delivered to all replicas of a given instance, they will converge to the same state. (More details about CRDTs can be found in Chapter 4 or by referring to [96–98].) CRDTs naturally tolerate node problems, namely, nodes going offline and online and node crashes, and network problems, namely, partitions, message loss, message reordering, and message duplication. Node crashes are tolerated as long as the desired state exists on at least one correct node. The following results on CRDT computations are summarized from [110].

CRDT definition. For the purposes of this section, we define a *CRDT instance* to be a replicated object that satisfies the following conditions:

- Basic structure: It consists of n replicas where each replica has an initial state, a current state, and two methods, query and update, that each executes at a single replica.
- Eventual delivery: An update delivered at some correct replica is eventually delivered at all correct replicas.
- Termination: All method executions terminate.
- Strong eventual consistency (SEC): All correct replicas that have delivered the same updates have equal state.

This definition is slightly more general than the one given in the original report on CRDTs [96]. In that report, an additional condition is added: that each replica will always eventually send its state to each other replica, where it is merged using a join operation. This condition is too strong for CRDT composition, since it no longer holds for a system containing more than one CRDT instance. We explain the conditions needed for CRDT composition in the next section.

CRDT composition. The properties of CRDTs make them desirable for computation in distributed systems. It is possible to extend these properties to full programs where the nodes are CRDTs and the edges are monotonic functions. To achieve this, it is sufficient to add the following two conditions on the merge schedule, i.e., the sequence of allowed replica-to-replica communications:

- Weak synchronization: For any execution of a CRDT instance, it is always true that eventually every replica will successfully send a message to each other replica.
- Determinism: Given two executions of a CRDT instance with the same set of updates but a different merge schedule, then replicas that have delivered the same updates in the two executions have equal state.

The first condition allows each CRDT instance to send the merge messages it requires to satisfy the CRDT conditions. The second condition ensures that the execution of each CRDT instance is deterministic, which makes it a form of functional programming. We remark that SEC by itself is not enough for this, since the states of replicas *in different executions* that have delivered the same updates can be different, even though SEC guarantees that they are equal in the same execution. In practice, enforcing determinism is not difficult but it depends on the type of the CRDT instance. Meiklejohn and Van Roy [110] explain how to do it for a set that has add and remove operations (the so-called Observed-Remove Set).

We define a *CRDT composition* to be a DAG where each node is a CRDT instance, and each node with at least one incoming edge is associated to a function of all incoming edges arranged in a particular order. Given the first of the two conditions introduced above, we can show that the execution of a CRDT composition satisfies the same properties as a single CRDT instance. If the second condition is added, then the CRDT composition behaves like a functional program.

Hybrid Gossip Communication. Gossip is a well-known and effective approach for implementing robust and efficient communication strategies on highly dynamic and large-scale system [95,107]. In its most simple form, in a gossip protocol, each node periodically interacts with a randomly selected node. In this interaction both exchange information about their local state (and potentially merge it). Since all nodes do this in parallel and in an independent fashion, after approximately one round-trip time, all nodes will have performed, at least, one merge step, and on average two merge steps (one initiated by the node itself and another initiated by some peer). We usually call this period of interactions a *cycle*. After a small number of cycles, the network converges to a globally consistent vision of the system state. This simple approach can be used, for instance, to compute aggregate functions, such as inferring the network size or load. Interestingly, this can also be used for other, and more complex, purposes such as managing the membership of a large-scale system, which implies building and maintaining an overlay (i.e., logical) network topology, in a way that is both robust and scalable, but also to support robust data dissemination in such systems.

Gossip-based approaches have been shown to be highly resilient to network faults, due to the inherent redundancy that its core to the design of gossip protocols. Unfortunately, this redundancy also leads to efficiency penalties. Hybrid gossip addresses this aspect of gossip protocols. In a nutshell, the key idea of hybrid gossip is to leverage on the feedback produced by previous gossip interactions among nodes such that an effective and non-redundant structure of communication can naturally emerge. The topology of this *emergent structure* depends on the computation being performed by nodes, and it enables nodes significantly improve the communication and coordination cost by restricting the exchange of information among node to the logical links that belong to this structure, lowering the among of redundant communication.

Key to maintaining the fault tolerance of gossip protocols in hybrid gossip is the use of the remaining communication paths among nodes (those that are not selected to be part of the emergent structure) to convey minimal control information. This control information enables the system to detect (and recover) from failures that might affect the emergent structure. Moreover, in highly dynamic scenarios, the additional communication paths allow nodes to fall back to a pure gossip strategy, for instance, when there are a significant number of concurrent nodes crashes or network failures.

Interesting, hybrid gossip solutions naturally allow different components of the system to operate using either the emergent structure or a pure gossip approach simultaneously. Hence, components of the system that are in stable conditions (i.e., low membership dynamics and low failures) will operate resorting to the emergent structure, while components of the system that are subjected to high churn or network/node failure will fallback to use pure gossip while still being able to inter-operate with the components using the emergent structure.

Therefore, hybrid gossip approaches enable applications to, effectively and transparently, benefit from the resilience of a pure gossip approach entwined with the efficiency of a gossip approach that leverages an emergent communication topology. The hybrid gossip approach has been introduced in [94,111]. The Plumtree protocol, in particular, shows how to build an efficient and robust spanning tree connecting a large number of nodes to support reliable application-level broadcast. This solution is currently used in industry, for example, the Basho Riak database uses it to manage the underlying structure of its ring topology which is used to map data object keys into nodes (through consistent-hashing).

2.3.4   Runtime for edge scenarios

Above, we have discussed enabling technologies that can be leveraged to build new and exciting edge applications in the ultrascale domain. Tapping into these enabling technologies can, however, be a complex task for developers. Therefore, it becomes relevant to provide frameworks, tools, and other artifacts that exploit these technologies in a coherent way, providing high-level abstractions to programmers that aim at developing their ultrascale edge applications. We now discuss some existing runtime support tools and frameworks that have been recently proposed to this end.

Antidote. Antidote is a geo-replicated key-value store, designed for providing strong guarantees to applications while exhibiting high availability, thus providing a good compromise in the consistency versus availability trade-off in the design of cloud databases. These properties make antidote a strong candidate as an edge database, especially when edge nodes have non-scarce resources (e.g., commodity servers).

In particular, some cloud databases adopt a strong consistency model by enforcing a serialization in the execution of operation, leading to high latency and unavailability under failures and network partitions. Other databases adopt a weak consistency model where any replica can execute any operation, with updates being propagated asynchronously to other replicas. This approach leads to low latency and high availability even under network partition, but replicas can diverge. On the other hand, Antidote allows any operation to execute in any replica but provides additional guarantees to the application as we explain next.

First, Antidote relies on CRDTs for guaranteeing that concurrent updates are merged in a deterministic way. Antidote provides a library of CRDTs with different concurrency semantics, including registers, counters, sets, and maps. The applications programmer must select the most appropriate CRDT, considering its functionality and concurrency semantics (e.g., add-wins, remove-wins).

Second, Antidote enforces causal consistency, guaranteeing that whenever an update u may depend on update v, if a client observes update u he also observes update v. Applications can leverage this property to guarantee their correctness when the correctness depends on the order of updates, e.g., an update executed after changing the access control policies should not be visible in a replica with the old access control policies.

Third, Antidote provides a highly available form of transactions, where reads observe a causally consistent snapshot of the database and writes are made visible atomically. Unlike standard transactions, write–write conflicts are solved by merging the concurrent update. Applications can leverage these highly available transactions to guarantee that a set of updates is made visible atomically.

Fourth, Antidote provides support for efficiently enforcing numeric invariants, such as guaranteeing that the value of a counter remains larger than 0. To this end, it includes an implementation of a Bounded Counter CRDT [112], a shared integer that must remain within some bounds. The implementation uses escrow techniques [113] for allowing an operation to execute in a replica without coordination in most cases.

Finally, associated with Antidote, we have developed a set of tools to verify whether an application can execute correctly under weak consistency, and when this is not the case, what coordination is necessary. These tools are backed by a principled approach to reason about the consistency of distributed systems [114].

Antidote is designed to be deployed in a set of geo-distributed data centers. Within each cluster, data is shared among the servers. Data is geo-replicated across data centers. The execution of transactions in Antidote, and the replication of updates across data centers, is controlled by Cure [115], a highly scalable protocol that enforces transactional causality and consistency (combining CRDTs for eventual consistency, causal consistency, and highly available transactions).

Legion. Legion [2] is a new framework for developing collaborative web applications that transparently leverage on the principles of edge computing by enabling direct browser-to-browser communication. Legion was implemented in *JavaScript* and it uses the *Web Real-Time Communications* (https://webrtc.org) to establish direct communication channels among web application users. At its core, Legion enables applications to transparently replicate, in the form of CRDTs, relevant application state in clients. Clients can then modify the application state locally, and through the use of hybrid gossip mechanisms, synchronize directly among them, without the need to go through the web application server. The server, however, is still used both to ensure the durability of the application state and to assist in the operation of Legion, namely, to simplify the task of creating the initial webRTC connections among clients when they enter the application.

A simplified architecture of Legion is illustrated in Figure 2.12. Legion can be used by a web application simply by importing a JavaScript script. This script provides the application access to the *Legion API*. The API exposes to the application the ability to manipulate data objects that can be used to model the application state. These data objects include records, counters, lists, and maps. All of these objects are internally represented by Legion through CRDTs which simplifies the direct synchronization among clients of shared application state. This is provided by an extensible CRDT

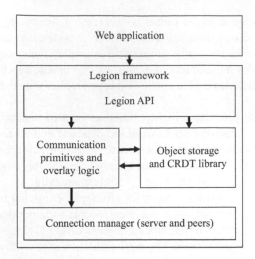

Figure 2.12 The Legion architecture

Library that is part of the *Object store* component of Legion . The synchronization of objects among clients (and that of a subset of clients with the server to ensure durability) is transparently managed by the Object Store.

To guide the synchronization process, Legion leverages on an unstructured overlay network, whose construction is guided by the principles of hybrid gossip, and takes into consideration the relative distance of each client among them. This allows clients to mostly interact and synchronize with clients that are in their vicinity. While the typical use case in Legion is to have clients interacting through the manipulation of shared data objects, web applications also have access to communication primitives that enable them to disseminate messages among the currently active clients of the application in a decentralized fashion. This is achieved by a gossip-based broadcast protocol that operates on top of the legion overlay network.

Finally, Legion also takes into account security, by ensuring that before clients can start to replicate and manipulate application data objects they authenticate on a server. Moreover, Legion exposes an adapter API that allows developers to integrate their Legion-backed applications with existing backends. The framework provides adapters to the Google Real Time API.[3] These adapters allow the developers to leverage this backend to do any combination of the following: authentication and access control, data storage for durability, and support to the WebRTC signaling protocol required to create webRTC connections among browsers. More details on the design and operation of Legion can be found in [2]. Legion is open source and available, alongside some demo applications through `https://legion.di.fct.unl.pt`.

Lasp. The Lasp language and programming system [116] was designed for application development on unreliable distributed systems, and in particular for edge

---

[3] https://developers.google.com/google-apps/realtime/application

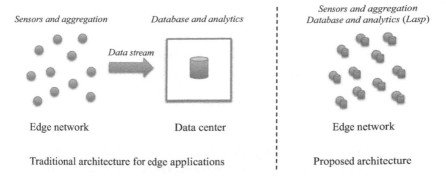

Sensors and aggregation   Database and analytics

Data stream

Edge network   Data center

Traditional architecture for edge applications

Sensors and aggregation
Database and analytics *(Lasp)*

Edge network

Proposed architecture

Figure 2.13   Proposed architecture for edge applications using Lasp

computing. Lasp allows developers to write applications by composing CRDTs, as explained above [110]. In addition to composition, Lasp also provides a monotonic conditional operation that allows executing application logic based on monotonic conditions on CRDTs. The Lasp implementation combines a programming layer based on synchronization-free computing with a communication layer based on hybrid gossip. This makes the implementation highly resilient and well adapted to edge networks.

Many of today's edge applications use the cloud as a database to store data coming from the edge. By using Lasp as their database, such applications can be translated to fully run on the edge (see Figure 2.13). This cannot be done with traditional cloud databases since they are not designed to run on unreliable edge networks. In the proposed architecture, the edge network runs everything: the sensors and aggregation software on individual edge nodes and the database (Lasp) on all edge nodes. Analytics computations can be run either as an internal Lasp computation or as an external to Lasp on individual nodes, using Lasp just as a database.

Example Lasp program. A typical application for Lasp is the scenario of advertisements counter that counts the total number of times each advertisement is displayed on all client mobile phones, up to a preset threshold for each. Figure 2.14 defines graphically part of the Lasp program for this application. The actual code is a straightforward translation of this graph. The application has the following properties:

- Replicated data: Data is fully replicated to every client in the system. This replicated data is under high contention by each client.
- High scalability: Clients are individual mobile phone instances of the application, thus the application should scale to millions of clients.
- High availability: Clients need to continue operation when disconnected as mobile phones frequently have periods of signal loss (offline operation).

This application can be implemented completely on the edge, as explained previously, or partly on the cloud. For this application, we have demonstrated the scalability of the Lasp prototype implementation up to 1,024 nodes by using the *Amazon* cloud computing environment to simulate the edge network [117].

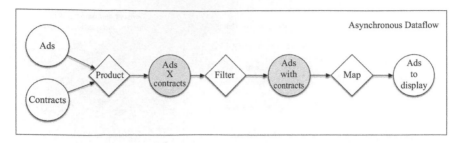

Figure 2.14   A Lasp computation to derive the set of displayable advertisements in the advertisement counter scenario. On the left, Ads and Contracts give information for the advertisements, including how many times they have been displayed, and their contracts, including the threshold for each advertisement. On the right are the advertisements that can be displayed. All data structures are sets, similar to database relations, and the computation is similar to an incremental SQL query.

2.3.5   Future directions

Building additional tools and support for a new generation of ultrascale edge applications is quite relevant and challenging. The varied nature of edge computing environments, which can combine small private clouds and data centers, specialized routing equipment and 5G towers, users' desktops, laptops and even cellphones, to small things sensors and actuators, makes it a daunting task to build a single runtime support that can efficiently operate on all such devices and deal with their heterogeneity.

While we presented a set of tools and frameworks that can ease the development of ultrascale edge computing applications and services, these do not cover all possible execution scenarios. That path to build such support requires not only the development of specialized runtimes for different edge settings, but also devising standard protocols and data representation models that allow the natural integration of different runtimes in a cohesive and effective edge architecture.

Current solutions for data replication and management are also unsuitable for the ultrascale that one is expected to find in emerging edge computing applications. The use of CRDTs to address the requirements of data management in this setting presents a viable approach. However, further efforts have to be dedicated in designing new and efficient synchronization mechanisms that can naturally adapt to the heterogeneity of the execution environment.

2.4   Spectral graph partitioning for process placement on heterogeneous platforms

It is customary in the literature to model a distributed application as a graph, whose vertices are processes, or computing tasks, and an edge between tasks denotes a communication between them. The edges are weighted with a positive value to mark the magnitude of this communication. Frequently used magnitudes to measure the communications are the data volume, in total number of bytes, or the number of messages interchanged [118].

In this setting, spectral techniques divide the set of vertices into two parts, equal in number of vertices, in such a way that the total communication from one part to the other is lesser than between the two parts of any other partition. The practical interest for this is to assign each part to a computation node, so the slow communication link between two nodes is used less than the quick intra-node links. It is imposed that the computational nodes are similar in performance, and also similar in the computational requirements of the vertices, in order for the assignation be balanced. The theoretical resource that allows one to compute this in an effective way is the Fiedler eigenvector of the Laplacian matrix of the graph [119]. The study of the eigenvalues and eigenvectors of a matrix is called spectral resolution [120], hence the name of the method.

In this section, we describe the spectral method as it is customarily used. We also propose to extend the previous scheme in two directions. First, we consider that each vertex has assigned a volume or weight, positive but possibly different depending on the vertex. To divide the set of vertices into two parts so that the part have the same volume (possibly with a different number of vertices), we consider the Fiedler eigenvalue of a generalized Laplacian (that we will define) which has similar properties to the standard Laplacian. The practical interest of this extension comes from the fact that the computational requirements of each vertex (process) can be different, and we are interested in a partition in vertex subsets with equal computational load (not necessarily equal number of vertices).

A second extension is to consider the division in two parts, where the fraction of total volume assigned to each part is not the same but can be predefined to p and $1 - p$ to each part, for a fraction p of the total of vertices. The Fiedler eigenvector of the generalized Laplacian can be used to this end. This is of interest for the case where the two subsets of vertices/processes will be assigned to computational units that are not equal in speed, being instead proportional to p and $1 - p$. Hence, the partition of tasks is conformal with the speed of the intended processors. We also discuss the problem of partitioning in more than two parts. We find difficult to put it in this scheme.

For the structure of the section, in the following section, we describe notation about graphs and linear algebra. Then, we introduce the spectral partitioning technique using the Laplacian . The material is standard but our presentation emphasizes the operator view (that is, avoid references to coordinates as much as possible). Section 2.4.3 is our work about weighted graph partitioning using a potential over the vertices. We use a finite element model as example. After a numerical comparison of performance against other partition methods, using the software Scotch, we draw some conclusions.

2.4.1 *Graphs and matrices: examples*

A graph $G = (V, E)$ consists of a set V of *vertices*, and a set E of *edges*, being each edge a set $\{u, v\}$ of two vertices $u, v \in V$. Each edge $\{u, v\}$, also defined as $u \sim v$, is said that joins u and v. Note that this structure does not model loops or directed arrows.

A *weight on edges* is a map

$$w : E \to \mathbb{R}$$

The weight of the edge $u \sim v$ is denoted $w(u, v)$. If a weight on the edges is not specified, implicitly the constant unit weight must be considered (that is, $w(u, v) = 1$ for each $(u \sim v) \in E$).

The *degree* of a vertex is the number of vertices adjacent to it.

A *potential on vertices* is a map

$$p : V \to \mathbb{R}$$

The set of all potentials (that is, of all functions $V \to \mathbb{R}$) is denoted $\mathbb{R}^V$.

We choose an ordering of the set of vertices, $V = \{v_1, \ldots, v_n\}$. The *adjacency matrix* of G (for this conventional ordering) is the $n \times n$ symmetric matrix A:

$$A = \begin{pmatrix} a_{11} & a_{12} & \cdots & a_{1n} \\ a_{21} & a_{22} & & a_{2n} \\ \vdots & & \ddots & \vdots \\ a_{n1} & a_{n2} & \cdots & a_{nn} \end{pmatrix} \quad \text{with } a_{ij} = \begin{cases} 1 & \text{if } v_i \sim v_j \\ 0 & \text{if not} \end{cases} \quad \text{for } i, j \in \{1, \ldots, n\}.$$

For an edge weight w, its *weighted adjacency matrix* is A_w with entries a_{ij} where

$$a_{ij} = \begin{cases} w(v_i, v_j) & \text{if } v_i \sim v_j \\ 0 & \text{if not} \end{cases}$$

The adjacency matrix is the matrix of the constant unit weight $w(u, v) = 1$ if $u \sim v$. We will consider mainly *positive edge weights* (that is, weights w such that $w(u, v) > 0$ for each $(u \sim v) \in E$), with the notable exception of the Laplacian.

We represent a vertex potential $p : V \to \mathbb{R}$ as the vector $p = (p(v_1), p(v_2), \ldots, p(v_n))$. A weighted adjacency matrix A_w operates in $\mathbb{R}^V$, the set of vertex potentials, as a matrix multiplication.

$$A_w : \mathbb{R}^V \longrightarrow \mathbb{R}^V$$

$$p \longmapsto A_w p$$

That is, the vector $A_w p$ has as j-entry the value $\sum_{j=0}^{n} a_{ij} p(v_j)$.

To give an intuitive interpretation of this setting, we consider a easily visualizable graph: the vertices are a square lattice of dots, and four edges join each one with those placed up, down, left and right (three edges for lateral vertices and two for the corners, Figure 2.15). This type of graph is used in finite elements computations. It is symmetric.

As example of weight in this graph, let us take that each edge has weight one, so $A_w = A$ is the adjacency matrix. As an example of potential p_0, we consider that $p_0(v_0) = 1$ in one vertex v_0, and $p_0(v) = 0$ in the other ones, $v \neq v_0$. The application of A to that potential, $A p_0$, transfers the value 1 to the vertices adjacent to v_0. That is, $p_1 = A p_0$ takes the value 1 in vertexes adjacent to v_0, and 0 in others. A second

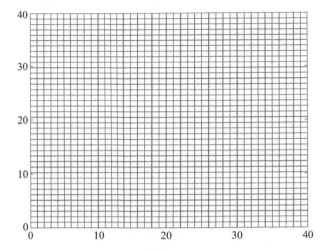

Figure 2.15   Square mesh of size 40× 41

application $p_2 = A^2 p_0$ widens the circle of influence: $p_2(v)$ is the number of paths of two edges from v_0 to v. The iterated application $p_k = A^k p_0$ produces a sequence $p_0, p_1, p_2, ...,$ in a transfer process. We can assign to the sum of potential $\sum_{i=0}^{n} p_k(v_i)$ the meaning of the total amount of material that comprises p_k. In the process induced by A the total amount of material is not constant, but is multiplied by four in the majority of the vertices, the inner vertices. Therefore it is not exactly a diffusion process. Taking another weight on edges, being $w(u, v)$ the inverse of the number of arrows that come out of u, it can be seen that $\sum_{i=0}^{n} p_k(v_i)$ (with $p_k = A_w^k p_0$) is constant, and the process is properly a diffusion process.

It is pertinent to mention iterations in the above example because the eigenvalues p are those potentials that verify $Ap = \lambda p$ (equivalently $A^n p = \lambda^n p$). And they are precisely the potentials invariant (except for a factor λ^n) under iterations of A.

2.4.2   Laplacian and partitions

A *partition of a set* V is an array (V_1, V_2) of two subsets of V such that

$$V_1 \cup V_2 = V \quad \text{and} \quad V_1 \cap V_2 = \emptyset$$

A *partition of a graph* $G = (V, E)$ is a partition of the underlying set of vertices. An edge $u \sim v$ in G is *cut* by a partition (V_1, V_2) if $u \in V_1$ and $v \in V_2$ or vice versa ($u \in V_2$ and $v \in V_1$). If the graph is weighted, the *total weight of the cut*, or total cut, is $\text{cut}(V_1, V_2) = \sum_{\substack{u \in V_1 \\ v \in V_2}} w(u, v)$.

If there are several partitions in a graph, usually it is preferable to have a minimum number of cuts (or total cut, if weighted). We are interested in partitions with minimal cut, but with a balanced number of vertices, that is, $|V_1| = |V_2|$ (if $|V|$ is even, $|V_1| = |V_2| \pm 1$ if it is odd). We express the combinatorial problem of finding these partitions using linear algebra, in particular the spectrum (that is, eigenvalues and eigenvectors[4]) of the Laplacian matrix, later defined.

Let us suppose given an order $V = \{v_1, v_2, \ldots, v_n\}$ in the set of vertices. A vector $x = (x_1, \ldots, x_n)$ corresponding to a potential of $\mathbb{R}^V$ has an entry x_i for each v_i. The *characteristic vector* c_S of a set $S \in V$ is $c_S = (c_1, \ldots, c_n)$ with

$$c_i = \begin{cases} 1 \text{ if } v_i \in S \\ 0 \text{ if } v_i \notin S \end{cases}$$

Sometimes it is preferable to use values other than 0 or 1 in the vector expression of a combinatorial object like a subset or partition [119]. For two real values b_1, b_2, the (b_1, b_2)-*indicator vector* of a partition (V_1, V_2) is the vector $(x_1, \ldots, x_n)$ with

$$x_i = \begin{cases} b_1 \text{ if } v_i \in V_1 \\ b_2 \text{ if } v_i \in V_2 \end{cases}$$

For example, the $(0,1)$-indicator is the characteristic of the second set of the partition. We use mainly $(1,-1)$-indicators.

The following proposition summarizes some graph and combinatorial properties expressed in linear algebra language. We denote with a dot $\cdot$ the inner product in $\mathbb{R}^V$, and with $\mathbf{1} = (1, \ldots, 1)$ the vector all whose entries are 1. The *degree* of a vertex $u \in V$ is the cardinal of the set $\{v \in V$ such that $u \sim v\}$, that is, the number of vertices adjacent to u. The *degree vector* is $(d_1, d_2, \ldots, d_n)$, where d_i is the degree of v_i.

Proposition 2.1. *Let* $G = (V, E)$ *be a graph of adjacency matrix A. For two sets* $S, T \subset V$ *of characteristics* c_S, c_T:

1. $\mathbf{1} \cdot c_S$ *is the cardinal of S, that is,* $\mathbf{1} \cdot c_S = |S|$. *Also* $c_S \cdot c_S = |S|$.
2. $c_S \cdot c_T = |S \cap T|$.
3. *The vector A$\mathbf{1}$ has, in the i-th entry, the degree of* v_i, *that is, A$\mathbf{1}$ is the degree vector*

   $$A\mathbf{1} = (d_1, d_2, \ldots, d_n)$$

   Also $\mathbf{1} \cdot A\mathbf{1} = \sum_i d_i$.
4. *Ac$_S$ has, in entry i-th, the number of edges to* v_i *from a vertex in S. That is, calling* $S \sim v = \{s \in V$ *such that* $s \sim v$ *and* $s \in S\}$,

   $$Ac_S = (x_1, x_2, \ldots, x_n) \quad \text{with} \quad x_i = |S \sim v_i|$$

   If A_w *is a weighted adjacency matrix, the i-th entry of* $A_w c_S$ *is the sum of the weight of the edges of the form* $s \sim v_i$ *with* $s \in S$. *That is,*

   $$A_w c_S = (x_1, x_2, \ldots, x_n) \quad \text{with} \quad x_i = \sum_{u \in S \sim v_i} w(u)$$

---

[4]We recall that, given a matrix A, λ is an eigenvalue of A if there exists an vector v such that $Av = \lambda v$. In this case, v is the associated eigenvector of λ.

Proof. It is easy to do the computations for these claims from the definitions. For example, for *c*), we have that the *i*-th entry of $A1$ is $\sum_{j=0} na_{ij} \cdot 1$. As a_{ij} is 1 if $v_i \sim v_j$ (and 0 in other case), then $\sum_{j=0}^{n} a_{ij} = \sum_{j|v_i \sim v_j} 1$, that is precisely the number of vertices adjacent to v_i. $\qquad\square$

If we call D_g the matrix with the degree vector in the diagonal and zero off-diagonal:

$$D_g = \begin{pmatrix} d_1 & 0 & \cdots & 0 \\ 0 & d_2 & & 0 \\ \vdots & & \ddots & \vdots \\ 0 & 0 & \cdots & d_n \end{pmatrix}$$

from a similar easy computation we have $1 \cdot D_g 1 = \sum_i d_i$. For any partition, if x is it $(1, -1)$-indicator, we also have $x \cdot D_g x = \sum_i d_i$, because the minus signs compensate in the entries where them appear.

In this context, it is traditional to define the Laplacian matrix L as

$$L = D_g - A$$

See, for example, [121] or [122]. The rationale behind this definition is the following relationship between the cut of a partition and the transform by L of its characteristic vectors.

Theorem 1. *For a partition* (V_1, V_2), *of* $(1, -1)$-*indicator* x, *we have*

$$cut(V_1, V_2) = \frac{x \cdot Lx}{4}$$

Proof. For a partition (V_1, V_2), with c_1 and c_2 being characteristic vectors of its sets, the sum of the weight of the edges $u \sim v$ with $u \in V_1$ and $v \in V_2$ is $c_1 \cdot Ac_2$. Therefore, $cut(V_1, V_2) = c_1 \cdot Ac_2$. By the symmetry of A, it is also equal to $c_2 \cdot Ac_1$.

If x is the $(1, -1)$-indicator of (V_1, V_2), then $x = c_1 - c_2$, and

$$x \cdot Ax = (c_1 - c_2) \cdot A(c_1 - c_2)$$
$$= c_1 \cdot Ac_1 + c_2 \cdot Ac_2 - (c_1 \cdot Ac_2 + c_2 \cdot Ac_1)$$
$$= c_1 \cdot Ac_1 + c_2 \cdot Ac_2 - 2cut(V_1, V_2)$$

Besides, as $c_1 + c_2 = 1$, that is $c_1 = 1 - c_2$, then $c_1 \cdot Ac_1 = c_1 \cdot A(1 - c_2) = c_1 \cdot A1 - c_1 \cdot Ac_2$. Likewise, $c_2 \cdot Ac_2 = c_2 \cdot A1 - c_2 \cdot Ac_1$, hence

$$c_1 \cdot Ac_1 + c_2 \cdot Ac_2 = c_1 \cdot A1 - c_1 \cdot Ac_2 + c_2 \cdot A1 - c_2 \cdot Ac_1$$
$$= (c_1 + c_2) \cdot A1 - (c_1 \cdot Ac_2 + c_1 \cdot Ac_2) = 1 \cdot A1 - 2cut(V_1, V_2)$$

Hence

$$x \cdot Ax = c_1 \cdot Ac_1 + c_2 \cdot Ac_2 - 2cut(V_1, V_2)$$
$$= 1 \cdot A1 - 2cut(V_1, V_2) - 2cut(V_1, V_2) = \sum_i d_i - 4cut(V_1, V_2)$$

That is, $4\mathrm{cut}(V_1, V_2) = \sum_i d_i - x \cdot Ax$. As $\sum_i d_i = x \cdot D_g x$, we can express $\sum_i d_i - x \cdot Ax = x \cdot D_g x - x \cdot Ax = x \cdot Lx$. Therefore,

$$\mathrm{cut}(V_1, V_2) = \frac{x \cdot Lx}{4}$$

$\square$

We have deduced this well-known identity in matrix form, instead of summatory form as usual, to avoid the index chasing. This way also makes explicit the role of the values b_1, b_2 using in indicators (as it is done in [119]). For example, if x is a $(\frac{1}{2}, -\frac{1}{2})$-indicator of (V_1, V_2), then $\mathrm{cut}(V_1, V_2) = x \cdot Lx$. In general, if x is a (b_1, b_2)-indicator the cost of its cut is $x \cdot Lx/(b_2 - b_1)^2$. This deduction also shows the role of the diagonal degree matrix.

In addition to the expression of cost as a bilinear form with matrix L, we express the requirement that the partition (V_1, V_2) be balanced as $\mathbf{1} \cdot x = 0$. Hence, the problem of finding the balanced partition of minimal cost is the following problem of combinatorial optimization:

$$\begin{aligned} &\underset{x}{\text{minimize}} \quad x \cdot Lx \\ &\text{subject to} \quad x_i = \pm 1, \; i = 1, \dots, n \\ &\qquad\qquad\quad \mathbf{1} \cdot x = 0 \end{aligned}$$

To solve this combinatorial problem, it is customary to relax the restrain $x_i = \pm 1$. The relaxed problem has several features that ease its numerical resolution: L is symmetric; hence, its eigenvalues are real and there are an orthonormal basis of eigenvectors [123]. Besides, $\mathbf{1}$ is an eigenvector of eigenvalue 0, because $D_g \mathbf{1} - A\mathbf{1} = 0$. Also, the eigenvalues are non-negative [124] $0 = \mu_0 \le \mu_1 \le \cdots \le \mu_{n-1}$ (numbering then without multiplicity $0 = \lambda_0 < \lambda_1 < \cdots < \lambda_k$). These features of L are generally deduced from its expression as summatory of squares that we have avoided. Here, we derive them from standard facts of numerical matrix analysis.

The main result in numerical eigenvalue computation is the min–max theorem [120]. In our case, this implies $\lambda_1 = \min_{x \neq 0} (x \cdot Lx)/(x \cdot x)$, the minimum is reached in a vector x_1 of norm 1, that is eigenvalue for λ_1. As the eigenvectors of different eigenvalues are orthogonal, $\mathbf{1} \cdot x_1 = 0$. That is, x_1 is a solution of the relaxed problem.

The first non-null eigenvalue λ_1 is the Fiedler value and its eigenvector x_1 is the Fiedler vector [125]. It solves the relaxed problem, numerically with computational complexity of $O(n^3)$. Rounding x_i gives a $(1, -1)$-indicator of a partition. The solution of the relaxed problem is an approximation of the combinatorial problem. This problem is *NP*-hard [118], hence the interest of a relaxed approximation. A bound of the error of this approximation, involving λ_1, is given by the bound of Mohar [126]. With Δ_g being the maximum vertex degree of G, $\Phi(G)$ the cost of the minimal cut, and $Sp(G)$ the cut obtained by the Fiedler eigenvector:

$$\Phi(G) \le Sp(G) \le \sqrt{\lambda_1 (2\Delta_g - \lambda_1)}$$

These properties, included the bound of Mohar, can be translated for Laplacians with vertex potential, a generalization of the Laplacian that we define in the next subsubsection and that allows us to extend the spectral partition to unequal vertex load.

2.4.3 *Laplacian with potential of vertex weights*

A *potential* is a function $p : V \longrightarrow \mathbb{R}$, and its diagonal form is the matrix $D_p = (d_{ij})$ with $d_{ii} = p(x_i)$, $d_{ij} = 0$ if $i \neq j$. The *Laplacian with potential p* (or p-Laplacian) is

$$L_p = L + D_p$$

That is $L_p = D_g - A + D_p$. Some properties of the p-Laplacian are similar to those of the Laplacian.

If the potential p is non-negative, L_p has a real eigenvalue that is positive and of maximum absolute value between the eigenvalues (known as *Perron eigenvalue*). There is an eigenvector of the Perron eigenvalue that is positive (the *Perron eigenvector* ρ).

The max–min theorem for the operator L_p gives us that $\lambda_1 = \min_{\substack{x \neq 0 \\ x \cdot \rho = 0}} (x \cdot L_p x)/$ $(x \cdot x)$, and the minimum is reached in its eigenvectors. Conventionally, the eigenvector of λ_1 of norm 1 and with a greater number of non-negative values is the *Fiedler vector* ϕ.

The spectral decomposition of L_p assure that $\phi \cdot \rho = 0$. This can be viewed, like in the previous Laplacian, that the positive and negative values of the Fiedler vector is an indicator of two sets of vertices that cut V in two parts of equal sum of Perron values.

To build potential p in such a way that the Perron vector ρ have predetermined values ρ_i, we have developed the following result. $A = (a_{ij})$ is the adjacency matrix and $(A\rho)_i$ the i-th component of the vector $A\rho$.

Theorem 2. *The potential*

$$p(x_i) = 1 + a_{ii} - \frac{(A\rho)_i}{\rho_i}$$

has ρ as Perron vector.

By the above discussion, the p-Laplacian of this potential has a Fiedler vector orthogonal to the Perron vector (that is, it produces a partition in parts of equal total load at the vertices), and that in addition, by the extremal max–min property, minimizes the cost of communications in the relaxed problem.

Also, by taking this Fiedler vector as an approximation to the combinatorial solution, that is, the unrelaxed problem, the error can be bounded with an expression similar to that of Mohar. As above with $\Phi(G)$ being the cost of the minimal cut, and $Sp_p(G)$ the cut obtained by Fiedler eigenvector of L_p:

$$\Phi(G) \leq Sp_p(G) \leq \sqrt{2\lambda_1 \max_i \frac{d_i - a_{ii}}{\rho_i}}$$

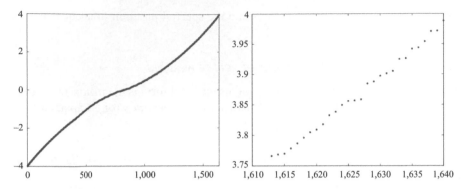

Figure 2.16   Eigenvalues of the mesh. The area of main eigenvalues is zoomed

With these results, we can mimic the traditional partition techniques, but incorporating the load at the vertices. In addition, the division into two parts can be done by assigning unequal proportions of the load (for example, 30%–70%).

The unequal load has been addressed in the literature either by modeling as a generalized eigenvalue problem [127], or by using several eigenvectors [128]. Both approaches have their own drawbacks [118]. For our purposes, the main disadvantage is that the vertex load is not embodied in the Laplacian. As we want to consider mappings from application graph to machine graph, the loads should be included in the model.

2.4.4 Mesh graph

In this subsection, first we give an example of spectral decomposition of the mesh graph of Figure 2.15. We will see that the eigenvector of the dominant eigenvalue partitions the square. In this example of Cartesian graph, the adjacency matrix has side $40 \times 41 = 1,640$. The 1,640 eigenvalues, in increasing order, are plotted in Figure 2.16, and as the matrix is symmetric, the Jordan form is diagonal [129].

Each vector is a value in every vertex, so we can plot it as a z value of height above the xy plane where the square lattice is displayed. With this convention, the first and second eigenvectors (with respect the ordering eigenvalues) can be seen in Figure 2.17.

Note that these are the eigenvectors of the adjacency matrix, not the Laplacian. However, the first eigenvector, bell-shaped and positive, is symmetrically posed in the square. We consider that each vertex has a load proportional to the corresponding entry of this first eigenvector. The second eigenvector, orthogonal to it, has positive and negative entries defining a partition of the mesh, whose two parts are equal in total load (measured by the first eigenvector).

In the case of the Laplacian, first and second eigenvectors (Perron and Fiedler) are in Figure 2.18. And there are also, as in the adjacency matrix, one positive and the other partitioning the vertices in two sets of vertices. The sets have equal load,

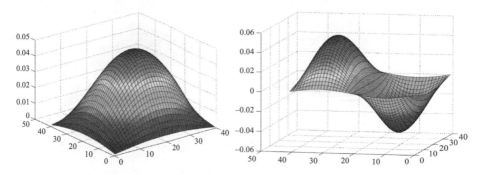

Figure 2.17   The first two eigenvectors of the mesh

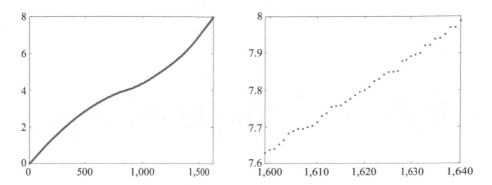

Figure 2.18   Laplacian eigenvalues of square lattice. The area of main eigenvalues is zoomed.

measured by the first eigenvector, such that being constant gives us an equal number of vertexes in each part (Figure 2.19).

The adjacency matrix and the Laplacian matrix have been taken as examples. They differ only in the diagonal, so the adjacency matrix is a particular type of p-Laplacian: one that has as potential the degree at each vertex. This example has been considered because it is easy to represent the eigenvectors and to see that the first eigenvector (Perron in the case of the adjacency matrix) corresponds to a load at each vertex (uniform in the case of Laplacian).

2.4.5   Numerical experiment

In this subsection, we describe a comparison, using the partitioning software Scotch [130], of the spectral method described above against the other method of graph partition. We have integrated the spectral bipartition method (with vertex loads) in Scotch. We resorted to the LAPACK library [131] for the eigenvector computation due to their availability, but it is preferable to use libraries specialized in sparse matrices,

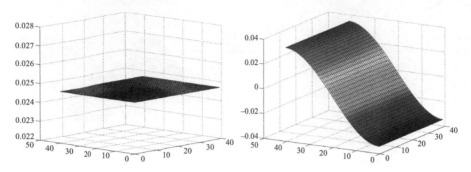

Figure 2.19   Eigenvectors of square lattice

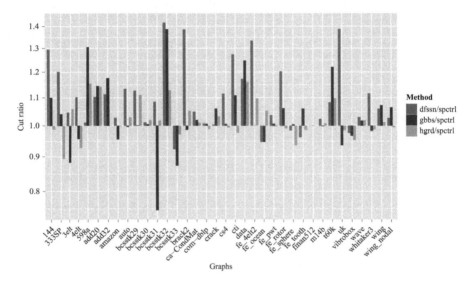

Figure 2.20   Ratio of cut improvement of the spectral method against others

such as [132]. The Fiedler eigenvector is used as an initial method in a multilevel approach (see [118] for technical background). In Figure 2.20, we do a
comparison with some of the initial methods present in Scotch (Diffusion, Gibbs-
Pole-Stockmeyer, H-greedy) over the graphs of the Walshaw collection [133], and
also some bigger graphs from the dataset of [134]. The cut produced with the spectral
method, for bipartitions, is about 10% better than the other methods. There are some
cases where the spectral method behaves equal or worse. In the figure, we plot the
value "cost of the cut of other method/cost of the spectral cut," hence a value of 1
means equal cost, greater than 1 means that spectral has lower cost.

The tests are meant to compare initial methods, leaving the contribution of
coarsening–uncoarsening as equal as possible between methods. To be precise,

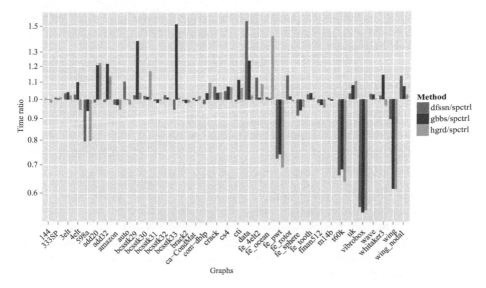

Figure 2.21   Ratio of time improvement of the spectral method against others

the tests include, for each graph of Walshaw benchmark (excluding fe_body and MemPlus, which are not connected), five different coarsening processes: up to 64, or 128, or 256, or 512, or 1,024 vertices. Then, each of these initial graphs is bipartitioned by diffusion, Gibbs, greedy, and spectral methods and then are uncoarsened with the Fiduccia-Mattheyses algorithm [135]. The final measure is the cost of the cut obtained. Unit loads and weights of the input graph are considered. In the plot, we use the mean of the five measures for each pair graph method.

In Figure 2.21, we also compare the timing of running each method compared to the spectral method. We plot the ratio of the time of three other ones compared to the spectral method. We see balanced results here where in some cases the spectral method is much faster but for some graphs (e.g., vibrobox) the ratio is lower than 0.6. However, the geometric mean of the ratio is 0.986, which means that, on average, the spectral method is comparable in terms of timings to the other methods. This is a good result as computing the eigenvectors can be very long. Actually, the coarsening phase that happens only in the other methods takes also a lot of time that has a strong impact on the timings.

2.4.6   Conclusions

The bipartition through the Fiedler eigenvector can be done by incorporating the loads of the vertices in the model of the graph, without the need to introduce these loads a posteriori in the resolution process. The classical techniques of analysis of the error of the approximation can be generalized to this new approach. Bipartition can be done in unbalanced parts, with a predetermined ratio, minimizing communications. However, extending this scheme to partitions in three or more parts does not seem straightforward. The numerical results, in comparison with the more usual methods, are favorable to the spectral method, especially in graphs of a certain type, such as those from social networks.

2.5 Summary

This chapter has shown some works related to UCS and the variety of systems that could be integrated in those complex environments. However, there are still several research topics and challenges that must be faced to cope with such complexity. Some of them are shown below:

Cloud/fog/dew big data computing: In the future, the highest opportunities lie in the availability of massive scale cloud infrastructure which will be omnipresent. To effectively use these available resources, massively federated and scalable software with orchestration through network awareness will be necessary. As an extension of links between UCS and Clouds, data access models for data mining in Exascale systems will be a key research topic. The integration will be between Cloud systems but also Fog and future type of infrastructure, leading to need on machine-to-machine computing and Cloud computing integration. Heterogeneity of such system will continue to increase, leading to the need to be able to integrate warehouse-scale computing using purpose-designed chips. Integrating the lowest, Dew-level devices will present additional challenges due to the extreme quantities of Physical Edge Devices, their severely low processing power and communication means, and the huge amounts of data generated.

HPC: One of the key points will be the availability of programming abstractions for the different fields of Exascale such as data analysis, machine learning, scientific computing, Big Data management, and smart cities that will be based on asynchronous algorithms for overlapping communication and computation. To reach this overlap, parallel applications (such as the MPI-based one) will need to be optimized using platform topology and performance information. One crucial research topic will be programmability of UCS as applications will run millions of parallel execution flows. New workflow programming for very large plate forms will be needed. But interoperability and sustainability will only be reached when code will be prevented to be platform specific and still efficient on different platforms. From a broader point of view, the scale of UCS will lead to Supercomputing on demand leading to a better use of the vast amount of available resources. The efficiency will be linked to researches on performance evaluation, modeling, and optimization of data parallel applications on heterogeneous HPC platforms. Management of such large distributed systems will be based on future researches on complex systems modeling, self-organizing systems, (interface and cellular automata.

Application-driven topics: With the aim of harnessing the power of UCS, scientific community will be able to improve dramatically the quality of models. One key example will be the research focus on meteorology beyond wind simulation (interfacing between different software packages and data formats, necessary for integration of simulations for complex tasks). New tools will be needed to use UCS for scientists from diverse fields, but tools only available to computer scientists will be needed such as the hardware/software co-design models to guide together the development of hardware and software infrastructure.

Tool-driven: Several tools will be needed to use efficiently UCS. Some tools can be provided by software, and also abstract models and new programming paradigms helping programmers to better use the available resources are helpful. Due to the scale of the systems, one key element will be resource-efficient models for automatic recovery from minute-to-minute failures. As security is often forgotten by programmers, software-defined security models will be needed on large-scale distributed infrastructure to simplify its usage. One way to increase security and privacy will be to create new secure privacy-preserving data management algorithms such as machine learning. To address code sustainability and adaptation evolution on code production, such as source-to-source translators and model-driven engineering, is needed in order to adapt to the underlying hardware.

In order to support some of these challenges, several breaktroughs are expected in order to reach proper support for programmers and users in the Ultrascale context as described in the NESUS research roadmap[6]:

Improve the programmability of complex systems: Due to the size of these systems, it is no more possible for the programmer to have a precise and detailed global view of the state of its application. Thus, he/she needs to have support from programming frameworks to simplify this view;

Break the wall between runtime and programming frameworks: Exascale systems are so complex that runtime need high-level information from the programmers and the programmer need some information on the runtime to understand how to harness its power;

Enabling behavioral sensitive runtime: Runtime cannot run application as black boxes anymore as large-scale systems are composed of a large number of interconnected elements. Network profile must be known to reduce impact on neighbor applications, for example.

Chapter 3
Resilience and fault tolerance

Pascal Bouvry[1], Sebastien Varrette[1], Tuan Anh Trinh[2],
Muhammad Umer Wasim[1], Abdallah A.Z.A. Ibrahim[1],
and Xavier Besseron[1]

As discussed in the Introduction, ultrascale computing is a new computing paradigm that comes naturally from the necessity of computing systems that should be able to handle massive data in possibly very large-scale distributed systems, enabling new forms of applications that can serve a very large amount of users and in a timely manner that we have never experienced before. It is very challenging to find sustainable solutions for ultrascale computing system (UCS) due to their scale and a wide range of possible applications and involved technologies. For example, we need to deal with cross fertilization among high-performance computing (HPC), large-scale distributed systems, and big data management.

One of the challenges regarding sustainable UCS is resilience. Traditionally, it has been an important aspect in the area of critical infrastructure protection (e.g. the traditional electrical grid and the smart grids). Furthermore, it has also become popular in the area of information and communication technology (ICT), ICT systems, computing and large-scale distributed systems. The existing practices of dependable design deal reasonably well with achieving and predicting dependability in systems that are relatively closed and unchanging. Yet, the tendency to make all kinds of large-scale systems more interconnected, open, and able to change without new intervention by designers, makes existing techniques inadequate to deliver the same levels of dependability. For instance, evolution of the system itself and its uses impairs dependability: new components 'create' system design faults or vulnerabilities by feature interaction or by triggering pre-existing bugs in existing components; likewise, new patterns of use arise, new interconnections open the system to attack by new potential adversaries, and so on. Another one, which attracted less interest in the literature, but becomes more and more crucial with the expected convergence with the Cloud computing paradigm, is the notion of regulation in such a system to assess the quality of service (QoS) and SLA proposed for the use of these platforms. This chapter covers both aspects through the reproduction of two articles: [3] and [136].

[1]University of Luxembourg, Parallel Computing and Optimization Group (PCOG), Luxembourg
[2]Corvinus University of Budapest, Corvinus Fintech Center, Budapest, Hungary

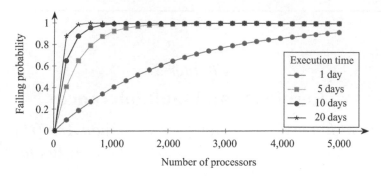

Figure 3.1   Typical probability of failure with increasing number of processors in a computing system

In this chapter, we show an introduction to resilience in UCS from two facets: technical and legal. Thus, the rest of this chapter is organized as follows: Section 3.1 reviews the basic notions of faults, fault tolerance, and robustness. Applications and implementations within UCS are also proposed, while novel challenges and opportunities linked to the development of distributed ledger technologies (DLT). Then regulation compliance aspects are covered in Section 3.2. Finally, Section 3.3 concludes the paper and provides some future directions and perspectives opened by this study.

3.1   Security and reliability in ultrascale system

3.1.1   Faults, fault tolerance, and robustness

As illustrated in Figure 3.1 and due to their inherent scale, UCS is naturally prone to errors and failures which are no longer rare events [137–140].

There are many sources of *faults* in distributed computing and they are inevitable due to the defects introduced into the system at the stages of its design, construction, or through its exploitation (e.g. software bugs, hardware faults, problems with data transfer) [138–141]. A fault may occur by a deviation of a system from the required operation leading to an *error* (for instance, a software bug becomes apparent after a subroutine call). This transition is called a fault activation, *i.e.* a *dormant* fault (not producing any errors) becomes *active*. An error is *detected* if its presence is indicated by a message or a signal, whereas not detected, present errors are called *latent*. Errors in the system may cause a (service) *failure*, and depending on its type, successive faults and errors may be introduced (*error/failure propagation*). The distinction between faults, errors, and failures is important because these terms create boundaries allowing analysis and coping with different threats. In essence, faults are the cause of errors (reflected in the state) which without proper handling may lead to failures (wrong and unexpected outcome). Following these definitions, *fault tolerance* is an ability of a system to behave in a well-defined manner once an error occurs.

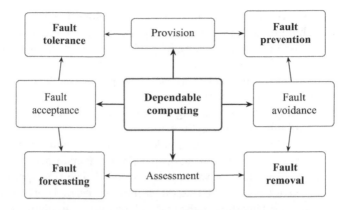

Figure 3.2　Means for dependable computing

There are five specific fault models relevant in distributed computing: *omission*, *duplication*, *timing*, *crash*, and *byzantine failures* [141,430].

Omission and *duplication* failures are linked with problems in communication. Send-omission corresponds to a situation when a message is not sent; receive-omission – when a message is not received. Duplication failures occur in the opposite situation – a message is sent or received more than once.

Timing failures occur when time constraints concerning the service execution or data delivery are not met. This type is not limited to delays only, since too early delivery of a service may also be undesirable.

The *crash* failure occurs in four variants, each additionally associated with its persistence. Transient crash failures correspond to the service restart: amnesia-crash (the system is restored to a pre-defined initial state, independent on the previous inputs), partial-amnesia-crash (a part of the system stays in the state before the crash, where the rest is reset to the initial conditions), and pause-crash (the system is restored to the state it had before the crash). Halt-crash is a permanent failure encountered when the system or the service is not restarted and remains unresponsive.

The last model – *byzantine* failure (also called *arbitrary*) – covers any (very often unexpected and inconsistent) responses of a service or a system at arbitrary times. In this case, failures may emerge periodically with varying results, scope, effects, etc. This is the most general and serious type of failure [141,430].

3.1.1.1　Dependable computing and fault-tolerance techniques

Faults, errors and failures are *threats* to system's *dependability*. A system is described as dependable, when it is able to fulfil a contract for the delivery of its services avoiding frequent downtimes caused by failures.

Identification of threats does not automatically guarantee dependable computing. For this purpose, four main groups of appropriate methods have been defined [141]: *fault prevention*, *fault tolerance*, *fault removal*, and *fault forecasting*. As visible in Figure 3.2, all of them can be analysed from two points of view – either as means of avoidance/acceptance of faults or as approaches to support/assess dependability. Fault-tolerance techniques aim to reduce (or even eliminate) the amount of service failures in the presence of faults. The main goal of *fault prevention* methods is to minimize the number of faults occurred or introduced through usage and enforcement of various policies (concerning usage, access, development, etc.) The next group – *fault removal* techniques – is concentrated around testing and verification (including formal methods). Finally, *fault forecasting* consists of means to estimate occurrences and consequences of faults (at a given time and later).

Fault-tolerance techniques may be divided into two main and complementary categories [141]: *error detection* and *recovery*. Error detection may be performed during normal service operation or while it is suspended. The first approach in this category – *concurrent detection* – is based on various tests carried out by components (software and/or hardware) involved in the particular activity or by elements especially designated for this function. For example, a component may calculate and verify checksums for the data which is processed by it. On the other hand, a firewall is a good illustration of a designated piece of hardware (or software) oriented in detection of intrusions and other malicious activities. *Preemptive detection* is associated with the maintenance and diagnostics of a system or a service. The focus in this approach is laid on the identification of latent faults and dormant errors. It may be carried out at a system start-up, at a service bootstrap or during special maintenance sessions. After an error of a fault is detected, recovery methods are applied. Depending on the problem type, *error or fault handling* techniques are used. The first group is focused on the elimination of errors from the system state, while the second is designed to prevent activation of faults. In [141], the specific methods are separated from each other, where in practice this boundary is fuzzy and depends on the specific service and system types. Generally, error handling is solved through:

1. *Rollback* [142]: the system is restored to the last known, error-free state. The approach here depends on a method used to track the changes of the state. A well-known technique is *checkpointing* – the state of a system is saved period-ically (e.g. the snapshot of a process is stored on a disk) as a potential recovery point in the future. Obviously, this solution is not straightforward in the case of distributed systems and there are many factors to consider. In such an environ-ment, checkpointing can be coordinated or not – with differences in reliability and the cost of synchronization of the distributed components – see [430–432]. Rollback can also be implemented through the *message logging*. In this case, the communication between the components is tracked rather than their state. In case of an error, the system is restored by *replaying* the historical messages, allowing it to reach global consistency [430]. Sometimes both techniques are treated as one, as usually they complement each other.

2. *Rollforward*: the current, erroneous system state is discarded and replaced with a one newly created and initialized.

3. *Compensation*: an approach based on components' *redundancy* and *replication*, sometimes referred to as *fault masking*. In the first case, additional components (usually hardware) are kept in reserve [432]. If failures or errors occur, they are

used to compensate for the losses. For example, a connection to the Internet of a cloud platform should be based on solutions from at least two different Internet service providers.

Replication is based on the dispersion of multiple copies of the service components. A schema with replicas used only for the purpose of fault tolerance is called a *passive (primary-backup) replication* [432]. On the other hand, an *active replication* is when the replicas participate in providing the service, leading to increased performance and applicability of load balancing techniques. Coherence is the major challenge here, and various approaches are used to support it. For instance, read-write protocols are crucial in active replication, as all replicas are expected to have the same state. Another worth to note example is clearly visible in volunteer-based platforms. An appropriate selection policy of the correct service response is needed when replicas return different answers, *i.e.* a method to reach quorum consensus is required.

These techniques are not exclusive and can be used together. If the system cannot be restored to a correct state, thanks to the compensation, rollback may be attempted. If this fails, then rollforward may be used.

The above methods may be referred to as *general-purpose* techniques. These solutions are relatively generic, which aids their implementation for almost any distributed computation. It is also possible to delegate responsibility for fault tolerance to the service (or application) itself, allowing tailoring the solution for specific needs – therefore forming an *application-specific* approach. A perfect example in this context is ABFT, originally applied to distributed matrix operations [143], where original matrices are extended with checksums before being scattered among the processing resources. This allows detection, location, and correction of certain miscalculations, creating a *disk-less checkpointing* method. Similarly, in certain cases, it is possible to continue the computation or the service operation despite the occurring errors. For instance, unavailable resource resulting from a crash-stop failure can be excluded from further use. In this work, the idea will be further analysed and extended to the context of byzantine errors and the nature-inspired distributed algorithms.

Fault handling techniques are applied after the system is restored to an error-free state (using the methods described above). As the aim now is to prevent future activation of detected faults, four subgroups according to the intention of the operation may be created. These are [141]: *diagnosis* (the error(s) are identified and their source(s) are located), *isolation* (faulty components are logically or physically separated and excluded from the service), *reconfiguration* (the service/platform is reconfigured to substitute or bypass the faulty elements), and *reinitialization* (the configuration of the system is adapted to the new conditions).

3.1.1.2 Robustness

When a given system is resilient to a given type of fault, one generally claims that this system is *robust*. Yet defining rigorously robustness is not an easy task and many contributions come with their own interpretation of what robustness is. Actually, there exists a systematic framework that permits to define a robust system unambiguously.

In fact, this should be probably applied to any system or approach claiming to propose a fault-tolerance mechanism. This framework, formalized in [144], answers the following three questions:

1. What behavior of the system makes it robust?
2. What uncertainties is the system robust against?
3. Quantitatively, exactly how robust is the system?

The first question is generally linked to the technique or the algorithm applied. The second – explicitly lists the type of faults or disturbing elements targeted by the system. Answering it is critical to delimit the application range of the designed system and to avoid counter examples selected in a context not addressed by the robust mechanism. The third and the last question is probably the most difficult to answer and, at the same time, the most vital to characterize the limits of the system. Indeed, there is nearly always a threshold on the error/fault rate above which the proposed infrastructure fails to remain robust and breaks (in some sense).

3.1.2   Fault tolerance in UCS

3.1.2.1   Computing hardware resilience

As mentioned before, any implementation of fault tolerance (or indeed of fault detection) in hardware implies compensation, *i.e.* the use of *redundancy* and *replication*. In terms of data or information redundancy, a general approach consists in the use of non-minimal coding to represent the data in a system. By far the most common implementation of data redundancy implies the use of *error detecting codes*, when the objective is fault detection, and of *error correcting codes* (ECC), when the objective is fault tolerance [145].

Memory elements, for instance, are probably the hardware components that require the highest degree of fault tolerance: their extremely regular structure implies that transistor density in memories is substantially greater than in any other device (the largest memory device commercial available in 2015 reaches a transistor count of almost 140 billion, compared, for example, to the 4.3 billion of the largest processor). This level of density has resulted in the introduction of fault-tolerant features even in commonly available commercial memories. Reliability in memories takes essentially two forms: to protect against single faults, the use of redundant ECC memory is common and well advertised [146], while marginally less known is the use of spare memory locations to replace permanently damaged ones. The latter technique, used extensively at fabrication for laser-based permanent reconfiguration, has also been applied in an on-line self-repair setting [147].

At the level of the computing elements, the development of high-performance processors has been driven by both performance and energy efficiency. As a result and due to their redundancy requirements and thus their negative implications both for performance and for power consumption, relatively little research into fault-tolerant cores has reached the consumer market, leading to limited developments. The situation is somewhat different outside of the high-performance market (typically in the spatial domain), where examples of processors specifically designed for fault tolerance exist.

More recently, the RAZOR approach [148] represents a fault-tolerance technique aimed specifically at detecting (and possibly correcting) timing errors within the processor pipelines using a particular kind of a time redundancy approach that exploits delays in the clock distribution lines.

3.1.2.2   Network resilience

Networks are a crucial element of UCS and more generally any system where processors have to share information, and therefore they represent a fundamental aspect of any multi-processor system. Often rivalling in size and complexity with the processing units themselves, networks and their routers have traditionally been a fertile ground for research on fault tolerance. Indeed, even when limiting the scope of the investigation to on-chip networks, numerous books and surveys exist that classify, describe, and analyse the most significant approaches to fault tolerance [149–151]. Very broadly, most of the fundamental redundancy techniques have been applied, in one form or another, to the problem of implementing fault-tolerant on-chip networks, ranging from data redundancy (*i.e.* parity or ECC encoding of transmitted packets), through hardware redundancy (*i.e.* additional routing logic), to time redundancy (*i.e.* repeated data transmission).

Recent studies [152] also consider a change in the communication pattern, typically using self-healing protocols based on *gossiping*. Gossip protocols define a pure P2P network over a large set of computing resources and exploit randomness to virally disseminate information while maintaining connectivity in a self-organized (independent of the initial state) equilibrium. Such equilibrium emerges from the loosely coupled and distributed run of the protocol within different and independent communicating components. The epidemic nature provides high fault-resilience and self-healing properties meant to be crucial for large-scale computing platforms as UCS, at the cost of an overhead in terms of messages routing performance [153].

3.1.2.3   Software and message passing interface resilience

We have mentioned previously that application specific approaches relying on ABFT which permit one to tailor the fault-tolerant mechanism solution for specific needs, therefore forming an *application-specific* approach.

More generally, the compute units of current and future HPC systems are more and more complex and diverse (including co-processors or graphics processing unit accelerators) such that smarter ways to efficiently program them are required. At this level, programming models that were introduced to abstract from the compute resources and leverage available parallelism, have to be adapted. In particular, parallel programming models, meant as ways to express parallelism inside applications, have to be compliant with a common programming language, which comes with a compiler and a runtime to ensure an efficient execution.

Various programming models have emerged as parallel machines evolved, and they follow different paradigms; yet, the most popular one is based on Message Passing oriented toward distributed and interconnected memory systems. In this model, multiple instances of the program (or processes) allow one to share computational resources. A process contains everything needed for executing a program: its own address space, a set of instructions, and a context. They communicate with each other through messages passed over the network.

The main implementation of this model is, of course, message passing interface (MPI), a standard library introduced in 1991. It is designed for distributed memory machines, and it involves processes running concurrently and parallelizing the program. Communications are to be made explicit by the user and MPI supports both point-to-point and collective communications. It is now widely and largely adopted for most scientific codes, having interfaces in many programming languages. The standard has been revised in multiple versions, the most recent being the MPI 3.1 [154] standard which introduced Non Blocking Collectives, allowing asynchronous communications between processes.

Numerous implementations of MPI are available, such as OpenMPI, MPICH2, MVAPICH2, Intel MPI, or MPC (Multi-Processor Computing).

Nowadays, MPI remains a straightforward and effective way to program large-scale MPI. Fault-tolerance aspects are reviewed in [155] as the MPI standard does not clearly define behavior of MPI implementation if one or several processes of an MPI application are abnormally aborted. There is a dedicated working group[1] covering this topic, and several MPI implementations embed fault-tolerance mechanisms. First attempts rely on a complete checkpointing and message logging to enable replacement of aborted processes – the checkpoints avoid reconstructing computations from the beginning through the message logs. This requires a reliable subsystem for the checkpoints and message logs, as well as for the 'dispatcher' process leading to a *coordinated* checkpoint. More recent approaches try to mitigate this requirement, such as the one proposed in ULFM 2.0, Intel MPI, or MPICH. For instance, ULFM enables user-level deployment of in-memory diskless checkpoints, stored on other compute nodes. It features reduced I/O activities to offer a decreased the failure-free overhead while enabling better restart speed. Yet, its development remains at an early stage. In all cases, building a resilient MPI program encompasses a minimal set of features:

- *Detection and notification of failures.* Typically, only processes involved in a communication with a failed process might detect the occurrence of a failure to limit the scope and noise induced by the detection operations.
- *Definition of a failure scope to enable error propagation.* This is typically left to application-specific settings.
- *Error recovery strategy.* This remains, of course, the main issue to solve and a work in progress, for instance, to define who should be in charge of defining the fault-tolerant strategy and the type of feedback the application receives. As an illustration, at the moment of writing, ULFM is not a recovery strategy, but a minimalistic set of building blocks for implementing complex recovery strategies.

---

[1] See http://mpi-forum.org/mpi-30/ft-wg

Table 3.1   Overview of the main consensus models used within DLT

Consensus model	Example
Proof-of-Authority (PoA)	POA Network, Kovan and Rinkeby *testnets*, etc.
Proof-of-Work (PoW)	Bitcoin, Ethereum (until version 3), Litecoin, Primecoin, Monero, Zcash, Namecoin, etc.
Proof-of-Stake (PoS)	Peercoin (PoST), Ethereum (starting version 4), Netcoin (PoU), etc.
Delegated Proof-of-Stake (DPoS)	Nano / Raiblocks (block lattice), etc.
Proof-of-Retrievability (PoR)	Spacemint, etc.
Direct Acyclic Graph (DAG)	IOTA (Tangle), Hashgraph, etc.
Byzantine Fault Tolerance (BFT)	PBFT, Ripple (FBA), Algorand (BA ⋆), etc.

3.1.3   Blockchains and DLT

Blockchains are immutable DLT system implemented in a distributed fashion (*i.e.* without a central repository) and usually without a central authority [156]. At their most basic level, they enable a community of users to record transactions in a ledger that is public to that community such that no transaction can be changed once published. This technology became widely known starting in 2008 when it was applied to enable the emergence of electronic currencies where digital transfers of money take place in distributed systems. It has enabled the success of e-commerce systems such as Bitcoin, Ethereum, Ripple, and Litecoin [157]. Because of this, blockchains are often viewed as bound to Bitcoin or possibly e-currency solutions in general. However, the technology is more broadly useful and is available for a variety of applications.

Indeed, at the heart of DLT resides a consensus algorithm which is responsible for maintaining the data structure, *i.e.* define the way new blocks representing sets of transactions are added. Each node maintains a copy of the blockchain and may propose a new block to the other participating nodes (called miners in the traditional PoW consensus model). Thus, the consensus model enables a group of mutually distrusting users to work together to decide which block is agreed to expand the structure and without any central authority. A list of the main consensus models currently available is proposed in Table 3.1.

The traditional PoW is not adapted for UCS – it involves intentionally resource-intensive tasks (taking large amounts of processing power, memory, or both); yet, using these systems for these duties is counter-productive and against energy efficiency objectives. More recent and alternative proposals seems more suited for an effective usage on UCS, typically the ones relying on PoS, direct acyclic graph (DAG), and the resolution of the BGP enabling BFT. The range of possible applications is wide, for instance, to securely store computing transactions or to enable QoS regulation from *smart contracts*.

A smart contract is a collection of code and data (sometimes referred to as functions and state) that is deployed to a blockchain such as Ethereum. Any future transactions sent to the blockchain can then send data to public methods offered by the smart contract. The contract executes the appropriate method with the user provided data to perform a service. The code, being on the blockchain, is immutable and therefore can be used (among other purposes) as a trusted third party for validating the SLA of the system. The next section demonstrates such a use case.

3.2   Regulation compliance in ultrascale system

Today's law-driven societies based on the use of smart contracts are transforming the way economies function around the globe. Regulation compliance is the common model used to ensure the desired level of reliability in any system, which is expected to be more and more crucial for large-scale computing platforms such as UCS.

Leaving aside the technological details of the running a smart contract on top of such systems, this section presents the design and implementation of network for sustainable ultrascale computing systems (NESUS) Watchdog, a software bot/agent adapted from the one proposed in [136] and inspired from the work performed in [158]. The underlying concept of NESUS Watchdog is built upon the notion factor analysis and stochastic modeling from the disciplines of unsupervised machine learning and Data Science, respectively. The aim of NESUS Watchdog is to monitor a UCS as per pre-defined regulations (a *smart contract*) and penalize the system in the case of a breach that (a) has a potential to create substantial damage and (b) has high probability to occur in the future.

3.2.1   NESUS Watchdog and regulatory compliance

As seen in Section 3.1.3, a smart contract is a piece of code that resides on a blockchain network and is identified by a unique address. It includes a set of executable functions and state variables. The functions are executed when a transaction is invoked by a certain condition (or by an electronic event or data). These transactions include input parameters that are required by the functions in the contract. Upon the execution of a function, the state variables in the contract may change depending on the logic implemented in the function. This execution is self-enforceable, i.e. once a smart contract is concluded its further execution is neither dependent on intend of contractual parties or any unplanned third part, nor does it require any additional approvals or actions from their side [159]. Thus, breach of contract and mechanism addressing the breach becomes irrelevant during the execution of a smart contract [160]. However, even though the breach becomes irrelevant during the execution, what if an output of a smart contract results in a breach? For example, deviation in an output of a smart contract is a breach if a service provider of a UCS provides '90% actual uptime' on average as compared to agreed '95% uptime'.

The NESUS Watchdog, hereafter referred as a *bot*, reuses the concepts proposed in [158] and performs a two-phase validation process for the potential breach by a smart contract executed on top of a UCS. Initially, it assesses the significance of the breach to ensure that it has a potential to create substantial damage. Afterward, if the significance is high, it assesses the probability of the breach. In case the probability is also high, i.e. the breach frequently occurred in the past and there is certainty for it

Smart Contract for QoS	Bot based Smart Contract for QoS
Condition If latency of a service goes beyond a pre-defined threshold or throughput falls below pre-defined threshold, the client machine sends a maintenance request. **Transaction** For sending the maintenance request, a transaction is sent to the *request_service_function* of the *Service_Smart_Contract* between the client machine and the service provider machine.	**Condition (or Breach)** If latency of a service goes beyond a pre-defined threshold or throughput falls below pre-defined threshold, A bot at the client machine applies following logical operations to send a penalization request. φ is a high significance of the breach ϑ is a high probability of the breach **PNL** is a penalization request $(\neg \varphi \lor (\varphi \land \neg \vartheta) \rightarrow \neg \textbf{PNL}) \land (\varphi \land \vartheta \rightarrow \textbf{PNL})$ **Transaction** For sending the penalization request, a transaction is sent to the *request_service_function* of the *Breach_Service_Smart_Contract* between the client machine and the service provider.

Figure 3.3   The Bot-enabled smart contract

to occur in the future, the bot invokes a transaction and executes a function in a smart contract that results in the penalization. Figure 3.3 presents an example of a smart contract for QoS in an UCS and a context where the contract is implemented using the bot.

3.2.1.1   Assessing significance of breach

To assess the significance of a breach within the system, the bot relies on the notion of *communality* [161], a measure of variance a broader concept of probability-based factor model (PFM) from the discipline of unsupervised machine learning [162,163]. In the example provided in Figure 3.3, it would correspond to the measure of the relationship between contract (QoS) and its output e.g. latency. Its high value indicates a strong relationship between the two and endorses the related breach (e.g. latency threshold) to be considered as significant.

Communality is estimated by using structural equation modeling (SEM). SEM is a statistical approach used to examine the association between a *latent* variable (or goal) and an observed variables (or criteria) [162,163]. Latent variable is a theoretical construct that is inferred from the variables that are observed in the field. In Figure 3.3, QoS is a latent variable, which is inferred from the variables (throughput or latency) that are observed during in the field. In SEM, the most popular and frequently used methods to estimate communality are principal factor analysis (PFA) and maximum likelihood (ML) [162,163]. Considering that ML estimation assumes normal distribution of observed variables and that the bot deals with observed variables without making any prior assumption, PFA was used to estimate communality. In PFA, the relationship vector $\Lambda = (\lambda_1 \lambda_2 \ldots \lambda_n)'$ between a latent variable F and observed variables vector $Y = (y_1 y_2 \ldots y_n)'$ is expressed in a variance–covariance matrix notation as follows:

$$cov(Y) = cov(\Lambda F) + \Psi,$$

where Ψ is a vector that represents the uniqueness of observed variables not shared with the latent variable. By using covariance property $cov(AZ) = Acov(Z)A^T$,

$cov(\Lambda F)$ on the right-hand side of the above equation can be expanded to $\Lambda cov(F)\Lambda^T + \Psi$.

Moreover, since we consider here only a *single* latent factor (the QoS), F is simply an identity matrix, thus $cov(F) = 1$. It follows that

$$cov(Y) = \Lambda\Lambda^T + \Psi.$$

Within HPC and UCSs, Y is generally not *commensurated*, i.e. observed variables (throughput, latency, etc.) are measured in different units and scales. In this case, standardized Y has to be used. After standardization, the covariance becomes correlation (r), and subsequently, the covariance matrix $cov(Y)$ becomes a correlation matrix $R = \Lambda\Lambda^T + \Psi$, which can be expanded as

$$\begin{bmatrix} 1 & \cdots & r_{1n} \\ \vdots & \ddots & \vdots \\ r_{1n} & \cdots & 1 \end{bmatrix} = \begin{bmatrix} \lambda_1 \\ \lambda_2 \\ \vdots \\ \lambda_n \end{bmatrix} \begin{bmatrix} \lambda_1 & \lambda_2 & \cdots & \lambda_n \end{bmatrix} + \begin{bmatrix} \Psi_1 & \cdots & 0 \\ \vdots & \ddots & \vdots \\ 0 & \cdots & \Psi_n \end{bmatrix}$$

Bringing Ψ to the left-hand side and performing subtraction,

$$\begin{bmatrix} 1 - \Psi_1 & \cdots & r_{1n} \\ \vdots & \ddots & \vdots \\ r_{1n} & \cdots & 1 - \Psi_1 \end{bmatrix} = \begin{bmatrix} \lambda_1 \\ \lambda_2 \\ \vdots \\ \lambda_n \end{bmatrix} \begin{bmatrix} \lambda_1 & \lambda_2 & \cdots & \lambda_n \end{bmatrix} = \Lambda\Lambda^T$$

Subtracting unique variance from one $(1 - \Psi)$ will yield shared variance of an observed variable for the latent variable, which is equal to square of λ_i [162,163]. Respectively, $(\lambda_i)^2$ can replace $(1 - \Psi)$ and the above equation will become

$$\begin{bmatrix} (\lambda_1)^2 & \cdots & r_{1n} \\ \vdots & \ddots & \vdots \\ r_{1n} & \cdots & (\lambda_1)^2 \end{bmatrix} = \Lambda\Lambda^T$$

Accordingly, in a reduced form, we obtain the following equation:

$$\begin{bmatrix} (\lambda_1)^2 & \cdots & r_{1n} \\ \vdots & \ddots & \vdots \\ r_{1n} & \cdots & (\lambda_1)^2 \end{bmatrix} = R - \Psi = \Lambda\Lambda^T$$

where $R - \Psi$ is a 'reduced correlation matrix.' If $R - \Psi$ is a positive semi-definite matrix, i.e. it satisfies $R - \Psi = (R - \Psi)^T$, then this implies that $R - \Psi$ has the following spectral decomposition (i.e. a factorization into a canonical form, whereby the matrix is represented in terms of its eigenvectors to identify latent variable and corresponding eigenvalues to show the strength of identified latent variable):

$$R - \Psi = UDU^T$$

In this equation, U is the matrix of eigenvectors of $R - \Psi$ and D is the diagonal matrix of corresponding eigenvalues $\Theta_1 \Theta_2 \ldots \Theta_n$

$$D = \begin{bmatrix} \Theta_1 & \cdots & 0 \\ \vdots & \ddots & \vdots \\ 0 & \cdots & \Theta_n \end{bmatrix}$$

The important property of a positive semi-definite matrix is that its eigenvalues are always positive or null. Hence, $\Theta_i \geq 0$, and consequently, D can be factored into $D^{1/2} D^{1/2}$. In particular:

$$R - \Psi = \left(U D^{\frac{1}{2}} \right) \left(D^{\frac{1}{2}} U^T \right) = \Lambda \Lambda^T$$

In a general expanded form:

$$\Lambda = \left(U D^{\frac{1}{2}} \right) = \begin{bmatrix} u_{11} & \cdots & u_{1n} \\ \vdots & \ddots & \vdots \\ u_{n1} & \cdots & u_{nn} \end{bmatrix} \times \begin{bmatrix} \sqrt{\Theta_1} & \cdots & 0 \\ \vdots & \ddots & \vdots \\ 0 & \cdots & \sqrt{\Theta_n} \end{bmatrix}$$

Yet, it can be observed that in the above form, Λ (or $UD^{\frac{1}{2}}$) is presented as a $n \times n$ matrix; however, as we consider here a single latent variable (the QoS within a UCS), Λ must be $n \times 1$ matrix representing $\Lambda = (\lambda_1 \lambda_2 \ldots \lambda_n)'$. Hence, from the right-hand side of above equation, the largest eigenvalue Θ_i and corresponding eigenvector U_i are used for calculation of Λ, i.e., $\Lambda = U_i \sqrt{\Theta_i}$. The squared value of Λ is called communality (ζ) and can be written as

$$\zeta = \Lambda^2 = \begin{bmatrix} (u_1)^2 \\ (u_2)^2 \\ \vdots \\ (u_n)^2 \end{bmatrix} \Theta_i$$

In the above equation, the eigenvector contains estimated unit-scaled loadings or weights (u_i) that are associated with each observed variable. The eigenvalue ζ is a shared variance among all the observed variables that represent the latent variable. Communality is obtained by multiplying the squared value of u_i with ζ, which represents the relationship of latent variable with observed variable.

Coming back to the concrete example proposed in Figure 3.3 to assess the QoS of a UCS, let us assume that the communality obtained for 'QoS and latency' is 0.87, when the one collected for 'QoS and throughput' is 0.14. The low value received in the second case indicates a weak relationship and therefore declares that the related breach (*i.e.* throughput < threshold) is insignificant and unlikely to create substantial damage.

3.2.1.2 Assessing probability of breach

To assess the probability of breach $P(x)$, the bot uses the notion of stochastic modeling from the domain of Data Science. A stochastic model predicts a random event weighted by its probability [164]. The bot, based on the distribution model of the previous breaches $(x_{t-1}, x_{t-2}, \ldots, x_{t-n})$, suggests a stochastic model with minimum 'square error' to find $P(x)$. In distribution modeling, square error as criteria with the minimum value indicates the best possible approximation (stochastic model) for the data. However, it also requires verification in terms of accuracy, i.e. how precisely a stochastic model can represent the data.

For example, during the distribution analysis, if the bot observes that *previous* breaches are lognormal increasing with minimum square error, then the probability of breach $P(x)$ is

$$P(x) = \frac{1}{\sigma x \sqrt{2\pi}} e^{-(ln(x)-\mu)^2/2\sigma^2} \quad \text{if} (x_{t-1}, x_{t-2}, \cdots, x_{t-n}) \sim LOGN(\mu, \sigma)$$

To verify the accuracy of the above model, the bot performs a Paired Sample T-Test. In the test, it determines whether the mean difference between two samples, i.e. previous breaches and random data generated using $LOGN(\mu, \sigma)$ in (2), is zero or not. For the latter case, i.e. $\neq 0$ (when the difference between the two is not negligible), the bot dismisses the use of the expected stochastic model.

3.2.2 Illustration: penalization by NESUS Watchdog

This subsection presents an empirical illustration of penalizations by the bot in UCS for three HPC workflows: Redis, MongoDB, and Memcached Servers access. The HPC facility of the University of Luxembourg and Docker containers were used to emulate the contractual environment of these workflows. Each of these scenarios was operated under a workload generated from the Yahoo Cloud Service Benchmark (YCSB) [165] which was deployed to continuously monitor the QoS of the system in terms of throughput (operations per second), read latency (time to read data from database), and update latency (time to update data in database). For the experiments described in the sequel, the input parameters given to be passed to the YCSB benchmark for evaluation correspond to the different number of operations (ranging from 0 to 10,000), an increasing number of records (ranging from 0 to 10,000), and a number of threads ranging from 0 to 100. Python (for scripting) and R (for data visualization) were used to identify the smart contract breach, in which case the bot was activated to request penalization. In addition, several data analysis tools were used to assist the PFM analysis such as Arena Input analyser, STATA or IBM Statistical Analysis Software Package (SPSS).

Figure 3.4 presents YCSB monitoring of service providers in terms of unit-scaled throughput, read latency, and update latency. The YCSB data of all three service providers was used by the bot to calculate communality for throughput (0.38), read latency (0.46), and update latency (0.33). It can be observed that read latency has the highest value and consequently, the strongest relationship with QoS. Therefore, the related breach, i.e. read latency > threshold, is significant and most likely to create substantial damage.

For each workflow, the following operations were performed: (a) the threshold was set to average read latency, which was calculated from its YCSB data,

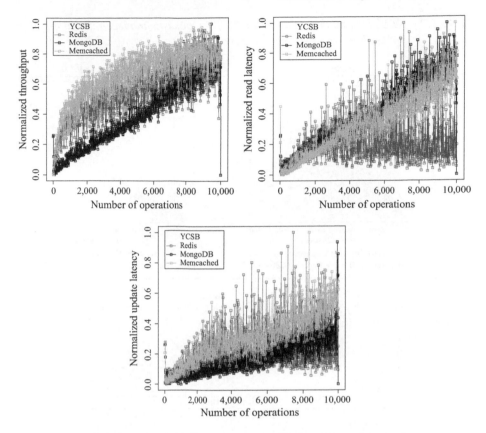

Figure 3.4   YCSB (version 0.12.0) Monitoring of Redis, MongoDB, and Memcached

(b) based on the condition, i.e. read latency > average read latency, previous breaches $(x_{t-1}, x_{t-2}, \ldots, x_{t-n})$ were identified, (c) distribution modeling of previous breaches was performed, and (d) stochastic model with minimum square error was identified and further verified for accuracy using the paired sample T-Test. The stochastic models for read latency of Redis and Memcached successfully passed the T-Test. However, for MongoDB (as it failed the prior T-Test) the procedure in the preceding paragraph was repeated for throughput (with the second highest communality value of 0.38) and stochastic model identified successfully passed the T-Test.

Tables 3.2 and 3.3 present the implementation and results of the PFM analysis conducted within the NESUS Watchdog for the considered workflows. For instance, the top figures show previous breaches based on the two conditions: 'read latency > average read latency' for Redis and Memcached, and 'throughput < average throughput' for MongoDB. The obtained distribution models are exhibited in each case, as well as the parameters of the stochastic models. It can be observed that for Redis and Memecached, previous breaches in read latency are lognormal

Table 3.2   NESUS Watchdog (a software bot) – stochastic models and penalization
for the Redis and Memcached workflows

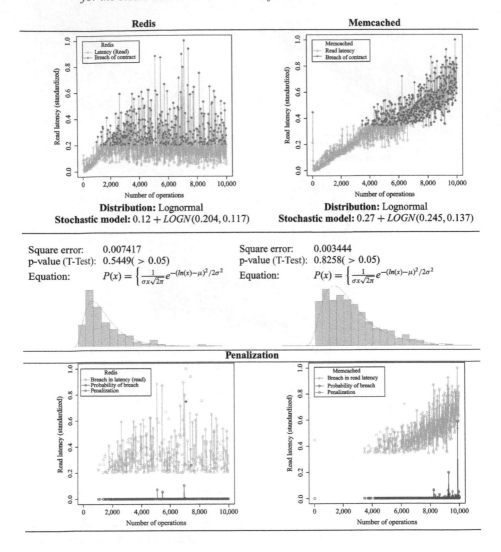

increasing and for MongoDB, previous breaches in throughput are beta increasing. We propose within each HPC workflow the measured square error (Redis: 0.007417, Memcashed: 0.003444, and MongoDB: 0.018634). Moreover, as p-values of Paired Sample T-Test (Redis: 0.5449, Memcashed: 0.8258, and MongoDB: 0.4788) are greater than 0.05, the null hypothesis (the two samples are the same) is accepted as compared to the alternate hypothesis (the two samples are different). Hence, the stochastic models for Redis (read latency), i.e. $0.12 + LOGN(0.204, 0.117)$, Memcached (read latency), i.e. $0.27 + LOGN(0.245, 0.137)$, and MongoDB (throughput),

Table 3.3   NESUS Watchdog (a software bot) – stochastic models and penalization for the MongoDB workflow

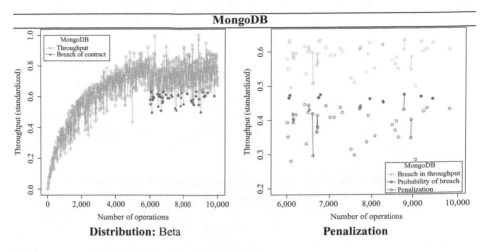

Stochastic model: $0.48 + 0.17 * BETA(2.49, 1.48)$

Square error:	0.018634
p-value (T-Test):	0.4788(> 0.05)
Equation:	$P(x) = \begin{cases} \dfrac{x^{\beta-1}(1-x)^{\alpha-1}}{\int_0^1 t^{\beta-1}(1-t)^{\alpha-1}\,dt} \end{cases}$

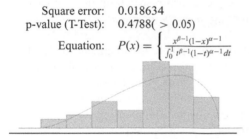

i.e. $-0.48 + 0.17 * BETA(2.49, 1.48)$, can be used by PFM to find the probability of breach $P(x)$. In particular, a lognormal $P(x)$ for Redis and Memcached and beta $P(x)$ for MongoDB was demonstrated.

Penalization aspects are also illustrated. For Redis and Memcached, the penalization request was issued by the bot based on the condition: $P(x) > 0.70$, whereas, for MongoDB, the condition was $P(x) > 0.45$. It can be observed that only Redis and MongoDB Servers were penalized. Technically, this difference could be attributed to the fact that Memcached is simply used for caching, and therefore, it is less prone to breach of contract. Whereas Redis and MongoBD as databases and message brokers are performing more complex operations and are more likely to cause a breach.

3.3   Conclusion

Due to their scale and the wide range of possible applications and involved technologies, UCS requires adapted frameworks to enable resilient and secure executions.

In this chapter, we have reviewed the general concepts of faults, fault tolerance and robustness before detailing the main approaches suitable for large scale HPC systems. New opportunities and challenges have been highlighted, in particular at the level of hardware, network, and MPI resilience. Novel data structures based on DLT have been introduced as a new field worth further investigations for large-scale experiments and validations. A potential illustration on regulatory compliance within UCS has been proposed.

What emerges is the need for the apparition of additional disruptive paradigms and solutions at all levels: from hardware, languages, compilers, operating systems, middleware, services, and application-level solutions. In these aspects, there are several research challenges for resilience in ultrascale systems that should be faced in a near future:

Characterization of hardware and software faults in ultrascale systems.
Characterization of hardware and software faults is essential for making the informed choice about research needs for the resilience of ultrascale systems. From the hardware perspective if silent hardware faults are exceedingly rare, then the hard problem of detecting such errors in software or tolerating their impact can be ignored. If errors in storage are exceedingly rare, while errors in computer logic are frequent, then research on mechanisms for hardening data structures and detecting memory corruptions in software is superfluous.

Development of a standardized fault-handling model. Development of a standardized fault-handling model is the key to provide guidance to application and system software developers about how they will be notified about a fault, what types of faults they may be notified about, and what mechanisms the system provides to assist recovery from the fault. Applications running on today's HPC systems are not even notified of faults or given options as to how to handle faults. If the application happens to detect an error, the computer may also eventually detect the error and kill the application automatically, making application recovery problematic.

Improved fault prediction, containment, detection, notification, and recovery.
Scale is a major opportunity for applications ultrascale computing systems. However, the larger the scale, the higher the probability of a failure in some part of the system. To build such a system, resilience is a must, and that means we need better fault prediction mechanisms, containment measures and recovery from failures to allow the applications keep-on working even if a specific component fails.

Programming abstractions for resilience in ultrascale systems. Programming abstractions for resilience will be able to grow out of a standardized fault handling model. Several programming abstractions will need to be developed and supported in order to develop resilient ultrascale applications. The development of fault-tolerant algorithms requires various resilience services.

Standardized evaluation of fault-tolerance approaches. Standardized evaluation of fault-tolerance approaches will provide a way to measure the efficiency of a new approach compared with other known approaches. It will also provide a way to measure the effectiveness of an approach on different architectures and at different scales. The latter will be important to determine whether the approach can scale to serve the needs of ultrascale systems.

Offering a global view on the reliability/resilience issues will allow us to define the right level of information exchange between all layers and components in order to have global (cross-layer/component) solution.

Chapter 4
Data management techniques

Angelos Bilas[1], Jesus Carretero[2], Toni Cortes[3], Javier Garcia-Blas[2], Pilar González-Férez[4], Anastasios Papagiannis[1], Anna Queralt[5], Fabrizio Marozzo[6], Giorgos Saloustros[1], Ali Shoker[7], Domenico Talia[6], and Paolo Trunfio[6]

Today, it is projected that data storage and management is becoming one of the key challenges in order to achieve ultrascale computing for several reasons. First, data is expected to grow exponentially in the coming years and this progression will imply that disruptive technologies will be needed to store large amounts of data and more importantly to access it in a timely manner. Second, the improvement of computing elements and their scalability are shifting application execution from CPU bound to I/O bound. This creates additional challenges for significantly improving the access to data to keep with computation time and thus avoid high-performance computing (HPC) from being underutilized due to large periods of I/O activity. Third, the two initially separate worlds of HPC that mainly consisted on one hand of simulations that are CPU bound and on the other hand of analytics that mainly perform huge data scans to discover information and are I/O bound are blurring. Now, simulations and analytics need to work cooperatively and share the same I/O infrastructure.

This challenge of data management is currently being addressed from many different angles by a large international community, but there are three main concepts in which there is a wide agreement:

- First, data abstractions need to change given that traditional parallel file systems are failing on adapting to the new needs of applications and especially to their scalability characteristics. For this reason, abstractions such as object stores or KVs are positioning themselves in the lead to become the new storage containers.

[1]Institute of Computer Science (ICS), Foundation for Research and Technology – Hellas (FORTH), Greece
[2]Computer Science and Engineering Department, Universidad Carlos III de Madrid, Madrid, Spain
[3]Barcelona Supercomputing Center (BSC), Barcelona, Spain
[4]Department of Computer Engineering, University of Murcia, Spain
[5]Barcelona Supercomputing Center (BSC), Barcelona, Spain
[6]Dipartimento di Ingegneria Informatica, Modellistica, Elettronica e Sistemistica (DIMES), Università della Calabria, Italy
[7]Institute for Systems and Computer Engineering, Technology and Science (INESC-TEC), Portugal

Examples such as Dynamo, BigTable or Cassandra, among others, are being used by companies such as Facebook or Twitter that need to manage and process incredibly huge amounts of data.

- Second, data needs to be replicated in order to both become resilient to errors in the vast amount of hardware needed to store it and to offer fast enough access to it. Unfortunately, this replication implies significant overheads in both the space needed and the access/modification time of the data, which were the original challenges.

- Third, the use of HPC is becoming more necessary than ever in order to be able to analyze the huge amount of data that is generated everywhere (i.e., smart cities, cars, open data, etc.); thus traditional HPC systems cannot be the only ones used to analyze this data because they are scarce and very expensive to use. For this reason, cloud environments are becoming closer to HPC in performance and cheaper to use taking an active role in solving HPC problems of standard users.

In this chapter, we will present three techniques that address the aforementioned challenges. First, we will present Tucana, a novel KV store designed to work with fast storage devices such as Solid State Drives (SSDs). In addition to presenting its rich features including arbitrary dataset sizes, variable key and value sizes, concurrency, multithreading, and versioning, we will evaluate its performance compared with similar KV components with respect to throughput, CPU usage, and IO. This novel KV system advances in the idea that new abstractions to store data are needed in ultrascale computing.

Second, we present Hercules and the benefits of integrating it and a data mining Cloud framework (DMCF) as an alternative to classical parallel file system enabling the execution of data-intensive application on cloud environments. Furthermore, we detail a data-aware scheduling technique that can reduce the execution time of data-intensive workflows significantly. This platform combination, in addition to the new data scheduler, puts a step forward in the use of cloud infrastructures for ultrascale computing by a larger community whose needs are growing.

Finally, this chapter discuss the idea of conflict-free replicated data types (CRDT), a methodology that helps implementing basic types that can be replicated without the overhead of synchronization on the critical path of data update, but with the guarantee that, at some point in time, all replicas will see unequivocally all updates done in the other replicas. Furthermore, basic CRDT can be combined to construct larger datatypes with the same properties. This methodology enables the proliferation of replicas without the overhead of accessing/modifying them which will be key in ultrascale computing.

4.1　Intra-node scaling of an efficient KV store on modern multicore servers

Tucana is a KV store designed for fast storage devices, such as SSDs, that reduces the gap between sequential and random I/O performance, especially under a high degree of concurrency and relatively large I/Os (a few tens of KB). It supports variable size keys and values, versions, arbitrary data set sizes, concurrency, multithreading, and persistence. *Tucana* uses a B$^\epsilon$-tree approach that only performs buffering and batching at the lowest part of the tree, since it is assumed that the largest part of the tree (but not the data items) fits in memory. Compared to RosckDB, *Tucana* is up to 9.2× more efficient in terms of CPU cycles/op for in-memory workloads and up to 7× for workloads that do not fit in memory.

This section analyzes in detail host CPU overhead, network and I/O traffic of H-*Tucana*, a modification of HBase that replaces the LSM-based store engine of HBase with *Tucana*. Several limitations to achieve higher performance are identified. First, network path, inherited from HBase, becomes a bottleneck and does not allow *Tucana* to saturate server cores. Second, lookups for traversing the tree represent up to 78% of the time used by *Tucana*, mainly due to key comparisons. Finally, when mmap, used by *Tucana* for allocating memory and device space, runs out of memory, *Tucana* exhibits periods of inactivity and stops serving requests, until the system replenishes available buffers for mmap.

4.1.1 Introduction

Currently, KV stores have become an important building block in data analytics stacks and data access in general. Today's large-scale, high-performance data-intensive applications usually use KV stores for data management, since they offer higher efficiency, scalability, and availability than relational database systems. KV stores are widely used to support Internet services, for instance, Amazon uses Dynamo, Google uses BigTable, and Facebook and Twitter use Cassandra and HBase.

The core of an NoSQL store is a KV store that performs (key,value) pair lookups. Traditionally, KV stores have been designed for optimizing accesses to hard disk drives (HDDs) and with the assumption that the CPU is the fastest component of the system (compared to storage and network devices). Indeed, KV stores tend to exhibit high CPU overheads [166].

Tucana [166] is a KV store designed for fast storage devices, such as SSDs, that reduces the gap between sequential and random I/O performance, especially under a high degree of concurrency and relatively large I/Os (a few tens of KB). *Tucana* is a full-feature KV store that achieves lower host CPU overhead per operation than other state-of-the-art systems. It supports variable size keys and values, versions, arbitrary data set sizes, concurrency, multithreading, and persistence. The design of *Tucana* centers around three techniques to reduce overheads: CoW, private subsection allocation, and direct device management.

Tucana is up to 9.2× more efficient in terms of CPU cycles/op for in-memory workloads and up to 7× for workloads that do not fit in memory [166]. *Tucana* outperforms RocksDB for in-memory workloads up to 7×, whereas for workloads that do not fit in memory both systems are limited by device I/O throughput.

Tucana is used to improve the throughput and efficiency of HBase [167], a popular scale-out NoSQL store. The LSM-based storage engine of HBase is replaced with *Tucana*. Data lookup, insert, delete, scan, and key-range split and merge operations are served from *Tucana*, while maintaining the HBase mapping of tables to KV pairs, client API, client-server protocol, and management operations (failure handling and load balancing). The resulting system, called H-*Tucana*, remains compatible with other components of the Hadoop ecosystem. H-*Tucana* is compared to HBase using Yahoo Cloud Serving Benchmark (YCSB) and results show that, compared to HBase, H-*Tucana* achieves between $2 - 8\times$ better CPU cycles/op and $2 - 10\times$ higher operation rates across all workloads.

This section uses *Tucana* to study the behavior of H-*Tucana* by using two datasets, one that fits in memory and one that does not. In addition, H-*Tucana*'s behavior is compared with HBase and with two ideal versions of H-*Tucana* that do not perform I/O. The aim is to understand the overheads associated with efficient KV stores for fast storage devices.

The aspect examined are host CPU overhead, network and I/O traffic, the use of RAM, and write amplification problem, i.e., whether the same data is written multiple times. Results show that there are several important limitations to achieve higher performance. Although the average CPU utilization is low, a few (one or two) cores, that execute tasks of the network path, become bottleneck. The analysis for network traffic shows that network devices are far from achieving their maximum throughput. Therefore, the network path, inherited from HBase, does not allow *Tucana* to achieve better performance. Regarding index metadata, traversing the *Tucana* tree represents up to 78% of the time used by *Tucana* mainly due to the key comparisons. In addition, when mmap runs out of memory, the KV store exhibits periods of inactivity and stops serving requests, until the system replenishes available buffers for mmap. Next, these issues are analyzed and evaluated in more detail.

4.1.2   Background

KV stores have been traditionally designed for HDDs and use LSM-tree structure at their core. LSM-trees [168] are a write-optimized structure that is a good fit for HDDs where there is a large difference in performance between random and sequential accesses. LSM-trees organize data in multiple levels of large, sorted containers, where each level increases the size of the container.

Their advantages are (1) they require a small amount of metadata, since data containers are sorted; (2) I/Os can be large, resulting in optimal HDD performance. The drawback is that for keeping large sorted containers they perform compactions which incurs high CPU overhead and results in I/O amplification for reads and writes.

Going forward device performance and CPU-power trends dictate different designs. *Tucana* uses as a basis a variant of B-trees, broadly called B^ϵ-trees [169].

B^ϵ-trees are B-trees with an additional per-node buffer. These buffers allow one to batch insert operations to amortize their cost. In B^ϵ-trees the total size of each node is B and ϵ is a design-time constant between [0,1]. ϵ is the ratio of B that is used for buffering, whereas the rest of the space in each node ($1-\epsilon$) is used for storing pivots.

Buffers contain messages that describe operations that modify the index (insert, update, delete). These operations are initially added to the tree's root node buffer. When the root node buffer becomes full, a subset of the buffered operations are propagated to the buffers of the appropriate nodes at the next level. This procedure is repeated until operations reach a leaf node, where the KV pair is simply added to the leaf. Leaf nodes are similar to B-Trees and they do not contain an additional buffer, beyond the space required to store the KV pairs.

A get operation traverses the path from the root to the corresponding leaf by searching at the buffers of the internal nodes along the path. A range scan is similar to a get, except that messages for the entire range of keys must be checked and applied as the appropriate subtree is traversed. Therefore, buffers are frequently modified and searched. For this reason, they are typically implemented with tree indexes rather than sorted containers.

Compared to LSM-trees, B^ϵ-trees incur less I/O amplification. B^ϵ-trees use an index to remove the need for sorted containers. This results in smaller and more random I/Os. As device technology reduces the I/O size required to achieve high throughput, using a B^ϵ-tree instead of an LSM-tree is a reasonable decision.

4.1.3 Tucana Design

Tucana [166] is a feature-rich KV store that provides persistence, arbitrary dataset sizes, variable key and value sizes, concurrency, multithreading, and versioning.

Tucana uses a B^ϵ-tree approach to maintain the desired asymptotic properties for inserts, which is important for write-intensive workloads. B^ϵ-trees achieve this amortization by buffering writes at each level of the tree. *Tucana*'s design assumes that the largest part of the tree (but not the data items) fits in memory and *Tucana* only performs buffering and batching at the lowest part of the tree.

Figure 4.1 shows an overview of the tree index organization of *Tucana*. The index consists of internal nodes with pointers to next level nodes and pointers to variable size keys. A separate buffer per internal node stores the variable size keys. Pointers to keys are sorted based on the key, whereas keys are appended to a buffer. The leaf nodes contain sorted pointers to the KV pairs. A single append-only log is used to store both the key and values. The design of the log is similar to the internal buffers of B^ϵ-trees. However, note that *Tucana* avoids buffering at intermediate nodes. For each key, leaves store as metadata a fixed-size prefix of the key and a hash value of the key, whereas the key itself is stored in the KV log. These prefix and hash values of the keys will help while traversing the tree.

Insert operations traverse the index in a top-down fashion. At each index node, a binary search is performed over the pivots to find the next level node to visit. When the leaf is reached, the KV pair is appended to the log and the pointer is inserted in the leaf, keeping pointers sorted by the corresponding key. If a leaf is full, a split operation is triggered prior to insert. Split operations, in index or leaf nodes, produce two new nodes each containing half of the keys and they update the index in a bottom-up fashion. Delete operations place a tombstone for the respective keys, which are removed later. Deletes will eventually cause rebalancing and merging.

Point queries locate the appropriate leaf traversing the index similar to inserts. At the leaf, a binary search is performed to locate the pointer to the KV pair. Finally, range queries locate the starting key similar to point queries and subsequently use the index to iterate over the key range.

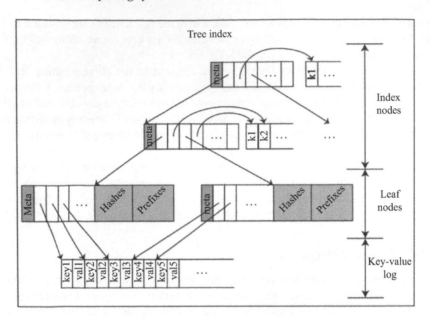

Figure 4.1　Design of the tree index of Tucana

Tucana manages the data layout as a set of contiguous segments of space to store data. Each segment is composed of a metadata portion and a data portion. The metadata portion contains the superblock, free log, and segment allocator metadata (bitmap). The superblock contains a reference to a descriptor of the latest persistent and consistent state for a segment. Each segment has a single allocator common for all databases (key ranges) in a segment. The data portion contains multiple databases. Each database is contained within a single segment and uses its own separate indexing structure. *Tucana* keeps persistent state about allocated blocks by using bitmaps.

Tucana directly maps the storage device to memory to reduce space (memory and device) allocation overhead. *Tucana* leverages mmap to use a single allocator for memory and device space. mmap uses a single address space for both memory and storage and virtual memory protection to determine the location (memory or storage) of an item. This eliminates the need for pointer translation at the expense of page faults. Additionally, mmap eliminates data copies between kernel and user space.

Tucana uses CoW to achieve recovery without the use of a log. CoW maintains the consistency of both allocator bitmap and tree metadata. The bitmap in each segment consists of *buddy pairs* with information about allocated space. Only one buddy of the pair is active for write operations, whereas the other buddy is immutable for recovery. A global per segment increasing counter, named ***epoch***, marks each buddy. A successful commit operation increments the epoch denoting the latest instant in which the buddy was modified.

For the tree structure, each internal index and leaf node has epochs to distinguish its latest persistent state. During an update, whether the node's epoch indicates that it is immutable, a CoW operation will take place. After a CoW operation for inserting a key, the parent of the node is updated with the new node location in a bottom-up fashion. The resulting node belongs to epoch+1 and will be persisted during the next commit. Subsequent updates to the same node before the next commit are batched by applying them in place. Since keys and values are stored in buffers in an append-only fashion, CoW is only performed on the header of each internal node.

Tucana's persistence relies on the atomic transition between consistent states for each segment. Metadata and data in *Tucana* are written asynchronously to the devices. However, transitions from state to state occur atomically via synchronous updates to the segment's superblock with `msync` (commits). Each commit creates a new persistent state for the segment, identified by a unique epoch id. The epoch of the latest persistent state of a segment is stored in a descriptor to which the superblock keeps a reference.

HBase [167] is a scale-out columnar store that supports a small and volatile schema. HBase offers a table abstraction over the data, where each table keeps a set of KV pairs. Each table is further decomposed into regions, where each region stores a contiguous segment of the key space. Each region is physically organized as a set of files per column. At its core HBase uses an LSM-tree to store data [168]. *Tucana* is used to replace this storage engine, while maintaining the HBase metadata architecture, node fault tolerance, data distribution, and load-balancing mechanisms. The resulting system, H-*Tucana*, maps HBase regions to segments, and each column to a separate tree in the segment. To eliminate the need for using HDFS under HBase, HBase is modified so that a new node handles a segment after a failure. It is assumed that segments are allocated over a reliable shared block device, such as a storage area network (SAN) or virtual SAN and are visible to all nodes in the system. In this model, the only function that HDFS offers is space allocation. *Tucana* is designed to manage space directly on top of raw devices, and it does not require a file system. H-*Tucana* assumes the responsibility of elastic data indexing, while the shared storage system provides a reliable (replicated) block-based storage pool.

4.1.4   Experimental evaluation

The experimental platform consists of two machines each equipped with a 16 core Intel(R) Xeon(R) E5-2630 CPU running at 2.4 GHz and 64 GB DDR4 DRAM. Both nodes are connected with a 40 Gbits/s network link. As a storage device, the server uses a Samsung SSD PRO 950 NVMe of 256 GB.

The open-source YCSB [170] is used to generate synthetic workloads. The default YCSB implementation executes gets as range queries and therefore exercises only scan operations. For this reason, YCSB is modified to use point queries for get operations. Two standard workloads proposed by YCSB with the default values are run. Table 4.1 summarizes these workloads. The following sequence is run: Load the database using workload A's configuration file and then run workload C. In this way, the experiment has two phases an initial one with only puts operations (write requests), and a second phase with only gets operations (read requests). However, due to the commits at the beginning of the run phase, the run uses 32 YCSB threads and eight regions.

Table 4.1   *Workloads evaluated with YCSB. All*
workloads use a query popularity that
follows a Zipf distribution

	Workload
A	50% reads, 50% updates
C	100% reads

Two datasets are used, a small one that fits in memory and a large one that does not. The small dataset is composed of 100M records, and the large dataset has 500M records. The load phase creates the whole dataset and the run phase issues 10 million operations.

The analysis uses four engines: HBase, H-*Tucana*, NW-H-*Tucana*, and Ideal-H-*Tucana*. H-*Tucana* is cross-linked between the Java code of HBase and the C code of *Tucana*. NW-H-*Tucana* is a modification that does not perform any I/O by completing all the I/O requests without issuing them to the storage device. The *Tucana* tree is used, and the get and put operations are performed, but all the data remains in memory. Ideal-H-*Tucana* is a modification in which *Tucana* completes put requests without doing the insert operation and get requests return a dummy value. The *Tucana* tree is not used and no I/O is performed either. For NW-H-*Tucana* and Ideal-H-*Tucana*, only the small dataset is used.

Graphs for CPU utilization depict values given by `mpstat` and include (i) User that corresponds to %usr + %nice; (ii) Sys that corresponds to %sys + %irq + %soft, where %irq and %soft correspond to the percentage of time spent by the CPUs to service hardware interrupts and software interrupts, respectively; and (iii) IOW that corresponds to %iowait the percentage of time that the CPUs were idle during which the system had an outstanding disk I/O request.

4.1.4.1   Throughput analysis

Figure 4.2 depicts the throughput, in Kops/s, achieved by HBase and H-*Tucana* with both datasets and by NW-H-*Tucana* and Ideal-H-*Tucana* with the dataset that fits in memory. Regarding H-*Tucana* and comparing both operations, the run phase (get operations) outperforms the load phase (put operations) by 33.7% and 3.4× with the small and large datasets, respectively. There are several reasons for this difference in performance. First, *Tucana* uses a lock for inserting new KV pairs, therefore put operations require a lock to ensure exclusive access when modifying the tree. On the contrary, *Tucana* provides lock-less gets. Second, the amount of I/O traffic during the load phase is significantly larger than during the run phase. During the load phase, I/O write operations are issued to ensure that the dataset is stored on the device, whereas during the run phase there are almost not writes with the exception of a snapshot at the beginning of the phase. In addition, for the small dataset, during the run phase there are no reads since the dataset fits in memory, and for the large dataset, the amount of data read is smaller than during the load phase. Finally, for the large dataset, the

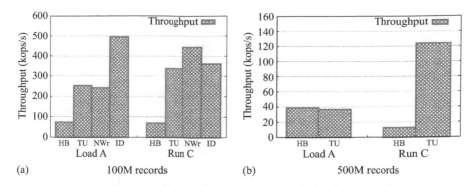

*Figure 4.2　Throughput (kops/s) achieved by HBase, H-*Tucana*, and the NW and Ideal versions of H-*Tucana *with the 100M dataset and by HBase and H-*Tucana *with 500M records*

memory pressure has a huge impact during the load phase, since index and leaf nodes are evicted from memory and they have to be re-read several times, and they are written multiple times.

Comparing performance to HBase, with the small dataset, H-*Tucana* significantly outperforms HBase by up to 3.4× and 4.8× during the load and run phases, respectively. Thanks to its B$^{\epsilon}$-tree approach, when dataset fits in memory H-*Tucana* is able to significantly improve HBase performance. However, with the large dataset, H-*Tucana* exhibits up to 5.7% worst performance than HBase during the load phase, whereas H-*Tucana* outperforms HBase by up to 9.9× during the run phase.

HBase stores data on the device as HFiles, and the dataset is only sorted per HFile. New insert operations do not need to read previous values. HBase usually issues large write operations achieving good I/O performance. The size of the dataset does not significantly impact on its write performance. However, for get operations, this organization exhibits poor read performance when the dataset does not fit in memory, since all HFiles have to be checked for each get. HBase (and LSM trees in general) mitigate these overheads with the use of compactions and bloom filters.

With the large dataset and during the load phase, the problem of H-*Tucana*, as Section 4.1.4.3 shows, is the significant amount of data written, and the bad I/O pattern produced. This problem is not inherent to the design of *Tucana* tree, but rather due to mmap. Section 4.1.4.3 shows that H-*Tucana* writes less amount of data than HBase, but it issues smaller requests that ends in worst I/O performance.

During the load phase, NW-H-*Tucana* provides quite similar performance than H-*Tucana*, the reason is that for small datasets and fast devices, the role of the device is reduced and the differences between NW-H-*Tucana* and H-*Tucana* are small. However, during the run phase, NW-H-*Tucana* improves H-*Tucana* performance by up to 32%. This difference in performance is due to the snapshot performed by H-*Tucana* at the beginning of the tests that issues I/O traffic and reduces H-*Tucana* performance.

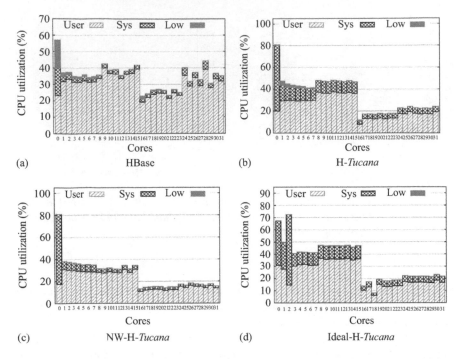

Figure 4.3   *CPU utilization per core at the server side during the execution of the load phase with 100M records*

When comparing both phases, get operations outperform by up to 84% put operations. Since NW-H-*Tucana* does not perform any I/O, the reason is again that gets are lock-less operations, whereas puts are not.

Ideal-H-*Tucana* outperforms H-*Tucana* by up to 2× and 14.2% during the load and run phase by avoiding lookups over the tree, insertions, and I/O operations. NW-H-*Tucana* outperforms Ideal-H-*Tucana* by up to 23% during the run phase. The reason is that Ideal-H-*Tucana* has to do an allocation for each get operation, but the NW-H-*Tucana* version just returns an existing value. The allocation cost more than the work done by the NW-H-*Tucana* version. Due to this allocation, with Ideal-H-*Tucana*, the load phase outperforms by up to 27% the run phase.

4.1.4.2   CPU utilization analysis

For the small dataset, Figures 4.3 and 4.4 depict, for the server, the CPU utilization per core produced during the execution of the load and run phases, respectively, with the four engines. For the client, Figure 4.5 provides the average CPU utilization for both phases, also for the smaller dataset. Figure 4.6 depicts, for HBase and H-*Tucana*, the average CPU utilization for both phases with the 500M dataset. For the server, Table 4.2 provides the average number of cores that has a CPU utilization larger than 80%, the average CPU utilization achieved, and also the percentage of time during which this saturation occurs.

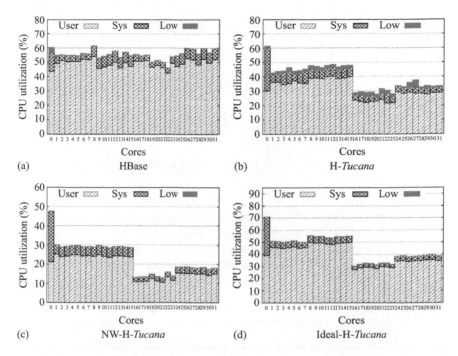

Figure 4.4   CPU utilization per core at the server side during the execution of the run phase with 100M records

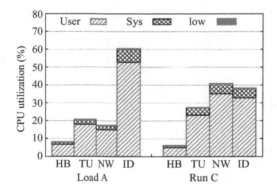

Figure 4.5   For the 100M dataset, average CPU utilization at the client side during the execution of both phases for the four engines

Regarding the 100M records dataset, for HBase, the CPU utilization is, on average, 34.6% and 55.3% for the load and run phases, respectively. However, Table 4.2 shows that, during both phases, there are several cores (2 and 13) that achieve a CPU utilization close to or above 90%. This effect does not appear on Figures 4.3 and 4.4, because the cores saturated are not always the same. These cores become a bottleneck

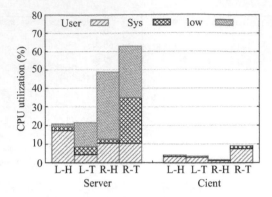

*Figure 4.6   For the 500M dataset, average CPU utilization at the server and client,
during the execution of the load and run phase for HBase and
H-Tucana. L-H and R-H represent the load and run phase with HBase,
and L-T and R-T represent the load and run phase with H-Tucana*

*Table 4.2   Number of cores with a CPU utilization larger than 80%, average CPU
utilization, and duration (in time percentage) of this saturation*

Size	Phase	Engine	CPU util.	# Cores	% Time
100M	**Load**	HB	89.4	2.0	94.1
		TU	88.3	1.0	61.5
		NW	99.0	1.1	68.3
		ID	90.0	1.0	65.0
	Run	HB	86.1	13.0	97.2
		TU	80.7	1.3	55.2
		NW	80.2	1.0	59.1
		ID	0.0	0.0	0.0
500M	**Load**	HB	90.8	1.8	96.0
		TU	86.5	1.9	66.7
	Run	HB	86.9	12.3	99.9
		TU	84.2	14.4	97.5

and do not allow HBase to provide better performance. Some of these cores are usually executing tasks related to the network path, as the analysis for Ideal-H-*Tucana*
shows. On the contrary, the client has an average CPU utilization lower than 10%.

H-*Tucana* has an average CPU utilization of 33.6% and 39.1% for the load and
run phases, respectively. Being more lightweight in CPU utilization than HBase,
H-*Tucana* provides a significant better performance. During the run phase, a small
percentage of the CPU utilization is for I/O wait time due to the commit that occurs at
the beginning of this phase. However, there is no I/O due to get operations because the
dataset fits in memory. For both phases, one core presents an average CPU utilization

above 80% during more of the half of the execution time. Consequently, during this time, H-*Tucana* cannot provide a better performance. As results for Ideal-H-*Tucana* show, these cores are executing tasks related to the network path (inherited from HBase). The client still provides a low CPU utilization.

NW-H-*Tucana* provides an average CPU utilization of 33.5% and 44.4% for the load and run phases, respectively. The load phase has one core with a CPU utilization of 99% during two-thirds of the time. The run phase also has saturation problem, since during half of its execution time one core has a CPU utilization of 80%. It can be considered that one core becomes a bottleneck, and NW-H-*Tucana* cannot provide better performance. In addition, although the client presents a low CPU utilization, during the run phase, two cores present a CPU utilization above 80% during 70% of the execution time (this data is not presented due to space constraint).

Ideal-H-*Tucana* provides a low CPU utilization: on average, 26.1% and 23.1% for the load and run phases, respectively. But, Table 4.2 shows a saturation problem during the load phase, because the CPU utilization of one core is over 90%. Since Ideal-H-*Tucana* does not execute any code from *Tucana*, this bottleneck appears due to HBase that mainly executes network tasks. Therefore, it can be claimed that HBase has a problem on its network path that implies a serialization of the code. The client average CPU utilization is larger than the server. Indeed, during the load phase, it is 60.1%, and four cores achieve an average CPU utilization close to 88%. Therefore, it can be considered that the client is close to saturation as well. Ideal-H-*Tucana* cannot provide a better performance when inserting KV pairs.

During the run phase, Ideal-H-*Tucana* does not have saturation problem at the server. The client presents an average CPU utilization of 40.6%, and six cores have a utilization above 80% but only 25% of the time. Therefore, during this phase, the CPU is not a bottleneck.

With the 500M dataset, Figure 4.6 shows that H-*Tucana* presents a low CPU utilization at the server during the load phase. The problem is the memory pressure because the dataset does not fit in memory, and the system spends most of the time managing pages faults. *Tucana* uses mmap as a single allocator for memory and device space, and *Tucana* cannot decide which pages are evicted from memory and which are kept. Therefore, pages containing index and leaf nodes are evicted, and they have to be re-read from the devices. This behavior is analyzed in Sections 4.1.4.3 and 4.1.4.4.

During the run phase, the percentage of time used for I/O wait is significantly increased due to the amount of data that has to be read for the get operations since the dataset does not fit in memory.

With HBase, the server presents a low average CPU utilization during the load phase; however, almost two cores present more than 90% during the execution of the test. The run phase presents a higher average CPU utilization, with a high I/O wait percentage due to the I/O read operations. But, again, the CPU becomes a bottleneck with 12 cores having a CPU utilization close to 87%. Therefore, it can be claimed that HBase cannot provide better performance.

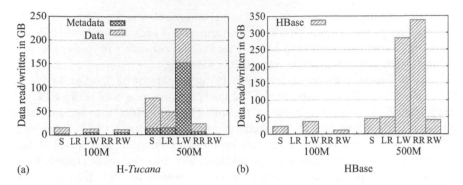

*Figure 4.7   Total size, in GB, of the dataset (metadata plus data) and amount of
data, in GB, read and written during the execution of the test with
H-*Tucana *and HBase, for both phases. S stands for Size, LR and LW for
reads and writes performed during the load phase, and RR and RW for
reads and writes performed during the run phase*

With the large dataset, the client provides a quite low CPU utilization with both
HBase and H-*Tucana*. The reason is the drop of performance due to the lack of
memory at the server.

4.1.4.3   I/O analysis

Figure 4.7 depicts the total size of the dataset and the amount of data read and
written during the execution of the test with H-*Tucana* and HBase. For H-*Tucana*,
metadata represents blocks used for internal and leaf nodes, and data represents
blocks used for the KV log. For HBase, it is not able to distinguish between data and
metadata.

H-*Tucana* presents a total write amplification of up to 37% and 2.2× for the
100M and 500M records, respectively. However, several things should be highlighted.
During the load phase, the amount of data blocks written is almost equal to the total
size of KV log. The extra data blocks are written because a block could be written
several times on the device due to commits. But once a data block is full and written
on the device, it is never re-written again. However, the amount of metadata blocks
written is up to 11.8× larger than the actual size of the metadata. The reason is that
internal and leaf nodes are modified several times and in a different instant of time.
In addition, with mmap modified disk blocks are written to the device not only during
Tucana's commit operations but also periodically, by the flush kernel threads when
they are older than a threshold or when free memory shrinks below a threshold, using
an LRU policy and madvise hints. This policy also increases the times a metadata
block is written on the device.

During the run phase, the blocks written to the device are due to the *Tucana*'s
commit operations issued at the beginning of this phase. This commit writes on the
device blocks modified at the end of the load phase but not written to the device yet.

During the load phase, with 100M records, no data is read from the storage device. However, with 500M records, metadata blocks are read because internal or leaf nodes are evicted from memory. On the contrary, the data blocks are read to make key comparisons. The problem is that mmap controls which pages are evicted from memory due to memory pressure, and the current implementation of *Tucana* cannot modify this behavior. As a result, mmap evicts not only data pages, but also metadata pages. This behavior reduces the amount of I/Os that can be amortized for inserts due to the limited buffering in the B^ϵ-tree.

During the run phase, no data is read with the small dataset. However, the large dataset implies a larger amount of data read from the SSDs, since the whole dataset does not fit in memory.

HBase presents a write amplification problem due to the compactions performed that is shown in Figure 4.7. Its total write amplification is up to $2.1\times$ and $7.1\times$ for the 100M and 500M records, respectively. With respect to the amount of data read, HBase does not read any data with the smaller dataset. With the large dataset, HBase reads up to $8.5\times$ the size of the dataset.

Tucana has better inherent behavior with respect to amplification, thanks to its B^ϵ-tree. Indeed, *Tucana* does not require compactions at the expense of more random and small I/Os. HBase introduces compactions and ends up issuing larger requests. With 500M records, during the load phase, the average request size is 239 and 641 kB for H-*Tucana* and HBase, respectively. Consequently, although HBase writes by up to 45% more data than H-*Tucana*, HBase outperforms H-*Tucana*, thanks to its I/O access pattern. With 100M records, during the load phase, the average request size is 493 kB and 478 kB for H-*Tucana* and HBase, respectively, and therefore, there is almost no difference in I/O performance between them.

4.1.4.4 Network and I/O traffic analysis

For H-*Tucana*, Figure 4.8 depicts the throughput and network traffic during the execution of both phases, whereas Figure 4.9 depicts the throughput and I/O traffic.

Figure 4.8 shows that the network devices are not a bottleneck, since they are able to provide up to 40 Gbit/s, but the maximum in-coming throughput achieved is 380 MB/s during the load phase, and the maximum out-going throughput achieved is 853 MB/s during the run phase. Therefore, as Section 4.1.4.2 says, the network path of HBase does not allow *Tucana* to achieve better network throughput.

Regarding I/O traffic, with the small dataset, the storage devices provide up to 515 MB/s of write throughput, achieving a 100% of disk utilization. Therefore, in this case, *Tucana* is achieving almost its maximum performance, with high utilization, and the devices can become a bottleneck. During the run phase, there is write traffic due to the commit. Both phases do not have read traffic.

With the 500M records dataset, during the load phase storage devices provides up to 512 MB/s of write throughput; however, the write performance drops as the system runs out of memory and achieves on average 163 MB/s. Regarding reads, at the beginning of the execution, there is not read traffic, since the dataset still fits in memory. However, when the dataset does not fit in memory, the read traffic is significantly increased. Due to the read and write traffic, the storage device is 100%

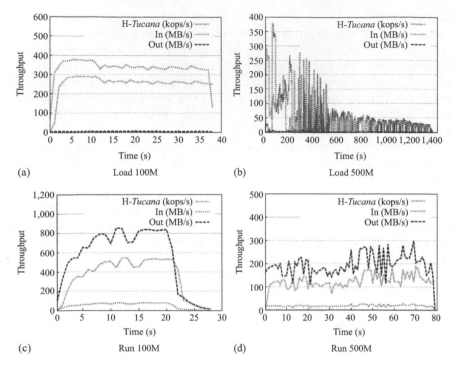

*Figure 4.8   For H-*Tucana, *throughput (kop/s) and network traffic (MB/s) during the execution of the load and run phase for 100M and 500M records. In and Out stand for input and output network traffic, respectively*

utilized. During the run phase, the storage device provides up to 378 MB/s of read throughput, and it is close to a 100% of disk utilization.

4.1.5   Summary

This section analyzes host CPU overhead, network, storage, and memory limitations of an efficient KV store, *Tucana*, designed for fast storage devices. *Tucana* is a feature-rich KV store that supports variable size keys and values, versions, arbitrary data set sizes, concurrency, multithreading, and persistence and recovery from failures. The issues analyzed include host CPU overhead, network and I/O traffic, and memory use.

4.2   Data-centric workflow runtime for data-intensive applications on Cloud systems

In the last decade, the scientific computing scenario is greatly evolving in two main areas. First, the focus on scientific computation is changing from CPU-intensive jobs, like large-scale simulations or complex mathematical applications, toward a

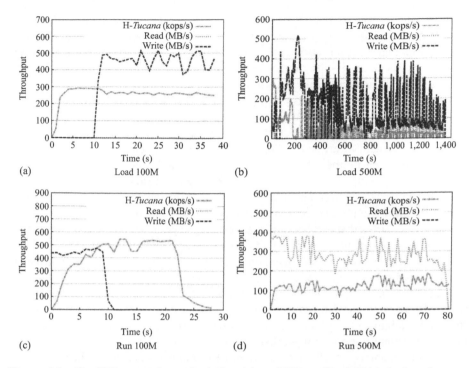

Figure 4.9 *For H-*Tucana, *throughput (kop/s) and I/O traffic (MB/s) during the execution of the load and run phase for 100M and 500M records*

data-intensive approach. This new paradigm greatly affects the underlying architecture requirements, slowly vanishing the classical CPU bottleneck and exposing bottlenecks in the I/O systems. Second, the evolution in computing technologies and science funding restrictions are changing the available computing resources in the scientific community.

In current approaches, the interfaces and management solutions of the different infrastructures present notable differences, requiring different programming models, even for the same application. On the other side, the future ultrascale systems should take advantage of every possible resource available in a transparent way for the user [171].

Workflow management systems are computing platforms widely used today for designing and executing data-intensive applications over HPC systems or distributed infrastructures. Data-intensive workflows consist of interdependent data processing tasks, often connected in a DAG style, which communicate through intermediate storage abstractions, typically files [172].

Current trends in scientific computing and data-intensive applications are involved in the use of Cloud infrastructures as a flexible approach to virtually limitless computing resources on a pay-per-use basis. Additionally, several research centers complement their private computing infrastructure (usually HPC systems) with public

Cloud resources. The systems from both HPC and Cloud domains are not efficiently supporting data-intensive workflows, especially because their design was thought for individual applications and not for ensembles of cooperating applications. Given this current scenario, a solution that combines characteristics typical of HPC, data analysis, and Cloud computing is becoming more and more necessary.

This section describes a data-aware scheduling strategy [173] for exploiting data locality in data-intensive workflows executed over the DMCF [174] and Hercules [175] platforms. Some experimental results are presented to show the benefits of the proposed data-aware scheduling strategy for executing data analysis workflows and for demonstrating the effectiveness of the solution. Using a data-aware strategy and Hercules as temporary storage service, the I/O overhead of workflow execution has been reduced by 55% compared to the standard execution based on the Azure storage Cloud infrastructure, leading to a 20% reduction of the total execution time. This evaluation confirms that our data-aware scheduling approach is effective in improving the performance of data-intensive workflow execution in Cloud platforms.

Some existing solutions focused on the use of in-memory storage as a different approach for solving the bottlenecks in highly concurrent I/O operations, such as Parrot and Chirp [176]. Our in-memory approach takes hints from all these solutions, by (i) offering popular data access APIs (POSIX, put/get, MPI-IO), (ii) focusing on flexible scalability through distributed approaches for both data and metadata, (iii) the use of compute nodes (or worker virtual machines (VMs)) to enhance the I/O infrastructure, and (iv) facilitating the deployment of user-level components.

The remainder of this section is structured as follows. Section 4.2.1 describes the main features of DMCF. Section 4.2.2 introduces Hercules architecture and capabilities. Section 4.2.3 emphasizes the advantages of integrating DMCF and Hercules. Section 4.2.4 details the data-aware scheduling technique proposed. Section 4.2.5 presents the experimental results. Finally, Section 4.2.6 concludes this section.

4.2.1 DMCF overview

The DMCF [174] is a software system implemented for designing and executing data analysis workflows on Clouds. A Web-based user interface allows users to compose their applications and submit them for execution over Cloud resources, according to a Software-as-a-Service approach.

The DMCF architecture has been designed to be deployed on different Cloud settings. Currently, there are two different deployments of DMCF: (i) on top of a Platform-as-a-Service Cloud, i.e., using storage, compute, and network APIs that hide the underlying infrastructure layer; (ii) on top of an Infrastructure-as-a-Service (IaaS) Cloud, i.e., using VM images that are deployed on the infrastructure layer. In both deployment scenarios, we use Microsoft Azure[1] as Cloud provider.

The DMCF software modules can be grouped into *web components* and *compute components* (see top-left part of Figure 4.10). DMCF allows users to compose, check, and run data analysis workflows through an HTML5 web editor. The workflows can

---

[1] http://azure.microsoft.com

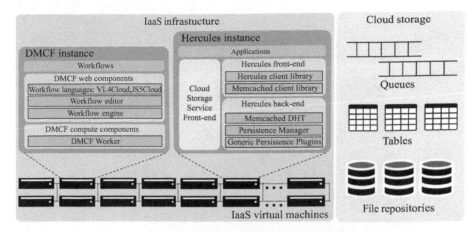

Figure 4.10   DMCF+Hercules architecture. Under an IaaS infrastructure, DMCF acts as a workflow engine while Hercules accelerates I/O accesses

be defined using two languages: *VL4Cloud* (Visual Language for Cloud) [174] and *JS4Cloud* (JavaScript for Cloud) [177]. Both languages use three key abstractions:

- *Data* elements, representing input files (e.g., a dataset to be analyzed) or output files (e.g., a data mining model).
- *Tool* elements, representing software tools used to perform operations on data elements (partitioning, filtering, mining, etc.).
- *Tasks*, which represent the execution of Tool elements on given input Data elements to produce some output Data elements.

The DMCF editor generates a JSON descriptor of the workflow, specifying what are the tasks to be executed and the dependency relationships among them. The JSON workflow descriptor is managed by the DMCF workflow engine that is in charge of executing workflow tasks on a set of workers (virtual processing nodes) provided by the Cloud infrastructure. The workflow engine implements a data-driven task parallelism that assigns workflow tasks to idle workers as soon as they are ready to execute. Further details on DMCF execution mechanisms are given in Section 4.2.3.

4.2.2   Hercules overview

Hercules [175] is a distributed in-memory storage system based on the key/value Memcached database. The distributed memory space can be used by the applications as a virtual storage device for I/O operations. Hercules has been adapted for being used as an alternative to Cloud storage service, offering in-memory shared storage for applications deployed over Cloud infrastructures.

Hercules architecture (see top-center part of Figure 4.10, labeled Hercules instance) has two main layers: front-end (Hercules client library) and back-end (server layer). The user-level library is used by the application (or DMCF workers) for

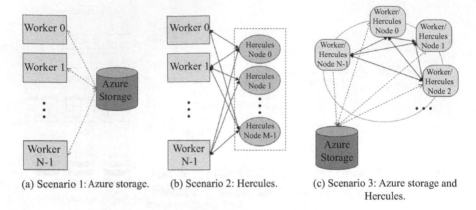

(a) Scenario 1: Azure storage.   (b) Scenario 2: Hercules.   (c) Scenario 3: Azure storage and Hercules.

Figure 4.11   Integration scenarios between DMCF and Hercules

accessing to the Hercules back-end. The library features a layered design, while back-end components are based on enhanced Memcached servers that extend basic functionality with persistence and tweaks.

Hercules offers four main advantages: scalability, easy deployment, flexibility, and performance.

Scalability is achieved by fully distributing data and metadata information among all the available nodes, avoiding the bottlenecks produced by centralized metadata servers. Data and metadata placement is completely calculated at the client side by a hashing algorithm. The servers are completely stateless.

Easy deployment and flexibility at the worker side is provided by a POSIX-like user-level interface in addition to the classic put/get approach existing in current NoSQL databases. This approach supports legacy applications with minimum changes. Servers can also be deployed without root privileges.

Performance and flexibility are targeted at the server side by exploiting I/O parallelism. The capacity of dynamically deploying as many Hercules nodes as necessarily provides the flexibility feature. The combination of both approaches results on each node being accessed independently, multiplying the total throughput peak performance.

4.2.3   Integration between DMCF and Hercules

DMCF and Hercules can be configured to achieve different levels of integration, as shown in Figure 4.11.

Figure 4.11a shows the original approach of DMCF, where every I/O operation is carried out against the Cloud storage service offered by the Cloud provider (Azure storage). There are, at least, four disadvantages about this approach: usage of proprietary interfaces, I/O contention in the service, lack of configuration options, and persistence-related costs unnecessary for temporary data. Figure 4.11b presents a second scenario based on the use of Hercules as the default storage for temporary

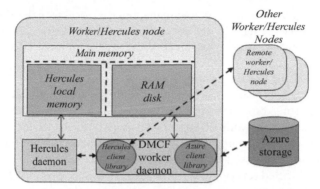

Figure 4.12   DMCF and Hercules daemons

generated data. Hercules I/O nodes can be deployed on as many VM instances as needed by the user depending on the required performance and the characteristics of data. Figure 4.11c shows a third scenario with a tighter integration of DMCF and Hercules infrastructures [178]. In this scenario, initial input and final output are stored on persistent Azure storage, while intermediate data are stored on Hercules in-memory nodes. Hercules I/O nodes share virtual instances with the DMCF workers.

Current trends in data-intensive applications are extensively focusing on the optimization of I/O operations by exploiting the performance offered by in-memory computation, as shown by the popularity of Apache Spark Resilient Distributed Datasets. The goal of this subsection is strengthening the integration between DMCF and Hercules by leveraging the co-location of compute workers and I/O nodes for exposing and exploiting data locality. In order to simplify the implementation of the solution, some workarounds were used: each time that one worker needed to access data (read/write operations over a file), it copied the whole file from Hercules servers to the worker local storage. This approach may greatly penalize the potential performance gain in I/O operations for two main reasons:

- *Data placement strategy*. The original Hercules data placement policy distributes every partition of a specific file among all the available servers. This strategy has two main benefits: avoids hot spots and improves parallel accesses. In an improved DMCF-Hercules integration, whole files can be stored on the same Hercules server.
- *Data-locality agnosticism*. Data locality will not be fully exploited until the DMCF scheduler is tweaked for running tasks on the node that contains the necessary data and/or the data is placed where the computation will be realized.

Figure 4.12 describes an improvement to the third scenario of integration between DMCF and Hercules, which is exploited as the base for the proposed data-aware scheduling strategy. Four main components are present: DMCF worker daemon, Hercules daemon, Hercules client library, and Azure client library. The DMCF worker daemons are in charge of executing the workflow tasks; Hercules daemons act as

I/O nodes (storing data in-memory and managing data accesses); the Hercules client library is intended to be used by the applications to access to the data stored in Hercules (query Hercules daemons) and the Azure client library is used to read/write data from/to the Azure storage.

In this model, we use an RAM disk as generic storage buffer for I/O operations performed by workflow tasks. The objective of this approach is to enable the support of DMCF to any existing tool, allowing even binaries independently of the language used for their implementation, while offering in-memory performance for local accesses.

The logic used for managing this RAM disk buffer is based on the full information about the workflow possessed by the DMCF workers. When every dependency of an specific task is fulfilled (every input file is ready to be accessed), the DMCF worker brings the necessary data to the node from the storage (Azure storage in the first scenario or Hercules in the second scenario).

Based on this approach, every existing tool is capable of accessing transparently data, without the need of modifying the code. After the termination of the task, every data written in the RAM disk is transferred to Hercules/Azure by the DMCF worker. Every data transfer to/from Hercules is performed by the DMCF worker through the Hercules client library.

4.2.4   Data-aware scheduling strategy

This subsection presents the data-aware scheduling strategy that combines DMCF load-balancing capabilities and Hercules data and metadata distribution functionalities for implementing various locality-aware and load-balancing policies.

Before going into details of the purposed scheduling mechanism, we recall the high-level steps that are performed for designing and executing a knowledge discovery application in DMCF [174]:

1. The user accesses the website and designs the workflow through a Web-based interface.
2. After workflow submission, the system creates a set of tasks and inserts them into the Task Queue.
3. Each idle worker picks a task from the Task Queue and concurrently executes it.
4. Each worker gets the input dataset from its location. To this end, a file transfer is performed from the Data Folder where the dataset is located to the local storage of the worker.
5. After task completion, each worker puts the result on the Data Folder.
6. The Website notifies the user whenever each task has completed, and allows her/him to access the results.

Algorithm 1 describes the data-aware scheduler employed by each worker. Compared to the original scheduler described in [174], this novel scheduling algorithm relies on a local list within each worker, called *locallyActivatedTasks*. This list contains all the tasks whose status was changed by this worker from "*new*" to "*ready*" at the end of the previous iteration. The worker cyclically checks whether there are tasks ready to be executed in *locallyActivatedTasks* or in the Task Queue (lines 2

```
1  Procedure main()
2  |  while true do
3  |  |  if locallyActivatedTasks.isNotEmpty() or TaskQueue.isNotEmpty() then
4  |  |  |  task ← selectTask(locallyActivatedTasks, TaskQueue);
5  |  |  |  TaskTable.update(task, 'running');
6  |  |  |  foreach input in task.inputList do
7  |  |  |  |  transfer(input, DataFolder, localDataFolder);
8  |  |  |  transfer(task.tool.executable, localToolFolder);
9  |  |  |  foreach library in task.tool.libraryList do
10 |  |  |  |  transfer(library, ToolFolder, localToolFolder);
11 |  |  |  taskStatus ← execute(task, localDataFolder, localToolFolder);
12 |  |  |  if taskStatus = 'done' then
13 |  |  |  |  foreach output in task.outputList do
14 |  |  |  |  |  transfer(output, localDataFolder, DataFolder);
15 |  |  |  |  TaskTable.update(task, 'done');
16 |  |  |  |  foreach wfTask in TaskTable.getTasks(task.workflowId) do
17 |  |  |  |  |  if wfTask.dependencyList.contains(task) then
18 |  |  |  |  |  |  wfTask.dependencyList.remove(task);
19 |  |  |  |  |  |  if wfTask.dependencyList.isEmpty() then
20 |  |  |  |  |  |  |  TaskTable.update(wfTask, 'ready');
21 |  |  |  |  |  |  |  locallyActivatedTasks.addTask(wfTask);

22 |  |  |  else //Manage the task's failure;
23 |  |  else //Wait for new tasks in TaskQueue;

24 SubProcedure selectTask(locallyActivatedTasks, TaskQueue)
25 |  bestTask ← Hercules.selectByLocality(locallyActivatedTasks, TaskQueue);
26 |  if bestTask in TaskQueue then
27 |  |  TaskQueue.removeTask(bestTask);
28 |  foreach task in locallyActivatedTasks do
29 |  |  if task != bestTask then
30 |  |  |  TaskQueue.addTask(task);
31 |  empty(locallyActivatedTasks);
32 |  clean(localDataFolder);
33 |  clean(localToolFolder);
34 |  return bestTask;
```

Algorithm 1   Worker operations

and 3). If so, a task is selected from one of the two sets (line 4) using the *selectTask* subprocedure (lines 24–34), and its status is changed to "*running*" (line 5). Then, the transfer of all the needed input resources (files, executables, and libraries) is carried out from their original location to two local folders, referred to as *localDataFolder* and *localToolFolder* (lines 6–10). At line 11, the worker locally executes the *task* and waits for its completion. If the *task* is "*done*" (line 12), if necessary the output results are copied to a remote data folder (lines 13 and 14), and the *task* status is changed to "*done*" also in the Task Table (line 15). Then, for each *wfTask* that belongs to the same workflow of *task* (line 16), if *wfTask* has a dependency with *task* (line 17), that dependency is deleted (line 18). If *wfTask* remains without dependencies (line 19), it becomes "*ready*" and is added to the Task Queue (lines 20 and 21). If the *task* fails (line 22), all the tasks that directly or indirectly depend on it are marked as "*failed*."

The *selectTask* subprocedure works as follows. First, it invokes the *selectByLocality* function provided by Hercules, which selects the best task that this worker can manage from *locallyActivatedTasks* and the Task Queue (line 25). To take advantage of data locality, the best task selected by this function is the one having the highest number of input data that are available on the local storage of the worker, based on the information available to Hercules. This differs from the original data-locality-agnostic scheduling policy adopted in DMCF, in which each worker picks and executes the task from the queue following an FIFO policy. If such a best task was chosen from the Task Queue, then that task is removed from the Task Queue (lines 26 and 27). All the tasks in *locallyActivatedTasks* that are different from the best task are added to the Task Queue, thus allowing the other workers to execute them (line 28–30). Finally, *locallyActivatedTasks* is emptied, and localDataFolder and localToolFolder are cleaned from the data/tools that are not used by bestTask (lines 31–33).

4.2.5   *Experimental evaluation*

This subsection presents the experimental evaluation of the data-aware scheduling strategy used to improve the integration between DMCF and Hercules. For this evaluation, we have emulated the execution of a data analysis workflow using three alternative scenarios:

- *Azure-only*: every I/O operation of the workflow is performed by DMCF using the Azure storage service.
- *Locality-agnostic*: a full integration between DMCF and Hercules is exploited, where each intermediate data is stored in Hercules, while initial input and final output are stored on Azure. DMCF workers and Hercules I/O nodes share resources (they are deployed in the same VM instance); however, every I/O operation is performed over remote Hercules I/O nodes through the network.
- *Data-aware*: based on the same deployment as in the previous case, this scenario is based on a full knowledge of the data location and executes every task in the same node where the data are stored, leading to fully local accesses over temporary data. Based on this locality exploitation, most I/O operations are performed in-memory rather than through the network.

The evaluation is based on a data mining workflow that analyzes n partitions of the training set using k classification algorithms so as to generate kn classification models. The kn models generated are then evaluated against a test set by a model selector to identify the best model. Then, n predictors use the best model to produce in parallel n classified datasets. The k classification algorithms used in the workflow are C4.5, support vector machine (SVM) and Naive Bayes, which are three of the main classification algorithms [179]. The training set, test set, and unlabeled dataset

Listing 4.1   Classification JS4Cloud workflow

```
 1: var TrRef = Data.get("Train");
 2: var STrRef = Data.define("STrain");
 3: Shuffler({dataset:TrRef, sDataset:STrRef});
 4: var n = 20;
 5: var PRef = Data.define("TrainPart", n);
 6: Partitioner({dataset:STrRef, datasetPart:PRef});
 7: var MRef = Data.define("Model", [3,n]);
 8: for(var i = 0; i <n; i++){
 9:     C45({dataset:PRef[i], model:MRef[0][i]});
10:     SVM({dataset:PRef[i], model:MRef[1][i]});
11:     NaiveBayes({dataset:PRef[i], model:MRef[2][i]});
12: }
13: var TeRef = Data.get("Test");
14: var BMRef = Data.define("BestModel");
15: ModelSelector({dataset:TeRef, models:MRef, bestModel:BMRef});
16: var m = 80;
17: var DRef = Data.get("Unlab", m);
18: var FDRef = Data.define("FUnlab", m);
19: for(var i = 0; i <m; i++)
20:     Filter({dataset:DRef[i], fDataset:FDRef[i]});
21: var CRef = Data.define("ClassDataset", m);
22: for(var i = 0; i <m; i++)
23:     Predictor({dataset:FDRef[i], model:BMRef, classDataset:CRef[i]});
```

that represent the input of the workflow have been generated from the *KDD Cup 1999*s dataset,[2] which contains a wide variety of simulated intrusion records in a military network environment.

Listing 4.1 shows the JS4Cloud source code of the workflow. At the beginning, we define the training set (*line 1*) and a variable that stores the shuffled training set (*line 2*). At *line 3*, the training set is processed by a shuffling tool. Once defined parameter $n = 20$ at *line 4*, the shuffled training set is partitioned into n parts using a partitioning tool (*line 6*). Then, each part of the shuffled training set is analyzed in parallel by $k = 3$ classification tools (*C4.5*, *SVM*, *NaiveBayes*). Since the number of tools is k and the number of parts is n, kn instances of classification tools run in parallel to produce kn classification models (*lines 8–12*). The kn classification models generated are then evaluated against a test set by a model selector to identify the best model (*line 15*). Then, $m = 80$ unlabeled datasets are specified as input (*line 15*). Each of the m input datasets is filtered in parallel by m filtering tools (*lines 19 and 20*). Finally, each of the m filtered datasets is classified by m predictors using the best model (*lines 22 and 23*). The workflow is composed of $3 + kn + 2m$ tasks. In the specific example, where $n = 20$, $k = 3$, $m = 80$, the number of generated tasks is equal to 223.

Figure 4.13 depicts the VL4Cloud version of the data mining workflow. The visual formalism clearly highlights the level of parallelism of the workflow, expressed by the number of parallel paths and the cardinality of tool array nodes.

---

[2]http://kdd.ics.uci.edu/databases/kddcup99/kddcup99

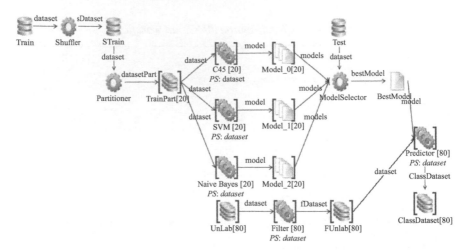

Figure 4.13   Classification of VL4Cloud workflow

Table 4.3   Bandwidth micro-benchmark results (in MB/s)

Operation	Hercules local access	Hercules remote access	Azure storage data access
Read	800	175	60
Write	1,000	180	30

Once the workflow is submitted to DMCF using either JS4Cloud or VL4Cloud, DMCF generates a JSON descriptor of the workflow, specifying which are the tasks to be executed and the dependency relationships among them. Thus, DMCF creates a set of tasks that will be executed by workers. In order to execute a given workflow task, we have provisioned as many D2 VM instances (CPU with 2 cores and 7GB of RAM) in the Azure infrastructure as needed and configured them by launching both the Hercules daemon and the DMCF worker process on each VM. In order to better understand the performance results, we have performed a preliminary evaluation of the expected performance of both Azure storage and Hercules. Table 4.3 presents bandwidth performance of an I/O micro-benchmark consisting in writing and reading a 256 MB file, with 4 MB chunk size. Latency results are not relevant for data-intensive applications. Due to the usual large file size, the latency-related time is negligible in comparison with the bandwidth-related time.

After the initial setup, DMCF performs a series of preliminary operations (i.e., getting the task from the Task Queue, downloading libraries, and reading input files from the Cloud storage) and final operations (e.g., updating the Task Table, writing the output files to the Cloud storage). Table 4.4 lists all the read/write operations performed during the execution of the workflow on each data array. Each row of the

Table 4.4   Read/write operations performed during the execution of the workflow

Data node	No. of files	Total size	No. of read operations	No. of write operations
Train	1	100 MB	1	–
Strain	1	100 MB	1	1
TrainPart	20	100 MB	60	20
Model	60	≈20 MB	60	60
Test	1	50 MB	1	–
BestModel	1	300 kB	80	1
UnLab	80	8 GB	80	–
FUnLab	80	≈8 GB	80	80
ClassDataset	80	≈6 GB	–	80

table describes: *i*) the number of files included in the data array node; *ii*) the total size of the data array; *iii*) the total number of read operations performed on the files included in the data array; and (iv) the total number of write operations performed on the files included in the data array. As can be noted, all the inputs of the workflow (i.e., *Train, Test, UnLab*) are never written on persistent storage, and the final output of the workflow (i.e., *ClassDataset*) is not used (read) by any other task.

Figure 4.14a shows the turnaround times of the workflow executed in the three scenarios introduced earlier: *Azure-only, locality-agnostic, data-aware*. In all scenarios, the turnaround times have been measured varying the number of workers used to run it on the Cloud from 1 (sequential execution) to 64 (maximum parallelism). In the Azure scenario, the turnaround time decreases from 1 h and 48 min on a single worker to about 2.6 min using 64 workers. In the Locality-agnostic scenario, the turnaround time decreases from 1 h and 34 min on a single worker, to about 2.2 min using 64 workers. In the data-aware scenario, the turnaround time decreases from 1 h and 26 min on a single worker to about 2 min using 64 workers. It is worth noticing that, in all the configurations evaluated, locality-agnostic allowed us to reduce the execution time in about 13% compared to the Azure scenario, while data-aware allowed us to reduce the execution time in about 20% compared to the Azure scenario.

We also evaluated the overhead introduced by DMCF in the three scenarios. We define as overhead the time required by the system to perform a series of preliminary operations (i.e., getting the task from the Task Queue, downloading libraries and reading input files from the Cloud storage) and final operations (e.g., updating the Task Table, writing the output files to the Cloud storage) related to the execution of each workflow task. Table 4.5 shows the overhead time of the workflow in the three analyzed scenarios. We observe that the overhead in the Azure-only scenario is 40 min, while in the locality-agnostic scenario is 26 min and in the data-aware is 18 min. This means that using Hercules for storing intermediate data, we were able to reduce the overhead by 36% using a locality-agnostic approach and by 55% using a data-aware approach.

Figure 4.14b presents the time required by the application to perform every I/O operation of the application, and Figure 4.14 increases the level of detail, showing

Table 4.5   Overhead in the three scenarios

	Total time (s)	Overhead (s)
Azure-only	6,487	2,382
Locality-agnostic	5,624	1,519
Data-aware	5,200	1,086

only the operations affected by the use of the Hercules service, i.e., I/O operations that work on temporary data. As shown in the figure, the difference between the three strategies is clear.

In order to better show the impact of the Hercules service, Figure 4.14 presents a breakdown of the total execution time, detailing the time spent on each of the tasks executed by the workflow application: computation tasks (CPU time), I/O tasks over input/results files stored in Azure storage, and I/O operations performed over temporary files. This figure clearly shows how the time required for I/O operations over temporary files, the only operations affected by use of Hercules services, are reduced to be almost negligible during the execution of the workflow, showing a great potential for increasing the I/O performance in data-intensive applications with large amounts of temporary data.

4.2.6   Conclusions

While workflow management systems deployed on HPC systems (e.g., parallel machines) typically exploit a monolithic parallel file system that ensures highly efficient data accesses, workflow systems implemented on a distributed infrastructure (most often, a public Cloud) must borrow techniques from the Big Data computing (BDC) field, such as exposing data storage locality and scheduling work to reduce data movement in order to alleviate the I/O subsystems under highly demanding data access patterns.

In this section, we proposed the use of DMCF+Hercules as an alternative to classical shared parallel file systems, currently deployed over the HPC infrastructures. Classical HPC systems are composed by compute resources and I/O nodes completely decoupled. Based on this approach, the available I/O nodes can scale with the number of compute nodes performing concurrent data accesses, avoiding the bottleneck of current parallel file systems. In extreme cases, our solution should also be provided over the I/O infrastructure of the parallel file system, taking advantage of the available resources (I/O nodes counting with large amounts of RAM and a dedicated high-performance network). DMCF+Hercules aims to achieve scalability to enhance four main aspects that contribute to the file I/O bottleneck illustrated as motivation above: metadata scalability, data scalability, locality exploitation, and file system server scalability. DMCF+Hercules will act as an I/O accelerator, providing improved performance for data accesses to temporary data.

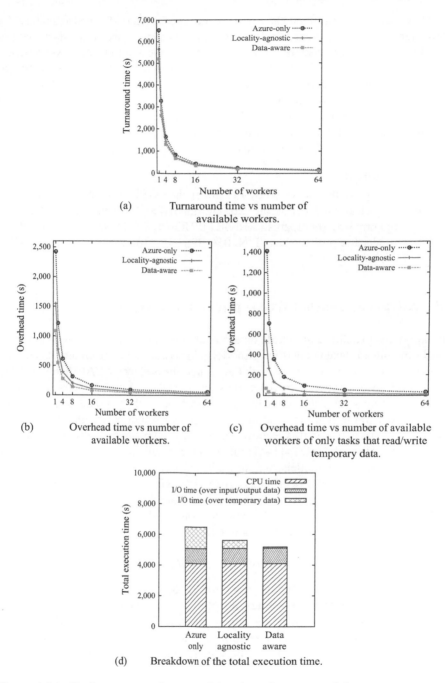

(a)   Turnaround time vs number of
available workers.

(b)   Overhead time vs number of
available workers.

(c)   Overhead time vs number of available
workers of only tasks that read/write
temporary data.

(d)   Breakdown of the total execution time.

*Figure 4.14   Performance evaluation of the classification workflow using
Azure-only, locality-agnostic and data-aware configurations*

This section also presented an experimental evaluation performed to analyze the performance of the proposed data-aware scheduling strategy executing data analysis workflows and to demonstrate the effectiveness of the solution. The experimental results show that, using the proposed data-aware strategy and Hercules as storage service for temporary data, the I/O overhead of workflow execution is reduced by 55% compared to the standard execution based on the Azure storage, leading to a 20% reduction of the total execution time. These results demonstrate the effectiveness of our data-aware scheduling approach in improving the performance of data-intensive workflow execution in Cloud platforms.

Acknowledgment

This section is partially supported by EU under the COST Program Action IC1305: Network for Sustainable Ultrascale Computing (NESUS). This section has been partially supported by the Spanish MINISTERIO DE ECONOMÍA Y COMPETI-TIVIDAD under the project grant TIN2016-79637-P "Towards unification of HPC and Big Data paradigms."

4.3   Advanced conflict-free replicated datatypes

One approach to achieve ultrascale data management is to use a full data replication paradigm with a relaxed consistency model. This is advocated given the tradeoffs of Availability, Consistency, and network Partition addressed by the CAP theorem [180]. While a relaxed consistency model allows for prompt local updates, this can lead to potential conflicts in the data once merged elsewhere. With the premise to eventually converge to a single state, manual and case-tailored solutions are unproven correct and cumbersome to use. In this section, we present a more generic and mathematically proven method though CRDTs [181] that guarantee eventual convergence. We present four variants of CRDT models: operation-based, pure operation-based, state-based, and delta-state-based CRDTs [97,98,181–183]. We aim to keep the presentation simple by addressing a common "set" datatype example throughout all CRDT variants to show their differences. We finally present a case study, on the *dataClay* [184,185] distributed platform, demonstrating how CRDTs can be used in practice.[3]

4.3.1   Scalability and availability tradeoffs

With the immense volumes of data generated by social networks, Internet of Things, and data science, scalability becomes one of the major data management challenges. To sustain such data volumes, a data management service must guarantee both a large data storage capacity and high availability. Although the former can be increased through scaling up, i.e., augmenting the storage capacity of a service though adding

---

[3]The research leading to these results has received funding from the European Union's Horizon 2020—The EU Framework Programme for Research and Innovation 2014–2020, under grant agreement No. 732505, LightKone project.

larger hard drives or using RAID technology, the availability challenge remains, due to bottlenecks and single points of failure. A typical alternative is to scale out through distributing, a.k.a., replicating, the data over distinct nodes either within a small proximity, like a cluster, or scattered over a large geographical space. This however raises a challenge on the quality of data, subject to the speed of Read/Write operations and data freshness, and often governed through a data consistency model [186].

Traditionally, the common approach was to fully replicate the data and use a strong consistency model, e.g., sequential consistency or total order protocols like quorum-based consensus [187,188]. However, the overhead of synchronization becomes intolerable under scale, especially in a geographically distributed setting or loosely coupled systems. In fact, the CAP theorem [180,189] forces to choose between (strict) data consistency and availability, given that network partitions are hard to avoid in practice. Consequently, the recent trend is to adopt a relaxed data consistency model that trades strict consistency for high availability. This is advocated by applications that cannot afford large response times on *reads* and *writes* and thus allow for stale reads as long as propagating local writes eventually lead to convergence [190]—assuming system quiescence.

The weakest consistency models that guarantee convergence often adopt a variant of Eventual Consistency (EC) [190] in which updates are applied locally, without prior synchronization with other replicas such that they are eventually delivered and applied by all replicas. In practice, many applications require stronger guarantees on time and order and advocate the causal consistency model, which enforces a *happens-before* relation [191]: A is delivered before B if A occurred before B on the same machine; or otherwise, A occurred before a *send* event and B occurred after a *receive* event (possibly by transitivity). To understand the need for causal consistency in applications, consider an example on a replicated messaging service where Bob commented on Alice's message, i.e., Alice's message happened before Bob's comment. Since, in a distributed setting, it can happen that different users read from different servers (a.k.a., replicas), without enforcing causal consistency some users may read Bob's comment before Alice's message.

Even if it boosts availability, a relaxed consistency model can lead to conflicts when concurrent operations are invoked on different replicas. Traditionally, conflicts are reconciled manually or left to the application to decide on the order (all concurrent versions are retained and exposed) [192]. This process is very costly and subject to errors which necessitates a systematic way instead. CRDTs [97,98,181] are mathematical abstractions that are proven to be conflict-free and easy to use, and they are recently being adopted by leading industry such as Facebook, Tom Tom, and Riak DB. In the rest of this section, we introduce CRDTs and present some of the recent advanced models.

4.3.2 Conflict-free replicated datatypes

CRDTs [97,98,181] are data abstractions (e.g., counters, sets, maps, etc.), that are usually replicated over (often loosely connected) network of nodes, and are mathematically formalized to guarantee that replicas converge to the same state, provided

$$\Sigma \qquad : \text{State type, } \sigma_i \text{ is an instance}$$

$\text{prepare}_i(o, \sigma_i)$: Prepares a message m given an operation o

$\text{effect}_i(m, \sigma_i)$: Applies a *prepared* message m on a state

$\text{val}_i(q, \sigma_i)$: Read-only evaluation of query q on a state

Figure 4.15   The general composition of an op-based CRDT

they eventually apply the same updates. The assumption is that state updates should be commutative, or designed to be so. This ensures that applying concurrent updates on different nodes is independent of their application order. For instance, applying "Add A" and "Add B" to a *set* will eventually lead to both elements A and B in the two replicas. Whereas concurrent non-commutative operations "Add A" and "Remove A" may lead to two different replicas (one is empty and the other has element A).

There are two main approaches to CRDTs: operation-based (a.k.a., op-based) and state-based. The former is based on disseminating operations, whereas the latter propagates a state that results from locally applied operations. In the systems where the message dissemination layer guarantees reliable causal broadcast (RCB), op-based CRDTs are desired as they allow for simpler implementations, concise replica state, and smaller messages. On the other hand, state-based CRDTs are more complex to design, but can handle duplicates and out-of-order delivery of messages without breaking causality, and thus are favored in hostile networks.

In the following, we elaborate on these models and their optimizations focusing on the Add-wins Set (AWSet) datatype (in which a concurrent add dominates a remove). We opt for AWSet being a very common datatype that has causality semantics, which helps explaining the different ordering guarantees in CRDT models. More formally, in an AWSet that retains add and rmv operations together with their timestamps t, the concurrent semantics can be defined by a read operation that returns the following elements:

$$\{v \mid (t, [\text{add}, v]) \in s \land \forall (t', [(\text{add}|\text{rmv}), v]) \in s \cdot t \not< t'\} \qquad (4.1)$$

Op-based CRDTs. In op-based CRDTs [181], each replica maintains a local state that is type-dependent. A replica is subject to clients' operations, i.e., *query* and *update*, that are executed locally as soon as they arrive. While query operations read the local (maybe stale) state without modifying it, updates often modify the state and generate some message to be propagated to other replicas through an RCB middleware. The RCB handles the exactly once dissemination across replicas, mainly through an API composed of causal broadcast function cbcast and causal deliver function cdeliver.

To explain the process further, we consider the general structure of an op-based CRDT in Figure 4.15 and convey Algorithm 1 in Figure 4.16 that depicts the interplay between the RCB middleware and the CRDT. In particular, when an update operation o is issued at some node i having state σ_i, the function $\text{prepare}_i(o, \sigma_i)$ produces a message m that includes some ordering meta-data in addition to the operation. This message m is then broadcast by calling $\text{cbcast}_i(m)$ and is delivered via

state:
| $\sigma_i \in \Sigma$
on operation$_i(o)$:
| $m := $ prepare$_i(o, \sigma_i)$
| cbcast$_i(m)$
on cdeliver$_i(m)$:
| $\sigma_i := $ effect$_i(m, \sigma_i)$

on query$_i()$:
| val$_i(\sigma_i)$

Algorithm 1: CRDT & RCB

state:
| $\sigma_i = (s, \pi) \in \mathcal{P}(O) \times (O, \leq)$
on operation$_i(o)$:
| tcbcast$_i(o)$
on tcdeliver$_i(m, t)$:
| $\pi_i := $ effect$_i(m, t, \pi_i)$

on tcstable$_i(t)$:
| $\sigma_i := $ prune$_i(\pi_i, s, t)$
on query$_i()$:
| val$_i(\sigma_i)$

Algorithm 2: Pure CRDT & TRCB

Figure 4.16   Distributed algorithms for node i showing the interplay of classical and pure op-based CRDTs given a standard versus tagged RCB middlewares, respectively

$$\Sigma = \mathbb{N} \times \mathscr{P}(I \times \mathbb{N} \times V) \qquad \sigma_i^0 = (0, \{\})$$
$$\text{prepare}_i([add, v], (n, s)) = [add, v, i, n+1]$$
$$\text{effect}_i([add, v, i', n'], (n, s)) = (n' \wedge (i = i') \vee n, s \cup \{(v, i', n')\})$$
$$\text{prepare}_i[rmv, v], (n, s)) = [rmv, \{(v', i', n') \in s \,|\, v' = v\}]$$
$$\text{effect}_i([rmv, r], (n, s)) = (n, s \setminus r)$$
$$\text{val}_i(n, s) = \{v \,|\, (v, i', n') \in s\}$$

Figure 4.17   Operation-based Add-Wins Set CRDT, at node i

cdeliver$_j$(m) at each destination node j (including i itself). cdeliver triggers effect$_j$(m, σ_j) that returns a new replica state σ_j'. Finally, a query operation q is issued, val$_i$(q, σ_i) is invoked, and no corresponding broadcast occurs.

Example. We further exemplify op-based CRDTs though an "Add-wins Set" (AWSet) CRDT design depicted in Figure 4.17. The state Σ is composed of a local sequence number $n \in \mathbb{N}$ and a set of values in V together with some meta-data in $I \times \mathbb{N}$ that is used to guarantee the causality information of the datatype. The prepare of an add operation produces a tuple, to be disseminated by RCB, composed of the element to be added together with the ID and the incremented sequence number of the local node i. The effect function is invoked on RCB delivery and leads to adding this tuple to the state and incrementing the sequence number only if the prepare was local at i. To the contrary, preparing an rmv returns all the tuples containing the removed item, which allows the corresponding effect to remove all these tuples. Finally, the val function returns all the elements in the set.

Pure Op-based CRDTs. Op-based CRDTs can be optimized to reduce the dissemination and storage overhead. Indeed, since op-based CRDTs assume the presence of and RCB, one can take advantage of its time abstractions, i.e., often implemented via version vectors (VVs), to guarantee causal delivery and thus avoid disseminating the meta-data produced by prepare. Consequently, this leads to disseminating the "pure" operations and possible arguments which makes the prepare useless, hence

$$\Sigma = \mathscr{P}(O) \times T \hookrightarrow O \qquad \sigma_i^0 = (s_i, \pi_i)^0 = (\{\}, \{\})$$

$$\text{effect}_i(o,t,s,\pi) \;=\; (s \setminus \{[\text{add},v] \mid o = [\text{rmv},v]\},$$
$$\pi \setminus \{(t',[\text{add},v]) \mid o = [\text{rmv},v] \wedge t' < t\} \cup$$
$$\{(t,o) \mid o = [\text{add},v] \wedge (\_,o) \notin \pi \wedge o \notin s\})$$

$$\text{val}_i(s,\pi) \;=\; \{v \mid [\text{add},v] \in s \vee (t,[\text{add},v]) \in \pi\}$$

$$\text{prune}_i(\pi,s,\tau) \;=\; (s \cup \{o\}, \pi \setminus \{(t,o)\}) \wedge t \leq \tau$$

Figure 4.18   Pure operation-based Add-Wins Set CRDT, at node i

the name Pure op-based CRDTs [98,183]. In addition, this "pure" mind-set leads to having a standard state for all datatypes: a partially order log: Polog. However, this will lead to storing the VV in the state which can be very expensive when the number of replicas in the systems is high. Fortunately, and contrary to the classical op-based approach, the time notion of VV is useful to transform the Polog into a sequential log which eventually helps to prune the—no longer needed—VVs.

Tagged reliable causal broadcast (TRCB). To achieve the above optimizations, we consider an extended RCB, called Tagged RCB (TRCB), that provides two functionalities through the API functions: `tcdeliver` and `tcstable` [98,183]. The former is an equivalent to the standard RCB `cdeliver` presented above with a simple extension to the API by exposing the VVs (used internally by the RCB) to the node upon delivery, which can be appended to the operation by the recipient. On the other hand, `tcstable` is a new function that returns a timestamp τ indicating that all operations with timestamp $t \leq \tau$ are *stable*: have been delivered on all nodes. The essence is that no concurrent operations to the stable operations in the Polog are expected to be delivered, and hence, the corresponding VVs in the Polog can be pruned without affecting the datatype semantics.

Given the TRCB, depicted in Algorithm 2 of Figure 4.16, the design of Pure CRDTs differs from the classical ones in different aspects. First, the state is common to all datatypes and is represented by a set of stable operations and a Polog. Second, `prepare` has no role anymore as the operations and its arguments can be immediately disseminated though the TRCB. Third, the significant change is with the `effect` function that discards datatype-specific "redundant" operations before adding to the Polog (e.g., a duplicate operation). However, to the contrary of classical op-based CRDTs, only one `effect` function is required per datatype. Finally, `prune` function is required to move stable operations (triggered via the TRCB's `tcstable`) to the sequential log after pruning the VVs.

Example. Using the same example of the AWSet, we provide the Pure CRDT version in Figure 4.18. The state is composed of a set of sequential operations s and Polog π: a map from timestamps to operations. The `prepare` does not exist due to the reasons mentioned above, and hence the operation and its arguments are sent to the destination. Once an `rmv` operation is delivered, the `effect` deletes the corresponding operation from s and those in the causal past of $\text{rmv} \in \pi$. (Remember that all operations in s are in the causal past of delivered operations.) Finally, `effect` only adds an `add` to π if the element is not in s or π. Once the `tcstable` triggers prune, given a stable timestamp τ, all operations with timestamp $t \leq \tau$ become stable and are thus removed by prune from π and added to s without the (now useless) timestamp.

Additional pedantic details. A catalog of many op-based CRDT specifications such as counters, sets, registers, and maps can be found in [183]. There are also several optimizations that are beyond the scope of this book. For instance, the pure op-based specifications can be generalized further to have a common framework for all CRDTs in such a way the user only needs to define simple datatype-specific rules to truncate the Polog. In addition, one can go deeper and optimize each datatype aside. An example is to replace the stable state with a classical datatype instead of retaining the set of operations. On the other hand, datatypes that are natively commutative can be easier to implement as classical op-based CRDTs. Finally, we avoid presenting the details of the TRCB for presentation purposes. The reader can refer to [98,183] for these details.

State-based CRDTs. While op-based CRDTs are based on the dissemination of operations that are executed by every replica, a "state" is disseminated in the state-based CRDTs [181]. A received state is incorporated with the local state via a *merge* function that, deterministically, reconciles any existing conflicts.

As depicted in Figure 4.19, a state-based CRDT consists of a state, mutators, join, and query functions. The state Σ is designed as a join-semilattice [193]: a set with a *partial order*, and a binary *join* operation $\sqcup$ that returns the *least upper bound* (LUB) of two elements in S and is always designed to be commutative, associative, and idempotent. On the other hand, mutators are defined as *inflation*: for any mutator m and state X, $X \sqsubseteq m(X)$. This guarantees that the state never diminishes, and thus, each subsequent state subsumes the previous state when joined elsewhere. Finally, the query operation leaves no changes on the state. Note that the specification of all these functions, and the state, is datatype specific.

Anti-entropy protocol. To the contrary of op-based CRDTs that assume the presence of RCB, state-based CRDTs can ensure eventual convergence using a simple *anti-entropy* protocol, as in Figure 4.20, that periodically ships the entire local state to other replicas. Each replica merges the received state with its local state using the *join* operation. (The algorithm in Figure 4.20 can be more sophisticated to include retransmissions, routing, or gossiping, but we keep it simple for presentation purposes.)

Example. Again, we exemplify on state-based CRDTs via Figure 4.21 that depicts the design of AWSet. The state Σ is composed of two sets. One set is for the addition of elements with unique tags defined by unique ID and sequence number, and another tombstones set that serves for collecting the removed tags. This design is crucial to

Σ	: State defined as *join semi-lattice*, σ_i is an instance
Mutators	: mutating operations that inflate the state.
$s \sqcup s'$	: LUB to merge states s and s'
$\text{val}_i(q, \sigma_i)$	: Read-only evaluation of query q on a state

Figure 4.19 The general composition of a state-based CRDT

inputs:
| $n_i \in \mathcal{P}(\mathbb{I})$, set of neighbors
durable state:
| $X_i := \perp \in S$, CRDT state
on receive$_{j,i}(Y)$
| $X_i' = X_i \sqcup Y$

on operation$_i(m)$
| $X_i' = m(X_i)$
periodically // ship state
| $j = \mathsf{random}(n_i)$
| $\mathsf{send}_{i,j}(X_i)$

1

Figure 4.20   A basic anti-entropy algorithm for state-based CRDTs

$$
\begin{aligned}
\Sigma &= \mathscr{P}(\mathbb{I} \times \mathbb{N} \times E) \times \mathscr{P}(\mathbb{I} \times \mathbb{N}) \\
\sigma_i^0 &= (\{\}, \{\}) \\
\mathsf{add}_i(e, (s,t)) &= (s \cup \{(i, n+1, e)\}, t) \\
&\quad \text{with } n = \max(\{k \mid (i, k, \_) \in s\}) \\
\mathsf{rmv}_i(e, (s,t)) &= (s, t \cup \{(j, n) \mid (j, n, e) \in s\}) \\
\mathsf{val}_i((s,t)) &= \{e \mid (j, n, e) \in s \wedge (j, n) \notin t\} \\
(s,t) \sqcup (s', t') &= (s \cup s', t \cup t')
\end{aligned}
$$

Figure 4.21   State-based AWSet CRDT, at node i

achieve the semi-lattice inflation properties subject to mutators: add and rmv. The former adds the new element to the addition set together with a new tag leaving the tombstones set intact. An element is removed by rmv through adding its unique tag to the tombstones set. Notice that the element must not be removed from the addition set which violates inflation. Given these specifications, the query function val will simply return all the added elements that do not have corresponding tags in the tombstones set. Finally, the merge function $\sqcup$ joins any two (disseminated or not) states by simply computing the union of the sets, thus respecting the semi-lattice properties.

Delta-state CRDTs. Despite the simplicity and robustness of state-based CRDTs, the dissemination overhead is high as the entire state is always propagated even with small local state updates. Delta-state CRDTs [97,182] are state-based CRDT variants that allow one to "isolate" the recent updates on a state and ship the corresponding *delta*, i.e., a state in the semi-lattice corresponding only to the updates, and shipped to be merged remotely. The trick is to find new delta-mutators (a.k.a., δ-mutators) m^δ that return deltas instead of entire states (and again, these are datatype specific). Given a state X, the relation between mutators m in state-based CRDTs and m^δ is as follows:

$$X' = m(X) = X \sqcup m^\delta(X) \tag{4.2}$$

This represents the main change in the design of state-based CRDTs in Figure 4.19.

Example. Considering the AWSet example, the only difference between the delta CRDT version in Figure 4.22 and its state-based counterpart in Figure 4.21 is with mutators. One can simply notice that add^δ returns the recent update that represents

$$
\begin{aligned}
\Sigma &= \mathscr{P}(\mathbb{I} \times \mathbb{N} \times E) \times \mathscr{P}(\mathbb{I} \times \mathbb{N}) \\
\sigma_i^0 &= (\{\},\{\}) \\
\mathsf{add}_i^\delta(e,(s,t)) &= (\{(i,n+1,e)\},\{\}) \\
&\quad \text{with } n = \max(\{k \,|\, (i,k,\_) \in s\}) \\
\mathsf{rmv}_i^\delta(e,(s,t)) &= (\{\},\{(j,n) \,|\, (j,n,e) \in s\}) \\
\mathsf{val}_i((s,t)) &= \{e \,|\, (j,n,e) \in s \wedge (j,n) \notin t\} \\
(s,t) \sqcup (s',t') &= (s \cup s', t \cup t')
\end{aligned}
$$

Figure 4.22 Delta-state AWSet CRDT, at node i

the added element, whereas add returns the entire state. A similar logic holds for the difference between rmv^δ and rmv. As for the $\sqcup$ and val, their design is the same in both versions; however, notice that the propagated and merged message is a delta-state in Figure 4.22 rather than a whole state. Indeed, although a delta-mutator returns a single delta, it is more practical to join deltas locally and ship them in groups (which must not affect the $\sqcup$ in any case) as we explain next.

Causal anti-entropy protocol. This delta CRDT optimization comes at a cost: it is no longer safe to blindly merge received (delta) states when the datatype requires causal semantics. Indeed, state-based CRDTs implicitly ensure per-object causal consistency since the state itself retains all the causality information, whereas a delta state includes the tags of individual changes without any memory about the causal past. This requires a little more sophisticated anti-entropy protocol that enforces causal delivery on received deltas and supports coarse-grained shipping of delta batches, called "delta-intervals." A delta-interval $\Delta_i^{a,b}$ is a group of consecutive deltas corresponding to a sequence of all the local delta mutations from a through $b - 1$, and merged together via $\sqcup$ before shipping:

$$
\Delta_i^{a,b} = \bigsqcup \{d_i^k \,|\, a \leq k < b\} \tag{4.3}
$$

Given this, an anti-entropy algorithm can guarantee causal order if it respects the "causal delta-merging condition": $X_i \sqsupseteq X_j^a$. This means that a receiving replica can only join a remote delta-interval if it has already seen (and merged) all the causally preceding deltas for the same sender. The algorithm in Figure 4.23 is a basic anti-entropy protocol that satisfies the causal delta-merging property. (We discarded many optimization to focus on the core concept.) In addition to the state, a node retains a sequence number that, together with the acknowledgments map, helps the node to identify the missing deltas to be sent to a destination. In addition, the delta-interval D serves to batch deltas locally before sending them periodically. Once an operation is received from a client, a corresponding delta is returned by m^δ, which is then merged to the local state and joined to D for later dissemination to a random node. Once a delta interval is received, it gets merged to the local state as well as the local delta-interval buffer—to be sent to other nodes. Finally, deltas that have been sent to all nodes are garbage-collected from D.

inputs:
  | $n_i \in \mathcal{P}(\mathbb{I})$, set of neighbors
durable state:
  | $X_i := \bot \in S$, CRDT state
  | $c_i := 0 \in \mathbb{N}$, sequence number
volatile state:
  | $D_i := \{\} \in \mathbb{N} \hookrightarrow S$, sequence of δs
  | $A_i := \{\} \in \mathbb{I} \hookrightarrow \mathbb{N}$, ack map
on operation$_i(m^\delta)$
  | $d = m^\delta(X_i)$
  | $X_i' = X_i \sqcup d$
  | $D_i' = D_i\{c_i \mapsto d\}$
  | $c_i' = c_i + 1$

on receive$_{j,i}$(delta, d, n)
  | if $d \not\sqsubseteq X_i$ then
  | | $X_i' = X_i \sqcup d$
  | | $D_i' = D_i\{c_i \mapsto d\}$
  | | $c_i' = c_i + 1$
  | send$_{i,j}$(ack, n)
on receive$_{j,i}$(ack, n)
  | $A_i' = A_i\{j \mapsto \max(A_i(j), n)\}$
periodically // ship delta-interval
  | $j = \mathsf{random}(n_i)$
  | $d = \bigsqcup\{D_i(l) \mid A_i(j) \le l < c_i\}$
  | send$_{i,j}$(delta, d, c_i)
periodically // garbage collect δs
  | $l = \min\{n \mid (\_, n) \in A_i\}$
  | $D_i' = \{(n, d) \in D_i \mid n \ge l\}$

1

Figure 4.23   Basic causal anti-entropy protocol satisfying the delta-merging condition

Additional pedantic details. A catalog of many delta-state CRDT specifications such as counters, sets, registers, and maps can be found in [97,182]. There are also several optimizations that are beyond the scope of this book. For instance, the tags in the tombstone set can be compressed further in a single VV and few tags. This helps generalizing the specifications to use a common causality abstraction per all datatypes [182]. Furthermore, the causal anti-entropy protocol can consider other conditions to improve performance, e.g., through considering transitive propagation of deltas or sending a complete state once a delta does not help, e.g., a node was unavailable for a long time. In this particular case, other useful alternatives to define deltas by *join decomposition* can be found in [194].

4.3.3   A case study: dataClay distributed platform

We now present a case study to demonstrate the practical use of CRDTs in a real distributed system: dataClay distributed platform [184,185]. The aim is to give the reader an applied example of CRDTs showing how they can make the developers life easier. For that purpose, we try to be direct and simple to help the reader getting started.

dataClay. A distributed platform aimed at storing, either persistently or in memory, Java and Python objects [184,185]. This platform enables, on the one hand, to store objects as in an object-oriented database and, on the other hand, to build applications where objects are distributed among different nodes, while still being accessible from any of the nodes where the application runs. Furthermore, dataClay enables several applications to share the same objects as part of their data set.

dataClay has three interesting properties. The first is that it stores the class methods in addition to the data. This functionality has several implications that help application developers use the data in this platform: (1) data can only be accessed using the class methods (no direct field modifications) and thus class developers can take care, for instance, of integrity constraints that will be fulfilled by all applications using the objects and (2) methods can be executed over the objects inside the platform, without having to move the data to the application. The second property is that objects in dataClay are not flat, and they can rather be composed of other objects, or language basic types, like in any object-oriented language. Finally, dataClay enables objects to be replicated to several nodes managed by the platform in order to increase tolerance to faults and/or execution performance by exploiting parallelism.

The case for CRDTs. Despite fully replicating the data (and class definitions) to improve tolerance to faults, dataClay does not natively implement any synchronization scheme between replicas since some applications (or modules of an application) cannot afford paying the synchronization price [186,195]. Consequently, to provide this flexibility, dataClay tries to offer mechanisms for class developers to implement the consistency model their objects may need. Nevertheless, building such mechanisms is always tedious and, most importantly, synchronization implies a performance penalty and lack of scalability [189]. Here is where CRDTs come into play to provide a relaxed consistency and seamless plug-and-play conflict resolution for the replicated objects across the platform. Furthermore, given that code is part of the replicated data, the class developers can implement CRDTs and dataClay itself will guarantee that the update rules will be followed regardless of the application using them.

Using CRDTs. For replicating objects, dataClay can provide the developer with a library for CRDTs to be used in the classes and maybe through composing objects. Given that dataClay's system model is a graph-like Peer-to-Peer system, it is more desirable to use the state-based CRDT model since no RCB middleware is required. By using CRDTs, any application can modify the data objects without prior synchronization with other replicas or applications. Once the changes are propagated, CRDTs can eventually converge to the same value. In order to show how CRDTs are mapped to dataClay, we provide a simple example on a Grow-only Counter (GCounter) CRDT [97,181]. We choose the counter being a simple example and at the same time shows how a semi-lattice can be different from the AWSet discussed before.

The GCounter specification is conveyed in Figure 4.24. In this design, the state Σ is defined as a map from node IDs to a natural number corresponding to the increments done locally. As `inc` mutator shows, a node can only increment its own key, whereas the `val` query function returns the sum of all keys from all nodes. Once a (whole) state is propagated, the merge is done by taking the maximum counter corresponding to each key. For instance, in a system of three nodes, the following two GCounters are merged as follows: $(1, 4, 5) \sqcup (3, 4, 2) = (3, 4, 5)$. In the *Java* implementation of

$$
\begin{aligned}
\Sigma &= I \hookrightarrow \mathbb{N} \\
\sigma_i^0 &= \{\} \\
\text{inc}_i(m) &= m\{i \mapsto m(i) + 1\} \\
\text{val}_i(m) &= \sum_{r \in \mathbf{dom}(m)} m(r) \\
m \sqcup m' &= \mathbf{max}(m, m')
\end{aligned}
$$

Figure 4.24   State based GCounter CRDT, on replica i

```
public class CRDTG_Counter extends DataClayObject {
    // To identify which replica I am.
    // The Key is the dataClay ID where the replica is stored.
    private String nodeID = System.getenv().get("nodeID");
    // The real set of counters.
    // We store it as a map to allow adding new replicas seamlessly
    private Map<String, Integer> counters;

    public CRDTG_Counter() {
    counters = new HashMap<String, Integer>();
    // Creating a new counter
    counters.put(nodeID, 0);
    }

    public synchronized void increment() {
     // Incrementing my "local" counter
     Integer counter = counters.get(nodeID);
     if(counter == null){
            counter = 0;
     }
    counter++;
    counters.put(nodeID, counter);
     // Propagate the update to all replicas
    for(String key: counters.keySet()){
            if(key.equals(nodeID)){
                    continue;
            }
            this.runRemote(new ExecutionEnvironmentID(key),
                    "merge", new Object[]{ counters });
    }
    }

    public int getValue(){
     int counter = 0;
     for(String key: counters.keySet()){
            counter = counter + counters.get(key);
    }
    return counter;
    }

   public synchronized void merge(Map<String, Integer> map){
       String[] keys = map.keySet().toArray(new String[map.size()]);
       for( String key: keys ){
               Integer current = counters.get(key), value = map.get(key);
           if(current == null || current < value ){
                   counters.put(key, value);
           }
       }
   }
  }
 }
```

Figure 4.25   An implementation for GCounter CRDT in dataClay

the GCounter presented in Figure 4.25, the state is coded as a *hash map* to enable the addition of new replicas on the fly, without any kind of synchronization and/or notification as part of the CRDT. In this code, the increment method pushes the new version of the hash map to all existing replicas to have the last up-to-date version and recover any potentially missed update from another node. We leave the details of the code as an exercise to the reader.

Class deployment. As mentioned above, dataClay also replicates the class definitions to be used by the applications across the systems and to allow method invocations close to the data. For this purpose, once a class is updated, the different versions must be coordinated to avoid conflicts in the semantics of the corresponding class instances. In order to allow for these updates in a loosely coordinated fashion, the classes can be designed as a Set CRDT associated with the class version. When a class update is made somewhere by any developer, the changes are deployed everywhere in the system, but they cannot be used until all replicas in the system see the new change. This concept is similar to the *causal stability* feature provided by the Tagged RCB presented before. In particular, although not all nodes detect causal stability of a version at the same time, once any node detects this, it is safe to start using that version. The reason is that causal stability ensures that the version has been delivered by all nodes in the system, and thus, the new class updates can be fetched to be used in the future. Notice that we are talking about class deployment here, but the designer must consider the compatibility between the old and the new versions, e.g., if some class instances already exist.

4.3.4 Conclusions and future directions

CRDTs make using replicated data less cumbersome to developers and correct being mathematically designed abstractions. However, they can only be useful when the application semantics allow for stale reads and favor immediate writes. CRDTs exist for many datatype variants of counters, sets, maps, registers, graphs, etc. They can however be extended to other types as long as operations are commutative or can be made so.

This section presented two main variants for CRDTs and their important optimizations. Some of the tradeoffs are understood, while others require future empirical investigation. Op-based CRDT designs are more intuitive to design and can be used once a reliable causal middleware is available. If it is possible to extend the middleware API, one can use pure op-based CRDTs to reduce the overhead of dissemination and storage. On the other hand, state-based CRDTs are more tolerant in hostile networks and gossip-like systems being natively idempotent: data can arrive though different nodes and get merged safely. Despite being easy to use in practice, state-based CRDTs can be expensive on dissemination when the state is not small. Consequently, it is recommended to use the delta-state CRDT alternative that significantly reduces the dissemination cost if a convenient causal anti-entropy protocol can be deployed. Furthermore, hybrid models of these variants can have tradeoff properties, and are interesting to study in the future work. Finally, it would be promising to investigate the feasibility of CRDTs in other system models and research areas like Edge Computing or Blockchain.

4.4 Summary

Given current projections for data growth and the needs for increased data processing, ultrascale systems face significant challenges for keeping up both with data storage and access. This chapter has examined approach to tackle the efficiency of data storage and access at three levels: the storage level via an efficient KV store, the workflow-level via a locality-aware workflow management systems, and the algorithmic-level via the use of conflict-free replicated data types.

Midterm challenges related to data management in ultrascale system will require more research in topics related to:

HPC and data analysis: Understand and realize the close relationship between HPC and data analysis in the scientific computing area and advances in both are necessary for next-generation scientific breakthroughs. To achieve the desired unification, the solutions adopted should also be portable and extensible to future ultrascale systems. These systems are envisioned as parallel and distributed computing systems, reaching two to three orders of magnitude larger than today's systems.

Embrace and cope with new storage device technologies: The appearance of new storage device technologies carry a lot of potential for addressing issues in these areas but also introduce numerous challenges and will imply changes in the way data is organized, handled, and processed, throughout the storage and data management stack.

Shift from performance to efficiency: Instead of only or mostly considering absolute performance as the driving force for new solutions, we should shift our interest in considering the efficiency at which infrastructures are operating. This is becoming more important as the size at which future infrastructures are required to operate continues to scale with application requirements.

To face those challenges, we will need to enforce the convergence of HPC, ultrascale and Big Data worlds. Storage, interconnection networks, and data management in both HPC and Cloud needs to cope with technology trends and evolving application requirements, while hiding the increasing complexity at the architectural, systems software, and application levels. Future work needs to examine these challenges under the prism of both HPC and Cloud approaches and to consider solutions that break away from current boundaries. Moreover, future applications will need more sophisticated interfaces for addressing the challenges of future ultrascale computing systems. These novel interfaces should be able to abstract architectural and operational issues from requirements for both storage and data. This will allow applications and services to easily manipulate storage and data, while providing the system with flexibility to optimize operation over a complex set of architectural and technological constraints.

Chapter 5

Energy aware ultrascale systems

Ariel Oleksiak[1], Laurent Lefevre[2], Pedro Alonso[3], Georges Da Costa[4], Vincenzo De Maio[5], Neki Frasheri[6], Victor M. Garcia[3], Joel Guerrero[7], Sebastien Lafond[8], Alexey Lastovetsky[9], Ravi Reddy Manumachu[9], Benson Muite[10], Anne-Cecile Orgerie[11], Wojciech Piatek[1], Jean-Marc Pierson[4], Radu Prodan[1,2], Patricia Stolf[4], Enida Sheme[6], and Sebastien Varrette[13]

Energy consumption is one of the main limiting factors for the design of ultrascale infrastructures. Multi-level hardware and software optimizations must be designed and explored in order to reduce energy consumption for these large-scale equipment. This chapter addresses the issue of energy efficiency of ultrascale systems in front of other quality metrics. The goal of this chapter is to explore the design of metrics, analysis, frameworks and tools for putting energy awareness and energy efficiency at the next stage. Significant emphasis will be placed on the idea of "energy complexity," reflecting the synergies between energy efficiency and quality of service, resilience and performance, by studying computation power, communication/data sharing power, data access power, algorithm energy consumption, etc.

[1] Poznan Supercomputing and Networking Center, Poland
[2] Ecole Normal Superior, France
[3] Universitat Politecnica de Valencia, Spain
[4] University of Toulouse, France
[5] Vienna University of Technology, Austria
[6] Polytechnic University of Tirana, Albania
[7] University of Genoa, Italy
[8] Abo Akademi University, Finland
[9] University College of Dublin, Ireland
[10] Institute of Computer Science, Tartu Ulikool, Estonia
[11] University of Rennes, Inria, CNRS, IRISA, France
[12] Alpen-Adria Universitat Klagenfurt, Austria
[13] University of Luxembourg, Luxembourg

5.1   Energy modeling and simulation

Energy consumption has become a significant issue for data centers. For this reason, many researchers currently focus on developing energy aware algorithms to improve their energy efficiency. However, due to the difficulty of employing real data centers' infrastructure for assessing the effectiveness of energy-aware algorithms, researchers resort to simulation tools. These tools require precise and detailed models for virtualized data centers in order to deliver accurate results. In recent years, many models have been proposed, but most of them do not consider some of the energy impacting components (e.g. CPU, network, storage). In this work, we provide a review of energy modeling and simulations for ultrascale systems and identify open issues and future challenges in the field.

First, we focus on energy consumption of physical nodes inside the data center. Since energy is the integral of power over time, those are the two main factors that are interested in energy modeling. Therefore, first we provide models for the component with the highest power draw inside the physical nodes, such as CPU, RAM, I/O, network, and cooling systems. After this, we focus on modeling the parameters affecting the running time of the data center, such as the data center's workload and the way computational resources are managed inside the data center.

Concerning the simulation part, we discuss different types of data center simulations, such as event-based simulation and statistical simulations, discussing the current state of the art in this area and the solutions that can fit the most the ultrascale scenario.

5.1.1   Related work

Global power and energy models of servers inside data centers are evolving. In [196], authors provide a global landscape of power consumption of servers in large-scale data centers and show the relative importance of each subpart (e.g. CPU, memory, network, etc.).

Concerning CPU modeling, existing papers either focuses on a specific CPU architecture [47,197,198] or assumes a linear relationship between CPU usage and energy consumption [199,200], which may lead to inaccurate results [201]. Moreover, most of these models do not consider the virtualization overhead, making it not suitable for virtualized data center.

Concerning memory modeling, works like [202,203] provide simulations of DRAM behavior, but neither the virtualization overhead nor the energy consumption is considered. Works like [204] provides modeling of memory resource management in VMWare ESX Server, but no energy modeling is provided. Similar works like [205,206] provide insights about memory management, respectively, for Xen and KVM hypervisor.

Storage energy modeling has been provided by [207] and other similar works like [208–210]. These works, however, do not consider the virtualization overhead, neither distributed storage systems.

Data centers network performances have been instead modeled in works like [211]. Other works like [212] propose data center network simulators, without considering energy consumption. Works like [213,214] target how to improve energy efficiency of networking in data centers, while works like [215,216] try to model energy consumption of network transfers, but do not use this model in simulations.

Works like [217–219] provide a joint approach to data center modeling. However, all these works have the problems previously outlined. Moreover, several features provided by the virtualization layer available in data centers are not modeled. We analyze them in detail in the following sections.

5.1.2 Actor definition

First of all, we define the actors involved in energy consumption. We define an ultrascale system $\mathscr{S}$ as

Definition 1. *A* **ultrascale system** *is a vector $\mathscr{S}$,*

$$\mathscr{S} = [\mathscr{H}, \mathscr{N}], \tag{5.1}$$

where

- *$\mathscr{H}$ is the set of physical machines (PMs) inside the system $\mathscr{S}$ during its whole lifetime. PMs are defined in Definition 2;*
- *$\mathscr{N}$ is the network infrastructure, composed of network switches connecting PMs. Network switches are defined in Definition 3.*

A PM is a hardware device, such as a personal computer or any other computing device. PMs can also be used to host virtual machines (VMs) that execute computation. Resources offered by the PMs are shared between all the VMs that are hosted by the PM. The sharing of the resources is managed by the hypervisor, a program running on the PM operating system (OS), or even a modified version of a PM's OS (e.g. Xen), that is responsible for allowing the different OSs running on the VMs to use the PM's resources. A PM can have a diverse amount of hardware resources. In this work, we mostly focus on CPU, RAM, storage and network. For this reason, a PM $h \in \mathscr{H}$ can be seen as a vector of its amount of resources and the set of VMs that are allocated on it.

Definition 2. *We define a PM h as follows:*

$$h = [\mathrm{CPU}_{max}(h), \mathrm{RAM}_{max}(h), \mathrm{BW}_{io}^{max}(h), \mathrm{BW}_{net}^{max}(h), s], \tag{5.2}$$

where

- *$\mathrm{CPU}_{max}(h)$ is the maximum CPU load that is possible to allocate to host h;*
- *$\mathrm{RAM}_{max}(h)$ is the maximum amount of RAM for host h;*
- *$\mathrm{BW}_{io}^{max}(h)$ is the maximum I/O bandwidth;*
- *$\mathrm{BW}_{net}^{max}(h)$ is the maximum network bandwidth;*
- *s is the network switch to which h is connected (see Definition 3).*

From now on, $\text{CPU}_{max}(h)$ is defined in MIPS (Millions of Instructions Per Second), $\text{RAM}_{max}(h)$ in bytes, $\text{BW}_{io}^{max}(h)$ and $\text{BW}_{net}^{max}(h)$ in bytes per second.

Definition 3. *A **switch** s is defined as*

$$s = [\text{BW}_{net}^{max}(s), \mathcal{H}_{(s)}, \mathcal{N}_{(s)}], \tag{5.3}$$

where

- $\text{BW}_{net}^{max}(s)$ *is the bandwidth of the switch s;*
- $\mathcal{H}_{(s)}$ *is the set of PMs, defining the hosts that are connected to s;*
- $\mathcal{N}_{(s)}$ *is the set of switches, defining the switches that are connected to s.*

Formally, $\exists x \in \mathcal{H}_{(s)} \iff$ *switch s connects x and* $\exists y \in \mathcal{N}_{(s)} \iff$ *switch s connects y. Clearly,* $\mathcal{H}_{(s)} \subset \mathcal{H}$ *and* $\mathcal{N}(s) \subset \mathcal{N}$.

Concerning the networking, We consider that in modern data centers there are many types of LAN technologies available. Such new technologies are different from the typical LAN technologies and offer an higher latency and throughput, to meet the growing needs of modern Cloud applications. Such technologies might need to rely on a different physical layer technology, different from the typical CSMA/CD used by Ethernet. Among them, the most successful one is Infiniband that is based on the RDMA technology. We will later on describe both technologies in detail.

5.1.3 Energy modeling

The computing oriented energy consumption in an ultrascale system E_s is given by the integral of its instantaneous power draw $P_s(t)$:

$$E_s = \int_{t_{start}}^{t_{end}} P_s(t)\, dt, \tag{5.4}$$

where $[t_{start}, t_{end}]$ is the interval for which energy consumption is calculated, and $P_s(t)$ is the sum of the idle power of data center infrastructure, consisting of the sum of the idle power of all PMs and switches in the system $P_{inf}(\mathcal{S})$ and the instantaneous power $P(h, t)$ of each node h at time instant t:

$$P_s(t) = P_{inf}(\mathcal{S}) + \sum_{h \in \mathcal{H}(t)} P(h, t). \tag{5.5}$$

$P_{inf}(\mathcal{N})$ can be approximated as a constant and includes the idle constants that will be described in the next sections. Concerning instantaneous PM's power consumption, it is the sum of the instantaneous power consumption of each of its components. While the consumption of some components (e.g. memory, PCI slots, motherboard) is constant over time, consumption of other components (CPU, RAM, I/O operations, network, thermal) varies depending on the load. Therefore, we distinguish two parts, $P_{idle}(h, t)$ and $P_{active}(h, t)$:

$$P(h, t) = P_{idle}(h) + P_{active}(h, t). \tag{5.6}$$

The idle power $P_{idle}(h)$ is a constant representing the consumption required by the machine just to be on. The active power $P_{active}(h, t)$ is instead dependent on the PM subsystems' load. Its value is comprised between 0 and $P_r(h) = P_{max}(h) - P_{idle}(h)$, where $P_r(h)$ is the size of the interval of values in which $P_{active}(h,t)$ is defined. $P_{max}(h)$ is the maximum power consumption on the PM h. For simplicity, it is assumed that P_{active} is influenced mostly by CPU, RAM, network, I/O operations and cooling system, as stated by [220]; therefore, it is defined as follows:

$$P_{active}(h,t) = P_{cpu}(h,t) + P_{ram}(h,t) + P_{net}(h,t) + P_{io}(h,t) + P_{cool}(h,t) \qquad (5.7)$$

where $P_{cpu}(h,t)$ is the power draw of CPU, $P_{ram}(h,t)$ is the power draw of the RAM, P_{net} is the power consumption of network and P_{io} is the power consumption of disk operations that are the components identified in Definition 2. As energy consumption is the integral of power draw, the active energy consumption of PM h, E_h is obtained in the following way:

$$E_{active}(h) = \int_{t_{start}}^{t_{end}} P_{active}(h,t)\, dt \qquad (5.8)$$

Then, by applying the linearity of the integral, we obtain the equation of the energy consumption of each component:

$$E_x(h) = \int_{t_{start}}^{t_{end}} P_x(h,t)\, dt \qquad (5.9)$$

where $x \in \{CPU, RAM, net, io, cool\}$.

In the next section, we describe the current state of the art in terms of power modeling for different hardware components and identify open challenges in adapting such models for ultrascale machines.

5.1.4 Power modeling

5.1.4.1 CPU modeling

CPU is the most impacting component on the energy consumption of a PM [221]; therefore, most work focus only on its model. Most works on energy modeling [40, 222] assume a linear relationship between the CPU use and its power consumption.

However, power consumption is more aligned with a piecewise linear trend according to our observations in Figure 5.1. The initial transition from idle to non-idle state, when several hardware components are simultaneously starting to consume power (e.g. caches), produce in a higher growth in power consumption at low load levels. Once all components are powered up, the power grows at a different trend:

$$P_{low\text{-}cpu}(h,t) = \alpha(h) \cdot P_r(h) \cdot \boldsymbol{load}_{cpu}(h,t) \qquad (5.10)$$

$$P_{high\text{-}cpu}(h,t) = \beta(h) \cdot P_r(h) + (1 - \beta(h)) \cdot P_r(h)$$
$$\cdot load_{cpu}(h,t)$$

$$P_{cpu}(h,t) = \begin{cases} P_{low\text{-}cpu}(h,t), & load_{cpu}(h,t) \leq \mathscr{L}(h) \\ P_{high\text{-}cpu}(h,t), & \text{otherwise} \end{cases} \qquad (5.11)$$

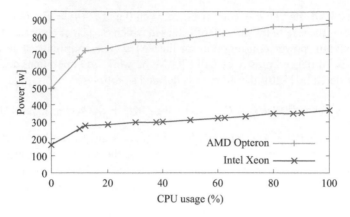

Figure 5.1   Instantaneous power consumption of a host in relation to CPU utilization. Traces coming from the measurements of instantaneous power draw from an AMD Opteron 8356 and an Intel Xeon E5-2690 using a Voltech PM1000+ power measurer

where $\mathscr{L}(h)$ is the load at which the trend changes on host h, $load_{cpu}(h, t)$ is the CPU load on host h at time instance t, modeled as

$$load_{cpu}(h, t) = \frac{CPU(h, t)}{CPU^{max}(h)} \tag{5.12}$$

$P_{\max}(h)$ and $P_{\text{idle}}(h)$ are the maximum and idle power consumptions of host h, and $\alpha(h)$ and $\beta(h)$ are the coefficients for low (i.e. $\leq \mathscr{L}(h)$) and high (i.e. $> \mathscr{L}(h)$) CPU load levels.

Memory modeling

Workloads for Cloud also include applications such as multimedia, video image processing, and speech recognition, which are extremely memory-intensive. These applications consume a considerable amount of power during memory accesses that also needs to be modeled. In power modeling for memory, the model described in [223,224] is employed. Since power consumption varies according to write and read access, we define power function as

$$P_{mem}(h, t) = \beta_{read} \, access_{read}(h, t) + \beta_{write} \, access_{write}(h, t) + \mathscr{C}_{memory} \tag{5.13}$$

where $access_{read}(h, t)$ and $access_{write}(h, t)$ are, respectively, the number of read and write access on the PM h, β_{read} and β_{write} the power consumption for each access (respectively, write and read access) and $\mathscr{C}_{memory}$ is the idle power consumption for memory.

5.1.4.2 Network modeling

A network transfer occurs in two different directions: sending and receiving. Power draw of the network transfer is different if the transfer is a send or a receive. Therefore, the power draw of network transfer can be modeled as

$$P_{net}^x(h, t) = \delta_x \cdot load_{net}(h, t) + K_x(c_x(t)) \tag{5.14}$$

where $x \in \{s, r\}$ and s, r refer, respectively, to send and receive. $load_{net}(h)$ models the network load on host h and δ_x the linear relationship between network load and power draw. Concerning the $K_x(c_x(t))$, it models the hardware-related constant of the NIC, plus the overhead $O_{net}(c_x(t))$ given by the number of simultaneous connections at time t, $c_x(t)$, formally

$$\mathscr{K}_x(c_x(t)) = \mathscr{K}_x + O_{net}(c_x(t)) \tag{5.15}$$

When modeling network transfer, further parameters that affect the time t_{end} at which the network transfer ends need to be considered. This time is determined by (1) the network bandwidth on host h, $BW_{net}^{max}(h)$ and (2) the delay caused by transfer patterns, modeled by the parameters b_x and t_x, as in

$$t_{end} = \frac{DATA_x}{BW_{net}^{max}(h)} \tag{5.16}$$

$DATA_x$ is the real number of bytes transferred, that is, the sum of actual data transferred by the application, and the additional data needed for routing and transfer control, that is calculated according to

$$DATA_x = PAYLOAD_x + \frac{PAYLOAD_x}{p_x} \cdot HEADER \tag{5.17}$$

where $PAYLOAD_x$ is the quantity of data to be sent/received, p_x is the payload per packet and $HEADER$ the size of the header of each packet, whose size depends on the network protocol.

5.1.4.3 I/O modeling

Modeling of energy consumption of I/O components is very important for data-intensive applications that need to constantly read and write a big amount of data from/to I/O devices. In this work, we focus on I/O from disk. For power draw of disk operations, we use the model proposed by [207,225]

$$P_{io}(h, t) = \gamma(h)load_{io}(h, t) + \mathscr{C}_{io}(h) \tag{5.18}$$

where $\gamma(h)$ models the linear relationship between disk load and power draw coefficients. Concerning $load_{io}(h, t)$, it is modeled as

$$load_{io}(h, t) = \frac{BW_{io}(h, t)}{BW_{io}^{max}(h)} \tag{5.19}$$

where $BW_{io}^{max}(h)$ is the maximum storage bandwidth on the PM h and $BW_{io}(h, t)$ is the bandwidth at the time instance t.

5.1.4.4   Thermal modeling

Modeling the thermal behavior of data centers is an essential first step to the design of effective thermal management techniques. In [226], authors present a *spatio-temporal* analytical model to characterize the thermal behavior of data centers, thus allowing the resource management system to make fast and online scheduling decisions in real time. The spatial model describes the correlated behavior for the inlet temperatures of all the servers in the room, while the temporal model describes the temperature evolution for an individual computing node inside each server. Traditionally, these two different types of temperatures have not been considered simultaneously by the literature: the inlet temperature is often linked to cooling optimization, while the node temperature often comes as an optimization objective or constraint. Energy consumption of cooling systems mostly depends on the technology used, as described by [227]. In our work, we focus only on air-cooled ultrascale systems, as in [228]. Power consumption of cooling on a host h depends on two main quantities: the heat generation, that is proportional to CPU utilization, and the consumption generated by fans. To model its power consumption, we slightly modify the model provided by [229] as described below:

$$P_{cool}(h,t) = \zeta\, load_{cpu}(h,t) + c_2 T_{die}(t) + c_3 T_{die}^2(t) + P_{fan}(h,t) + \mathscr{C}_{cool}(h) \quad (5.20)$$

where $load_{cpu}(h,t)$ is modeled as in (5.12). $T_{die}(t)$ and $T_{die}^2(t)$ represent the temperature of the die at time instant t, $P_{fan}(h,t)$ is the power consumption of the fans at instant t, and $\mathscr{C}_{cool}(h)$ is a constant related to the idle consumption of the cooling system. Regarding $P_{fan}(h,t)$, it is modeled as in [229]

$$P_{fan}(h,t) = 0.0012 RPM(h,t) - 12 \times 10^{-8} RPM(h,t)^2$$

$$+ 28 \times 10^{-2} RPM(h,t)^3 \quad (5.21)$$

where $RPM(h,t)$ are the revolutions per minute of the fans on host h at time t.

5.1.5   Runtime modeling

Precise models of the runtime conditions are needed for performance evaluation purposes. These models encompass the whole utilization and context of ultrascale infrastructures: workload and resource management systems.

5.1.5.1   Workload modeling

The workload modeling consists of providing the laws and characteristics of possible tasks submitted in Exascale infrastructure.

As described in [230], most known workloads are quite small as they are acquired on currently existing infrastructure, meaning only several Petaflops of computing power. Due to the envisioned large number of processing elements in Exascale computers, it is necessary to use alternate sources of data in order to propose adaptation to existing laws.

As an example, in [231], authors use traces from a large computing cluster of Google in order to evaluate tendencies on workload laws. One of the main teaching comes from a large number of failing tasks which is aligned with the expected high failure rate in multi-million core systems.

Overall, the classical laws for workload modeling are task dynamism (the inter-arrival time of tasks), and for each category, frequency (the sum of all frequencies of a particular workload must be 1); mass which represents the mean amount of computation, i.e. the makespan; disparity which is the ratio between the mean and median makespan and thus must be greater than 1.

Usually, the models used in the literature [230,231] are

Task dynamism : Inter-arrival time follows an exponential law
Makespan follows a lognormal law taking into account the mass and disparity
Frequency follows usually a normalized powerlaw between all the classes

One of the key missing elements of the classical approach is the missing link between the quality of service of past tasks and the submission of future ones. In [232], authors demonstrate that depending on the efficiency of past decisions of the scheduling, authors will submit more or less tasks. They propose to have a feedback between the quality of service of past tasks and the submission rate of present tasks.

5.1.5.2   Model evaluation

In this section, we perform a preliminary validation of the selected model. First, we compare our model with other state-of-the-art models, by measuring energy consumption during the execution of benchmarks described in [225]. For measurements, we employ Voltech PM1000+ power measurer. Concerning non-live traces, we show the consecutive execution of CPULOAD-SOURCE and CPULOAD-TARGET benchmarks. Concerning live migration, we show the consecutive execution of CPULOAD-SOURCE, MEMLOAD-VM, CPULOAD-TARGET, MEMLOAD-SOURCE, and MEMLOAD-TARGET. The comparison is performed by implementing different models inside the DISSECT-CF simulator and comparing their results with our model. For this reason, we consider only CPU, network and I/O coefficients, since data about memory and thermal are not available in the simulator. Validation results shown in Table 5.1 are obtained using a test set of 80% of the measurements and show an NRMSE below 7% for both Opteron and Xeon data set, with an average

Table 5.1   Model coefficients and errors

Model	Machine set	$\mathscr{L}$	α	β	γ	δ	P_{idle} (W)	P_{max} (W)	MAE (W)	NRMSE (%)
Our model	Opteron	0.12	5.29	0.68	0.05	0.1	501	840	18.28	6.2
	Xeon	0.12	4.33	0.47	0.05	0.1	164	382	11.5	6.8
Linear	Opteron		284.974	618.67					47.8	15.6
	Xeon		165.08	212.563					23.7	13.9
Cubic	Opteron		209.317	695.684					69.2	23.6
	Xeon		140.753	235.776					37.3	20.4

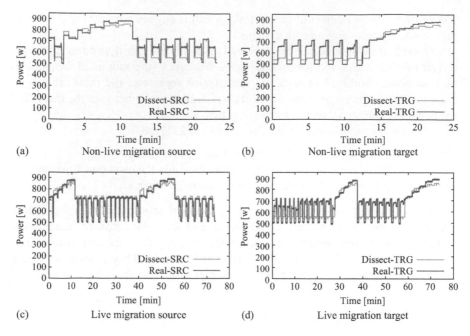

Figure 5.2   Results for the Opteron machine set

MAE of 18.28 W on the Opteron machines, and of 11.5 W on the Xeon machines. First, we compare the piecewise linear prediction with the linear model in [233] showing a reduction in NRMSE of 9.4% (15.6% vs. 6.2%) on Opteron machines and of 7.1% (13.9% vs. 6.8%) on Xeon machines. The improvement is even higher compared with the cubic model in [234], with a reduction in NRMSE of 17.4% (23.6% vs. 6.2%) on the Opteron machines and of 13.6% (20.4% vs. 6.8%) on Xeon. Secondly, we see in detail the results obtained by our model with the real energy traces. The MAE and NRMSE error metrics is computed on both instantaneous power and energy consumption on both sets of machines. We also compare in Figure 5.2 (for the Opteron set) and Figure 5.3 (for the Xeon set) the power traces obtained from the simulator with the real measurements.

We observe that the simulation is able to provide power values with an MAE not higher than 67.3W compared to the real ones. This value is, however, influenced by the fact that in some cases the power consumption is underestimated by around 100W like in Figure 5.2a (between 12 and 24 minutes and Figure 5.2b (between 0 and 14 minutes), because the test scenarios active during those minutes perform non-live migrations while both hosts are idle.

In these situations, the simulator only considers the power consumption caused by the network and storage despite some inherent CPU consumption caused by these two operations. Thus, the simulator considers idle CPU consumption for both hosts, despite slight CPU load caused by the need for supporting the storage operations. This slight load, on the other hand, leads to significant offsets in the power consumption

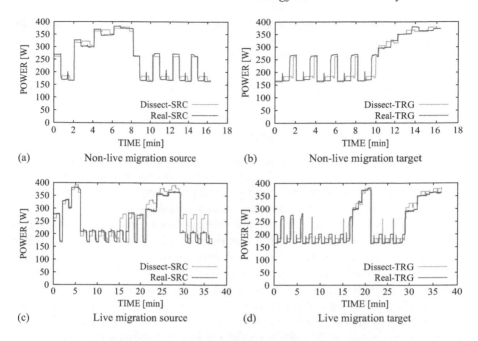

Figure 5.3 Results for the Xeon machine set

model according to Figure 5.1. Nevertheless, NRMSE is in each case between 8% and 22% for instantaneous power consumption and between 8% and 25% for energy consumption, showing that our model is able to provide good accuracy, that will be even higher by including data from other subsystems.

5.1.6 Simulation

In order to be able to evaluate the quality of decision-making systems, it is also important to have a clear framework of analysis. Due to the scale of Exascale systems, it is difficult to evaluate actual infrastructures. Simulation is complex at these sizes and thus a large variety of techniques have been developed. Several simulation frameworks propose models for resource management. Simgrid [235] and CloudSim [236] propose to simulate tasks and the infrastructure they run on from the point of view of raw computing power. GroudSim [237] propose a simulation engine for Grid and Cloud, but energy of thermal management is not taken into account. On the Cloud federation side, DISSECT-CF [238] proposes a model for energy consumption considering different components of PMs, without however considering RAM and thermal management. Some other simulators such as DCWorms [239] also propose to take into account during the simulation the thermal effects.

Current simulation frameworks have mainly two limitations:

Scale: Most simulators simulate independently each computing element, such as the cores, leading to consuming too much time to simulate ultrascale systems [240,241].

Coverage: No simulator is able to cover all the needed elements for ultrascale simulations. Some works are trying to add the missing elements such as power and energy [242], dynamic voltage and frequency scaling (DVFS) [243] or thermal simulation [239]. These improvements are in different simulators leading to difficulties to obtain a precise and global simulation taking into account all phenomenon.

5.1.7 Issues and open challenges

In this section, we identify the issues and open challenges in energy modeling and simulations for ultrascale systems. The main issues with energy modeling rely on the fact that while a lot of literature covers modeling for energy consumption of CPU, very few work covers with the same accuracy the modeling for other components of PMs, such as RAM, network, I/O, and thermal. The main reason behind this is that until the latest years, computation, and therefore CPU has been the most energy impacting component. However, with the advent of big data and IoT, always more data are transferred through the Internet to be processed and extract meaningful knowledge out of them. For this reason, it is reasonable to believe that the transfer of data over the network, and consequently I/O and RAM, will have an increasing importance for energy consumption. Therefore, there is a strong need for precise models also for these components, to be able to model the energy consumption of applications handling big quantities of data. Also, thermal modeling is often neglected in ultrascale systems modeling, regardless of its impact on energy consumption. Such modeling would enable the use of effective thermal management systems that would allow to increase energy efficiency. Moreover, at the moment there are different models for energy consumption of ultrascale systems, with a consequent lack of a unified reference model about their energy consumption. As a consequence, each system employs different energy models, making difficult to identify energy consumption of ultrascale systems. For this reason, it is important for the ultrascale system research community to develop a reference model for energy consumption of each one of these components and therefore for energy consumption of complete ultrascale systems.

This lack of a unified view is reflected also by the current state-of-the-art simulators for ultrascale systems: at the current state, the existing simulator either focus on specific sources of energy consumption or on very specific scenarios. Also, there are several scalability issues for this type of systems, targeting both event-based and stochastic simulations. For this reason, research on simulators for ultrascale systems should provide a unified simulation framework for this type of systems. Such a unified framework should be able to simulate the behavior of all the sources of energy consumption in these systems, providing an accurate simulation that will help both scientists and application designers in identifying energy consumption of these systems.

5.1.8 Conclusion

In this work, we have identified the state of the art in terms of energy modeling and simulations for ultrascale systems. First, we describe a model for an ultrascale system, with special focus on Cloud data centers, then we move to modeling of individual PMs and switches. Once identified the main components to be modeled and the main challenges in their modeling, we describe how to perform simulations of energy consumption in ultrascale systems. Finally, we identify open challenges in energy modeling and simulation. In the future, we aim at proposing a holistic view of energy modeling, in order to capture the energy consumption of all components of ultrascale systems. In this way, we aim at having a fine-grained precise modeling of the whole system, in order to identify sources for energy leakages and pro-actively take actions to reduce them, thus increasing ultrascale systems' energy efficiency. Concerning simulations, we aim at bringing such a holistic view of modeling in the design of ultrascale simulations. In this way, it will be possible to identify energy consumption in ultrascale systems and applications before they are running and improve them before the time they are deployed.

Acknowledgments

The work described in this book chapter has been funded through the Haley project (Holistic Energy Efficient Hybrid Clouds) as part of the TU Vienna Distinguished Young Scientist Award 2011 and Rucon project (Runtime Control in Multi Clouds), FWF Y 904 START-Program 2015.

5.2   Evaluation of renewable energy usage for an Exascale computer

Supplying data centers with clean-to-use renewable energy is essential to help mitigate climate change. With renewable energies in data centers, Exascale can then be achieved without (or with less) greenhouse gases' emissions. Renewable energies include solar panels, wind turbines; most of them are intermittent and difficult to predict in the long term. Storage elements such as batteries, fuel cells, and supercapacitors are then necessary. These storage units are complementary. Supercapacitors, with their low energy but high power, handle very short-term fluctuations of power and ensure the stability of the system. Batteries, with a much higher energy capacity, enable shifting load or generation through time, but only over a few minutes or hours. Finally, to account for longer term variations and seasonal trends, hydrogen storage (combining an electrolyzer to generate hydrogen from electricity, hydrogen storage tanks, and fuel cells to generate electricity from hydrogen) is also used. Many works have been made on power sources modeling: the models proposed define the characteristics and behavior of the components. These models must be sufficiently representative of reality while remaining easily usable. Different models are possible depending on the use and the needed granularity. For example, an aged fuel cell only delivers a fraction of the output of a newer one. To account for this phenomenon, aging can be considered in the proposed models. These models are then used in works concerning tasks placement and energy saving; depending on the models used, decisions can include capital (replacement) costs, and not only operation costs [244].

Lot of researches are currently done on optimization of the IT load under renewable energy constraints. It aims to manage the workload in such a way that power consumption matches as closely as possible to the power available through renewable energies. For example, batch jobs may be delayed, in order to run when more energy will be available. Most of the approaches propose a centralized optimization with global knowledge from the IT load and electrical point of view. Contrary to this, the approach presented in [245] considers the power supply as a black box which only provides an energy budget to the IT side where the IT load is optimized under renewable energy constraints. In [246], the authors propose to separate the optimizations of electrical infrastructure from the optimizations of the computing resources. They designed an online greedy scheduling algorithm (called Attractiveness-Based Blind Scheduling Heuristic, or ABBSH), which exchanges information with the electrical management system in order to take the availability of energy in consideration. Along with this algorithm, several multi-objective functions are proposed to handle the trade-off between energy and performance considerations.

More and more data centers are built in cold climate areas for cheaper cooling and increased energy efficiency of the facilities. However, such geographical locations have highly varying availability of renewable energy (especially solar energy), and fitting the data centers completely with renewable energy is challenging. In this subsection, we analyze the feasibility of using renewable energies for a data center located on 60° north latitude and discuss the competitiveness of deploying green data centers in different geographical locations. We also provide an analysis of the impact of battery size on the green coverage percentage, green energy loss, and brown energy taken from the traditional grid. Figure 5.4 represents an overview of the energy sources included in the following.

The remaining of this chapter presents some examples of renewable energy modeling and an algorithm to schedule tasks in this context.

5.2.1   Renewable energy modeling

This subsection outlines the total amount of renewable energy produced in one year for a 60° geographical location: Turku, Finland. In order to calculate the amount of renewable energy, we consider only renewable energy produced by wind turbines and solar panels. Since the weather and the season directly influences the production of renewable energy, we must utilize a weather model to predict the production rate. The weather data are collected from a weather station located at Åbo Akademi University in Turku, Finland. To describe the production rate of a solar panel, we acquire the data containing the solar power radiance on a horizontal 1 m^2 solar panel, and we calculated the produced power in Watts. We also acquire the data regarding the wind speed in [m/s] and model the resulting power production for a wind turbine.

5.2.1.1   Solar power model

The power incident on a solar panel depends not only on the power contained in the sunlight but also on the angle between the module and the sun. Referring to [247], we calculate that for a 60° of northern latitude, representing the location of Turku,

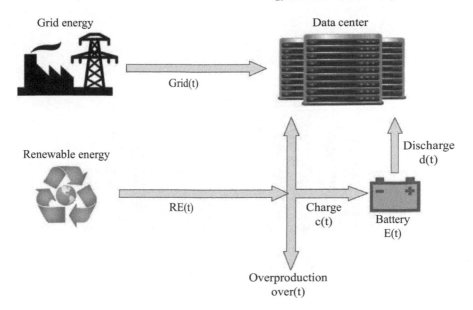

Grid energy

Grid(t)

Data center

Renewable energy

RE(t)

Charge
c(t)

Discharge
d(t)

Battery
E(t)

Overproduction
over(t)

Figure 5.4   Illustration of energy sources balance in our study

the angle at which a solar array should be tilted in order to achieve maximum energy through all the year is 45° with respect to the horizontal plane. We assume that the solar array tracks the sun on the vertical axis (east to west, but is fixed on the horizontal axis). Equation (5.22) shows the power generation of a 1 m² solar panel as

$$P_{solar} = e \cdot ie \cdot P_{solar\_h} \cdot \frac{\sin(\alpha + \beta)}{\sin(\alpha)} \tag{5.22}$$

where P_{solar_h} is the solar radiance in the horizontal plane we already have from weather data, α is the sun elevation angle through the year, and β is the tilt angle of the module measured from horizontal plane, 45°. The value for α is calculated according to

$$\alpha = 90 - \phi + \delta \tag{5.23}$$

where ϕ is the latitude (60°) and δ is the declination angle computed in (5.24) as

$$\delta = 23.45\text{o} \cdot \sin\left[360 \cdot \frac{(284 + d)}{365}\right] \tag{5.24}$$

where d is the day of the year. In addition, e represents the solar panel efficiency which is the percentage of the sunlight energy that is actually transformed into electricity because of limitations in the solar panel cells. In order to achieve realistic data, and according to the latest research, a value of 0.18 is chosen to multiply all hourly solar energy values. The Solar inverter efficiency ie represents the efficiency of the inverter connected between the solar panel cells and the AC grid. The average coefficient of the DC–AC power converting today is 95%. This value is taken into account to assure accurate and realistic power values.

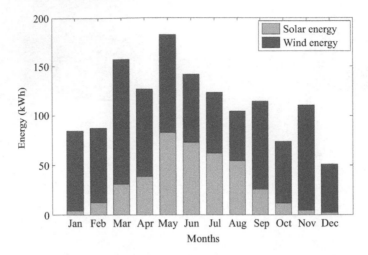

*Figure 5.5   Monthly available renewable energy over a year produced by 1 m²
          solar panel and 1 HY 1000 wind turbine*

5.2.1.2 Wind power model

The wind power model describes the power generation from the wind turbines in the
system. To produce the wind energy, we have chosen an HY 1000, 5 blade wind turbine generating a peak output power of 1,200 W. The wind power model is constructed
by taking into consideration the following key features:

Wind turbine power curve: According to the power profile in the technical specifications, we constructed the mathematical model of power as a function of wind speed.
Equation (5.25) describes the power production of a wind turbine as follows:

$$P_{wind} = ie \cdot 1,151 \cdot exp\left[-\left[\frac{(speed_{wind} - 14.28)}{6.103}\right]^2\right] \tag{5.25}$$

where $speed_{wind}$ is the wind speed in [m/s] and *ie* represents the solar inverter efficiency,
typically reaching a value of 95%. The parameters in (5.25) were obtained by using
curve fitting tools in MATLAB® and using the power data from [21] as a reference.
Having this formula, we obtain the annual hourly wind energy.

Finally, the total renewable power model is given as the sum of the total solar and
total wind production:

$$P_{renewable} = P_{solar} + P_{wind} \tag{5.26}$$

The overall annual renewable energy is calculated to be 1,358.27 kWh: 402.2 kWh
generated by 1 m² solar panel and 956.07 kWh by one HY 1000 wind turbine,
respectively (Figure 5.5).

5.2.1.3 Renewable quantity model

The energy consumption, which represents the total energy consumed by the servers
and the cooling system, is evaluated through simulation and equals 253 MWh per year.

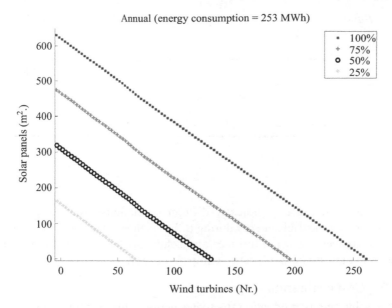

Figure 5.6   *The number of m² solar panel over the number of turbines for four*
green coverage levels over one year

The data center is composed of 1,000 PMs and 2,000 VMs running a synthetic workload. Detailed information about the used model is available from [248]. We build the
model which describes the relation between the number of wind turbines and square
meters of solar panels required to ensure a desired value of coverage with renewable
energy. Figure 5.6 shows the relation between the number of turbines and number of
m² solar panel needed for green coverage of 25%, 50%, 75%, and 100%, over one
full year.

5.2.1.4   Minimum percentage supply

A new metric is introduced in order to measure the ratio between the renewable
energy being produced by 1 turbine and a 1 m² solar panel and the data center energy consumption. It is called *Minimum Percentage Supply* (MPS), and it is
calculated as

$$MPS = \frac{RenewableEnergyProduction(kWh)}{TotalEnergyConsumption(kWh)} \cdot 100 \qquad (5.27)$$

For five different experimental scenarios, with PMs varying from 500 to 2,500,
we calculate the average value of MPS over a year, and for specific months in Finland
when renewable energy hits the maximum (May) and the minimum (December). As
energy consumption increases, MPS decreases nearly linearly. Table 5.2 presents the
annual, minimum, and maximum month MPS values, for five different data center
size. As seen in Table 5.2, there is a threefold difference between minimal and maximal

Table 5.2   MPS annual, maximal, and minimal months values in percentage

Nr. of PMs	500	1,000	1,500	2,000	2,500
Annual MPS (%)	1.10	0.54	0.36	0.27	0.21
May MPS (%)	1.70	0.85	0.57	0.42	0.34
December MPS (%)	0.47	0.24	0.16	0.12	0.09

MPS values, which clearly indicates different operational costs for producing the same amount of renewable energy during different times of the year. Obviously, more physical resources, i.e. wind turbines and solar panels, are needed in December to produce the same amount of energy compared to May.

5.2.1.5   Cost evaluation

The renewable energy production fluctuates between different time intervals depending on the weather conditions. The data center consumption fluctuates between different time intervals depending on the workload as well. This means that occasionally there is a higher production rate than consumption rate and occasionally it is the opposite. We refer to the difference between renewable available energy and the workload energy consumption as ΔE, given as follows:

$$\Delta E = Renewableenergy - Energyconsumption \tag{5.28}$$

We refer to $\Delta E > 0$ as *surplus* (or overproduction), meaning that more renewable energy is produced than what is consumed. This additional energy can, for example, be stored or be sold back to the grid if allowed. And, we refer to $\Delta E < 0$ as *deficit*, meaning that consumption of energy is higher than the production, and consequently, external *brown* energy must be bought from the grid.

Referring to periods of time during a year when renewable exceeds the consumption as surplus hours, the results of the study show that combining wind and solar energy sources provides greater surplus hours compared to using only one source of renewable energy. Meanwhile, increasing the number of solar panels and decreasing the number of wind turbines lead to decreasing the surplus hours in a year. However, during these shorter surplus periods, the excessive energy surpasses the value of energy consumption by 6–13 times. This brought us to two logical interpretations. The excessive energy represents wasted energy in case it will not be reused or income in case it will be stored in batteries and/or sold back to the grid.

In this perspective, we further investigate the cost aspect of using renewable energy, calculating overall income and expenses of combined grid and renewable energy in a data center, over one year. We show that using only solar energy source leads to extreme energy and cost values. This results in high income during short surplus periods of the year. Also, when solar energy is lacking, expenses are high in

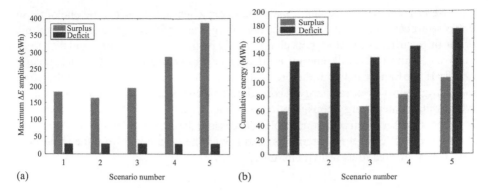

Figure 5.7 (a) Amplitude of DE over one year. (b) Amplitude and cumulative energy over one year

Table 5.3 Number of wind turbines and solar panels for five selected case study scenarios

Scenario Nr.	1	2	3	4	5
Wind turbines Nr.	195	150	100	50	0
Solar panels Nr.	0	108	228	348	465

order to provide for the data center energy need. The results also show that mixing wind energy source with a certain portion of solar, to compensate for the lack of wind, is the opposite. Therefore, there is less but more stable income.

Figures 7a and 7b present, respectively, the achieved ΔE amplitudes and annual cumulative energy surplus and deficits for the scenarios defined in Table 5.3. Values are based on a data center composed by 1,000 PMs and 2,000 VMs running a synthetic workload. Detailed information about the used simulation environment is available from [248].

5.2.2 Battery modeling

The production of energy from renewable resources, such as sunlight and wind, is variable over time and dependent on weather conditions. One common way to address this problem is to use batteries, not only as a backup in the case of energy outage or as a power peak shaving but as an energy storage device. The latest research proposes the usage of batteries as a key source of energy for the energy system supply of a data center. In this case, the main question to be tackled is: how to choose the battery capacity to maximize the renewable energy usage thus minimize the green energy loss. The concept of green coverage mentioned also in section 5.2.1.3 represents the percentage of total energy consumption provided by renewable energy.

We consider a data center consuming energy, which is provided by one of these three sources: renewable energy, battery energy, and grid energy, according to this order of priority. The battery gets charged only by the renewable source and it charges only when the renewable energy is of greater amount than the data center energy needs. If the battery is full and there is still renewable energy produced and therefore not being used, this extra energy is considered overproduction. The battery discharges when data center energy consumption is higher than what is provided by renewable sources. In cases when both renewable sources and the battery are not enough to fulfill the data center energy requirements, additional energy is taken from the traditional grid (also referred to as brown energy).

5.2.2.1   Simulator tool

In order to analyze and being able to predict the amount of available energy in the battery over specific moments in a chosen time period, we developed a simulation tool. The simulator is based on the concept of the battery as a finite state machine, whose trigger conditions are related to the available amount of solar energy and data center energy consumption at a specific time t.

There are four possible states that the battery can be at any time t: full, discharging, charging, or empty. Therefore, there are 16 possible state transition combinations. Practically, all of these combinations are feasible except for the Full–Empty and Empty–Full transitions which are generally limited by the charge/discharge rate of the battery during a certain period of time. Possible triggers from one state to the other depend on the amount of available solar energy in a moment of time t, referred to as $RE(t)$ (Renewable Energy) and the data center energy needs at that moment t, referred to as a $consum(t)$. Other affecting factors are the value of the stored energy in the battery, $E(t)$, and the maximum energy capacity of the battery named $Efull$. There are four possible states that the battery can be at any time t: full, discharging, charging, or empty. Therefore, there are 16 possible state transition combinations. Practically, all of these combinations are feasible except for the Full–Empty and Empty–Full transitions which are generally limited by the charge/discharge rate of the battery during a certain period of time. Possible triggers from one state to the other depend on the amount of available solar energy in a moment of time t, referred to as $RE(t)$ (Renewable Energy) and the data center energy needs at that moment t, referred to as a $consum(t)$. Other affecting factors are the value of the stored energy in the battery, $E(t)$, and the maximum energy capacity of the battery named $Efull$.

Implementation: The pseudocode for developing the simulator is given below as a set of eight steps. $BS(0)$ refers to the initial Battery State assigned to Full, assuming that the battery is fully charged when the simulation begins running (Figure 5.8). Each of the 16 "current–next" state combinations is assigned a combination number (named *combinationNr*), which calculates the energy ($E(t)$) the battery will have on every t. The green coverage is calculated according to (5.30) and printed out. The loop repeats 8,760 times for every hour of the year, resulting in outputs of total charging and discharging amount of the battery, overproduction, and grid energy for every hour.

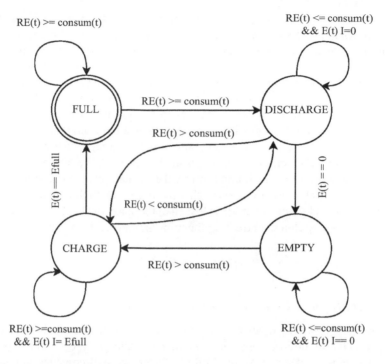

Figure 5.8 Battery states over time represented as a finite state machine

---

Algorithm 1: Simulator tasks

1: $BS(0) \leftarrow FULL, t \leftarrow 1$
2: **repeat**
3:     Define $BS(t) = f[BS(t-1), RE(t), consum(t)]$
4:     Define $combinationNr = f[BS(t-1), BS(t)]$
5:     Calculate $E(t) = f[E(t-1), combinationNr]$
6: **until** $t \leq 8,760$
7: $greenCoverage = $ annual $[RE(t) - over(t)]/$annual $[consum(t)]$
8: Print $charge(t), discharge(t), overproduction(t), grid(t), greenCoverage$

Equation (5.29) is checked by the simulator to be true for every moment of time t during the simulation time period

$$RE(t) + d(t) + grid(t) = consum(t) + c(t) + over(t) \qquad (5.29)$$

On the left side of (5.29) are listed the providing energy sources, and on the right side is listed drawn energy. $RE(t)$ represents the renewable energy being produced at moment t, $d(t)$ is the amount of energy discharged from the battery in the time period $(t-1)$ to t, and $grid(t)$ represents the amount of energy taken from the traditional grid at that moment t, in case it is needed to fulfill the data center energy needs. The variable *consum(t)* refers to the data center energy consumption at moment t, $c(t)$ is the amount of energy charged to the battery in the time period $(t - 1)$ to t, and *over(t)* represents the part of the produced renewable energy which is consumed neither by the data center nor from used to charge the battery. Based on (5.29), we calculate the green coverage metric of our specified data center over a year, as described in (5.30). The sum is composed of 8,760 hourly values for each of the metrics: *RE(t)*, *over(t)*, and *consum(t)*. We can distinguish two different scenarios from this equation. First, theoretically we evaluate the green coverage simply as total renewable energy over the year divided by total energy consumption over the year. We have no information regarding the overproduction without running the simulations, so we assume it is zero. Second, experimental simulations show that the overproduction is greater than zero, meaning that the real green coverage is less than the theoretical calculated value. The battery size is the key element affecting the minimization of the overproduction value

$$greenCoverage = \sum_{t=1}^{8,760} [RE(t) - over(t)] / \sum_{t=1}^{8,760} consum(t) \tag{5.30}$$

5.2.3   Geographical location competitiveness

In this subsection, we investigate how different geographical locations affect the green coverage and the required battery size to reach a certain green coverage. Given that only solar energy is affected by the latitude factor, we will consider as renewable energy only the solar energy produced. To highlight the differences to northern latitudes, we choose Crete, Greece, at 35° latitude because of its typically solar intense southern European climate, and Ilorin, Nigeria, at 8.5° latitude to cover the equatorial extreme point. Details on the renewable energy production for each of the countries can be found in [249].

5.2.3.1   Solar energy availability

The total amount of renewable energy provided over a year by each of the three selected countries: Finland, Crete, and Nigeria, is given in Figure 5.9. Table 5.4 presents numerically the total amount of annual solar energy provided by a 1 m² solar panel and the required quantity of solar panels in m² for the three countries, aiming for half of the data center energy consumption to be provided by the solar energy source. On the closer observance of the data, we notice a fair similarity between Nigeria and Crete, with only a 17% difference. Almost twice (45%) the number of solar panels needed in Nigeria are needed in Finland to achieve the same target of solar energy production.

5.2.3.2   Battery size for three different locations

Experiments and results: To perform the experiments, we have run the simulation tool by changing the input of battery size from 0 to 10MWh, separately for each of the countries. The first run, under battery size equal to 0, shows how much of the produced solar energy is spent in vain as overproduction. Increasing the size of the battery means increasing the amount of stored solar energy. The yield of this is

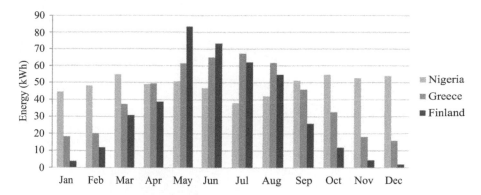

Figure 5.9   *Solar energy produced by 1 m² solar panel in three geographical locations monthly over a year*

Table 5.4   *The total amount of annual solar energy provided by 1 m² solar panel and the number of solar panels in m² needed to cover 50% of energy consumption for Finland, Crete, and Nigeria*

Country	Annual solar energy/1 m² (kWh)	Required solar panels (m²)
Finland	402	324
Crete	500	260
Nigeria	585	222

reduction in the amount of overproduction and energy taken from the grid, translating to an overall higher renewable energy usage. The optimization concept based on the battery size is related to the fact that as battery size increases, the amount of energy taken from the grid and the overproduced energy is decreased. The decreasing rate depends on the battery capacity and of the energy production pattern, which differs in the selected geographical locations. The simulation time covers a period of 1 year (8,760 h), taking as input the hourly solar energy records and the hourly energy consumption values over the year. The data center is composed of 100 servers and we assume in this paper a synthetic variable workload over one week repeated over the whole year. The annual energy consumption for this data center equals 260 MWh. The used synthetic variable workload is obtained as presented in [250].

Through empirical simulations, we found that to achieve no solar overproduction over a year, a 230 kWh battery capacity is needed for the data center located in Nigeria, a 292 kWh battery capacity for the Greece location, and a 9.3 MWh battery capacity if the location is Finland. According to a typical Tesla Powerwall 2 battery chosen as a template with a capacity of 13.5 kWh [251], the overall battery size needed is equal to 17, 21, and 688 of such batteries for Nigeria, Crete, and Finland, respectively.

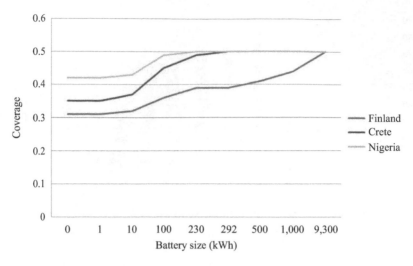

Figure 5.10   The value of achieved average green coverage over a year with increasing battery size for Finland, Crete, and Nigeria

According to (5.30), the real green coverage is decreased from the theoretical one in proportion to the overproduction amount. For a theoretical green coverage for the three countries, we chose to assign the same value of 50%. The first simulation with battery size 0 for each of the countries shows lower values of green coverage because of the overproduction energy, illustrated in Figure 5.10. The achieved values are 42%, 35%, and 31%, for Nigeria, Crete, and Finland, respectively. This means that out of a desired annual renewable energy usage of 50%, there is an 8%, 15%, and 19% drop from this desired usage because of the total overproduction energy over the whole year. The way to recover from this problem is increasing battery size. Figure 5.9 graphically shows higher values of green coverage rising toward 0.5 (50%) with increasing battery size. The rate by which this increase happens changes by country, referring to the annual values.

5.2.4   Renewable energy and Exascale computing

One of the constraints limiting the development of Exascale computing is the power consumption. To achieve an Exaflop computer, a limit of 20 MW was set on its maximal power dissipation by the U.S. Department of Energy (DOE) to stay behind cost feasibility limits. When looking at the current power efficiency of supercomputers from the Top500 [46] and Green500 [252] lists, it clearly illustrates how ambitious is this challenge. On average the five most powerful computers from the Top500 list achieve around 36 teraflops for a power dissipation of 5.6 MW. Scaling these to an Exaflop, taking into account the 20 MW limit, would require seven times more power efficiency computing technologies. On the other hand, when taking as reference the average efficiency of the five most efficient computers from the Green500 list, it

Table 5.5   Required wind turbines and solar panels to provide a 50%
renewable energy coverage

Scenarios	1	2	3	4
Wind turbines (Nr)	0	33,300	60,000	86,500
Nr. Solar panels (m^2)	220,000	133,000	66,600	0

would require 3.5 times more power efficiency computing technologies to provide an Exaflop with a power budget of 20 MW.

Even if the 20 MW limit might sound a challenging goal, Koomey *et al.* established that electrical efficiency of computation has doubled roughly every year and a half for more than six decades [253]. This observed trend indicates that it could be possible to provide an Exascale computer dissipating 20 MW from 3 to 6 years from now.

When scaling the results from [248], we can evaluate the required number of solar panels and wind turbines to provide a different coverage of renewable energy sources for an Exascale computer dissipating a maximum power of 20 MW and deployed in Turku, Finland. Here, we assume a workload of users' requests uniformly distributed over a 24 h time window. This workload is replicated for every day of the year, assuming an homogeneously distributed workload pattern over the year. The assumed wind turbine is a 1 kW HY 1000 wind power characteristics. A detailed description about the simulation settings and assumptions are available from [248]. Table 5.5 provides the number of required solar panels and wind turbine to cover 50% of the energy consumption of the Exascale computer over a one-year period. Without any wind turbine, the required surface of solar panel would be 220,000 m^2, which is equivalent to 31 football pitchs.

5.2.5   Policy for renewable-powered data centers

As seen in the previous subsections, the problematic of renewable energy is becoming a major focus for powering data centers. Several international actions show this importance.

5.2.5.1   European Commission

Due to the European climate and energy package called 20-20-20, there is a goal to reach the following targets:

- A 20% reduction in EU greenhouse gas emissions from 1990 levels;
- Raising the share of EU energy consumption produced from renewable resources to 20%;
- A 20% improvement in the EU's energy efficiency.

These goals are not only for reducing the ecological footprint of European activities but also with an economical goal of creating jobs.

In this context, several funding programs were created in order to improve the overall energy efficiency of European Community countries with one on the focus of large-scale data centers: *Datacenters in Smart Cities* funded in 2013. This funding schema came after the success of several independent EU-funded projects for energy-efficient data centers such as Fit4Green[254], Games[255], All4Greens[256], CoolEmAll[257], and Eco2Clouds[258].

These European projects focus on the interaction of data centers with their electrical surroundings such as battery, solar panels, etc.

5.2.5.2   USA

One of the main drivers of the USA policy comes from the National Strategic Computing Initiative which assigned the U.S. DOE Office of Science (SC) and the National Nuclear Security Administration to create a framework to build an Exascale supercomputer.

Several funding schemes came from this objective but the main focus was put on energy efficiency and energy- and power-capping, not on using renewable sources.

5.2.5.3   Collaborative projects

A large number of international or national projects have the focus to evaluate the possibility of powering data centers with renewable energy.

DataZero [259]: French-funded project aims at powering a large-scale data center using only renewable energies without an access to an electricity grid. It focuses on the task scheduling and electrical infrastructure reconfiguration.

CtrlGreen [260]: This French project addressed the autonomic management of a data center partly operated by renewable energy. It focused on the scheduling side of the problem.

GreenWare [261] is an NSF-funded project taking into account the cooperation of a federation of data center to optimize renewable energy consumption.

5.2.5.4   Companies

Several large companies (Apple, Google, etc.) announced using renewable energy equivalent to the energy consumed by their data centers. At the moment, each of their data centers is not directly consuming this renewable energy but their owners are funding this production for other usages. Thus, the described interconnection between renewable electrical sources and data centers is not yet actually used.

5.3   An introduction to cooling in data centers

Data centers can require up to several megawatts of power, which are dissipated as heat. Dissipating this heat requires careful planning to minimize costs. Converged high-performance and big data computing infrastructures [262] typically also require cooling. This can be a significant part of the fixed and operational costs and typically needs to be customized to the climatic and infrastructure conditions available at a data center site. There is at present no standard methodology to do this, although there is a growing body of knowledge in this area. It has been recognized as an area of importance for the European Union with awards for the best European data centers being given out annually [263]. There are also standardization efforts underway in other parts of the world [264–267].

The motivation for improved knowledge of cooling strategies is the higher density of computing units, which can make traditional fan-driven air cooling a suboptimal choice. Unfortunately, most people with a high-performance computing background do not have a large background in heat transfer and building design, though some engineers do use supercomputers to design thermofluid systems. The aim of this review is to introduce the main technologies and problems to be overcome in data center cooling.

The efficiency of a data center is often characterized by the power usage effectiveness (PUE), which is the ratio of the energy used for the data center to the ratio of the energy used for the computing equipment [268–272]. Use of the PUE as a data center efficiency metric has made cooling considerations important in data center operation since chillers and refrigeration have used up to 30% of system power [269,273].

Previous work has focused on understanding the impact of data center loads on required cooling [274,275]. This is therefore not reviewed in detail here. The data center load is an important design consideration; however, for the mechanical cooling design, the most important initial consideration is being able to sustain maximum performance of the data center. More comprehensive information is available at [276]. This is a valuable openly accessible collection of resources that also targets small data centers. In addition, the Greengrid [277] and American Society of Heating, Refrigerating and Air-Conditioning Engineers (ASHRAE) handbooks [264] are useful resources, though less accessible to the casual reader.

5.3.1   Overview of data center cooling methodologies

In this section, there will be no distinction between data centers mostly targeted for cloud workloads and those targeted to high-performance computing workloads. For the purposes of data center cooling, they are very similar.

The largest distinction is between air and liquid cooled data centers. A primary reason for using liquid cooling is that it allows for a higher computation density since liquids typically have a higher heat capacity than air. Liquid cooling however typically needs a more complicated infrastructure and thus may have higher setup costs.

The design of air-cooled systems has stabilized. Typically, an air-conditioned room is used and the cabinets are arranged to have a design that would enable high heat transfer rate—usually racks are arranged to have hot and cold aisle between them to ensure good transport of hot air to the air cooling system.

There are several liquid cooling options, and this is an area still undergoing rapid innovation, though many data centers would like some standardization to enable lower site fixed costs with liquid cooling infrastructure being used for several generations of compute units. Some methods for liquid cooling that are currently of interest are

1. Heat loop pipes, siphons, liquid cooled heat sinks, and cold plates (for example, produced by Asetek [278], Aquaris [279], and CoolIT [280])

2. Fully immersed forced convective cooling (for example, as produced by Green revolution cooling [281] and investigated by Eiland *et al.* [282] for the Open Compute project [267])
3. Fully immersed free convective cooling (for example, the Rugged POD [283])
4. Phase change cooling (for example, using low boiling point liquids produced by 3M [284–287])

For each of these, one can consider keeping the primary cooling fluid temperature either close to room temperature or significantly above room temperature (*warm water cooling* [288]). When the primary cooling fluid is significantly above environmental conditions, seasonal temperature changes have negligible effects on the efficiency of the conversion of heat for other uses and the generated heat can be more effectively recycled.

Important considerations in choosing a cooling solution are maintenance costs and ease of maintenance. In fully immersed cooling solutions, careful design is required to make component replacement easy. Furthermore, the cooling fluids need to be chosen to enable high heat transfer rates as well as ensuring system cleanliness.

In a liquid cooled system, choosing the coolant and cooling system components is again only half of the work. In many cases, a secondary heat exchanger is used to transport the heat away from the computing system. Typically, the secondary exchanger will use water as the heat transportation medium. This allows for a reduction in cost and also easy integration into the building heating/cooling system, or for easy exhaust of the materials. Some of the heat may also be used to generate electricity using thermoelectric materials.

Surface properties are of great importance in heat transfer [289]. It can be challenging to model this; however, such properties can be measured and the materials or material coatings carefully chosen to ensure a high heat transfer rate.

The design of data center cooling systems typically involves cooperation between computer scientists, electrical engineers, mechanical engineers, civil engineers, and plumbers — most of whom have very different technical skills. A few engineers will use simulation to help design data center cooling systems [290]; however, in many cases, standard design rules will be used [291]. ASHRAE has formulated data center building standards [264], though rapid innovation in this area and the adjustment to local conditions make these difficult to adopt in every possible situation.

For a simple liquid cooled design, once the data center power needs are known, the maximum, average, and minimum power consumption can be estimated. Since almost all the power is dissipated into heat, one can then estimate the amount of heat that needs to be transported away. If the heat capacity of the transporting fluid is known, and the efficiency of heat generation and heat transport from the CPU, GPU, and RAM to the fluid estimated, then an appropriate fluid flow rate can be calculated to ensure that the system remains within a reasonable operating temperature range. The effectiveness of the secondary heat exchanger can then be determined. Typically, an electronic heat control system with temperature feedback would be used to regulate the cooling of the data center. This would move some of the implementation details for the cooling system from the design phase to the operational phase and also allow for adaptation of the system to the computational load at the data center.

In phase change cooling, the operating temperature of the chips needs to be estimated. A fluid with a low boiling point that is compatible with the electronic components is then chosen. The evaporated fluid transfers heat from the hot electronic surfaces to a liquid cooled condenser. The heat required to create a phase change from liquid to gas is known, if heat transfer between the hot electronic components and the cooling fluid, and between the evaporated cooling fluid and condenser is fast enough, the flow rate in the condenser can be adjusted to ensure adequate cooling of the electronic components. Condensers are typically custom made [292].

As concrete examples of existing deployments, Table 5.6 details the characteristics of several data centers and their cooling technologies.

5.3.2 Cost estimation

Cooling can be a significant part of a data center fixed and running costs. Liquid cooling will typically have a higher fixed infrastructure cost but lower running costs. When setting up or upgrading a data center, the choice of cooling options is usually different at every site and needs to be designed specifically for that site. An understanding of local conditions (climatic conditions, electricity costs, possibilities for heat reuse) is of great importance. Also of importance is whether a new data center is being constructed or whether an old data center is being upgraded. Efficient upgrading of an old data center will try to reuse existing infrastructure and may be more difficult to adapt to a liquid cooled solution. For upgrading of old data centers, common options are to use indirect liquid cooling by utilizing cooling doors on enclosed cabinets which have components or to directly attach liquid cooled heat sinks to hot components such as the CPU, GPU, and memory modules. These allow for easy servicing of the electronic components and do not require much retraining of data center personnel. They also allow for reuse of the airflow cooling infrastructure to cool components such as motherboards and storage, which require significantly lower air flows. Newer data centers which use liquid cooling can have a much better integration with building/environmental infrastructure to ensure better reuse of heat generated by the data center as well as initial training of the new personnel on best practices for operating and maintaining a liquid cooled infrastructure.

The total cost of ownership (TCO) model is a popular methodology for choosing data center infrastructure [270,291]. The choice of cooling infrastructure may be easier to model than the choices of CPU, GPU, interconnect, storage, and other compute components since only a few key system properties are needed.

Some considerations are

- the outside temperature, in particular does it allow for free cooling
- can the heat be used in electricity generation
- can the heat be used to provide hot water
- can the heat be used for building heating

In cold climates, all the above uses are possible (and building heating is particularly attractive [293–295]), but in hot climates or in the hotter seasons, only

Table 5.6   Example of cooling technologies deployed in existing HPC data centers. DLC—direct liquid cooling, ILC—indirect liquid cooling, PSNC—Poznan Supercomputing center, UL—University of Luxembourg, UT—University of Tartu, JSCC RAS—Joint Supercomputer Center of the Russian Academy of Science, SSCC RAS—Siberian Supercomputer Center of the Russian Academy of Science, PDC—PDC Center for High Performance Computing at the KTH Royal Institute of Technology, RIKEN—Advanced Institute for Computational Science Kobe, KAUST—King Abdullah University of Science and Technology, NSCC—National Supercomputing Center in Wuxi, DLTM—Distretto Ligure delle Tecnologie Marine

Site and system	Release date	Cooling technology	Power capacity (kW)	Heat reuse	Hot water	PUE
UL, BioTech, Luxembourg	2011	Airflow	200	None	None	?
UL, CDC S02-1, Luxembourg	2016	Airflow	300	None	None	?
UL, CDC S02-2, Luxembourg	2016	Airflow	280	None	None	?
UL, CDC S02-3, Luxembourg	2019	DLC	1,050	None	?	?
UL, CDC S02-4, Luxembourg	2019	DLC	1,050	None	?	?
UL, CDC S02-5, Luxembourg	2016	Airflow	300	None	None	?
PSNC, Eagle, Poland	2016	DLC	450	Building heating	?	1.05
UT, Rocket & Vedur, Estonia	2014 2011	Airflow	88	None	None	?
JSCC RAS, Russia	2017	DLC	300	None	+45°C	1.025–1.06
SSCC RAS, Russia	2017	DLC	100	None	+45°C	1.05
Beskow PDC, Sweden	2015	Airflow, Water Cooled Doors	1,000	Building warming	+19°C	?
K computer, RIKEN, Japan	2012	DLC	12,700	Electricity co-generation	+17°C	1.36
Shaheen, KAUST, Saudi Arabia	2015	Airflow, Liquid Cooled Cabinet	2,800	No	+23°C	?
Taihulight, NSCC, China	2016	ILC,	15,371	No	?	?
Ajax1, SKY, United Kingdom	?	Airflow	?	No	None	1.25
eigen, ENGIE, Netherlands	?	Airflow	?	No	None	1.28
Facebook, Lulea, Sweden	?	Airflow	?	No	None	1.1
DLTM Italy	2014	Airflow	5	No	None	?

electricity generation and hot water generation can be done. Each of these will likely have a different economic value.

As an example, for a 500kW data center, assuming an electricity cost of 0.05€ per kWh, electricity costs are about 300,000€ per year. With free cooling or exhaust to the atmosphere, no electricity costs are recovered—for a warm water system, chillers are not required. If hot water or building heating is provided, then only losses in heat conversion need be accounted for, these may be between 10% and 20% of system costs, thus operating costs are up to 60,000€ per year. If electricity is co-generated, assuming 35% efficiency ([296]), then electricity costs are 195,000€ per year. In cases where electricity costs are significantly less, for example, electricity is generated on site, operational costs will be much less significant than the fixed cost of establishing the infrastructure.

The additional concerns are component lifetimes and failure rates. Not all hardware components will be compatible with all liquid cooling solutions—in particular for fully immersed cooling solutions [297]. The cooling solution may also change the expected failure rates of computer components. On small systems, component failure rates will be infrequent; an extended warranty or similar insurance policy may be the best way to cover component failure. On large systems, component failure rates and component replacement should be considered part of the operational costs as it will be possible to apply statistical methods.

5.3.3 Simulation tools

5.3.3.1 Electrical load simulation and prediction

Due to its significant importance, cooling optimization has been the subject of studies done within a number of research and development projects. One of them was CoolE-mAll [274,298] which involved several authors of the current paper and investigated how cooling, heat transfer, IT infrastructure, and applications influence the overall energy and cooling efficiency of data centers. CoolEmAll provided advanced planning and optimization tools—SVD Toolkit (Simulation, Visualization, and Decision support toolkit) enabling analysis and optimization of data center infrastructure in a holistic manner. The toolkit consists of several modules supporting IT infrastructure designers, decision makers, and administrators in the process of planning new data centers or improving existing ones. In particular, the tools allow for detailed modeling of IT infrastructures, evaluating how they react to various load and power conditions and simulate the corresponding cooling facilities behavior.

The core of the SVD Toolkit is Data Center Workload and Resource Management Simulator (DCworms) [299] and the CFD simulation module. The former tool combines scheduling and management policies with power profiles and cooling models of data center infrastructure [275], while the latter one provides heat flow model supporting hot spots detection. In this way, SVD Toolkit allows evaluation of various arrangements and configuration of racks and cooling components until an optimal airflow through the server room is achieved. Models available within DCworms allow for estimating thermal load at different hardware levels (ranging from single chassis, through the whole rack up to the data center) and analysis of various cooling approaches based on fans, chillers, computer room airside handlers, and dry coolers (free cooling).

DCworms is still developed by Poznan Supercomputing and Networking Center and used for the evaluation of energy efficiency and different cooling strategies within other, ongoing, EU funded projects and is available for use under open-source-based license.

5.3.3.2   Thermofluid simulations

One of the earliest uses of supercomputers was for thermofluid coupled simulations. There are a large number of software packages that can do thermofluid simulation . However, detailed simulations are computationally costly; therefore, simpler simulation models are often used. A modular approach is often used, with low-level details from one simulation being fed into a larger less well-resolved simulation.

For an air-cooled system in a hot aisle cold aisle data center, one can start at the level of a simple rack in an air-cooled cabinet. If the rack is operating at maximum capacity, then one can calculate the required air flow rate to keep the system temperature at a sustainable level. In such an application, the air flow speed will be much less than the speed of sound, and so the low speed compressible Navier–Stokes equations or the incompressible Navier–Stokes equations can be used. The dominant heat transport mechanism will be convection, so once the heat has been transferred to the fluid, it can be considered as a turbulently mixed passive scalar. The room can be initially modeled as a source of cold air and a sink for hot air. Thus, a single simulation can be used to model all the racks in the data center. With this information, the required airflow in the room can be calculated using the low speed compressible Navier–Stokes equations or the incompressible Navier–Stokes equations with the Boussinesq approximation to allow for both free and forced convection and conduction.

Simulation of liquid cooled systems is more complicated because the details of heat transfer between different components are challenging. In cases where phase changes occur, accurate thermofluid simulation is extremely challenging and it may be best to use tables and correlation functions to estimate heat transfer rates. For liquid cooled systems with immersion, low-speed compressible Navier–Stokes equations or the incompressible Navier–Stokes equations with the Boussinesq approximation can again be used. Accurate meshing of all the geometry is complicated, thus a simpler representative model of the heat generating units would likely be sufficient for design purposes. The heat exchanger also need not be fully simulated, provided it is adequately characterized, in particular by having some model for heat absorbed from the primary cooling fluid as a function of temperature and circulation velocity and heat transmitted to the secondary cooling fluid. Engineering tables can be used to aid building design and/or integration with the building heating/cooling system to ensure for adequate operating conditions.

Example thermofluid simulation packages include

- OpenFOAM [300]
- OpenLB [301]
- Palabos [302]

- ANSYS Fluent [303]
- COOLSim [304]
- COMSOL Multiphysics [305]
- STAR-CCM+ [306]
- 6SigmaRoom [307]
- FloTHERM [308]
- TileFlow [309]

Specific data center simulation tools such as COOLSim, 6SigmaRoom, FloTHERM, and TileFlow can make it easy to design a data center. Data center simulations are also good educational computational modeling projects. Typically, simulations will not include all rack details but will instead consider a hierarchy of models. Thus, experimental confirmation will be required to validate the calculations before using them for design.

The simulation tools can be used to ensure that the operational environment will be suitable before deployment or upgrade of a data center. They can also be used in cost optimized design of a data center. Due to the long data enter building lifetimes, careful design choices are required since retrofitting costs for data center computer hardware upgrades should be minimized. Design optimization is an area that still needs to be fully applied to data centers, though it seems that some existing tools such as Dakota [310] for design optimization, can be coupled to the data center simulations, for example, one can couple Dakota to OpenFOAM to optimize cabinet placement for air-cooled data centers, or component placement in an immersed forced convectively cooled cabinet.

Modular pod data centers that are entirely self-contained are attractive for cloud computing applications [290]. Due to their limited size, airflow in these can be carefully optimized and validated to ensure sufficient cooling is obtained at a minimal cost, provided the heat can be exhausted efficiently.

5.3.4   Future challenges

In this chapter, we have given an overview of liquid cooling strategies for data centers. One of the challenges that remains is to determine which of these strategies data centers follow and how effective they are. There are a number of data collection and dissemination activities related to high-performance computing data centers, in particular VI4IO [311] which has as an additional component the comprehensive data center list and the Energy Efficiency working group [312], which is aiming to standardize liquid cooling deployments. It will be challenging to have plumbers and computer scientists work well together, but this will be required for effective data center design. A long-lived repository with computer center cooling strategies is also of interest. Such developments would allow for the development of a shared body of knowledge on data center design and operation.

Of particular interest in a survey are

- Data center location
- Data center layout

- Number of server rooms
- Characteristics of the server rooms
  - surface area
  - number of hosted racks/cabinets
  - CPU used and maximum operating watts
  - power distribution (number of PDU feeds, etc.)
  - rack capacity (kW), type, vendor and usage (high-performance computing (HPC), HPC hybrid (incl. accelerators), storage, interconnect, etc.)
  - servers in a rack with particular cooling technologies
  - Computer-aided design diagrams of the motherboard
    * airflow—also specify the type (hot/cold aisle, etc.)
    * Indirect Liquid cooling (such as airflow with water-cooled doors)
    * Direct Liquid Cooling (DLC)—also specify the type (immersive, heat loop, phase change, etc.)
  - expected/measured PUE (if measured, explain how):
  - inlet water temperature
  - ambient room temperature
  - outlet air/water temperature
  - Type of Heat recycling
    * building warming
    * electricity generation
    * none
    * other
- Heat exchanger (type(s) and capacity):
- Seasonal temperature variation accommodation:
- Fire Protection technology (argonite, etc.)
- Idle power consumption
- Maximum power consumption
- Was simulation used to help design your data center and/or integrated cooling solution?

Our initial attempt at data collection for a small subset of data centers indicates that such a survey will be difficult to fully populate and establish reliable entries for, though would be useful for the environment and for the high performance, big data and cloud computing industries. The PUE is a simple metric to collect, but because simple well-resolved component-wise power measurement techniques are not yet part of many data center deployments PUE reporting is not always easy to obtain. Awards do seem to encourage and highlight innovation [263], but care is required to ensure they lead to long-term best practices.

5.3.5 Conclusion

Some options and considerations for data center cooling have been presented. Data centers are expected to use up to 3% of all electricity generated worldwide. Depending on the data center, cooling can be up to 30% of the electricity costs for the data center. Thus, a good cooling solution which has a high initial setup cost can pay for itself quite quickly. While data center design specifications have not fully standardized, open-source hardware will force some standardization. Measurements of PUE, though not a good indicator on its own, has raised awareness of inefficient data center cooling methodologies that lead to high operating costs. A better measure of data center cooling effectiveness is needed, but may take time to develop. To do so, it is helpful to collect and curate information on cooling strategies used in different data centers.

Acknowledgments

We thank Natalie Bates, Jean-Jacques Chanot, Davide Marini, Alexander Moskovsky, Dale Sartor, Gert Svenson, Phil Tuma, Siddarth Venugopal, Jean-Marie Verdun, Andrew Winfer, Wilbert Yuque, Jason Zeiler, members of the Energy Efficiency Working Group https://eehpcwg.llnl.gov/, and members of the OpenCompute project http://www.opencompute.org/ for helpful discussions.

5.4 A full-cost model for estimating the energy consumption of computing infrastructures

Since its advent in the middle of the 2000s, the *CC* paradigm is increasingly adver-tised as a price-effective solution to many IT problems. This seems reasonable if we exclude the pure performance point of view as many studies highlight a non-negligible overhead induced by the virtualization layer at the heart of every Cloud middleware when subjected to an HPC workload. When this is the case, traditional HPC and ultrascale computing systems are required, and then comes the question of the real cost-effectiveness, especially when compared to instances offered by the Cloud providers.

Many public or private organizations have departments and workgroups that could benefit from HPC resources to analyze, model, and visualize the growing volumes of data they need to conduct business. From a general perspective, HPC is essential for increased competitiveness and stronger innovation. There are two realistic scenarios today to access HPC capacities beyond what is available from the desktop systems. One option is to acquire and operate an HPC system. However, for many companies and especially SMEs, this is seen as a non-viable solution since the TCO is perceived as too high, and additional skills and manpower are needed to operate and maintain such a system. With the rapidly growing enthusiasm around the *CC* paradigm, and more particularly of the *IaaS* model which is best suited for HPC workload, a second viable option is foreseen and attracts more and more attention due to the massive advertisement toward the cost-effectiveness of this approach. In this model, users rent to providers a *resource* that may be computing, storage and network or higher level services. At present, many large actors of the Cloud Computing market propose an IaaS service to their users. The cost model of IaaS is based on the actual resource usage of the user, who is thus billed depending on his activity. The computing resources are operated upon VMs and ran on a multi-tenant mode on the physical hardware. Characterized by their scalability and high-availability, IaaS platforms tend to be more and more efficient and are now sliding toward the territory of the traditional HPC facilities. Because of these interesting characteristics, many IaaS implementations have been largely studied and benchmarked in the context of an HPC usage.

While it is now widely established that running an HPC workload on top of IaaS resources induces a non-negligible performance overhead due to the hypervisor at the heart of every Cloud middleware, many people assume that this performance impact is counter-balanced by the massive cost savings brought by the Cloud approach. *But is it true?* Since 2007, the *UL* operates a medium size HPC facility [313] ($\simeq$ 10,100 computing cores, 346 CPU TFlops and a shared storage capacity of 8.8 PB over parallel and distributed File Systems as of May, 2018) addressing the needs of academic researchers coming from many different fields (physics, material sciences, economy, life science, etc.). While developing our own expertise in the management of such a platform, it also gave us the opportunity to scrutinize on a daily basis and over a significant period of time its associated operating costs.

In this context, [314] proposed a TCO analysis for this in-house HPC facility for the time period 2007–2014 which is reported in the next sections. Also, although the comparative performance of Cloud vs. HPC systems received a wide audience in the recent literature, the analogous analysis covering the costs remains at an early stage, with very few contribution from the academic community. This is also due to the constant and rapid evolution of the Cloud instances offered by the different providers and the frequent price changes, making it hard to establish a fair comparison of the Cloud usage price with regards the equivalent HPC infrastructure operational costs. Furthermore, the direct comparison of a given Cloud instance price with an HPC operating cost is biased and should be taken with precautions as it omits the performance aspect where the Cloud instance performance does not match with the one of an HPC node. To feed this gap and allowing a fair cost analysis, the approach proposed in [314] was twofold. First a theoretical price–performance model was established based on the study of the actual Cloud instances proposed by one of the major Cloud IaaS actors (Amazon). Then, based on the owned facility TCO and taking into account all the *OPEX*, an hourly price comparison is proposed.

Electricity is becoming a major expense in current Cloud and HPC data centers, even chasing the IT hardware cost [315]. Three main approaches can help reducing this energy consumption: improving the infrastructure's energy efficiency, exploiting renewable sources, and increasing the utilization rates. While the two first solutions partly rely on investments, the last one only depends on the facility's management policy. Energy-aware policies could rely on users' willingness to decrease their electricity usage. Yet, users are unaware of the energy consumption induced by their resource's utilization. It is thus crucial to provide the energy models for data centers. This was covered in two other studies [316,317] summarized in this chapter.

In this section, and inspired by the work proposed in [314], we propose a TCO analysis of an in-house academic HPC facility of medium-size (in particular, the one operated at the University of Luxembourg since 2007, or within the Grid'5000 project [318]) and compare it with the investment that would have been required to run the same platform (and the same workload) over a competitive Cloud IaaS offer.

This rest of this chapter is organized as follows: Section 5.4.1 reports the TCO analysis conducted in [314]. Then, the refinement of the model specialized for energy cost modelization [316] with recent cooling technologies is depicted in Sub-section 5.4.2. Finally, section 5.4.3 concludes the paper and provides some future directions and perspectives opened by this study.

5.4.1 Total cost of ownership analysis for a medium-size academic HPC facility

The *UL* operates since 2007 an HPC facility [313] and the related storage by a rel-atively small team of system administrators. The aspect of bridging computing and storage is a requirement of UL service—the reasons are both legal (certain data may not move) and performance related. Nowadays, people from three faculties, as many interdisciplinary centers within the UL, are users of this facility.

As of May 2018, it consists of 5 clusters spread across 2 geographic sites featuring a total of 662 computing nodes (for 10,108 cores) and a cumulative shared storage capacity of 8.8 PB over parallel and distributed File Systems. In the reported study, the data and metrics collected are restricted to two clusters (namely, *chaos*, *gaia*) that compose part of the UL HPC facility. Within these clusters, the internal interconnect is based on an Infiniband QDR (40Gb/s) network built on top of and adapted topology ("fat tree" and/or "star" depending on the situation) to ensure the best performances for the process communications. It is worth to note that such a technology outperforms by far all Ethernet-based network in use among major Cloud providers (including Amazon). A more recent cluster (*iris*) acquired on 2017 features up-to-date hardware (Infiniband EDR, broadwell and skylake processors) but is not part of the reported study, which restricts to the time period 2007–2015. In all cases, the cumulative hardware investment has reached 6.34 M€ by the end of 2014 (7.38 M€ by 2015) and its evolution is depicted in Figure 5.11.

The manpower is also a crucial piece of information often missing in many cost analysis. In Table 5.7, these costs are highlighted in the case of our facility. They reflect a reality where despite all efforts, the local team managing the facility were outnumbered. While the TCO analysis proposed in this section relies on these numbers (more precisely, on the normalized prices for the year 2014), we estimate to 7.35 **FTE** (thus $\simeq$ 88 **PM**) the ideal manpower that would be required to maintain the platform at its sizing in 2015, in the repartition reported in Table 5.8.

Another crucial question when performing a TCO analysis is the hypothesis linked to the usage of the platform. In our case, we have the chance to ensure a consistent and precise monitoring of the HPC resource usage (CPU, memory, etc.) with regard to the submitted jobs. For instance, a typical usage of the *gaia* cluster resources is illustrated in Figure 5.12. It permits one to derive an accurate ratio in terms of *used resources* with regard to the available computing components.

From this information, the TCO of the local HPC facility can be estimated, more precisely for the two clusters `chaos` and `gaia`. These clusters are heterogeneous and composed of different node classes as reported in Table 5.9; the hourly cost of a node belonging to each node class is computed accordingly and reported. In all cases for the calculation of the TCO, we take into account the amortized node purchase price, network and server equipment price, room equipment, manpower and energy

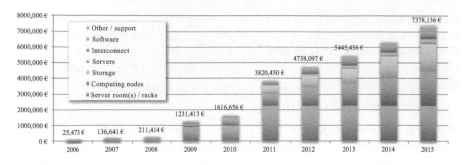

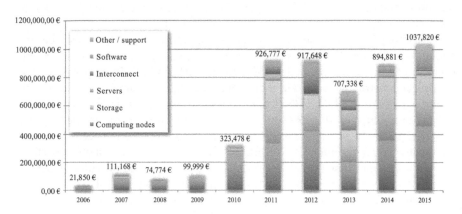

*Figure 5.11   Investment in the UL HPC facility for the time period 2007–2015.
Top: cumulative, incl. server rooms; bottom: yearly, excl. server rooms*

Table 5.7   UL HPC manpower

Year	PM effort	Total annual cost (€)
2006	1	11,553.63
2007	4	32,118.40
2008	19	64,200.24
2009	13	60,450.24
2010	9	57,864.00
2011	13	87,379.20
2012	25	136,947.68
2013	49	194,280.10
2014	40	173,026.90
2015	54	254,619.13

(power and cooling) costs. Computing nodes are considered amortized on a four-year basis, network equipment for eight years and server equipment for three years. Server rooms on their side are supposed to be amortized in 15 years. Unfortunately, the only thing that could not be integrated into this TCO analysis is the building cost itself as

Table 5.8   Ideal manpower repartition to operate a medium-size HPC facility

SMP Services	**1 *FTE***
Operating systems	10%
Compilers	10%
COTS applications	15%
Open source applications	30%
Storage	20%
Change management	10%
Hardware	5%
SAN storage and parallel file system	**1 *FTE***
Hardware	30%
Software (GPFS, Lustre, OneFS, etc.)	50%
Allocation and provisioning	10%
Capacity planning	10%
Parallel cluster	**1.6 *FTE***
Operating systems	10%
Compilers	10%
COTS applications	20%
Open-source applications	30%
Storage	20%
Change management	10%
Hardware	5%
Queuing systems	10%
Internal cluster network	5%
Monitoring	20%
Database	**1 *FTE***
Installation and configuration	10%
Tuning and optimization	20%
Backups and DR	10%
Database design	40%
Database administration	20%
Web services	**40% *FTE***
Operating systems	10%
Apache	10%
Application server	10%
Server-based security	10%
Backup/recovery	**35% *FTE***
Server admin	20%
Client admin	10%
Capacity planning	5%
Scientific programming	**2 *FTE***
Development	100%
Debugging/testing	60%
Profiling/optimization	40%

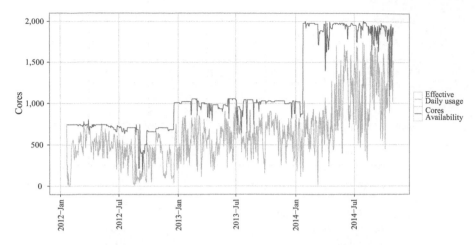

Figure 5.12   Example of used vs. available computing resources within the gaia *cluster*

Table 5.9 chaos *and* gaia *computing nodes characteristics (as of 2015) and estimated TCO evaluation per computing node*

	Node	CPUs/GPU	Memory [GB]	Nodes	CPU Family	GFLOPS	Hourly cost ($)
CHAOS	d-cluster1	12	24	16	westmere (2.26 GHz)	108.48	0.386
	e-cluster1	16	32	16	sandybridge (2.20 GHz)	281.60	0.380
	h-cluster1	12	24	32	westmere (2.26 GHz)	108.48	0.375
	r-cluster1	32	1,024	1	nehalem (2.26 GHz)	289.28	1.760
	s-cluster1	16	32	16	sandybridge (2.20 GHz)	281.60	0.380
GAIA	gaia-[1-60]	12	48	60	westmere (2.26 GHz)	108.48	0.400
	gaia-[123-154]	12	48	32	westmere (3.07 GHz)	147.36	0.291
	gaia-[61-62]	12/1,792	24	2	westmere (2.26 GHz)	108.48	0.588
	gaia-[63-72]	12/10,240	24	10	westmere (2.26 GHz)	108.48	0.545
	gaia-[75-79]	16/12,480	64	5	sandybridge (2.20 GHz)	281.60	0.524
	gaia-[83-122]	12	48	40	westmere (2.93 GHz)	140.64	0.291
	gaia-73	160	1,024	1	sandybridge (2.00 GHz)	2,560.00	2.596
	gaia-74	32	1,024	1	sandybridge (2.40 GHz)	614.40	1.463

the HPC center is hosted within a university which, as research institutions, benefits from governmental funding for its buildings. For obvious privacy reasons, the detailed buying price of the machines cannot be disclosed. Yet, the final amortized node hourly costs are reported in the last column of Table 5.9. To facilitate the comparison with Amazon EC2 instances prices, this TCO is reported in US Dollar rather than in Euro.

Amazon EC2 instances for HPC and equivalent cost models

Since its launch in 2006 with the *m1.small* instance, Amazon has largely expanded the variety of instances and features it provides through its EC2 offer. They are now

Table 5.10   EC2 instance types—grouped by family

Instance family	Instance type	Processor microarchitecture	Introduction date
General purpose	m1	Xeon Family	2006-08-23
	m3	Ivy Bridge-EP	2012-10-31
	t2	Xeon Family	2014-07-01
	m4	Haswell-EP	2015-06-11
	m5	Skylake	2017-11-28
Memory optimized	m2	Xeon Family	2010-02-22
	cr1	Sandy Bridge-EP	2013-01-21
	r3	Ivy Bridge-EP	2014-04-10
	r4	Broadwell	2016-11-30
Compute optimized	c1	Xeon Family	2008-08-08
	cc1	Nehalem-EP	2010-07-13
	cc2	Sandy Bridge-EP	2011-11-14
	c3	Ivy Bridge-EP	2013-11-14
	c4	Haswell-EP	2014-11-13
	c5	Skylake	2017-11-06
Storage optimized	hi1	Xeon Family	2012-07-18
	hs1	Sandy Bridge-EP	2012-12-21
	i2	Ivy Bridge-EP	2013-12-20
	i3	Broadwell	2017-02-23
Dense storage	d2	Haswell-EP	2015-03-30
GPU	cg1	Nehalem-EP	2010-11-14
	g2	Sandy Bridge-EP	2013-11-05
	g3	Broadwell	2017-07-13
Micro	t1	Xeon Family	2009-10-26
	t2	Haswell	2014-07-01

proposed in several families, each corresponding to a different computing need. Along the years and at new instance type releases, Amazon decreased the prices of the already existing ones.

To ensure backward compatibility, most older instances are still distributed; however, they do not provide a good price/performance ratio anymore regarding the most recent ones.

Table 5.10 presents all the available instance types and their release dates as of early 2018 (except for the *cc1.4xlarge* which is not available anymore). An instance type, e.g. *m1* or *c1*, belongs to an instance family, e.g. *General Purpose* or *Compute Optimized*. For each instance type, there exist one or several models available that are not presented in this table. Instance models are described by an extension of the instance type (e.g. *m1.small*), possible values are micro, small, medium, large, xlarge, 2xlarge, 4xlarge, and 8xlarge. A given instance model corresponds to a particular performance of the instance in terms of vCPU, Memory, Storage, Network, or such other performance characteristics.

To summarize, the cloud characteristics (which are also valid for EC2) that may impact HPC applications are the following:

1. Clouds are run in *virtualized environments*. Although the virtualization overhead is not so important for CPU bound applications, the virtualized networking is still an important drawback for applications that need communications (i.e. a large part of HPC applications). Even though the networking uses virtualization improvements such as *SRIOV*, there exists a performance drop for inter-node communications.
2. There is generally no high-performance network such as Infiniband yet available. This is still a problem for many applications whose performance is highly linked with the network performance.
3. Cloud by default uses multi-tenancy. This is a real problem as it does not ensure a reliable and stable behavior for applications. In particular, I/O operations in multi-tenancy platforms can face high I/O jitter. However, EC2 also provides a charged *Dedicated Instances* service to ensure the user will have the exclusive access to the nodes reserved.
4. Spatial and link proximity of the reserved VM is not guaranteed by default. Because of this intrinsic characteristic, inter-node bandwidth and latency can vary a lot. As for multi-tenancy, EC2 also provides for some instances the *placement group* feature, a logical grouping of instances within the same Availability Zone (isolated location within the same region) ensuring a low-latency, 10 Gb network between the nodes.

If we now aim at the execution of an HPC workload, one of the key constraints to address is the need for a reliable and efficient underlying network. Not all EC2 instances offer such a guarantee; however, there exists a mechanism called *placement group* available for some of them and that allows the user to group a set of instances in the same cluster. This is an important requirement for HPC applications that use several nodes. Here, we consider that most *classical* HPC applications fall into that category and thus need to be placed within the same cluster.

It is also important to say on an HPC point of view that the nodes that host the EC2 instances have HyperThreading (HT) activated; thus, each vCPU on an instance is actually a HyperThread. In all cases, Amazon's EC2 provides several mechanisms to target high performance in its cloud instances.

1. Enhanced networking with *SRIOV*. This hardware feature, proposed on the most efficient instances, provides higher network performance for the VM: higher bandwidth and lower network latency and jitter. The instances where this feature is available are *c3, c4, r3, i2*, and *d2*. Unfortunately, GPU instances do not provide the Enhanced Networking feature but we have to consider them anyway for an HPC environment.
2. Placement groups (or cluster networking). This feature provides high bandwidth performance with a full bisection Ethernet network.
3. Dedicated instances. By default on EC2, cloud instances are multi-tenant VM hosted on the same physical node. By opting for the dedicated instance

option (paying) at launch time, the instance will have exclusive access to the underlying PM.

4. EBS-optimized. EBS is Amazon's persistent storage for EC2 instances (as opposed to instances local storage which is destroyed after the instance termination). It can be purchased with a provisioned IO option to increase and guarantee data transfer rates. EBS volumes have a maximum throughput of 128 MiB/s that can be attained only with instances proposing the EBS-optimized option.

5. One of the latest instance types released by Amazon at this time, the *c4* and *c5* instances, proposes EBS storage with no additional costs but does not provide local storage.

In practice, EC2 instance performances are provided in **ECU**. This metric represents the relative measure of the integer processing power of a given instance. Amazon does not give precisely how they measure ECU, the only information available is that one ECU is equivalent to one Intel Xeon core running at 1.0–1.2 GHz. It is also clearly stated by Amazon that this metric might be revised in the future by adding or substituting measures that go into the definition of an ECU. According to Amazon, the goal of providing instance performance as ECU is to make it easier to compare CPU capacity between different instance types and thus to "*provide a consistent amount of CPU capacity no matter what the actual underlying hardware.*" Although the claim of using several benchmarks and tests to manage the consistency and predictability of the performance from an EC2 Compute Unit, it seems that this information might be sometimes misleading. In [319], the authors showed that for several instance types the performance measured experimentally was unreliable, unpredictable, and not reflecting the ECU provided by EC2. This was due to the fact that the instances that were tested in this study were running indifferently on several types of CPU and it seems that for instance whose CPU model is described as being a *Xeon Family*, there is no guarantee of the actual *CPU* model on which the instance will be run.

In another study driven by Iosup *et al.* in [320], the authors experimentally compared the actual GFLOPS regarding the announced ECU for *m1* and *c1* instances and observed a real performance comprised between 39% and 44% of the advertised performance for *m1* instances and most of *c1* instances with an exception of 58.6% for the *c1.xlarge* instance. It follows that ECU is a non-standard way to measure a processor performance and it actually makes it difficult to fairly compare the computing performance of an EC2 instance with an HPC node. Moreover, as this metric is not provided with a strict definition and as it was observed performance mismatch between the announced ECU and actual performance, we need another metric such as FLOPS which is the traditionally used theoretical processor computing performance metric. As according to its definition, an ECU is equal to one Xeon core at 1.0–1.2 GHz, the ECU should reflect the processor FLOPS value.

In [314], the authors offered an accurate linear model exhibiting the relationship between ECU and GFLOPS. Based on multiple linear regression, an automated stepwise selection was first performed. Then, from the meaningful parameters detected, a manual assessment of the ones that are the most representative in the model via R^2 shrinkage is executed. Among many parameters evaluated, we established that the

*Table 5.11   Coefficients of the new EC2 price model for on-demand instances, with
fitting performance evaluation*

Generation	GFLOPS (α)	MemGiB (β)	DiskGiB (γ)	GPUs (δ)	Adj. R^2	P-value
1st (m1, c1, m2, cg1)	0.0039522	0.0061130	0.0000670	0.0015395	0.9999909	0e+00
2nd (cc2, m3, hi1)	−0.0035266	0.0355353	0.0007284	0.0000000	0.9999785	1e−07
3rd (hs1, cr1, g2, c3)	0.0017209	0.0106101	0.0000655	0.0001644	1.0000000	0e+00
4th (i2, r3, c4)	0.0009952	0.0081883	0.0007605	0.0000000	0.9998832	0e+00
5th (m4, d2)	0.0000000	0.0173750	0.0000342	0.0000000	1.0000000	0e+00

significant ones are processor speed (GFLOPS), memory size (GB), disk size (GB), and number of GPU cores. It follows that the new price model for EC2 instance prices can be described through the following equation:

$$Instance\_Price = \begin{cases} \alpha * GFLOPS \\ +\beta * Memory\_GB \\ +\gamma * Disk\_GB \\ +\delta * Nb\_GPUs \end{cases}$$

It appears that instances that were released in the same time period could be grouped in the same price model without changing significantly the fitting—this assessment would probably need to be checked against recent instances (*i.e.* after 2016). Table 5.11 provides the parameters for the refined on demand pricing models obtained for five successive *generations* (*i.e.* release period) of Amazon instances.

These five models have been evaluated individually, leading to very low error rates, or even perfect linear fitting [314].

From this price model, it is possible to provide accurate EC2 equivalent prices for a given class of node within a local HPC facility. This means that even though not all the cluster computing nodes have a perfect cloud instance match, we are still able to determine what would be its equivalent price on EC2 if that matching instance was available. This information is later used to assess the interest of operating a given node class regarding renting an on-demand instance with the same performance on the cloud. Such an estimation is proposed in Figure 5.13 which presents the ratio, for each node class in the cluster, of the *EC2 Equivalent Price* based on the closest possible existing EC2 instance, vs. the operating cost of the considered node as evaluated previously (see Table 5.9). It can be observed that for a few node classes, the ratio is close to 1, meaning that operating in-house these HPC nodes costs about the same price as renting the corresponding instance on Amazon. Thus, it may be interesting to rent these kind of resources instead of operating them locally. However for *all the other ones*, renting cloud instances is simply too costly. Let us also remind that the operating cost provided in Table 5.9 represents the *maximum* cost scenario where the HPC infrastructure is used at 100%. For a lower utilization of

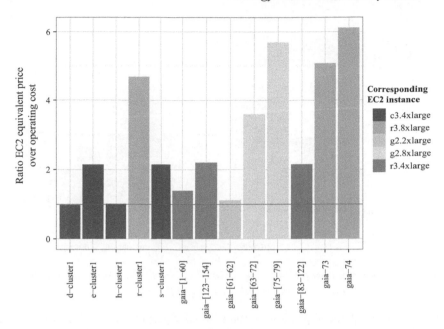

Figure 5.13   Ratio between the EC2 equivalent price of the UL in-house HPC resources with regard to their respective TCO estimation

the cluster, this operating cost will be decreased due to lower energy usage (see also section 5.4.2).

Finally, the pricing model can be extended as the above comparison is based on "on-demand" instance prices. In this purchase model, the customer pays a fixed rate by the hour with no commitment. In this scenario, the acquisition of an in-house HPC facility is probably a more cost-effective solution. However, cloud provider such as Amazon proposes cheaper options for the instance prices, in particular through *Reserved* instances which offer capacity reservation and a significant discount on the hourly charge of a given instance. There are three payment options in this case: (1) *No Upfront*: this option provides access to a Reserved Instance without requiring an upfront payment. (2) *Partial Upfront*: this option requires a part of the Reserved Instance to be paid upfront and the remaining hours in the term are billed at a discounted hourly rate, regardless of usage. (3) *All Upfront*: a full payment is made at the start of the term, with no other costs incurred for the remainder of the term regardless of the number of hours used.

It permits one to investigate how these instance prices impact the running costs on a yearly basis. For that purpose, all job requests scheduled on the UL HPC platform (as extracted from the logs of the batch scheduler) have been analyzed on a reference time period (the year 2014 in this case). The results are presented in Figure 5.14. It may seem surprising at first that the cost of operating the cluster locally is 40% cheaper than renting on EC2 with the all upfront reserved mode and 2.5 times less

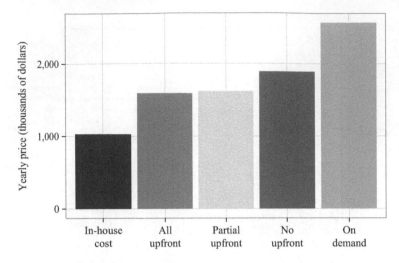

Figure 5.14 Annual cost for the year 2014 of UL workload if operated locally or rented on a cloud provider (Amazon EC2)

expensive for on demand pricing. Actually, a large part of the workload from *chaos* and *gaia* use nodes with a low local operating cost compared to their *EC2 relative price*. This result particularly shows that the migration of HPC workloads to the cloud is not only a problem of adaptability of the cloud performance to HPC needs but also a problem of correctly determining which types of job are good candidates to be run on the cloud in order to prevent such cost overheads.

5.4.2 Energy cost models for Clouds

Electricity lies among the costs incurred by a data center and this cost increases with the size of the data center. While it could be optimized with the help of users, they are often unaware of the actual energy consumption of their virtual resources. Indeed, the cost of renting a VM on a Cloud like EC2 (as presented in Table 5.10) depends mainly on the VM size and the resources' usage within the VM does not influence its price. Energy cost models are needed to increase users' energy-awareness and to provide an incentive toward a greener behavior.

The power consumption of a given device (computing, networking, or storage) is divided into two parts: a static part that corresponds to its energy consumption while being powered on but idle and a dynamic part that changes with the workload. Servers are not yet powered proportional: their static power consumption is high and the dynamic part does not depend linearly on the workload [321].

Figure 5.15 shows the power consumption of a synthetic workload running on a server (Nova node, detailed later in Table 5.12). The idle power consumption of this server is around 70 W.

Furthermore, devices are heterogeneous within the same data center as detailed for servers in Table 5.9. An energy cost model for VMs needs to consider both static and dynamic parts in order to discourage resource overprovisioning (costly due to

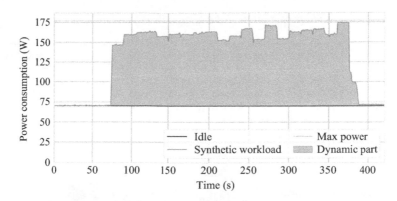

Figure 5.15   Power consumption of a server running a synthetic workload

the non-proportionality) and to promote dynamic energy-efficient techniques (such as dynamic voltage frequency scaling), respectively.

In addition to the electricity consumed by ICT resources, data centers contain other devices consuming electricity for a proper functioning of the infrastructure: cooling systems, power delivery components, and other miscellaneous elements such as the lighting. The deployment of VMs indirectly causes this additional consumption. Consequently, it should be included in the VM energy cost model.

Finally, when requesting VMs, users receive access to virtualized resources. Concretely, it implies that users may share physical resources and as previously explained, this sharing, combined with the virtualization layer may induce performance degradation and an increased energy consumption. A fair accounting is needed to attribute each Watt consumed by the data center to a user, including the Watts that cannot be measured by a software wattmeter that would monitor the VM (i.e. the indirect costs).

In order to be fair among users, an energy cost model for VMs needs to consider:

- the size of the VM to account for the booking of hardware resources
- the heterogeneity of servers, but the cost for a given VM should be independent from its physical allocation on a server (as users do not decide this allocation)
- the network and storage devices
- the non-IT equipment of the data center that consumes electricity (including cooling devices)

An energy-proportional model is proposed in [316]. This model is named EPAVE: Energy-Proportional Accounting in VM-based Environments. It consists of a power-aware attribution model for VMs taking into account the overall consumption of the data center and considering the heterogeneity of servers and VMs. To account for non-IT equipment, it uses the PUE, a widespread metric for measuring the infrastructure's energy efficiency for data centers. The PUE is given by the ratio between the overall data center power consumption over the power consumption of IT equipment (i.e. network devices, compute and nodes). The closer it is to 1, the more efficient is the data center infrastructure. It highlights the consumption impact of cooling system, power distribution units, and other non-IT systems.

Table 5.12   Servers characteristics of the Grid'5000 Lyon site

Hardware	Model	Cores	RAM (GB)
Nova: Dell PowerEdge R430	Intel Xeon E5-2620 (2.1 GHz)	2×8	64
Taurus: Dell PowerEdge R720	Intel Xeon E5-2630 (2.3 GHz)	2×6	32
Sagittaire: Sun Fire V20z	AMD Opteron 250 (2.4 GHz)	2	2

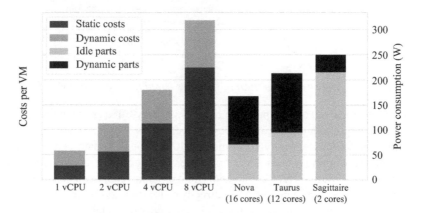

Figure 5.16   EPAVE cost model for servers only based on the Grid'5000 Lyon site

EPAVE comprises two parts: a static and a dynamic part. The static part deals with the idle consumption of servers hosting VMs, the power consumption of other IT equipment (including storage nodes and network devices) and the PUE.

We consider the Lyon site of Grid'5000 [318] as a use case to compute the energy cost given by EPAVE. Table 5.12 details its servers' characteristics: it consists of 3 clusters including 23 Nova nodes, 16 Taurus nodes, and 79 Sagittaire nodes. Based on their idle power consumption and their number of cores, we can compute the static part of EPAVE, which consists of the average static power consumption per core in the data center. The dynamic part is computed by using the maximal power consumption of each server.

Figure 5.16 presents the energy cost provided by EPAVE only for the server part depending on the size of the considered VM (from 1 to 8 virtual CPUs) using the server configurations presented in Table 5.12. It also displays the actual power consumption of each type of servers. We can observe that the server heterogeneity, and especially Sagittaire servers that are numerous, old and inefficient, causes a consequent increase in the static energy cost.

We consider that the electricity cost is around $0.2 per kWh in France from [322] and we use a PUE of 1.53 for the data center (PUE measured on Rennes site of Grid'5000 [323]). The full static costs (with PUE, network, and storage devices) are fairly distributed among the cores of the data center. It means that the energy cost determined by EPAVE for a VM with 1 vCPU hosted in this infrastructure is $0.02 per hour, so around $175 annually. This amount is similar to what can be found in [315].

If we consider the first node listed in Table 5.9, it is estimated to have an evaluated hourly TCO of $0.386 for 12 cores. In terms of performances, this node is really close to the Taurus nodes considered in our platform (Table 5.12). It means that if we consider this node to belong to our data center, its induced electricity cost (according to EPAVE) would represent around 60% of its overall TCO cost.

While this model can be an incentive for users to consume less energy, it does not take into account the electricity source. Most renewable energy sources (e.g. sun and wind) are intermittent and variable by nature. For favoring renewable energy sources, instead of computing a financial cost, we propose a CO_2-related cost [317].

This CO_2 emissions accounting framework gives flexibility to the Cloud providers, predictability to the users and allocates all the carbon costs to the users [317]. Similar to EPAVE, it considers the indirect costs induced by the user's utilization, like the consumption of the data center air-conditioning system. These indirect costs are fairly split among users over long time periods in order to ensure their predictability: they are provided to the users upon submission of their VMs' requests. Finally, the electricity consumption is translated into CO_2 emissions based on the provided electricity mix.

For the CO_2 computation, we rely on data provided by RTE, the French transmission system operator about the energy mix for France [4]. An example is provided in Figure 5.17 for one day (Friday, May 25, 2018). Current production status is updated every 15 minutes. RTE also provides the CO_2 emissions per kWh of electricity

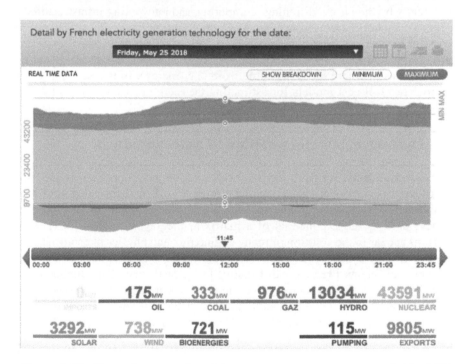

Figure 5.17   Example over a day of the energy mix in France provided by RTE

generated in France per day. On this day, it represents on average 26 g/kWh. This figure is low due to high dependence of the French electricity mix on nuclear power.

It means that for our 1 vCPU VM, it represents approximately 2.5 g of CO_2 generated per hour only for the utilization of this VM. This cost does not include the CO_2 emissions due to the manufacturing of data center devices.

In this section, we have pictured an overview of two energy costs models for VMs: EPAVE, which provides an energy-proportional accounting in data centers [316], and a CO_2 emissions accounting framework [317]. Both aim at fairly distributing all energy costs to the users, including indirect costs like the electricity consumption of cooling systems. They allow transparent, reproducible, and predictive cost calculation for users and providers. The two models indicate that electricity costs are of uttermost importance when considering TCO of a data center.

5.4.3   Conclusion

There are two realistic scenarios today to access HPC capacities beyond what is available from the desktop systems. One option is to acquire and operate an HPC system, the other option relies on the Cloud Computing paradigm, and more particularly of the IaaS model which is best suited for HPC workload. In this context, we have proposed a TCO analysis for a medium-size academic HPC facility, and we compare it to the Amazon EC2 cost model.

The costs of current data centers are mostly driven by their energy consumption specifically by the air conditioning, computing, and networking infrastructure. Yet, current cost models are usually static and rarely consider the facilities' energy consumption per user. Current pay-as-you-go models of Cloud providers allow users to easily know how much their computing will cost. However, this model is not fully transparent as to where the costs come from (e.g. energy). In this section, we have explored two full-cost models for estimating the energy consumption and the CO_2 emissions of VMs hosted in data centers.

5.5   Heterogeneous computation of matrix products

Matrix multiplication is one of the most essential computational kernels used in the core of scientific applications. An application is, for instance, the calculus of matrix polynomials. Matrix polynomials are used, e.g. for the computation of functions of matrices such as the exponential of a matrix by the Taylor method [324]. Matrix functions appear in the solution of many engineering and physics phenomena, which are governed by systems of linear first-order ordinary differential equations with constant coefficients [325], control theory [326], or theory of multimode electric power lines [327]. Some other engineering processes are described by second-order differential equations, whose exact solution is given in terms of the trigonometric matrix functions sine and cosine [328,329], for which efficient solutions have been proposed in [330,331].

Matrix multiplications has been highly studied in the past in order to improve the efficiency of its computation in both sequential and parallel computer architectures.

This operation has also received full attention in parallel heterogeneous environments. Some proposals use one of more GPUs in a node to improve the execution of matrix multiplications in order to accelerate applications like, for instance, the computation of the cosine of a matrix [332,333]. Many contributions that try to use all the devices of a heterogeneous environment basically propose irregular partitions of the factor matrices that can efficiently be mapped on the computing resources; see, for instance, [20,334,335]. However, it is difficult to find actual implementations of the matrix multiplication on heterogeneous nodes that feature very different devices. The MAGMA project, for instance, aims to develop a dense linear algebra library similar to LAPACK but for heterogeneous/hybrid architectures; it is one of the most active projects that implement BLAS routines for nodes featuring accelerators [336]. Currently, MAGMA implements a version for NVIDIA GPUs in which the matrix multiplication is carried out only by the GPUs, i.e. the CPU does not intervene. The MAGMA project also provides with a version, MAGMA MIC, which provides hybrid algorithms that involve the host CPU and one or more Intel Xeon Phi processors. However, this project does not use both NVIDIA GPUs and MICs processor all together in the same host. The authors of [337] propose a programming model for heterogeneous computers featuring CPU, a GPU, and a Xeon Phi with the aim to incorporate it to MAGMA library. However, they have not shown its proposal with matrix multiplication.

The work presented here is an experimental study of performance in execution time and energy consumption of matrix multiplications on a heterogeneous server. The server features three different devices: a multicore CPU, an NVIDIA Tesla GPU, and an Intel Xeon Phi coprocessor. Our implementation is based on a simple implementation using OpenMP sections. We have also devised a functional model for the execution time and energy consumption that allows one to predict the best percentage of workload to be mapped on each device.

The rest of the section is structured as follows. Section 5.5.1 shows the application implemented to carry out a square matrix multiplication on these three different devices. The following section shows experimental results in both time and energy consumption of our application. The section ends with conclusions.

5.5.1 A hybrid matrix multiplication application

In order to solve efficiently problems that intensively use matrix multiplications on a heterogeneous server, we propose an implementation for a matrix multiplication application and present an experimental study of its performance in both execution time and energy consumption.

5.5.1.1 The hardware and software used

The heterogeneous server we have been working with features the following devices:

- **CPU**: Two sockets with an Intel Xeon CPU E5-2670 v3 at 2.30 GHz each. This processor has 12 cores so the server contains a total of 24 threads. The main memory of the host is 64 GB.
- **GPU**: NVIDIA Tesla K40c with 2,880 cores and 12 GB of device memory.

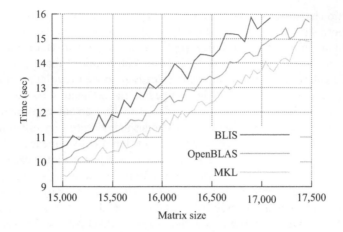

Figure 5.18   Execution time for a square matrix multiplication in one core using different libraries

- **PHI**: An Intel Xeon Phi 3120A coprocessor with 57 processors (228 cores) and 6 GB of device memory.

Although the term "device" is usually assigned to accelerators only, i.e. GPU and PHI, in the next and for the sake of simplicity, we will use it to denote all of them.

On the software side, we have within reach different implementations of Basic Linear Algebra Subprograms (BLAS) [338] to perform the matrix multiplication:

MKL: Intel Math Kernel Library is an optimized implementation of linear algebra routines contained in BLAS and LAPACK, and other mathematical functions like the FFT. This library is available for multicore x86 processors and also for the Intel Xeon Phi coprocessor [339]. There exist "threaded" routines, e.g. the matrix multiplication routine GEMM, for both devices.

OpenBLAS: OpenBLAS is an optimized BLAS library based on GotoBLAS2 1.13 BSD version [340]. Used in the CPU.

BLIS: This library is self-described as "a portable software framework for instantiating high-performance BLAS-like dense linear algebra libraries." In addition, the "framework was designed to isolate essential kernels of computation that, when optimized, immediately enable optimized implementations of most of its commonly used and computationally intensive operations" [341]. It has been used in the CPU.

CUBLAS: BLAS implementation for NVIDIA GPUs [342].

We performed a simple experimental analysis of the speed of the matrix multiplication (GEMM) in the CPU (Figure 5.18). For this test, we used the maximum available CPU cores, i.e. 24. (We ignored the fact that HT can be enabled to give a total of 48 logical processors. We observed that using just one thread per core is enough to fully exploit the execution resources of the core and not increase in performance can be achieved by activating HT.) It must be said that the performance of BLIS could be probably better by selecting the best parallel configuration. Contrary to the other two packages, BLIS is tuned by setting the value of up to four environment variables. That value corresponds to the number of threads that will be used to parallelize a given loop among the five nested loops in which the matrix multiplication is implemented in order to exploit the hierarchical set of intermediate memories of the most current architectures. In this test, only the outer loop was parallelized. A more suitable combination of values are likely to produce a better performance of BLIS, however, we decided not to test the large set of different combinations with the idea that barely the performance would outperform MKL in this machine. Consequently, we consider the performance of Intel MKL to be the best and, therefore, it is the only library used on the CPU side.

5.5.1.2 Implementation option

To proceed toward a heterogeneous matrix product, we started by implementing an application that partitions the problem into three concurrent pieces so that the three devices can cooperate in the solution. There exist different options to implement such an application. However, all the options can be gathered into two main classes standing for the use of light processes (threads) or heavy processes. The last option can be implemented, e.g. by using MPI [343]. Here, we decided to use a simple approach based on threads, which are spawned by means of OpenMP subsections.

The application has been implemented with OpenMP subsections so that each device code is included in a given subsection (Listing 5.1). The code for the Intel Xeon Phi, in lines 31 and 32, is implemented in a different source file (Listing 5.2) and compiled separately. This is because it is necessary to compile this code with the Intel C compiler (icc). For the compilation of the rest of the C code of the application, we used the GNU compiler (gcc) since there exists incompatibility between the available versions for the NVIDIA compiler (nvcc, version 7.5) and for the Intel compiler (icc, version 16.0).

The basics of the heterogeneous multiplication are easy. To perform the multiplication $C = AB$, matrix A is completely broadcast to the two accelerators from the Host computer. Matrix B, however, is partitioned into three blocks of consecutive columns. The second block is uploaded to the GPU, the third one is uploaded to the PHI, and the first one remains into the host memory. The amount of columns of each block is denoted in Listing 5.1 by the values of variables gpu_n, phi_n, and cpu_n for the GPU, the PHI, and the CPU, respectively. Currently, the application receives these values as arguments by a command line; in particular, the user sets the percentages for the GPU and for the PHI in the range [0, 1], the rest is computed by the CPU. Upon termination of the execution, the resulting matrix C appears partitioned and distributed among the three devices. We include in the application, and in the time measurement, the operation of gathering the result in the memory location allocated into the host to store the resulting matrix.

The code for the execution in the GPU is quite regular (lines 7–27). It includes the creation of the CUBLAS context, allocating memory for the three matrix factors, uploading matrices, executing the matrix product, downloading the result, and freeing the resources involved in the computation.

Listing 5.1   Code for the heterogeneous matrix multiplication

```
int gpu_n  = (int) (gpu_weight * n);
int phi_n  = (int) (phi_weight * n);
int cpu_n  = n-gpu_n-phi_n;
#pragma omp parallel sections num_threads(3)
{
#pragma omp section
{ // GPU
  if ( gpu_n ) {
  cublasHandle_t handle;
  CUBLAS_SAFE_CALL( cublasCreate(&handle) );
  double *gpu_A, *gpu_B, *gpu_C;
  CUDA_SAFE_CALL( cudaMalloc((void **) &gpu_A, n*n*sizeof(double) ) );
  CUDA_SAFE_CALL( cudaMalloc((void **) &gpu_B, n*gpu_n*sizeof(double) ) );
  CUDA_SAFE_CALL( cudaMalloc((void **) &gpu_C, n*gpu_n*sizeof(double) ) );
  CUBLAS_SAFE_CALL(cublasSetMatrix(n, n, sizeof(double), A, n, gpu_A, n ));
  CUBLAS_SAFE_CALL( cublasSetMatrix( n, gpu_n, sizeof(double),
                                 &B[n*cpu_n], n, gpu_B, n ) );
  CUBLAS_SAFE_CALL( cublasDgemm(handle, CUBLAS_OP_N, CUBLAS_OP_N, n, gpu_n,
                    n, &alpha, gpu_A, n, gpu_B, n, &beta, gpu_C, n ) );
  CUBLAS_SAFE_CALL( cublasGetMatrix( n, gpu_n, sizeof(double), gpu_C, n,
                                 &C[n*cpu_n], n ) );
  CUDA_SAFE_CALL( cudaFree(gpu_A) );
  CUDA_SAFE_CALL( cudaFree(gpu_B) );
  CUDA_SAFE_CALL( cudaFree(gpu_C) );
  CUBLAS_SAFE_CALL( cublasDestroy(handle) );
  }
}
#pragma omp section
{ // PHI
  if ( phi_n ) {
  gemmPHI( n, phi_n, n, alpha, A, n, beta, &B[n*(cpu_n+gpu_n)], n,
         &C[n*(cpu_n+gpu_n)], n );
  }
}
#pragma omp section
{ // CPU
  if ( cpu_n ) {
  dgemm( &transa, &transb, &n, &cpu_n, &n, &alpha, A, &n, B, &n,
                                   &beta, C, &n );
  }
}
}
```

Listing 5.2   Code for the heterogeneous matrix multiplication in the Xeon Phi
(offload mode)

```
void gemmPHI( int m, int n, int o, double alpha, double *A, int lda,
           double beta, double *B, int ldb, double *C, int ldc ) {
#pragma offload target(mic) in(m,n,o,alpha,beta,lda,ldb,ldc) \
             in(A:length(m*o)) in(B:length(o*n)) inout(C:length(m*n))
{
  cblas_dgemm(CblasColMajor, CblasNoTrans, CblasNoTrans, m, n, o,
                          alpha, A, lda, B, ldb, beta, C, ldc );
}
}
```

Table 5.13 *Meaning of shell variables used to execute the heterogeneous matrix*
multiplication application

Variable name	Meaning
OMP_NESTED:	Set to TRUE to ensure that MKL uses more than one thread when called inside an OpenMP subsection.
MKL_NUM_THREADS:	Number of threads used by MKL (CPU).
MKL_DYNAMIC:	Set to FALSE to avoid MKL automatically selects the number of threads (CPU).
MKL_MIC_ENABLE:	Set to 0 to avoid the Xeon Phi is used to accelerate the CPU computation.
MIC_ENV_PREFIX:	Specifies the environment variables with prefix MIC will address only the PHI.
MIC_OMP_NUM_THREADS:	Number of threads used by the PHI to execute MKL routines.
MIC_KMP_AFFINITY, MIC_USE_2MB_BUFFERS:	These variables control the efficiency of the Xeon Phi in the execution of the matrix multiplication routine. They have been set to such values according to the advice of Intel documentation.

For the Xeon Phi, we used the "offload mode" of computation, that is, data is explicitly uploaded to the device and the operation is also explicitly executed there. Thus, the programmer has control of what exactly is executing the coprocessor. Arguments in, out, and inout specify clearly the direction of variables characterized by those words. The operation is actually performed by calling to the BLAS matrix multiplication routine using the MKL version.

Finally, the code executed by the CPU only includes a call to the gemm routine (lines 38 and 39) for the matrix computation using MKL as well. We used the fortran interface instead of the C one used for the PHI for no specific reason but the application is oblivious of this.

Attention must be paid to the way in which the application is executed in our heterogeneous server. As it has been implemented, only three OpenMP threads are created so that each one will execute a different subsection. There will be, thus, one thread bound to each accelerator for data transference and control purposes. For the CPU case, however, the execution of the MKL routine will use only one thread. To use more threads (cores) collaborating in the matrix multiplication on the CPU side, the "nested parallelism" ability must be explicitly set. In addition, there are more environment variables that control the behavior of the application (Table 5.13).

This is an example of execution:

```
shell_$ MKL_NUM_THREADS=22 OMP_NESTED=TRUE MKL_DYNAMIC=FALSE
        MKL_MIC_ENABLE=0 MIC_ENV_PREFIX=MIC
        MIC_KMP_AFFINITY=balanced,granularity=fine
        MIC_OMP_NUM_THREADS=228 MIC_USE_2MB_BUFFERS=64K
        numactl --physcpubind=+0-11,12-23 program 10000 0.48 .15
```

The example executes the program program which generates two random matrices of order $n = 10,000$. The GPU performs 48% of the computation, 15% is carried out by the PHI, and the rest, 37%, is computed by the CPU.

It should also be noted that the server has the HT enabled, but we decided not to use all the 48 threads and always use 24 as a maximum number of threads instead. For instance, when operating with the three devices, two threads are bound to one accelerator each, leaving the other 22 for the execution of the matrix multiplication in the CPU.

In addition, we have always used core affinity. This is to prevent threads from leaping among the cores at runtime, so as to reduce the variability of the execution times and also to improve the performance of all the devices attached to the host. Concretely speaking, we use the tool numactl to bind threads to cores.

The following is an example of the output of the application:

```
n = 10,000 (CPU = 38.00
           (cpu = 1.17 s gpu = 1.14 s phi = 1.19 s)
           (1.30 s 1541.47 gflops)
```

for a random matrix of size $n = 10,000$. The weight used for each device in this example results in a workload rather well balanced.

5.5.1.3 Energy consumption

We are also interested in evaluating the energy consumption of the devices participating in the matrix multiplication with the aim at, first, understanding the power trace of each device and, second, exploring a workload distribution which can result in energy savings.

For the energy measurement, we have used a tool called powerrun [344]. This tool is a wrapper to other tools for measuring the power draw of the CPU (uses PAPI and Intel PCM), of the GPU (uses NVML [345]), and of the PHI (uses Intel's MPSS [346]). The tool gathers the power samples of all the devices under operation and dumps a power trace to a file to compute the energy consumed during the execution time. This tool provides a library to instrument the code under test with simple calls that frame the part of the code to be measured.

We provide here three tests that show the energy consumption (in joules) of the three devices, respectively. In each test, the three devices are operating concurrently. Only one of them is working on a matrix multiplication, while the other two remain idle. The test samples the energy of the three devices.

Figure 5.19 (a) shows the energy consumed by the system when only the CPU is "working" and is rather easy to interpret. The CPU is the most consuming device since it is the only one that performs useful work, while the other two consume the energy in the idle state. It is also quite clear the difference in energy consumption between the two accelerators when idle being very low in the case of the NVIDIA GPU compared with the Intel Xeon Phi.

Figure 5.19(b) shows the energy consumption when the GPU is the only device operating on a matrix multiplication. Note that one of the cores of the CPU is also

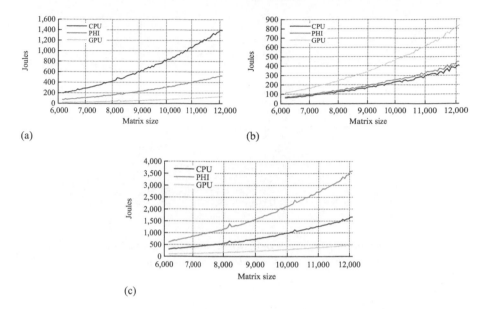

Figure 5.19   *Energy consumption when executing a matrix multiplication in the (a)
CPU, (b) GPU, or (c) PHI while the other two devices remain idle*

working since it is in charge of sending the two matrices to be multiplied and receiving
the resulting one. The consumption of the Intel Xeon Phi is very large in the idle state
when compared with the CPU.

As expected, the consumption of the Intel Xeon Phi is quite large when executing
the matrix multiplication (Figure 5.19(c)). Also in this case, one of the cores of the
CPU is working to feed the coprocessor with the two factor matrices and to receive
the solution matrix.

5.5.2   Experimental results of the matrix multiplication application

Figures 5.20 and 5.21 show the execution time in seconds spent by the application
to perform a matrix multiplication of two square matrices of sizes $n = 8,000$ and
$n = 14,000$, respectively. The two graphics show times for different weight combinations. The percentage of computation carried out by the GPU is shown on the y-axis,
while the work done by the PHI is shown on the x-axis. These two values are selected
by the user. The rest of the computation is performed by the CPU. The figure shows
less execution times (clearer cells) within the region between $\approx 25\%$ and $\approx 50\%$ for
the GPU, and $\lesssim 20\%$ for the PHI in the case of the problem sizes selected. There exists
more opportunity for the PHI to participate as long as the problem size increases.

Figure 5.22 shows the percentages of the minimum values obtained for the problem sizes $n = 8,000$, 10,000, 12,000, and 14,000, which are 0.72 s, 1.30 s, 2.08 s,
and 3.20 s, respectively. For large problems both the CPU and the GPU reduce their
weight to make room for the PHI, which does not contribute to the task with any size

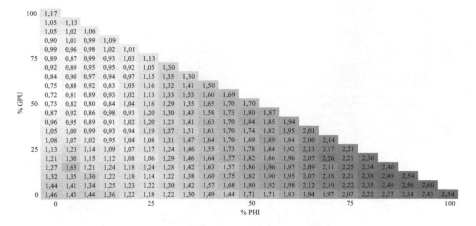

Figure 5.20   Execution time in seconds for a matrix product of size n = 8,000 varying the weight of workload on each device

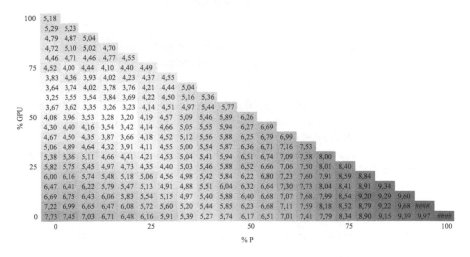

Figure 5.21   Execution time in seconds for a matrix product of size n = 14,000 varying the weight of workload on each device

smaller than $n = 12,000$. We can approximate the weight of each device, i.e. w_{cpu}, w_{gpu}, and w_{phi},[1] by the two linear functions shown in Table 5.14 for two intervals. By means of a larger experimental setup, we could easily devise a functional model that allows one to predict the best percentage of workload to be mapped on each device. However, we must take into account that there exist a problem size not very much smaller than $n = 2,000$ for which it is not worthwhile to use the GPU. Also, for problem sizes

---

[1]Note that the number of matrix columns assigned to a device d is $n_d = n \cdot w_d$, where d = cpu, gpu, phi.

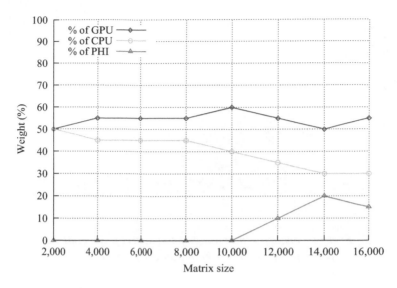

Figure 5.22   Functional model in graphics for the execution time of the matrix multiplication

Table 5.14   Functions of the weight for each device for the execution time of the matrix multiplication

	$n \in [2{,}000{,}10{,}000]$	$n \in [10{,}000{,}14{,}000]$
$w_{phi} =$	0	$\dfrac{n}{200} - 50$
$w_{gpu} =$	$\dfrac{n}{800} + 47.5$	$-\dfrac{n}{400} + 85$
$w_{cpu} =$	$100 - w_{gpu}$	$100 - (w_{phi} + w_{gpu})$

$n > 14{,}000$, the weight to be assigned to each device stabilizes around a fix value ($w_{phi} \approx 15\%$ and $w_{ghi} \approx 55\%$). However, as the problem size increases a little more, out-of-core algorithms are required and these functional models can significantly change.

Things are slightly different when we observe the total energy consumed by the matrix multiplication application. The minimum values of energy (in joules) are 379, 700, 1,177, and 1,783, for the problem sizes 8,000, 10,000, 12,000, and 14,000, respectively. Figures 5.23 and 5.24 show, as an example, the energy consumption with problem sizes $n = 8{,}000$ and $n = 14{,}000$, respectively. The corresponding weights of w_{gpu} in which we can find these minimum values are 55%, 60%, 60%, and 60%, for each problem size, respectively, and 0% for w_{phi}. These numbers show that while Intel

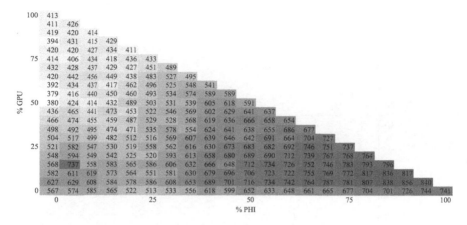

Figure 5.23   Energy consumption in joules for a matrix product of size n = 8,000 varying the weight of workload on each device

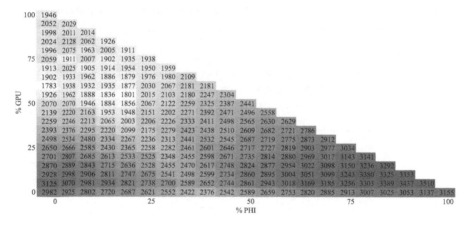

Figure 5.24   Energy consumption in joules for a matrix product of size n = 14,000 varying the weight of workload on each device

Xeon Phi can contribute a little to reduce the execution time, it can contribute nothing toward reducing the energy consumption in any case, as it was expected according to Figure 5.19(a)–(c). The NVIDIA GPU is, currently, a more efficient device for HPC. In this particular server and for large problem sizes ($n > 10,000$), the Intel Xeon Phi is used as a trade-off between execution time and total energy consumption.

We also figured out the dynamic energy of the application, i.e. the energy due to the execution of the application and that we obtain after taking away the energy consumed by each device in the idle state. The results showed that we can find the minimum value for the dynamic energy for all problem sizes when none of the accelerators are used. This is due, on one hand, to the high energy consumption of the PHI and, on the other hand, to that the NVIDIA GPUs has two different performance states (when idle) that are difficult to control and disturb the actual energy measurement when the device is idle.

5.5.3 Conclusions

This work has presented an application for matrix multiplications in a heterogeneous node composed by a multicore CPU and two very different accelerators. We have shown that it is not difficult to implement the application using OpenMP subsections. However, the incompatibility among compiler versions can make this task a bit cumbersome, and in addition, selecting the exact suitable value for the large number of environment variables is an arduous task that highly affects the performance of the application.

We have reduced the study of our application to a particular case in which all matrices involved are square. This case is motivated by the existence of many applications that involve only square matrices like, e.g. the evaluation of matrix polynomials, which is the core operation to obtain matrix functions using the Taylor method. However, the study can be extended to rectangular matrices with little effort. We have developed a functional model for the runtime so that we can select the proper amount of work to do by each device. In our node, the K40 is the most speedy device, far more than the Xeon Phi, which only has opportunity to contribute to the computation on matrices larger than $n = 10,000$. Furthermore, the Xeon Phi is currently the most expensive device in terms of energy consumption, and the K40 is the most energy efficient. Our study on the energy consumption resulted in a quite simple behavior, i.e. the lowest total energy consumption is achieved when the GPU is used in a similar proportion as that selected to achieve the lowest execution time, provided the Xeon Phi is not used at all. It was impossible to obtain an accurate measure of dynamic energy due to specific behavior of the GPU, which changes between two different performance states (when idle) in an unpredictable way. Finally, we proposed a heterogeneous matrix multiplication system to make easy the programmability of algorithms based on a heterogeneous matrix multiplication.

5.6 Summary

Energy is a challenge for very large-scale systems. Thus, there are several challenges that arise for midterm research, and possible approaches to address the future research topics and challenges:

Ultra-large-scale profiling and monitoring for reporting energy usage: Possible approaches include lightweight monitoring approaches using hardware support, accurate models allowing energy estimation (as in the case of RAPL), big data/machine learning techniques to cope with data sizes and complexity.

Multi-objective energy metrics: Metrics relevant for ultrascale, for example, power proportionality, scalability per J, trade-off with resilience, efficiency scalability, and data movement efficiency on all levels.

Models and simulation of energy consumption of UCS: In general, applying simulations to ultrascale systems will require simplified but accurate empirical modeling, stochastic approaches, and machine learning. Research may include machine learning approaches, such as decision trees, linear regression, regression trees and artificial neural network. Energy simulators should include models of energy consumption of heterogeneous hardware to simulate it in ultrascale. Such approaches will work with data collected in heterogeneous cloud infrastructure, running different types of hardware configurations (meaning different CPUs and different types of network hardware and topologies) and different types of virtualization technologies. Energy simulators should also model lightweight virtualization techniques.

Energy efficient resource management and scheduling: Possible approaches may include approximate algorithms taking into account risk of failures and assuming inaccuracy of information. They could use stochastic and machine learning methods for management. On single resources level today technology allows the logic isolation of jobs at a still significant performance costs. Therefore, low cost context switch and low cost process reallocation are features that need to be improved in order to achieve effective resource sharing policies. For virtualized infrastructures, the workload dynamic consolidation techniques should take advantage of very lightweight virtualization techniques and attempt to allocate large numbers of virtualized tasks in such a way to efficiently use the shared (possibly heterogeneous) resources. Additionally, adjusting execution to energy demand response and local renewables characteristics can help to significantly reduce energy costs and carbon footprint of ultrascale systems.

Energy efficient algorithms and eco-design of applications: Applications should be automatically analyzed and represented as a graph where nodes represent tasks that can be compiled and run in any of the computing elements of the system. Many bibliography addresses the scheduling of such kind of graphs but it is still a challenge to automatically generate quality graphs from application's code, especially with a focus on maximizing energy efficiency.

To face these challenges, we will need the adoption of intelligent methods for modeling and improving energy efficiency, to increase awareness and focus on energy efficiency in all UCS areas, and to design software taking the advantage of heterogeneous hardware and infrastructure.

Chapter 6
Applications for ultrascale systems

Svetozar Margenov[1], Thomas Rauber[2], Emanouil
Atanassov[1], Francisco Almeida[3], Vicente Blanco[3],
Raimondas Čiegis[4], Alberto Cabrera[3], Neki Frasheri[5],
Stanislav Harizanov[6], Rima Kriauzien[6], Gudula Rünger[7],
Pablo San Segundo[8], and Adimas Starikovicius[6], Sandor
Szabo[9], and Bogdan Zavalnij[9]

Many large-scale scientific applications have a need for ultrascale computing due to scientific goals to simulate larger problems within a reasonable time period. However, it is generally agreed that applications have to be rewritten substantially in order to reach ultrascale computing dimensions.

The needed reformulation of algorithms and applications from different areas of research toward their usage for ultrascale systems and platforms has to address different challenges that arise from the different application areas, algorithms and programs. The challenges include scalability of the applications using a large number of system resources efficiently, the usage of resilience methods to include mechanisms to enable application programs to react to system failures, as well as the inclusion of energy-awareness features into the application programs to be able to obtain an energy-efficient execution. The programming models should enable to concentrate on the algorithmic aspects and problem-specific issues of the specific application area such that program development is supported as far as possible.

Some of these topics are addressed in the previous chapters, while this chapter is concerned with the usage of corresponding results in the context of large-scale applications. An important issue is the integration of the techniques developed to

[1] Institute of Information and Communication Technologies, Bulgarian Academy of Sciences, Bulgaria
[2] Institute for Computer Science, University Bayreuth, Germany
[3] Departamento de Ingeniería Informática y de Sistemas, Universidad de La Laguna, Spain
[4] Faculty of Fundamental Sciences, Vilnius Gediminas Technical University, Lithuania
[5] Faculty of Information Technology, Polytechnic University of Tirana, Albania
[6] Institute of Data Science and Digital Technologies, Vilnius University, Lithuania
[7] Computer Science Department, Chemnitz University of Technology, Germany
[8] Center of Automation and Robotics, Universidad Politecnica de Madrid, Spain
[9] Institute of Mathematics and Informatics, University of Pecs, Hungary

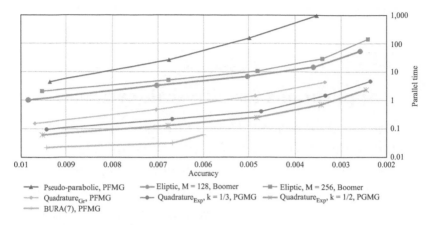

Figure 6.1　Application areas amendable for ultrascale computing

address the different aspects into the application programs. This chapter shows several aspects to adapt the former solutions to ultrascale applications, exploring algorithms, applications, and the impact of their translation into ultrascale systems.

The usage of ultrascale systems and platforms will allow for extension of existing application models and programs such that larger problems can be considered and more accurate solutions can be computed, giving the users from the different application areas a potentially significant benefit from ultrascale computing. However, the underlying algorithms, methods, and techniques have to be suitable for an execution on ultrascale systems and platforms, i.e. the required scalability, resilience, and energy-efficiency requirements have to be fulfilled at this level. Only if these requirements are fulfilled, it can be expected that the resulting application is suitable for ultrascale computing. A successful implementation of an ultrascale application may also require a switch to new algorithms and simulation techniques that are more suitable for ultrascale computing than existing approaches. Reasons may be a better inherent scalability of the new algorithms, a better locality of reference behavior, or less dependencies between the computations of the algorithm, thus enabling a more efficient parallelization also for heterogeneous ultrascale architectures. However, such a switch may involve a significant re-formulation of the application, since the algorithmic structure is usually deeply intertwined with program control.

A list of application areas and approaches that are likely amendable for ultrascale computing are summarized in Figure 6.1. The related present research topics and challenges include:

- **Methods and algorithms for coupled multiphysics problems:** (i) Operator splitting methods and algorithms; stable semi-implicit time stepping; splittings for multidimensional problems in space; splittings/decompositions with respect to physical processes; (ii) Monolithic methods; fully adaptive implicit time integration and asynchronous time integration; composite block preconditioned iterative methods for strongly coupled problems; (iii) Optimal control methods and multi-objective optimization;

- **Multilevel/multigrid methods and algorithms:** (i) Robust multilevel methods for ill-conditioned problems; hierarchical basis methods; local/additive Schur complement approximations; (ii) Multilevel methods for structured and unstructured grids; geometric and algebraic methods and algorithms; (iii) Meshless and particle-based methods; scalability and communication reduction by data locality; (iv) Model reduction methods; singular value decomposition and moment matching; parallel model reduction of large dynamical systems;
- **Parallelism:** (i) Balancing communications and computations for basic classes of numerical algorithms; (ii) Reducing global communications; avoiding transposition of data;
- **Data science methods:** (i) From big data mining to big data analytics, compressive sampling, matrix completion, low-rank models, and dimensionality reduction; efficient learning and clustering; robustness to outliers; scalable, online, active, decentralized, deep learning, and optimization; (ii) Big data analytics relying on MapReduce type methods; opportunistic/heterogeneous computing; (iii) From text ontologies to video and multimedia analytics: video semantic content analysis;
- **Simulation:** (i) Conservative methods for coupling quantum/particle and continuum methods; examples include extension of the chip analysis to the gate level, coupling with photon-based thermal models; (ii) Discrete event simulations of large circuits with conservative and optimistic methods; (iii) Scalable methods and algorithms for Internet of things problems; (iv) Break-through in simulation in molecular dynamics; (v) Stochastic simulations in systems biology; methods in computational chemistry and bioinformatics; drug discovery and in-silico drug design; simulations related to global climate changes.

The rest of the chapter is organized as follows. The next section is devoted to the topic of application-specific analytical energy models. Power and energy consumption have increasing importance with the scale of HPC applications, being an inherently integral part of the parallel efficiency. Scalable parallel algorithms for numerical solution of problems with fractional powers of elliptic operators are presented in Section 6.3. The non-local phenomena are concerned with materials whose behavior at any interior point depends on the state of all other points. The computational complexity of super-diffusion problems is one of the advanced application areas amendable for ultrascale computing. Another non-local problem is the topic of Section 6.4 where the HPC scalability of 3D relaxation gravity inversion is discussed. The numerical tests presented in last two sections are performed on the HPC system Avitohol at the Institute of Information and Communication Technologies, Bulgarian Academy of Sciences, once again demonstrating the cooperation of NESUS partners from several different countries. Advanced topics of graph algorithms in the spirit of ultrascale computing are included in Section 6.5. The problem of massive parallelization of the maximum clique problem is addressed. The theoretical estimates are supported by representative numerical tests. A brief summary is given in Section 6.6.

6.1   Application-specific analytical energy models

The energy consumption of application software is getting more and more important, especially for applications with a larger execution time. The hardware manufacturers have reacted to the growing interest in energy-efficient computing by developing energy-aware hardware features, such as dynamic voltage and frequency scaling (DVFS), core-independent functional units, multicore and hyperthreading, or on-chip power management units to control the power and energy consumption of the individual parts of the processor. Moreover, energy-efficient computing units such as GPUs (graphical processing units) or FPGAs (field programmable gate arrays) are employed for executing application codes.

The energy consumption of application codes also depends on the application-specific computational demands during execution. For example, even different implementations versions of an application code may lead to quite large differences in the resulting energy consumption due to a different usage of processor components or the memory hierarchy. Moreover, different applications or implementation versions may react differently to hardware parameters, such as the frequency or the numbers of cores of a multicore processor chosen for the execution run. In general, it is not a priori clear which application code is especially suited for an to energy-efficient execution and which parameter setting should be used. To guide the programming and the execution run toward energy efficiency, it would be beneficial to have information about the power and energy consumption expected. This information can be provided by a power and energy model which estimates the resulting energy consumption before execution. However, research has shown that it is difficult to capture all aspects and influencing factors for a large variety of application codes on a given hardware system within one model. Thus, application-specific energy models seem more appropriate. These models take the underlying architecture and application code characteristics into account.

This section describes analytical power and energy models that have been proposed to capture the power and energy behavior of different application classes. It is shown how the energy consumption of application codes can be measured and modeled, and how application-specific parameters can be integrated. Metrics that have been proposed to capture the energy efficiency of applications beyond the energy consumption given in Joule are described, such as the energy-delay product (EDP). A broad range of use cases are provided covering parallel applications and benchmarks for shared memory as well as message-passing distributed memory models. Their measured power and energy values as well as suitable models are presented.

6.1.1   Motivation

Power and energy models are often based on the architecture characteristics and the power consumption of their components. Examples are the modeling of the power and energy behavior for DVFS, which is described in more detail in Section 6.1.3.1, or the roofline model extended for energy. These kind of models can be very detailed and can give insight into the general power and energy behavior for the processor used, thus providing important information about the potential power and energy drawing of the architecture. The qualitative behavior of the power drawing with respect to some parameters is a useful tool for a first assessment of the power consumption to be expected. However, especially the amount of the dynamic power consumption for the active computation may vary for the specific application codes, as runtime experiments on various processors have shown. These differences in the power drawing stem from a specific exploitation of architecture components by the application code. For example, compute-bound applications occupy the compute facilities more intensely than memory-bound applications, which stress more on the communication facilities. In cases in which the quantitative behavior of the power and energy consumption is required, the particular application should be included in a prediction model if possible.

The power drawing of the Stanford Parallel Applications for Shared-Memory (SPLASH-2) can serve as a first motivation example of the diverse behavior of the power drawing. Figure 6.2 shows measurements of the power consumption of all SPLASH-2 applications on the Haswell architecture using eight threads. The shape of the power curves shows that all SPLASH-2 application programs have the same qualitative behavior of the power consumption. More precisely, the power consumption increases with the operational frequency and the highest power consumption is achieved for the highest frequency possible on that processor. However, the quantitative amount of power consumption varies strongly between the different applications with respect to the starting value and the gradient of the power curve. The behavior of the power curves indicate that an application-specific modeling is needed to capture

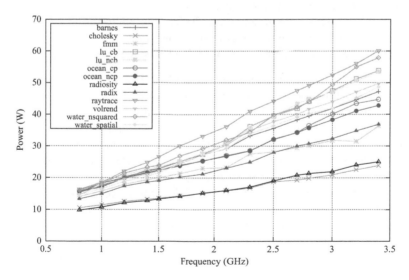

Figure 6.2   Power consumption of the SPLASH-2 benchmarks using eight threads on an Intel Core i7 Haswell processor

the quantitative power behavior with respect to the frequency. Also, an increase of the power consumption with the number of threads has been observed, not shown in this figure. Measurements have shown that there is a larger variation between the power consumption of the different applications when the number of threads is increased. Further details and an application-specific modeling of the power consumption of the SPLASH-2 benchmarks are discussed in Section 6.1.3.3.

6.1.2 Measuring power and energy

This section enumerates different measurement techniques and tools that are currently used to obtain energy and power measurements. Also, the different metrics used to represent energy efficiency and energy consumption in power-aware computing are summarized.

6.1.2.1 Energy measurement techniques

Energy consumption data and power monitoring capabilities of current high-performance computing (HPC) and ultrascale systems are often more limited. In many cases, only aggregate and approximate data are available. Portability also remains as an issue, as there exists plenty of interfaces that can be accessed at hardware and software levels.

Energy measurement hardware

Hardware sensors can be classified into three major categories, considering the scope of its implementation:

- Integrated sensors, where specific hardware components (such as a GPU or CPU) already contain measurement circuitry.
- Intra-node sensors, instrumentation devices placed inside the node that can perform probing at a component or power lane level.
- External power meters, measuring total load outside the power supply.

Each approach presents a tradeoff between precision of measurement, temporal resolution, cost of deployment, and intrusiveness.

Integrated processors require access a manufacturer specific interface. Intel processors from Sandy Bridge onward implement the Running Average Power Limit (RAPL) interface, which provides running counters of total energy consumed per package. Accelerators can also provide these interfaces to access to specific data at a hardware level. Nvidia GPUs provide instant power draw values through a CAPI, the Nvidia Management Library (NVML), while the Intel Xeon Phi exposes a greater number of power sensors through its System Management Controller chip. Some manufacturers also provide interfaces to access power data at a mainboard level; the Advanced Configuration and Power Interface (ACPI) open specification and the Intelligent Platform Management Interface (IPMI) are two examples of this type of interface.

For the purposes of dynamic application power profiling, the integrated sensors typically available often do not provide the necessary level of measurement accuracy and subsystem coverage. This has led to the development of intranode custom instrumentation by the scientific community. For example, the Linux Energy Attribution and Accounting Platform instruments a system's main board to provide power readings using a data acquisition board, PowerPack is composed of a collection of hardware sensors, meters and data acquisition devices and a software stack, and the Power-Mon line of devices is inserted between a system's power supply and motherboard, monitoring voltage and current on direct current rails to components.

Measurement performed through the power supply of a node is straightforward with no intrusion. However, the power draw values are very rough, as they contain no detail on which components are using the energy and have a very low polling rate. Dedicated power meters can be inserted between a system and a wall outlet and can also provide monitoring capabilities through multiple interfaces.

Energy measurement software

Many different software tools can be used for power and energy analysis, from low-level software interfaces to full-fledged analysis frameworks, including profilers, tracing and visualization systems, and estimation and modeling tools as shown in Figure 6.3.

The Performance API (PAPI), from the University of Tennessee, is well established as a library interface for hardware performance counters. In recent years, it has included support for many energy measurement sources.

The Energy Measurement Library (EML) is an open-source C library developed at Universidad de La Laguna providing a simple interface for acquisition of hardware energy consumption data through code instrumentation.

Pmlib is a software package developed at Universitat Jaume I to research the power-performance of parallel scientific code, using a client/server model.

PowerAPI is an attempt from Sandia National Laboratories to standardize access to power measurement data and power control at all levels of a given HPC facility, down to hardware components.

Larger profiling frameworks, with tracing and visualization systems, are usually built on top of PAPI and other libraries, using them as data providers for

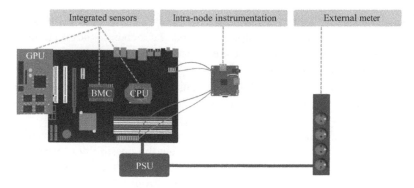

Figure 6.3   Overview of different measurement tools for energy measurement

larger analysis and visualization frameworks. These include Paraver, Vampir, or HPCView.

6.1.2.2   Metrics to capture energy efficiency

The traditional energy measurements for power (*Watts*) and energy (*Joules*) are not enough when we consider the multi-objective approach for energy and time that results in the energy efficiency of a system or an algorithm. For high-performance systems, more metrics have been used in the literature to characterize the level of efficiency achieved:

FLOP/s per unit of energy (*flops per watt, flops per joule*), the energy delay product (*EDP*), f (*timetosolution*) $\cdot$ *energy* (*FTTSE*), and The Green Index (*TGI*).

Flops per watt was introduced as a metric to take performance and energy efficiency into account. This metric was specified to rank high-performance computers different to the Top500 list, in the well-known Green500 list.

EDP was introduced to evaluate trade-offs between circuit-level power-saving techniques. It has been used to establish a relation between the energy and performance of processors at an architectural level.

FTTSE, f (*timetosolution*) $\cdot$ *energy* is proposed as a step forward from flops per watt, as the latter is focused in high sustained performance and does not consider the time spent to achieve a solution, a requirement of Exascale systems, in order to achieve a reasonable power draw.

Finally, **TGI** is introduced as a metric to aggregate the energy efficiency of a benchmark in a single number. It is a measurement similar to the *Standard Performance Evaluation Corporation (SPEC) rating*, in which the TGI represents the "greenness" of a system by providing a performance-to-watt metric relative to a reference system.

6.1.3   Application-specific energy models

Energy models describing the behavior of the energy consumption of specific applications are elaborated. General power and energy models are addressed first and then application-specific aspects are included.

6.1.3.1   General power and energy models for frequency scaling

The energy consumption E_A of an application code A depends on the execution time of A and the power P_A consumed during the execution. The power consumption P_A varies during the execution, which results in $E_A = \int_{t=0}^{T_A} P_A(t)dt$ for application A executed from time $t = 0$ to $t = T_A$. Since the variations of P_A during the execution time are difficult to capture, the average power consumption is often used as approximation, which leads to $E_A = P_A \cdot T_A$, where T_A is the execution time of A.

The DVFS mechanism influences the power consumption and the execution time of an application. DVFS systems typically provide the possibility to vary the operational frequency f of a processor in discrete steps between a maximum frequency f_{max} and a minimum frequency f_{min}. Typical values for desktop processors are $f_{min} = 0.8$ GHz and $f_{max} = 3.4$ GHz, e.g. for the Intel Haswell and the Skylake architecture.

Typical values for server processors are $f_{min} = 1.2$ GHz and $f_{max} = 3.0$ GHz for the Intel Broadwell processor. To capture the effect of DVFS on the power consumption, power models have been proposed which usually distinguish two contributions to the overall power consumption which are the dynamic power consumption P_{dyn} and the static power consumption P_{stat}, see [348,349] and the references therein. The dynamic power consumption P_{dyn} is intended to model the power consumption related to the computing activity of the processor, which may differ between applications due to different computational behavior and different usage of the computing resources of the processor. To model the dependence of P_{dyn} on the operational frequency f, the following formula:

$$P_{dyn}(f) = \alpha \cdot C_L \cdot V^2 \cdot f \qquad (6.1)$$

has been proposed with switching probability α, load capacitance C_L, and supply voltage V. The supply voltage depends linearly on f such that $V = \beta \cdot f$ and therefore (6.1) can be expressed as

$$P_{dyn}(f) = \alpha \cdot C_L \cdot \beta^2 \cdot f^3. \qquad (6.2)$$

According to (6.2), a modification of the operational frequency f can have a large influence on the resulting dynamic power consumption due to the cubic dependence, which is captured by

$$P_{dyn}(f) = \frac{P_{dyn}(f_{max})}{f_{max}^3} \cdot f^3 \qquad (6.3)$$

where $P_{dyn}(f_{max})$ denotes the dynamic power consumption for the highest frequency on the hardware system, which typically leads to the highest power consumption. The static power consumption P_{stat} is used to model the resulting leakage power. Different approaches have been proposed to model P_{stat}, including a linear dependency on f of the form $P_{stat}(f) = V \cdot N \cdot k_{design} \cdot I_{leak}$ with the number of transistors N, the hardware design parameter k_{design}, and the hardware technology parameter I_{leak} and an independence on f of the form $P_{stat}(f) = $ constant [348]. In the following, the constant application-specific static power model is assumed, which results in the total power for application A:

$$P_{total}^A(f) = P_{dyn}^A(f) + P_{stat}^A. \qquad (6.4)$$

The operational frequency also affects the execution time of an application A, expressed by $T_A = T_A(f)$. A reduction of the operational frequency f of a processor from f_{max} to f increases the execution time of A, which results in $T_A(f) = T_A(f_{max}) \cdot f_{max}/f$, if the dependence is linear. However, some applications exhibit a nonlinear behavior. The resulting energy consumption is modeled as

$$\begin{aligned} E_A(f) &= P_A(f) \cdot T_A(f) \\ &= \left(P_{dyn}^A(f_{max}) \cdot (f/f_{max})^2 + P_{stat}^A(f) \cdot (f_{max}/f) \right) \cdot T_A(f_{max}) \end{aligned} \qquad (6.5)$$

From (6.5), it is not a priori clear whether a reduction of f may lead to a reduction of the energy consumption, since the execution time increases and the power consumption decreases when the operational frequency is decreased. Runtime experiments have shown that a reduction is achieved until a threshold is reached, which is usually application specific. The actual effect depends on the application and its specific implementation as well as on the execution situation, including the number of threads or processes used and the setting of application-specific parameters. Sections 6.1.3.3 and 6.1.3.4 describe multithreaded applications and their power and energy modeling.

6.1.3.2 Theoretical and application-specific models

A wide variety of application-specific models has been developed in recent years. Different techniques have been applied to analyze the energy-efficiency applications in order to improve its efficiency, and therefore, reduce the overall power and energy consumption.

The Roofline Model of Energy [350] defined a model for algorithm designers and performance tuners, with high-level analytic insights into the relationship of energy, power, and time costs of an algorithm, expressing algorithms in terms of operations, concurrency, and memory traffic.

Analytical energy models have been achieved for master–slave applications, the high-performance Linpack (HPL) benchmark, and MPI communications OSU microbenchmarks, are models obtained for specific applications extending a time model with architectural and power parameters.

ALEPH is proposed to solve the bi-objective optimization problem for performance and energy ($BOPPE$) for manycore systems. Using energy and time models, it is able to determine a Pareto-optimal front of solutions.

6.1.3.3 Power modeling for the SPLASH-2 benchmarks

The Stanford Parallel Applications for Shared-Memory (SPLASH-2) is a collection of multithreaded benchmarks with different parallel workloads and execution characteristics. SPLASH-2 provides programs from a wide range of applications from scientific computing and graphics, including Cholesky and LU factorization or raytracing and radiosity algorithms. Thus, the SPLASH-2 benchmarks are ideal for demonstrating and testing the analytical energy models proposed. As hardware platforms, the Intel Haswell architecture is used for the experimental evaluation. Model-based power, energy, and EDP values are calculated and are compared with corresponding measurements on these processors [349].

The application-specific modeling is based on the energy consumption formula (6.5) by determining application-specific parameters for P_{dyn}^A and P_{stat}^A. This is done by using the least-squares method and the power model from (6.4), for which the values for $P_{dyn}(f)$ and P_{stat} are calculated based on the measured data on Intel multicore processors shown in Figure 6.2. The result of the power modeling for the benchmark barnes on the Intel Core i7 Skylake architecture is given in Fig 6.4. The static power, the dynamic power, and the overall power are depicted with respect to the operational frequency. Data for $p = 1$ and $p = 8$ threads are given. The constant behavior of the static power for both thread values can be observed as well as the increasing curves of the dynamic power. The level is higher for the parallel case with $p = 8$ threads. The curves denoted Power for $p = 1$ and $p = 8$ are the measured values. The total power

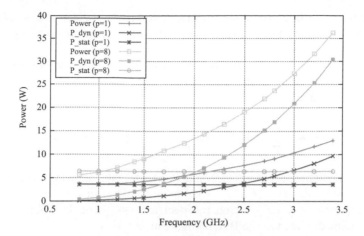

Figure 6.4   Modeling of the power consumption of the SPLASH-2 benchmark
barnes using one thread and eight threads of an Intel Core i7 Skylake
processor

of the model has to add the values of the curves P_{dyn} and P_{stat} for $p = 1$ and $p = 8$, respectively. The close match between the measurements and the model can be seen. When comparing the modeled power data for the benchmark barnes (which close to the measured data) with the measured data of barnes in Fig 6.2 on the Haswell architecture, it can be observed that the power level on the Skylake is lower than that on the Haswell architecture. This indicates that an application-specific power modeling has to take the application and the architecture used for the execution run into account.

6.1.3.4   Power modeling for multithreaded RK methods

Initial value problems of systems of first-order ordinary differential equations (ODEs) with system size $n \geq 1$ are given as

$$\mathbf{y}(x) = \mathbf{f}(x, \mathbf{y}(x)) \text{ with } \mathbf{y}(x_0) = \mathbf{y}_0 \tag{6.6}$$

The unknown solution function $\mathbf{y}(x)$ is a vector as is the right-hand side function $\mathbf{f}$ and the initial value $\mathbf{y}_0$ at point x_0. Runge–Kutta (RK) methods are numerical approximation methods for the solution of such ODEs, which result from including additional Euler steps into the well-known Euler method. The family of Runge–Kutta methods includes explicit and implicit approximation methods, which are applied with respect to the stiffness of the problem (6.6) to be solved.

Explicit RK methods compute a series of approximation vectors $\mathbf{y}_0, \mathbf{y}_1, \mathbf{y}_2 \cdots$ which approximate the exact solution at discrete x-values $x_0, x_1, x_2, \ldots$. One approximation step with s stages, which computes $\mathbf{y}_{\kappa+1}$ from $\mathbf{y}_\kappa$, $\kappa = 0, 1, 2, \ldots$, has the form:

$$\mathbf{k}_l = \mathbf{f}\left(x_\kappa + c_l h_\kappa, \mathbf{y}_\kappa + h_\kappa \sum_{i=1}^{l-1} a_{li} \mathbf{k}_i\right), \quad l = 1, \ldots, s \tag{6.7}$$

The vectors $\mathbf{k}_1, \ldots, \mathbf{k}_s$ are the stage vectors, the value h_κ is the step size used in the specific approximation step κ, i.e., $x_{\kappa+1} = x_\kappa + h_\kappa$, and $\mathbf{y}_\kappa$ is the previous approximation vector.

The stage vectors $\mathbf{k}_1, \ldots, \mathbf{k}_s$, computed in (6.7) are used to compute the next approximation vector $\mathbf{y}_{\kappa+1}$ and an additional approximation vector $\hat{\mathbf{y}}_{\kappa+1}$ for error control and step-size adaption:

$$\mathbf{y}_{\kappa+1} = \mathbf{y}_\kappa + h_\kappa \cdot \sum_{l=1}^{s} b_l \mathbf{k}_l, \quad \text{and} \quad \hat{\mathbf{y}}_{\kappa+1} = \mathbf{y}_\kappa + h_\kappa \cdot \sum_{l=1}^{s} \hat{b}_l \mathbf{k}_l. \tag{6.8}$$

The computation scheme (6.7) and (6.8) uses the following coefficients: the s-dimensional vectors $b = (b_1, \ldots, b_s)$, $\hat{b} = (\hat{b}_1, \ldots, \hat{b}_s)$ and $c = (c_1, \ldots, c_s)$, as well as the $s \times s$ matrix $A = (a_{il})$, which are specific for the particular RK method chosen and are usually depicted in the Butcher tableau.

For explicit RK methods, the matrix A is a strictly lower triangular matrix. The order r of the approximation vector $\mathbf{y}_{\kappa+1}$ and the order $\hat{r}$ of the second approximation vector $\hat{\mathbf{y}}_{\kappa+1}$ typically differ by 1 so that $r = \hat{r} + 1$ holds. An asymptotic estimate of the local error in the lower order approximation is computed by the difference between the two approximations $\mathbf{y}_{\kappa+1}$ and $\hat{\mathbf{y}}_{\kappa+1}$. This is used for stepsize control. The approximation vector of the current step κ is accepted, if a suitably weighted norm of the local error estimate lies within the predefined tolerance level. Although the estimate of the local error is in the lower order approximation, the more accurate approximation is usually taken to advance the integration (local extrapolation).

The coarse structure of an RK implementation is a while loop over the time steps, each of which computes a new approximation vector $\mathbf{y}_{\kappa+1}$ at time step $x_{\kappa+1}$. The computation of each new approximation vector comprises the computation of the arguments for the function evaluations that are required for the computation of the stage vectors $\mathbf{k}_1, \ldots, \mathbf{k}_s$, see (6.7), and the function evaluations of the right-hand side function $\mathbf{f}$ of the ODE system to be solved for these arguments.

There are several strategies to implement one time step, which differ in the way of the loop structures. More precisely, the loop over the stage vectors, the loop over the argument vectors, and the loop over the system size can be arranged in different ways, see [351]. Four different shared-memory versions implemented with Pthreads are chosen. All shared-memory versions of the RK methods distribute the computation of the different argument vectors, function evaluations, and approximation vectors among the threads. Synchronization operations are needed to ensure that the computation of the function evaluations is not started before all components of the argument vector have been computed by the different threads.

For these four versions, application- and implementation-specific power and energy models are derived from the models in Section 6.1.3. The derivation is based on measured power values to which the model from Section 6.1.3 is fitted by linear regression. Table 6.1 reports the resulting parameter values obtained by the modeling for the power function (6.4) along with the root-mean-square deviation (RMSD), which measures the standard deviation between the predicted and the measured power consumption values, i.e. smaller RMSD values indicate a better fit than

Table 6.1 Power modeling for the RD ODE on Broadwell

Version	Version 1	Version 2	Version 3	Version 4
$P_{dyn}(f_{max})$(W)	29.79	31.41	33.71	38.01
P_{stat}(W)	13.99	13.74	12.43	9.96
RMSD	1.29	1.32	1.42	1.03

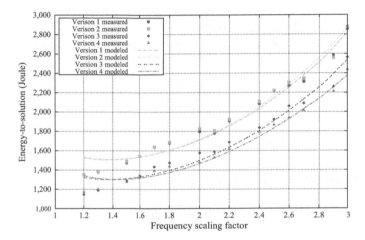

Figure 6.5 Comparison of measured and modeled energy consumption of the four RK implementation versions on an Intel Xeon Broadwell with 10 cores using 20 threads

larger RMSD values. The RMSD values are computed as $\sqrt{WSSR/ndf}$, where $WSSR$ is the weighted sum of squared residuals, also referred to as chi-square, and ndf is the number of degrees of freedom, which is 13 in our case, since 15 different frequencies are investigated and two parameters are to be determined. The result of the modeling and a comparison with the measured energy values is shown in Figure 6.5.

The results exemplify that the modeling of the power consumption not only depends on the application but also on the specific implementation version used.

6.1.3.5 Power modeling for MPI communications

The OSU microbenchmarks given by the Department of Computer Science and Engineering at The Ohio State University are tests designed to measure the performance of MPI implementations in a system. From all the tests included in the benchmark, two models were developed: Point-to-Point MPI communications and Collective MPI communications (*osu_latency* and *osu_bcast*, respectively).

Send/Recv (*osu_latency*) tests are carried out in a ping-pong fashion. The sender sends a message with a certain data size to the receiver and waits for a reply from the receiver. The receiver receives the message from the sender and sends back a replay with the same data size. Many iterations of this ping-pong test are carried out and average one-way latency values are obtained.

The Broadcast test (*osu_bcast*) measures the min, max, and the average latency of the *MPI_Bcast* collective operation across N processes, for various message lengths, over a large number of iterations.

Using intranode communications in a single Sandy Bridge processor, two models are proposed [352]: a model for predicting energy and a model for predicting energy consumption derived from a time model. Both functions depend on the number of processes (this does affect only *osu_bcast*), p, and the message size, n, and two different architectural parameters β and τ.

The different expressions for both time and energy in the broadcast configuration are

$$T_{bcast}(p, n) = \beta_{bcast}^t + \tau_{bcast}^t(p) \cdot n \tag{6.9}$$

$$E_{bcast}(p, n) = \tau_{bcast}^e(p) \cdot n \tag{6.10}$$

$$E'_{bcast}(p, n) = \sum_{i=1}^{p} P(p, c_i) \cdot T_{bcast}(p, n) \tag{6.11}$$

Analogous to these, the *MPI_Send/MPI_Recv* formula is

$$T_{send/recv}(n) = \tau_{send/recv}^t \cdot n \tag{6.12}$$

$$E_{send/recv}(n) = \tau_{send/recv}^e \cdot n \tag{6.13}$$

$$E'_{send/recv}(n) = \sum_{i=1}^{nc} P(c_i) \cdot T_{send/recv}(n) \tag{6.14}$$

For both cases, the architectural parameters are dependent on the process allocation in the underlying architecture. Equations (6.11) and (6.14) are derived from the basic energy equation of $E = P \cdot T$. However, by observing the experiments performed, three different states for the cores inside the processor were noticed: idle cores when the whole socket is idle, pseudo-idle cores that are not executing code, but belong to a socket where at least one process is allocated, and active cores where the communications are held.

These results obtained from both models are reflected in Tables 6.2 and 6.3. Table 6.2 presents the errors in % obtained from the experimentation for the Send/Recv operations. While the Energy model E is better overall, the maximum error obtained from the Energy model derived from Time E is 3.11%. In the broadcast experimentation, presented in Table 6.3, the results obtained for both models are pretty similar, with a maximum of 5.85% for the Energy model E, and 2.48% for the Energy Model derived from E.

6.1.3.6 Power modeling for the high-performance Linpack

The HPL is the standard benchmark to measure sustained computation in HPC systems. The importance of this benchmark comes from its usage to rank the capabilities

Table 6.2   Error comparison between Send/Recv models presented

	Error (%)			
	Config. A		**Config. B**	
N	**Model**	**Alt-Model**	**Model**	**Alt-Model**
2,000	0.57	3.11	−0.50	−1.59
3,000	0.02	2.58	−0.88	−1.97
4,000	−0.43	2.13	−0.05	−1.13
5,000	−0.17	2.39	−0.02	−1.11
6,000	−0.26	2.31	0.18	−0.90
7,000	0.23	2.78	−0.15	−1.23
8,000	0.08	2.64	−0.27	−0.81

Table 6.3   Error comparison between broadcast models presented for 16 processors (P = 16)

	Error (%)			
	Config. A		**Config. B**	
N	**Model**	**Alt-Model**	**Model**	**Alt-Model**
2,000	−2.99	−2.48	−0.59	−1.99
3,000	−2.01	−1.51	−1.09	−0.91
4,000	−1.62	−1.12	−0.08	−0.01
5,000	−0.90	−0.41	0.43	0.03
6,000	0.14	0.64	−5.85	0.10
7,000	0.30	0.79	1.07	1.22
8,000	0.02	0.52	0.18	1.16

of HPC systems in the Top500 list by measuring the achievable sustained number of double precision floating operations per second (*flops*). This list, updated every June and every November, serves as world reference to track the advances in computing capabilities of these HPC systems. Another list that serves also as reference is the Green500 list. In this case, measurement is focused on power-aware computing capabilities by taking into account flops per unit of energy (*flops/w* or *flops/J*) and thus obtaining a list of the most energy-efficient computers in the world.

In the HPL, data is distributed through the system using a two-dimensional layout for the processors, P and Q, in a cyclical scheme, to ensure the scalability and the balance of the parallel computers. A matrix of $Nx(N + 1)$ coefficients is separated in multiple blocks of NB by NB, and are assigned appropriately to the processes, in order to perform an LU factorization to solve a linear equation system, with multiple configurations available for broadcasting the partial results of every iteration.

The following model estimates the time consumed by a single execution of the HPL:

$$T_{HPL} = \frac{2N^3}{3\gamma PQ} + \tau \frac{N^2(3P+Q)}{2PQ} + \beta \frac{N((NB+1)log(P)+P)}{NB} \tag{6.15}$$

The three terms of (6.15) represent computation and communication separately. The first term represents the theoretical time for solving the linear system without communication, with γ representing the computing capabilities of a single node in the target architecture. The second and third terms represent the bandwidth and the latency, respectively, with the τ and β being architectural parameters for the most commonly used broadcast routine.

Since the time model is complex and contains many parameters, the authors decided to extend the time model by adding power measurements to obtain the energy consumption model [353]. This was done by characterizing the power consumption of the different phases of the HPL benchmark, which resulted in the inclusion of two new parameters, $P_i^{comp}(c)$ and $P_i^{comm}(c)$, for the computation and communication phases, respectively, of the i-th processor, when c cores are active.

$$E_i^{HPL}(c_i) = P_i^{comp}(c_i)\frac{2N^3}{3\gamma PQ}$$

$$+ P_i^{comm}(c_i)\left[\tau\frac{N^2(3P+Q)}{2PQ} + \beta\frac{N((NB+1)log(P)+P)}{NB}\right]$$

$$E^{HPL} = \sum_{i=0}^{np} E_i^{HPL}(c_i) \tag{6.16}$$

The resulting expression would have as many terms as processors are involved in the execution, which could be simplified to the different types of architectures involved in the benchmark, where each term would represent a concrete processor and would have its architectural parameter representing its energy consumption as shown in (6.16).

The validation of the model is illustrated in Figure 6.6. The model has very low error until the maximum amount of available memory is exceeded, the model no longer works as disk swapping is not considered in it. Table 6.4 allows a better visualization of the values measured and modeled, with their corresponding relative error.

6.1.4 Summary

The use cases presented in the previous section reflect the diversity and expressiveness of application-specific power and energy models. In particular, the following results are documented:

- Although application-independent energy models are well suited to give insight into the qualitative behavior of the energy consumption, e.g. in dependence on the degree of parallelism or the operational frequency, there is a need for

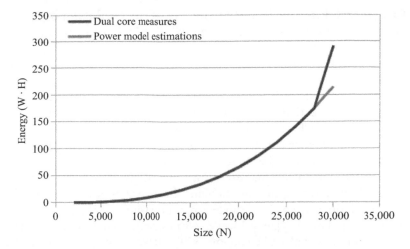

Figure 6.6 Energy consumption and energy estimated in W · h for HPL in an Intel Xeon Dual Core with 2 processes per node

Table 6.4 Energy consumption in W · h for 2 processes per node executions using 8 nodes (16 processes)

Size (N)	Time (s)	Measured (W·h)	Modeled (W·h)	E_{rel} (%)
4,000	1.20	0.71	0.68	5.02
8,000	7.42	4.82	4.61	4.49
12,000	23.26	15.45	14.7	5.07
16,000	51.11	34.49	33.87	1.84
20,000	96.76	66.04	65.03	1.55
24,000	162.76	111.55	111.09	0.41
28,000	253.68	174.68	174.98	0.17

application-specific energy models when the quantitative behavior is a concern. The investigations have shown that the result of the application-specific modeling mimics the qualitative behavior of the application-independent models but shows a significant variance in the amount of power or energy.

• The selection of application examples chosen in the investigation cover shared-memory applications, such as the multithreaded ODE-solvers, and message-passing applications as well as benchmarks being a black box for the end user. It has been shown that an application-specific power and energy modeling is possible for these use cases and that the models introduced can serve as power and energy prediction models for the respective class of application or benchmark.

6.2   On parallel algorithms for the numerical solution of problems with fractional powers of elliptic operators

It is known that Leibniz, in his correspondence with Bernoulli, L'Hospital and Wallis (1695), had several notes about the calculation of $D^{1/2}u(x)$. The further development of the theory of fractional calculus is due to the contributions of a plead of famous mathematicians such as Euler, Liouville, and Riemann. A bum of various results in this area has emerged in the last two decades. Presented study is strongly motivated by some particularly attractive numerical methods for problems with fractional powers of elliptic operators appeared during the last few years.

The nowadays remarkable interest in fractional diffusion models is provoked by numerous applications related to Hamiltonian chaos and non-local continuum physics [354,355], discontinuities and long-range forces in elasticity [356], anomalous diffusion in complex systems [357], non-local electromagnetic fluid flows [358], fractional Cahn–Hilliard models of phase separation [359], contaminant transport in multiscale porous media [360], materials science [361,362], modeling of fiber enforced soft tissues and related biomedical applications [363], image segmentation [364], denoising and deblurring [365,366], to name just a few.

The non-local continuum field theories are concerned with materials whose behavior at any interior point depends on the state of all other points, rather than only on an effective field resulting from these points. In some models, the contribution of the whole space $\mathbb{R}^d$ is accounted. Such kind of applications lead to fractional order partial differential equations that involve in general non-symmetric elliptic operators see, e.g. [367]. An important subclass of this topic is the fractional powers of self-adjoint elliptic operators, which are non-local but self-adjoint. In particular, the fractional Laplacian [368] describes an unusual diffusion process associated with random excursions. In general, if the power $\beta \in (0, 1)$, the parabolic equations with fractional derivatives in time are associated with sub-diffusion, while the fractional elliptic operators are related to super-diffusion.

There are several different definitions of fractional power of elliptic operators. In our studies, we use definition based on the spectral decomposition of the elliptic operator and the following solution approach. The non-local problem with fractional power of the Laplacian is transformed into some local differential problem, formulated in a space of a higher dimension. An important advantage of this approach is that, due to the common use of such partial differential equations, the related numerical solution methods are well developed, and the available software packages (including the parallel ones) are subject to a long-time development and permanent improvements. We use the finite volume method and multigrid methods for numerical solution of the arising local elliptic problems.

Four different transformations are considered in our works [369–371]. The first one leads to elliptic problem with singular weight [372]. For the second one, the non-local problem is transformed into a pseudo-parabolic problem [373]. In the third approach [374], exponentially convergent quadrature formulas are applied to the integral representation of a sought solution. The last method [375] we consider is based on the best uniform rational approximation (BURA) of a scalar function in the interval [0, 1]. This method conceptually differs from the previous three, as the original dimensionality of the problem is preserved. Computationally, it is based on solving independently several linear systems that are positive diagonal shifts of the (original, non-fractional) discretized elliptic operator.

The introduced space dimension causes an essential increase in computational complexity of fractional-in-space diffusion problems compared to the classical diffusion problems. Parallel computing is necessary to make application of such non-local models more feasible and attractive. In our works, we develop different parallel algorithms for the numerical solution of problems with fractional powers of elliptic operators. We use master–slave, domain decomposition methods and open source parallel multigrid libraries for numerical solution of systems of linear equations. It is important to note that the four considered transformations lead to very different properties of the developed parallel algorithms. We investigate and compare their scalability, efficiency, and accuracy.

Some initial results on the strong scalability of three developed 2D parallel solvers are presented in [369]. Only 1D partitioning of problem domain was considered and the parallel multigrid solver from AGMG package [376] was used to solve the linear systems. A more detailed analysis was done in our extended paper [370], where both weak and strong parallel scalability using 1D, 2D, and 3D partitioning was analyzed. In that study, we employed the parallel algebraic multigrid preconditioner BoomerAMG from the well-known HYPRE library of parallel high-performance preconditioners [377,378]. The performance of parallel preconditioner, load balancing, synchronization and communication overheads were considered.

In [371] we have started the analysis of parallel solvers for 3D problems. The strong scalability of the parallel algorithms was studied, taking into account the accuracy of the selected numerical methods. This analysis enables one to compare how the convergence rate of the numerical methods depends on the smoothness of the solution. It is well known that the solutions of fractional differential equations become less regular in the case of stronger super diffusion. For instance, there are well-expressed boundary layers where the regularity is degrading. The smoothness depends on the fractional power of the elliptic operator. This lack of regularity is responsible for the reduced rate of convergence. For more details, see [379,380] and the references therein. Finally, in recent work, [381], the accuracy of the pseudo-parabolic and integral representation methods is compared experimentally for elliptic equations with fractional order boundary conditions on unstructured 2D grids.

The rest of this section is organized as follows. The problem under consideration is introduced in Section 6.2.1. In Section 6.2.2, we describe four transformations, denoted by A1–A4. The parallelization of the considered algorithms is discussed in Section 6.2.3. The applicability of different parallelization techniques is discussed leading to different scalability results for the examined solution methods. The finite volume approximations of the PDEs corresponding to A1–A4 are presented in Sections 6.2.4–6.2.7. We address some specific issues related to the accuracy and computational costs. A well-known 2D test problem is used in this analysis. The right-hand side is a piece-wise constant checkerboard function (see, e.g. [374,375]) leading to additional interface boundary layers. In Section 6.2.8, we provide a comparative analysis of the accuracy and the related computational time. The goal is to examine the efficiency of the parallel algorithms accounting for the targeted accuracy. Brief concluding remarks are given in Section 6.2.9.

6.2.1 Definitions of fractional power of elliptic operators

There are different definitions of fractional power of elliptic operators. Let us start with several comments on the definition of fractional Laplacian in bounded domain $\Omega \subset \mathbb{R}^d$ introduced through the Riesz potential:

$$(-\Delta)^\beta u(x) = C(d, \beta) P.V. \int_{\mathbb{R}^d} \frac{u(x) - u(x')}{|x - x'|^{d+2\beta}} dx' = f(x) \tag{6.17}$$

$u = 0$ in $\Omega^c = \mathbb{R}^d \setminus \Omega$, where P.V. stands for the principle value. In [382], error bounds in the energy norm and numerical experiments (in 2D) are presented, demonstrating an accuracy of the order $O(h^{\frac{1}{2}} \ln h)$ for solutions obtained by means of linear elements on a quasi-uniform mesh. The numerical solution of problems involving such a non-local operator is rather complicated. There are at least two major reasons for that: the handling of highly singular kernels and the need to cope with an unbounded region of integration. The straightforward numerical methods lead to systems of linear equations with dense matrices. For real-life large-scale problems, this approach is computationally too expensive.

In our studies, we use another definition, based on the spectral decomposition of the elliptic operator. The research about the relations between these definitions is still ongoing. However, it is known [380] that they are not equivalent and may produce different solutions over bounded domains. The weak formulation of the elliptic problem is: find $u \in V$ such that

$$a(u, v) := \int_\Omega (\mathbf{a}(x)\nabla u(x) \cdot \nabla v(x) + q(x)) \, dx = \int_\Omega f(x)v(x)dx, \ \forall v \in V, \tag{6.18}$$

where $V := \{v \in H^1(\Omega) : v(x) = 0 \text{ on } \Gamma = \partial\Omega\}$.

We assume that Γ has positive measure, $q(x) \geq 0$ in Ω, and $\mathbf{a}(x)$ is an SPD $d \times d$ tensor product matrix, uniformly bounded in Ω. Then, fractional power of elliptic operator $\mathscr{L}^\beta$, $0 < \beta < 1$ is introduced through its spectral decomposition, i.e.

$$\mathscr{L}^\beta u(x) = \sum_{i=1}^\infty \lambda_i^\beta c_i \psi_i(x), \qquad u(x) = \sum_{i=1}^\infty c_i \psi_i(x) \tag{6.19}$$

where $\{\psi_i(x)\}_{i=1}^\infty$ are the eigenfunctions of $\mathscr{L}$, orthonormal in L_2-inner product and $\{\lambda_i\}_{i=1}^\infty$ are the corresponding positive real eigenvalues. Let us assume again that linear elements are used to get the FEM approximation $U_h \in V_h$, with h being the mesh-size and $V_h \subset H_0^1(\Omega)$ being the space of continuous piece-wise linear functions over the mesh. In the case of full regularity, the best possible convergence rate for $f \in L^2(\Omega)$ is, cf. [374],

$$\|u - U_h\|_{L^2(\Omega)} \leq Ch^{2\beta} |\ln h| \, \|f\|_{L^2(\Omega)} \tag{6.20}$$

This estimate illustrates well the low FEM accuracy, depending on $\beta \in (0, 1)$. Therefore, some additional mesh refinement is needed to get a given targeted accuracy. In any case, this means stronger requirements on the solution methods that strengthen the motivation of our study on the related parallel algorithms.

6.2.2 State of the art in numerical algorithms

In a very general setting, the numerical solution of non-local problems is rather expensive. The following four approaches A1–A4 lead to transformation of the original problem $\mathscr{L}^{\beta} u = f$ to some auxiliary local problems:

A1 Extension to a mixed boundary value problem in the semi-infinite cylinder $\Omega \times [0, \infty)$ [372]. The semi-infinite cylinder is truncated to allow numerical solution in a bounded domain.

A2 Transformation to a pseudo-parabolic problem [383]. Stability conditions are obtained for the fully discrete schemes under consideration. This approach is further applied to problems with fractional order boundary conditions [381].

A3 Integral representation of the solution is used in [374]. Then, different quadrature formulas are applied to evaluate numerically the related integrals in $(0, \infty)$.

A4 An alternative approach is followed in [375] where solution methods for algebraic systems $L_h^{\beta} \mathbf{u} = \mathbf{f}$ are proposed and analyzed. They are based on the BURA of $t^{1-\beta}$ in the interval $[0, 1]$. The stable implementation of the involved Remez algorithm is of a key importance for further development and usage of the BURA methods.

All A1–A4 are applicable to fractional diffusion problems in computational domains with general geometry.

6.2.3 Parallel algorithms

Our study is focused on the parallel implementation of solvers based on transformation to elliptic (A1) and pseudo-parabolic (A2) problems, two variants of the integral representation (A3), and approximate solution using BURA algorithms (A4). The related different parallel algorithms can be characterized by rather different properties. We present results of the parallel scalability tests. All tests were performed on the "Avitohol" cluster at the Institute of Information and Communication Technologies (IICT) of the Bulgarian Academy of Sciences (http://www.iict. bas.bg/avitohol/). The cluster consists of 150 HP Cluster Platform SL250S GEN8 servers. Each computational node has 2 Intel® Xeon® processors E5-2650v2 @ 2.6 GHz (8 cores each), 64 GB RAM and 2 Intel® Xeon® Phi 7120P coprocessors. The computational nodes are interconnected via fully non-blocking 56 Gbps FDR InfiniBand network. Up to 64 nodes (1,024 cores) were used in our parallel tests.

In order to implement the developed parallel algorithms, we use the two-level parallel programming templates [384]. The efficient parallel multigrid solvers from HYPRE numerical library [377,378] are applied as preconditioners in the parallel conjugate gradient method. A similar approach was used also in [370,371]. On the first level, we define a set of discrete problems, which can be solved independently in parallel and these tasks are statically or dynamically distributed. On the second level, each discrete problem is solved by using the domain decomposition method and a specified parallel linear system solver based on preconditioned CG method. Two types of multigrid solvers from HYPRE numerical library are used as preconditioners in the parallel conjugate gradient method. To study the performance of considered parallel numerical algorithms on structured grids, we use the geometric multigrid solver PFMG. To estimate their performance on general non-structured grids suitable for general domains, we use the algebraic multigrid solver BoomerAMG.

Also, we have compared selected numerical algorithms in terms of accuracy and computational costs using the following 2D test problem:

$$\mathscr{L}^\beta u = f(x), \quad x \in \Omega = (0,1) \times (0,1), \quad u(x) = 0, \ x \in \partial\Omega \tag{6.21}$$

with the Laplace operator $\mathscr{L} = -\Delta$, $\beta = 0.25$, where the right-hand side f is the well-known checkerboard function (see [374,375]):

$$f(x) = \begin{cases} 1 & \text{if } (x_1 - 0.5)(x_2 - 0.5) > 0 \\ -1 & \text{otherwise} \end{cases} \tag{6.22}$$

We use as reference (exact) solution, the numerical solution obtained via Fourier algorithm on sufficiently fine uniform grid with $N = 32768 = 2^{15}$ discretization points in each direction (see Figure 6.7). The discrete error values for different N are shown in Table 6.5. In this paper, the relative errors are used: Error $= \|u - U_h\|_\infty / \|u\|_\infty$. For the given example, $\|u\|_\infty = 0.3904$. In accordance with the theory (6.20), reduced convergence rate $O(h^{2\beta}) = O(h^{0.5})$ is observed.

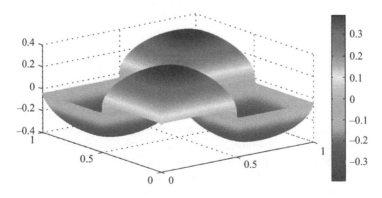

Figure 6.7   Solution $u(x)$ of the test problem (6.21)–(6.22)

Table 6.5 Accuracy of discrete solution U_h for problem (6.21)–(6.22)

Number of points N	128	256	512	1,024	2,048
Error		0.00946	0.00669	0.00473	0.00334	0.00236

6.2.4 Extension to a mixed boundary value problem in the semi-infinite cylinder $C = \Omega \times [0, \infty) \subset \mathbb{R}^{d+1}$

The non-local problem (6.21) is equivalent to the following classical local linear problem in the extended space $\mathbb{R}^{d+1}$ [372,385]:

$$-\frac{\partial}{\partial y}\left(y^\alpha \frac{\partial U}{\partial y}\right) + y^\alpha \mathscr{L}U = 0, \quad (x,y) \in C, \ \alpha = 1 - 2\beta \tag{6.23}$$

$$-y^\alpha \frac{\partial U}{\partial y} = d_\beta f, \quad (x,0) \in \bar{\Omega} \times \{0\}$$

$$U = 0, \quad (x,y) \in C_B = \partial C \setminus \bar{\Omega} \times \{0\}$$

where d_β is a positive normalization constant that depends only on β. Then, the solution of problem (6.21) is obtained by $u(x) = U(x,0)$.

In order to construct a finite volume approximation of (6.23), the semi-infinite cylinder is approximated by a truncated cylinder $C_Y = \Omega \times \{0, Y\}$ with a sufficiently large Y. A uniform mesh Ω_h is introduced in Ω and anisotropic mesh $\omega_h = \{y_j = (j/M)^\gamma Y, j = 0,\ldots,M\}$ is used to compensate the singular behavior of the solution as $y \to 0$, where $\gamma > 3/(2\beta)$ [372,385]. In this way, we obtain the mesh $C_{Y,h} = \Omega_h \times \omega_h$ for discretization of the extended problem.

Using the finite volume method and following the standard notations of the finite differences we define the discrete problem, which approximates (6.23):

$$-\left(y^\alpha_{j+1/2}\frac{U_{h,j+1} - U_{h,j}}{H_{j+1/2}} - y^\alpha_{j-1/2}\frac{U_{h,j} - U_{h,j-1}}{H_{j-1/2}}\right) \tag{6.24}$$

$$+\frac{y^{\alpha+1}_{j+1/2} - y^{\alpha+1}_{j-1/2}}{\alpha + 1}L_h U_h = 0, \quad (X_h, y_j) \in C_{Y,h}$$

$$-y^\alpha_{1/2}\frac{U_{h,1} - U_{h,0}}{H_{1/2}} + \frac{y^{\alpha+1}_{1/2}}{\alpha + 1}L_h U_h = d_\beta f_h, \quad X_h \in \bar{\Omega}_h \times \{0\}$$

$$U_h = 0, \quad (X_h, y_j) \in \partial C_{Yh} \setminus \bar{\Omega}_h \times \{0\}$$

where $y_{j+1/2} = \frac{1}{2}(y_j + y_{j+1})$, $H_{j+1/2} = y_{j+1} - y_j$.

The approximate PDE model (6.23) transforms the non-local fractional diffusion problem (6.21) into the well-studied case of elliptic PDE problems. However, this local differential problem is defined in a space of higher dimension. The finite volume discretization scheme (6.24) leads to a large system of linear equations. In the case of two-dimensional problem domain Ω, one has to solve a system with 7-point stencil of size $N_{x_1} \times N_{x_2} \times M$.

One standard approach for parallel solution of such problems is the domain decomposition method [386]. The discrete mesh of the problem domain and its associated fields are partitioned into sub-domains, which are allocated to different processes. Note that in our case, the discrete mesh $C_{Y,h}$ of the truncated cylinder $C_Y = \Omega \times \{0, Y\}$ has to be partitioned. We consider 1D, 2D, and 3D partitions in order to find the optimal decomposition.

We have used the parallel algebraic multigrid solver BoomerAMG from the well-known HYPRE numerical library [377,378] as a preconditioner for the parallel conjugate gradient method. The default parameter settings of BoomerAMG are applied, performing only a small tuning to adapt them to our problems. It is clear that the default parameters are optimized for the isotropic problems, thus there remains a potential possibility to improve the scalability of the solvers. The tolerance of the multigrid solver was set to 10^{-8} in all tests.

The accuracy and solution times of the parallel elliptic solver are shown in Table 6.6. The second order of convergence is observed in the introduced dimension and discrete error values from Table 6.5 are attained. Serial solution times T_1 are shown for the discrete problems that fit into single node's memory. Minimal parallel solution times T_p with optimal decomposition of the discrete mesh and corresponding speed-ups S_p are demonstrated using up to 512 parallel processes.

This parallel algorithm is very sensitive to the partitioning in the anisotropic y coordinate, which should be kept in one process. The parallel algebraic multigrid preconditioner is robust, and the number of iterations is stable for different numbers of the utilized processes and 2D topologies of grid partitioning. The solution time scales quite well for smaller number of processes. However, the setup costs of AMG preconditioner is taking the most of the total solution time (around 80% and more). For elliptic problems with grid aligned vertical anisotropy, it has been shown that geometric multigrid approach with horizontal semi-coarsening and vertical line smoothing is the most robust and efficient approach.

The detailed results of strong and weak scaling of the developed parallel solver are presented in [370]. The time per iteration scales well for our parallel solver up to

Table 6.6   The accuracy and solution times of the parallel elliptic solver on uniform space grid $N \times N$

N	M	Error	T_1	p	T_p	S_p
128	128	0.00985	13.03	48	1.02	12.80
128	256	0.00956	25.95	48	2.03	12.78
256	128	0.00703	56.36	64	3.29	17.11
256	256	0.00678	122.93	128	5.10	24.10
512	128	0.00503	236.95	256	6.86	34.56
512	256	0.00481	586.61	256	10.57	55.52
1,024	128	0.00360		512	14.85	
1,024	256	0.00341		512	29.36	
2,048	128	0.00258		512	53.95	
2,048	256	0.00241		512	144.19	

1,024 processes. The memory requirements of our elliptic problem solver, mostly of BoomerAMG preconditioner, are growing very fast. This limitation of the algorithm can be greatly improved by implementing some geometric multigrid algorithm based on a tensor-product approach with line smoothers over the vertical lines in the extended y direction.

6.2.5   Reduction to a pseudo-parabolic PDE problem

The solution of the non-local problem (6.21) is sought as a mapping [373,381]:

$$U(x,t) = (t(\mathscr{L} - \delta I) + \delta I)^{-\beta} f \qquad (6.25)$$

where $\mathscr{L} \geq \delta_0 I$, $\delta = \gamma \delta_0$, $0 < \gamma < 1$. Thus, it follows from (6.25) that function $U(x,1) = \mathscr{L}^{-\beta} f$ defines the solution of the non-local problem (6.21). The function U satisfies the evolutionary pseudo-parabolic problem

$$(tG + \delta I)\frac{\partial U}{\partial t} + \beta GU = 0, \quad 0 < t \leq 1 \qquad (6.26)$$

$$U(x,0) = \delta^{-\beta} f, \quad t = 0$$

where $G = \mathscr{L} - \delta I$. We see a typical property of such transformations, when instead of the non-local problem (6.21) a local pseudo-parabolic problem (6.26) is solved (in higher dimension space $\mathbb{R}^{d+1}$). By using the finite volume method for discretization in space and the Crank–Nicolson scheme for discretization in time, the problem (6.26) is approximated by the following discrete scheme [387]:

$$(t^{n-1/2}G_h + \delta I_h)\frac{\mathbf{U}_h^n - \mathbf{U}_h^{n-1}}{\tau} + \beta G_h \mathbf{U}_h^{n-1/2} = 0, \qquad 0 < n \leq M \qquad (6.27)$$

$$\mathbf{U}_h^0 = \delta^{-\beta} \mathbf{f}_h$$

where $G_h = L_h - \delta I_h$, $\mathbf{U}_h^{n-1/2} = (\mathbf{U}_h^n + \mathbf{U}_h^{n-1})/2$ and $t^{n-1/2} = (t^{n-1} + t^n)/2$.

The constructed finite volume scheme (6.27) implies that this numerical algorithm will advance in pseudo-time computing $\mathbf{U}_h^n$ from $\mathbf{U}_h^{n-1}$, solving one system of linear equations at each of M time steps. These systems are solved sequentially, one after another. Thus, the pseudo-parabolic numerical algorithm does not allow parallelism in the introduced new pseudo-time dimension. The usage of the proposed general two-level parallelization template is reduced only to the second level, at which discrete subproblems are solved in parallel. In the case, when the problem domain Ω is two-dimensional, the linear system will have 5-point stencil matrix, three-dimensional—7-point stencil matrix. We use a standard domain decomposition method for the parallel solution of pseudo-parabolic PDE problem (6.26). The discrete mesh of problem domain Ω and its associated fields are partitioned into sub-domains, which are allocated to different processes.

The errors and solution times of the parallel pseudo-parabolic solver are shown in Table 6.7. We see that the error values of the discrete solution from Table 6.5 are eventually obtained by increasing the number of time steps M. However, the numbers of time steps M for the uniform time grid should be taken quite large. This part of the algorithm can be improved if adaptive time stepping algorithms will be used.

Table 6.7   The accuracy and solution times of the parallel pseudo-parabolic solver on uniform space grid N × N

N	M	Error	T_1	p	T_p	S_p
128	592	0.00939	7.37	16	4.46	1.65
256	2,348	0.00676	102.76	16	26.29	3.91
512	9,216	0.00498	1,252.90	48	153.36	8.17
1,024	36,864	0.00353	24,712.00	96	950.42	26.00

One can easily see the similarities and differences between the (A1) and (A2) approaches. One of the important practical implications is the significantly smaller amount of memory required for the pseudo-parabolic algorithm—$O(N^2)$, compared to the elliptic approach—$O(N^2M)$. On the other hand, the parallel pseudo-parabolic algorithm does not have parallelism in the introduced additional dimension, i.e. in the pseudo-time. This structure of the algorithm poses restrictions on the size of the tasks that can be solved in parallel, thus leading to smaller sub-problems that are assigned to each of the parallel processes.

We have investigated both strong and weak scalability of the parallel pseudo-parabolic solver in our previous works [369–371]. The parallel multigrid preconditioner is robust for the solved problem, i.e. the number of iterations is quite stable. It increases only slightly with the number of parallel processes. The additional setup costs of the parallel BoomerAMG preconditioner for the pseudo-parabolic problem are not as large as for the elliptic problem solver, because of almost standard structure of the system matrix. It includes not only a diffusion term but also a positive diagonal matrix. Degradation of the efficiency of the parallel algorithm is clearly seen when the number of processes is increased. The efficiency of strong scaling is increasing when increasing the problem size.

6.2.6   Integral representation of the solution of problem (6.21)

The third numerical method is based on an integral representation of the solution of non-local problem (6.21) using the local elliptic operator $\mathscr{L}$ (cf. [374]):

$$\mathscr{L}^{-\beta} = \frac{2\sin(\pi\beta)}{\pi} \int_0^\infty y^{2\beta-1}(I + y^2\mathscr{L})^{-1}dy \tag{6.28}$$

Again, this problem is formally defined in a higher dimension space $\mathbb{R}^{d+1}$. To calculate integral in (6.28), three different numerical quadrature formulas are proposed in the literature, which we have used to develop three parallel numerical algorithms.

In the first algorithm [374], the integral (6.28) is first transformed to a sum:

$$\mathscr{L}^{-\beta} = \frac{2\sin(\pi\beta)}{\pi} \left[\int_0^1 y^{2\beta-1}(I + y^2\mathscr{L})^{-1}dy + \int_0^1 y^{1-2\beta}(y^2I + \mathscr{L})^{-1}dy \right] \tag{6.29}$$

Then, a quadrature scheme based on a graded partition of the integration interval $[0, 1]$ is applied to resolve the singular behavior of coefficient $y^{2\beta-1}$:

$$
y_{1,j} = \begin{cases} (j/M)^1/2\beta & \text{if } 2\beta - 1 < 0, \\ j/M & \text{if } 2\beta - 1 \ge 0, \end{cases} \qquad j = 0,\dots,M
$$

A similar partition is used to resolve the singularity of $y^{1-2\beta}$. The finite volume discrete operator L_h approximates the elliptic operator $\mathcal{L}$. Then, the integrals (6.29) to compute $L_h^{-\beta}\mathbf{f}_h$ are approximated as

$$
Q_{h,1}^{-\beta}\mathbf{f}_h = \frac{2\sin(\pi\beta)}{\pi}\left[\sum_{j=1}^{M}\frac{y_{1,j}^{2\beta} - y_{1,j-1}^{2\beta}}{2\beta}(I_h + y_{1,j-1/2}^2 L_h)^{-1}\mathbf{f}_h \right. \tag{6.30}
$$

$$
\left. + \sum_{j=1}^{M}\frac{y_{2,j}^{2-2\beta} - y_{2,j-1}^{2-2\beta}}{2 - 2\beta}(y_{2,j-1/2}^2 I_h + L_h)^{-1}\mathbf{f}_h\right]
$$

The second quadrature algorithm is defined on the uniform grid points $y_j = jh_y$ and $h_y = 1/\sqrt{M}$ [374]:

$$
Q_{h,2}^{-\beta}\mathbf{f}_h = \frac{2h_y\sin(\pi\beta)}{\pi}\sum_{j=-M}^{M}e^{2\beta y_j}\left(I_h + e^{2y_j}L_h\right)^{-1}\mathbf{f}_h. \tag{6.31}
$$

This approximation provides an exponential convergence to the discrete solution U_h. We note that for both quadrature algorithms (6.30) and (6.31) all $2M$ local discrete elliptic problems can be solved independently.

The third quadrature algorithm is defined as in [374]:

$$
Q_{h,3}^{-\beta}\mathbf{f}_h = \frac{2k\sin(\pi\beta)}{\pi}\sum_{j=-m_1}^{m_2}e^{2(\beta-1)jk}\left(L_h + e^{-2jk}I_h\right)^{-1}\mathbf{f}_h \tag{6.32}
$$

where $m_1 = \lceil \pi^2/(4\beta k^2)\rceil$ and $m_2 = \lceil \pi^2/(4(1-\beta)k^2)\rceil$. This approximation also provides an exponential convergence to the discrete solution U_h. The parameter $k > 0$ controls the accuracy of the approximation of integral and the number of local elliptic problems that need to be solved.

For parallel integral solvers, we have used the two-level parallel algorithm. The parallel processes are split into some number of groups. Values y_j of sums are distributed between these groups of processes statically or dynamically. For each received y_j value, the corresponding group of processes solves the discrete elliptic problem in parallel. We use the parallel programming templates [384] for master–slave parallelization on the first level.

The accuracy and solution times of the parallel quadrature solver with graded mesh (6.30) are shown in Table 6.8. The second order of convergence is observed in the introduced dimension, and discrete error values from Table 6.5 are attained. Minimal parallel solution times T_p with an optimal number of groups of processors and decomposition of the discrete mesh and corresponding speed-ups S_p are demonstrated using up to 256 parallel processes. Values of S_p till 114 are obtained for 256 processors.

Table 6.8   The accuracy and solution times of the parallel quadrature solver with graded mesh on uniform space grid $N \times N$

N	M	Error	T_1	p	T_p	S_p
128	128	0.009710	2.67	32	0.15	17.35
256	128	0.007041	9.90	64	0.47	20.87
512	256	0.004854	105.47	208	1.45	72.63
1,024	256	0.003517	505.51	256	4.41	114.50
2,048	512	0.002417	4,764.46			

Table 6.9   The accuracy and solution times of the parallel quadrature solver with exponential mesh on uniform space grid $N \times N$

N	m_1	m_2	k	Error	T_1	p	T_p	S_p
128	40	14	0.50	0.00956	0.43	16	0.062	6.90
128	89	30	0.33	0.00946	0.87	32	0.096	9.07
256	40	14	0.50	0.00678	1.56	32	0.13	11.89
256	89	30	0.33	0.00669	3.20	32	0.22	14.60
512	40	14	0.50	0.00482	7.97	96	0.25	31.81
512	89	30	0.33	0.00473	16.06	96	0.41	38.95
1,024	40	14	0.50	0.00343	38.66	256	0.71	54.58
1,024	89	30	0.33	0.00334	77.45	256	1.49	51.89
2,048	40	14	0.50	0.00245	185.00	256	2.37	78.01
2,048	89	30	0.33	0.00236	370.08	256	4.70	78.75

The accuracy and solution times of the parallel quadrature solver with exponential mesh (6.32) are shown in Table 6.9. The exponential order of convergence is observed in the introduced dimension, and discrete error values from Table 6.5 are attained. Minimal parallel solution times T_p with an optimal number of groups of processors and decomposition of the discrete mesh and corresponding speed-ups S_p are demonstrated using up to 256 parallel processes. Values of S_p till 78 are obtained for 256 processors.

Results of strong scaling for increasing problem sizes were shown in [370,371]. The parallel integral solver with one group ($g = 1$) is only slightly slower than the parallel pseudo-parabolic solver. The setup times are minimal when $g = p$, i.e. 2D or 3D elliptic subproblems are solved sequentially. Our tests have shown that a static cyclic distribution can be used for y_j tasks on the first level of parallelization, since obtained values of standard deviation s_g are quite small. We obtained a very good scalability and efficiency of the two-level parallel algorithm for 3D problem with speed-up S_p up to 248 using 512 processes (see in [371]).

We remind here that parallel BoomerAMG preconditioner was used in [370]. The setup times of parallel BoomerAMG preconditioner are relatively smaller for the quadrature solvers. However, they are still very significant and exceed the time of CG iterations. In this work, we have presented results obtained with geometric MG preconditioners, and thus the setup costs are minimal.

6.2.7 *Approximation of the solution of problem* (6.21) *using rational approximations*

The fourth algorithm is defined by using a different approach. Instead of transforming the non-local problem (6.21) to a locally defined classical PDE in a higher dimension space, the solution is directly approximated by a sum of discrete solutions of m local subproblems. The approximate solution is defined as in [375], namely,

$$\tilde{\mathbf{U}}_h = c_0 A_h^{-1} \tilde{\mathbf{f}}_h + \sum_{j=1}^{m} c_i (A_h - d_j I)^{-1} \tilde{\mathbf{f}}_h \qquad (6.33)$$

where the matrix and the right-hand side function are scaled as $A_h = h^2/8L_h$, $\tilde{\mathbf{f}}_h = (h^2/8)^\beta \mathbf{f}_h$. The coefficients of the rational function c_j and d_j are defined by solving the global optimization problem to find the BURA $r_m^*(t)$,

$$r_m(t) = c_0 + \sum_{j=1}^{m} \frac{c_j t}{t - d_j},$$

$$\min_{r_m} \max_{t \in [0,1]} |t^{1-\beta} - r_m(t)| = \max_{t \in [0,1]} |t^{1-\beta} - r_m^*(t)| =: \varepsilon_m(\beta)$$

The efficient modified Remez algorithm for computing BURA is proposed and investigated in [375].

Here, we remind some basic error estimates of such approximations. We have the following error bound:

$$\|\tilde{\mathbf{U}}_h - \mathbf{U}_h\|_{A_h} \leq \varepsilon_m(\beta) \|\tilde{\mathbf{f}}_h\|_{A_h^{-1}}$$

This estimate is quite nontrivial, since it is important to keep in mind that the matrix A_h defines a scaled operator L_h. Coefficients for $m \leq 7$ and some β values, approximation error estimates and results of numerical experiments are provided in [375]. For $\beta = \{i/8\}_1^7$ and $m \leq 30$, the errors $\varepsilon_m(\beta)$ are computed in [388] with high accuracy. The corresponding coefficients, however, are not available.

Solution of the non-local fractional diffusion problem (6.21) is transformed into a computation of sums (6.33). The corresponding $m + 1$ discrete elliptic subproblems again can be solved independently. Hence, the same two-level parallel algorithm can be used. However, the number of independent tasks is much smaller.

The accuracy and solution times of the BURA(m) solvers are shown in Table 6.10. By analyzing the accuracy of BURA(5) solutions, we see that the error values are close to values in Table 6.5 for $N \leq 128$, and BURA(6), BURA(7) for $N \leq 256$. The accuracy of BURA(m) solutions is decreasing with increased N due to the approximation error. Still we note that determination of coefficients c_j and d_j in (6.33) for arbitrary m and β is a non-trivial and computation demanding task [375].

6.2.8 *Comparison of accuracy*

Finally, we present the comparison in terms of the accuracy and parallel computational times for five numerical algorithms: elliptic (6.24), pseudo-parabolic (6.27),

Table 6.10   The accuracy and solution times of BURA(m) solver on uniform space grid N × N

	BURA(5)		BURA(6)		BURA(7)	
N	Error	Time	Error	Time	Error	Time
16	0.02697	0.009	0.02704	0.010	0.027025	0.010
32	0.01894	0.012	0.01893	0.013	0.018947	0.015
64	0.01339	0.022	0.01339	0.026	0.013380	0.029
128	0.00947	0.061	0.00946	0.072	0.009464	0.081
256	0.02775	0.209	0.00669	0.245	0.006691	0.280
512	0.07146	0.997	0.02804	1.164	0.006003	1.35
1,024	0.17077	4.82	0.05785	5.54	0.02803	6.43
2,048	0.06132	21.96	0.17017	26.11	0.05719	30.40

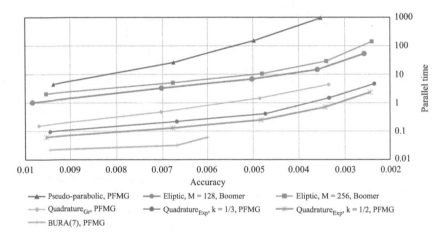

Figure 6.8   Comparison of parallel solvers in terms of accuracy

quadrature algorithm with graded mesh (6.30), quadrature algorithm with exponential mesh (6.32), and BURA(7) (6.33) algorithm. The reference (exact) solution was obtained for test problem (6.21)–(6.22) with $\beta = 0.25$ using the pseudo-spectral Fourier method [389] on uniform space grid with $N = 32,768$ points.

The parallel solvers are compared in terms of solution times T_p needed to achieve certain accuracy in Figure 6.8. Minimal parallel solution times are obtained with an optimal number of parallel processes and parameters of parallel algorithms. The corresponding speedups are shown in Figure 6.9.

6.2.9   Conclusions

Five different parallel numerical algorithms were developed for the numerical solution of problems with fractional powers of elliptic operators. The first four of them rely

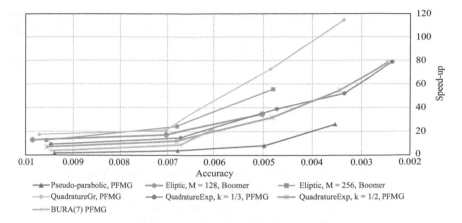

Figure 6.9 Speed-ups of parallel solvers

on transformations of the original non-local problem into well-known local PDE problems introducing an additional space dimension. The advantage of this approach is that due to the common use of these PDE models the related numerical solution methods are well developed. The available software packages (including the parallel ones) are subject to a long-time development and permanent improvements. However, the resulting parallel numerical algorithms have very different properties.

The performed analysis has shown that the selection of the best algorithm is problem dependent. The BURA method of rational approximation presents an attractive alternative if the high accuracy is not required and coefficients of the method for given fractional power β are known in advance. For the considered test problem, the relative accuracy of 0.006 can be achieved very cheaply with BURA(7) algorithm. Seeking more accurate solutions, the quadrature algorithm with exponential mesh has the smallest computational cost needed to achieve the required accuracy. However, it needs to be noted that the performance of some of the methods can be improved.

6.3 Scalability of 3D relaxational gravity inversion in HPC Avitohol

The old quest for the inversion of geophysical anomalies remains a difficult problem, with numerous methods developed in years, both manual and computer based. The difficulty is due to being a mathematically "ill-posed" problem [390]. In most of the engineering cases the traditional inversion implies generation of two-dimensional geo-section from one-dimensional data (case of 2D inversion) or three-dimensional geo-section from two-dimensional data (case of 3D inversion, the focus of this section).

The holographic principle cannot be fully applied for the traditional inversion because the field measured data is done in part of 3D geo-section boundary, usually in the ground surface that represents in average 1/6 of whole boundary; moreover, we used the simple formula of gravity potential $c*m/r$ and solution is not unique, the same anomaly may be obtained from different masses m in different depths r [391], [392]. And all this happens in geometrically and physically heterogeneous geo-sections.

There are numerous methods presented in the literature for 2D and 3D inversion, based on different ways the problem is attacked. A well-known practice is the reduction of calculations volume through mapping of 3D cases in 2D ones [393]. Other authors attempted simplification of geo-sections using 3D rectangular prisms [394] and convex geological structures [395]. "Exotic" methods are uses as well, for example, stochastic processes [396]. The multitude of methods indicates the difficulty of dealing with this "ill-posed" problem.

The uncertainty of inversion solutions is analyzed by authors as [397]. Typical negative phenomenon during the inversion is gradual variation in space of rocks physical parameters while in nature there is a clean contrast between different rocks. The other typical negative phenomenon is lack of separation for bodies in great depths, when the inversion creates an unreal in-depth single body instead of several ones, like a "bridge" between real bodies [398,399].

3D inversion is known to require huge computational capacities available in parallel systems. Different methods are experimented using parallel data processing by scholars as [400–403]. We have used a simple relaxational algorithm with the idea of reducing algorithmic complexities by compensating with the volume of computational time in parallel systems.

In this section, we describe scalability results from modified and simple relaxation algorithm for the 3D inversion of gravity anomalies in the HPC system Avitohol of Bulgarian Academy of Sciences. This algorithm was developed first during European Commission FP7 programme project HP-SEE, and the continuation of study was done for the COST IC1305 Action NESUS. The relaxation principle was implemented using a 3D mesh model representing the geo-section, updating in each iteration a single cell with a predefined "quanta" of mass density. Selection of the cell to be updated is based on weighted least squares method comparing observed anomaly with that of the model. Inversion was tested using simulations with one, two, three, and four vertical prismatic bodies. Scalability results confirmed the need for ultrascale computing systems in order to realize high-resolution inversions for engineering works.

The work started during the EC FP7 program project HP-SEE; first versions of the software were tested in several parallel systems made available during the project, starting with the local parallel system at Faculty of Information Technology, Polytechnic University in Tirana, the SGE system of the NIIFI Supercomputing Center at University of Pécs, Hungary, and the HP Cluster Platform Express 7000 operated by the Institute of Information and Communication Technologies, Bulgarian Academy of Sciences in Sofia, Bulgaria.

Results showed the need for higher parallel computing capacities, and the need for improving the algorithm in order to achieve a realistic separation of bodies in complex geo-sections. The actual work was done through collaboration of COST IC1305 action NESUS, aiming the scalability of algorithm using HPC system Avitohol at the Institute of Information and Communication Technologies, Bulgarian Academy of Sciences, also for trying some tuning of the algorithm to improve the quality of inversion.

6.3.1 Methodology of work

The idea of our relaxation method was obtained from the algorithm CLEAN for interpretation of radio-astronomy data, developed by Högbom [404]. The relaxation principle was applied generating step by step the discretized 3D geo-section through small "quanta" updates of mass density in one specific cell of the 3D mesh in each main iteration. This specific cell to be modified is selected scanning the whole 3D mesh, comparing the elementary anomaly of each cell with the shape of global anomaly, aiming for the best one that is subtracted from the latter. Following main iteration uses the reduced (i.e. relaxed) global anomaly as a goal to be reached.

Parallel programming was done with both techniques OpenMP and MPI, with the latter as a principal technique due to the lack of big HPC systems with shared memory as requested by OpenMP. Results of former work were published in [405–408]. The actual work was done using the HPC system Avitohol, a cluster of nodes each with 8 hyperthread processors (16 threads per node), where massive parallelization is possible with MPI.

Mathematically, the field observed data is represented by 2D points matrix G of dimensions $N_s N_t$, while the digitized 3D geo-section using 3D nodes matrix M of dimensions $N_i N_j N_k$.

Simple logic leads to the complexity of our iterative algorithm $O(N^8)$ for the same spatial extension of the geo-section, where N is the linear average dimension of used 2D and 3D matrices representing the spatial resolution of the geo-section. Main iterations are composed of $N^3 N^2$ *elementary iterations*, each of them calculates the impact of one 3D mesh cell at one of 2D surface measurement points.

Each 3D mesh cell represents an elementary *cuboid* composing the geo-section, and the change of N for the same spatial geo-section implies the change in size of mesh *cuboids* and the respective increase in the number of elementary iterations needed to generate the same mass distribution of the geo-section, which implies the complexity $O(N^8)$.

The identification in each main iteration of the 3D mesh cell to be updated was done scanning the 3D geo-section mesh. For each cell of the mesh (node M_{ijk}), its gravity impact A_{st} is calculated (an elementary iteration) for each surface point (s, t) where the anomaly G_{st} is measured.

The weighted least squares error was used as metrics to compare shapes of elementary anomalies (2D matrix A) generated by the 3D mesh cell (i, j, k), and that of the residual global anomaly (matrix G):

$$Err_{ijk} = \sum_{st} w_{st}(G_{st} - c * A_{st} - b_x x_{st} - b_y y_{st} - d)^2 \qquad (6.34)$$

where W is the 2D array of weights, c is the rock mass to be concentrated in the cell (i, j, k), and b_x, b_y, d are coefficients of the linear trend of the residual anomaly over the cell.

The role of subtracting linear trend from the residual anomaly was to avoid anomalous impact of the regional rock masses (case of multi-bodies geo-section) while considering the effect of a localized anomaly created by a single *cuboid* in the value of error Err_{ijk}.

Weights w_{st} were used to increase the weight of elementary anomaly central values in calculation of the error Err_{ijk}, and avoid peripheral values that tend toward zero.

The weights array W was calculated using the values of elementary anomalies:

$$w_{st} = \frac{A_{st}^{wc}}{\underset{count}{\sum_{st} A_{st}^{wc}}} \tag{6.35}$$

where *wc* is a constant defining the power of weights, and *count* is the number of counted elementary anomaly values ($count = N^2$ in our case).

In each main iteration, the best fit cell mass is increased or decreased with the predefined *quanta* of mass density, depending on the sign of constant c (6.34). After the contribution A of the elementary anomaly is subtracted from the residual observed one G, the absolute values summation of the latter was calculated and considered as the inversion error for the main iteration in course:

$$Err = \frac{\sum_{st} |G_{st}|}{N^2} \tag{6.36}$$

The algorithm as a function of mesh resolution was tested for geo-sections with one, two, three, and four vertical prismatic bodies (geo-sections with two and three body configurations are presented in Figure 6.10).

Theoretical field anomalies were calculated using the same software routines as used for the inversion. In Figure 6.11, the four bodies geo-section is presented together with the respective observed anomaly.

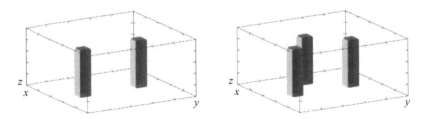

Figure 6.10   Geo-sections with two (left) and three body (right) configurations

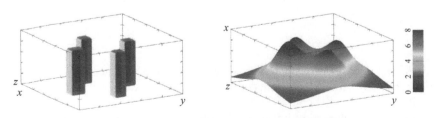

Figure 6.11   Four body geo-section (left) and its observed gravity anomaly (right)

For the inversion, we used geo-sections with dimensions 4,000 m × 4,000 m × 2,000 m, with mesh resolution 400, 200, and 100 m. Rectangular prismatic bodies were of dimensions 400 m × 400 m × 1,600 m situated from the bottom of geo-section up to the depth 400 m under the ground surface. Distance between bodies was 1,414 or 2,000 m depending on their reciprocal positions.

The iterative process was terminated when one of the conditions was fulfilled: until the best fit update of selected mesh cell (constant c in (6.34)) was less than half of predefined mass density *quanta*; or when the average error of last iterations experienced an increase.

6.3.2 Inversion quality results and discussions

Quality of the inversion resulted function of mesh resolution, number of bodies and weight power (the constant *wc* in (6.35)). Also, the constant c in (6.34) may be positive or negative, results indicated that accepting both or only positive updates impacted the quality of inversion. Scalability was calculated for the former case accepting both mass and density updates.

In Figure 6.12, the variation of inversion error as a function of weights power is presented. Oscillations of error, especially for the geo-section with four bodies, indicated the need for several runs of software for the same model in order to define the best weight power value. In our tests, we used the power value of 0.5.

In Figure 6.13, the increase of iterations number and the error variation as a function of geo-section bodies configuration and mesh resolution are presented.

While the increase of iterations number is apparently *normal*, the error experiences a sharp increase when the complexity of geo-section configuration changes from 1–2 to 3–4 bodies, especially for high-resolution meshes. We hypothesize that this increase of the error for three and four body geo-sections is related with the distances between prisms (Figures 6.10 and 6.11) compared with their heights and depths.

In Figure 6.14, results for two and three body inversion with mesh resolution 100 m are compared. The inversion of three bodies geo-section separates near-ground surface tops of prisms but fails in the depth, generating a single unreal body. One of the causes for such deformation is the fact that prisms are situated in corners of a horizontal triangle with two of edges shorter than their vertical length. When the software was run with the constraint of accepting only positive updates of mass density, and prisms positioned in distances relative to each other greater than their length, the results were much better (error reduced ten times) and inverted geo-sections are presented in Figure 6.15.

Such results show that for engineering purposes the calculations should be done for several combinations of parameters, in order to pick up the best achieved error. Our tests were done with a maximal resolution of 100 m that is insufficient for engineering purposes. Inversion of gravity is the simplest one compared with magnetism and electrometry methods of geophysics; in the case of magnetism the 3D distribution of a vector field is needed to compare with the scalar mass density field of gravity, while

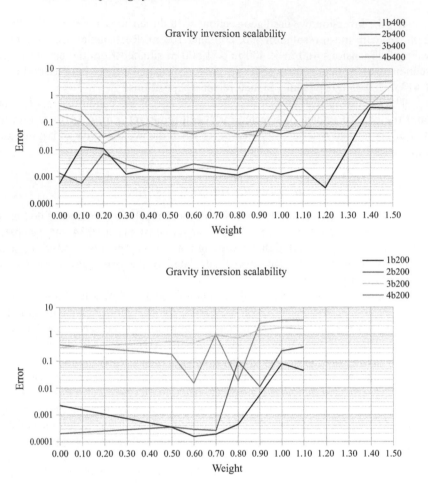

Figure 6.12   Error dependence on weight power for mesh with resolution 400 m (top) and 200 m (bottom)

in the case of electrometry methods the scattering of electrical field is modified by the properties of rocks and application of extra calculations (3D finite elements method, for example) are requested for each iteration. The scalability analysis indicates that ultrascale computing is necessary for practical purposes.

6.3.3   Scalability of inversion

Explained in the subsection of methodology, the theoretical complexity of the algorithm is $O(N^8)$, which was expected to be reflected in values of runtime.

Volume of data exchanged between MPI processes in each main iteration consists of few numbers—indices of the best fit cell, and the related weighted least squares error. Each process recalculates the new mass distribution into the geo-section mesh

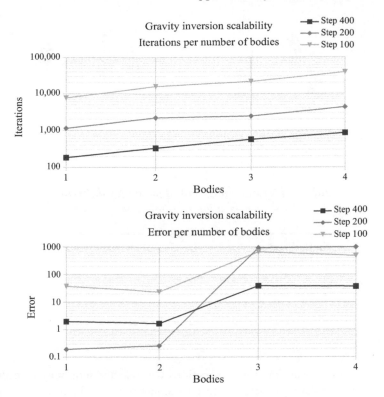

Figure 6.13 *Main iterations number (top) and error (bottom) as a function of number of bodies and mesh resolution*

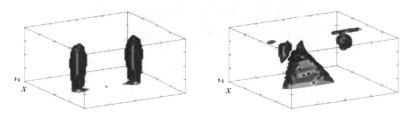

Figure 6.14 *Inversion of two body (left) and three body (right) geo-sections*

matrix *M* and the residual anomaly *G*. Because of small data exchange between processes, the impact of process communication is expected to be negligible.

At the same time, size of rock bodies that create anomalies should be proportional with the number of main iterations, each of them (iteration) increases the bodies mass with the predefined mass density *quanta*, as a result the size of rock bodies resulted proportional with the runtime as well.

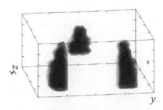 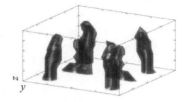

*Figure 6.15   Improved inversion of three body (left) and four body (right)
geo-sections*

*Table 6.11   Encoding spatial factors for different
geo-section resolution mesh*

Spatial factor	Mesh resolution (m)
1	400
2	200
4	100
8	50

The increase of runtime for geo-sections with one and four body configuration is shown in Figure 6.16. The spatial mesh resolution is encoded following the schema presented in Table 6.1 (runtime values for the models with spatial factor 8–50 m resolution, and for resolution 100 m in the case of four body model run in parallel with less than 32 processes are extrapolated).

Runtime data indicated that, when mesh cells sizes are divided by two, increase of runtime was increased at least 250 times. For the geo-section with four bodies and resolution 50 m running with 256 processes would take ≈1 day (86,400 s) in Avitohol. Practically, it would require 2,500 processing cores to achieve the calculation in a couple of hours and extrapolating for a resolution 25 m the runtime would increase to ≈26 days.

Decrease of runtime when increasing the number of parallel processes is shown in Figure 6.17 for geo-sections with one and four bodies. As expected from previous works, over-increasing of the ratio between processes number and model size is not effective, evident in the case of low-resolution models.

Speedup due to parallel execution is shown in Figure 6.18, for geo-sections with one, two, three, and four bodies, and resolution of 400 m (spatial factor 1) and 100 m (spatial factor 4). There is the expected degeneration of speedup for the low-resolution model. For a "reasonable" ratio between processes number and model size (case of spatial factor 4) speedup is the maximal possible one.

Speedup decrease for low-resolution models, when the number of parallel processes increases, is also reflected in plots of parallelization effectiveness in Figure 6.19.

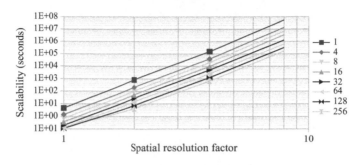

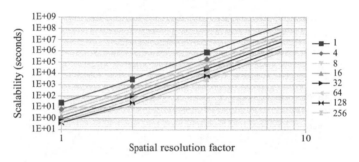

Figure 6.16   Runtime for one (top) and four body (bottom) geo-sections as a function of spatial mesh resolutions for different number of processes

Speedup of high-resolution 100 m is similar for geo-sections with different bodies, plot lines cover each other in Figure 6.18, and their minor variations are displayed "amplified" in plots of effectiveness.

At last, two tests were done accepting only positive changes of mass density for geo-sections of resolution 200 m with three and four bodies (inversion results shown in Figure 6.15). The error was improved ten times with a small increase in iterations and runtime; respective values are shown in Table 6.2. Improvement of the error varied 5–10 times for an increase of iterations and runtime up to 50%.

6.3.4   Conclusions

Quality of our relaxation algorithm can be evaluated from two pints of view, scalability related with the ratio between runtime and resolution, and quality of inverted geo-section related with separation ability of bodies in depth (ratios between their sizes, relative distances, and depths).

Complexity of the algorithm resulted $O(N^8)$ with effectivity over 90%, leading to a significant increase of runtime when the resolution of models increased for engineering purposes, requesting even days when running in thousand cores. Extrapolated

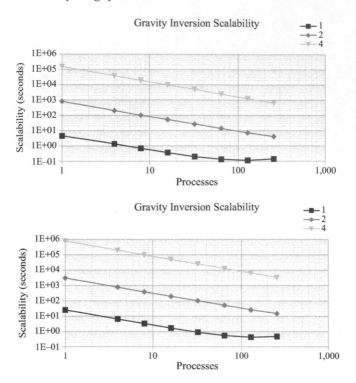

*Figure 6.17   Runtime for one (top) and four body (bottom) geo-sections as a
function of processes number, for different spatial mesh resolutions*

runtime for the inversion of a geo-section 4 km × 4 km × 2 km with resolution 25 m
resulted in 26 days in an HPC system as Avitohol.

The algorithm depends on parameters as least squares weights power and the mass
density *quanta*. Variation of inversion quality resulted complicated and difficult to be
evaluated a priori, requesting several runs of the software using different parameter
values in order to pick up the best possible error.

Comparing the simple gravity inversion from 2D ground surface data toward
3D geo-section, with seismic prospecting, the later consists of transforming 3D field
data (2D surface data multiplied by the third dimension—the time) to 3D geo-section.
In the case of electrometry methods, a redundancy of ground surface data obtained
through repeating measurements for different positions of power electrodes is used
traditionally to compensate the missing third dimension. In the case of gravity (and
magnetism), a third dimension may be obtained measuring the field intensity in
different heights through aerial surveys. The latter implies a complexity increase up
to $O(N^9)$.

The algorithm may be used for regional large-scale studies and anomalies from in-
depth structures, based on low- and medium-resolution geo-sections. High-resolution

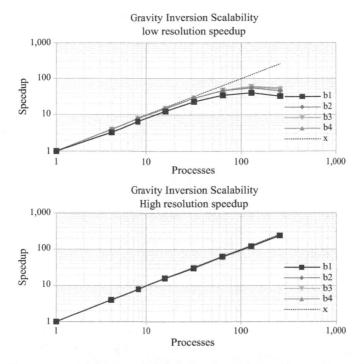

Figure 6.18   Speedup for resolution 400 m (top) and 100 m (bottom) as a function of processes number, for geo-sections with one, two, three, and four bodies

for small-scale shallow geo-sections may be used for engineering purposes, but for reasonable runtime of the algorithm HPC capacities are required. Also with interest to improve the scalability would be using GPU multicore hardware in desktop systems. Intensive calculations for high-resolution inversion of large-scale complex geo-sections may be only in ultrascale computing systems.

6.4   Massive parallelization of the k-clique problem using subchromatic functions[1]

In the near future problems arising from combinatorial optimization will be paramount for HPC and supercomputing. Today, only a few methods dealing with parallelization of such problems have been evolved. Also, most of them tend to divide the original problem into extremely unbalanced subproblems. It is also unclear which methods

[1]Acknowledgment: This report was supported by the NESUS STSM. Other support was by the Spanish Ministry of Economy and Competitiveness, grant DPI2017-86915-C3-3-R for Pablo San Segundo and by National Research, Development and Innovation Office—NKFIH Fund No. SNN-117879 for Sandor Szabo and Bogdan Zavalnij.

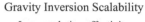

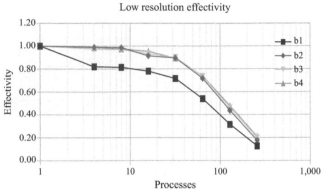

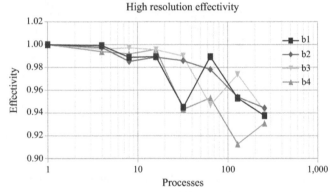

Figure 6.19   Effectiveness for resolution 400 m (top) and 100 m (bottom) as a function of processes number, for geo-sections with one, two, three, and four bodies

Table 6.12   Change of inversion quality for positive updates of mass density

Geo-section	Error	Iterations	Runtime
3 bodies	0.9355 => 0.0854	2,474 => 3,407	447.31 => 597.77
4 bodies	0.9916 => 0.1714	42,885 => 4,741	775.22 => 794.15

could be used for a more balanced partitioning, nor how to compare them. As a result there are only a few large-scale parallel programs available for combinatorial optimization. Motivated by these facts, ongoing research is concerned with new methods of research. The authors have chosen the k-clique problem as a representative combinatorial optimization problem. The aim of the present technical report is to

Table 6.13   The summary for the upper limit of $\omega(G)$ by different methods.

	$|V|$	Density	$\omega(G)$	Dsatur coloring	Iterated coloring	$\vartheta(\bar{G})$	pMax SAT	Edge coloring	5-fold coloring
1dc.512-c	512	92.56	52	83	74	53.03	136	65	56.8
1dc.1024-c	1,024	95.41	94	152	137	95.98	136	*	103
1dc.2048-c	2,048	97.22	172–174	304	268	*(174.73)	266	*	190.2
1et.1024-c	1,024	98.17	171	225	215	184.23	209	*	194.4
1et.2048-c	2,048	98.93	316	436	404	342.03	399	*	358.6
1tc.1024-c	1,024	98.48	196	241	229	206.3	225	*	217.2
1tc.2048-c	2,048	99.10	352	450	426	374.64	422	*	389.8
1zc.512-c	512	94.72	62	104	93	68.75	92	84	74.4
1zc.1024-c	1,024	96.82	112–117	201	177	128.67	176	*	138
2dc.1024-c	1,024	67.70	16	34	30	*	29	*	22.2
2dc.2048-c	2,048	75.93	24	65	54	*	53	*	38
brock800_2	800	65.13	24	134	118	*	117	79	107
brock800_4	800	64.97	26	136	118	*	117	79	106.4
C1000.9	1,000	90.11	68–	305	255	*	246	*	236.6
C250.9	250	89.91	44	92	78	56.24	71	70	76
C500.9	500	90.05	57–	164	140	84.2	132	123	131.8
hamm10-4	1,024	82.89	40	85	74	*	73	*	55.8
johns-10-4-4	210	88.52	30	48	41	30	40	37	32
johns-11-4-4	330	91.49	35	71	61	41.25	60	53	45
johns-11-5-4	462	93.49	66	97	88	66	87	81	66.4
johns-12-4-4	495	93.52	51	99	86	55	85	73	60.8
johns-12-5-4	792	95.58	80	161	138	99	137	128	99
johns-13-4-4	715	94.96	65	133	116	71.5	115	*	80.4
johns-13-5-4	1,287	96.89	123–	248	212	143	211	*	143
keller5	776	75.15	27	61	31	*	31	42	31
keller6	3,361	81.82	59	141	63	*	63	*	63
MANN_a45	1,035	99.63	345	369	360	356.05	359	*	360
MANN_a81	3,321	99.88	1,100	1,153	1,134	1,126.62	1,133	*	1,134
p_hat1500-3	1,500	75.36	94	270	265	*	263	*	244.8
p_hat700-3	700	74.80	62	143	134	*	131	105	125
monoton-9	729	83.52	28	53	47	*(34.41)	46	46	42.6
monoton-10	1,000	85.14	32–	71	60	*(41.83)	59	59	53.2
monoton-11	1,331	86.47	37–	84	72	*(49.96)	71	73	64.2
evil-N330	330	96.10	60	109	100	71.99	85	90	90.2
evil-N500	500	95.72	80	165	140	100	119	121	128.2

* indicates that the bound cannot be computed due to time or memory limit.

discuss and analyze the possibility of using different sub-chromatic methods to divide the k-clique problem into subproblems.

The structure of this section is the following. First, we describe the k-clique search problem, the upper bounds to be analyzed and the test graphs used for measurements. Second, we compare in detail the previously listed subchromatic upper bounds. The outcome of our experiments is summarized in Table 6.13. Third, we introduce the notion of *disturbing structures*, which will guide the partitioning of the problem. Finally, we discuss how the proposed bounds may be applied to partition the k-clique problem for massive parallelization.

6.4.1   Preliminaries

Several problems go under the heading of clique search in graphs. Specifically, this section is concerned with the well-known and deeply studied k-clique problem.

Problem 1. Given a simple finite graph $G = (V, E)$ and a positive integer k decide if the graph G has a clique of size k.

The term *finite* refers to the number of nodes. The adjective *simple* prohibits double and loop edges. A clique $\Delta \subset V$ is a subset of nodes that are all pairwise adjacent in G. Problem 1 is a decision problem and belongs to the NP-complete complexity class.

Finding a k-clique in a graph for which the clique number of G, $\omega(G)$, is greater or equal to k ($\omega(G) \geq k$), is relatively easy for moderate size graphs. The demanding problem is usually to prove the non-existence of a k-clique, when $k > \omega(G)$. On the other hand, if an upper bound below k can be found for this particular problem, the existence of a k-clique can be rejected trivially. Motivated by this fact, we study tight bounds for $\omega(G)$.

The most common method for establishing a bound for $\omega(G)$ is determining a legal coloring of the nodes of the graph G such that:

1.   Each node receives exactly one color.
2.   Two adjacent nodes cannot have the same color.

More formally, a node coloring of G with r colors, also an r-coloring, is a surjective map $f : V \rightarrow \{1, \ldots, r\}$. Here we identify the r colors with the numbers $1, \ldots, r$, respectively. The level sets of f are the so-called color classes of the coloring. The i-th color class $C_i = \{v : v \in V, f(v) = i\}$ consists of all the nodes of G that are assigned color i. The color classes $C_1, \ldots, C_r$ form a partition of V. Vice versa, the coloring is uniquely determined by the color classes $C_1, \ldots, C_r$.

The smallest number of colors required by any legal coloring of the nodes of the graph is called the chromatic number of the graph and denoted by $\chi(G)$. As the nodes of a clique Δ are all pairwise adjacent, any legal coloring of the nodes in Δ will require at least as many colors as the cardinality of the clique. Consequently, the chromatic number is always an upper bound for the size of the largest clique in the graph, that is, $\chi(G) \geq \omega(G)$.

Finding the chromatic number of a graph is well known to be NP-hard. In practice, approximate coloring algorithms are used as bound for the clique number. Specifically, we are interested in two coloring heuristics. The first is the well-known Dsatur algorithm from Daniel Brélaz [409]. The second one is the iterative coloring heuristic from Joseph C. Culberson [410], in the following IC.

In Section 6.4.2, we perform extended measurements on a carefully selected data set of 35 graphs and reported the results in Table 6.13. The first 11 graphs in the Table come from various error correcting code problems [411].[2] The next 19 graphs are

---

[2]https://oeis.org/A265032/a265032.html

taken from the second DIMACS Challenge [412].[3] The next 3 graphs are reformulated problems of monotonic matrices [413],[4] and the last 2 are from the so-called EVIL instances [414].[5] For the reported graphs, the clique number is extremely hard to compute, and in some cases these problems are still open. There are also instances where $\omega(G)$ is known but which cannot be determined by state-of-the-art solvers. Examples of these are the EVIL graphs, where $\omega(G)$ is known by construction, and a subset of the *Johnson* graphs. The latter are derived from code theory.

Table 6.13 reports the sizes and densities of the 35 selected graphs, along with their clique number, or alternatively the best known bounds. Also in the Table, the column *legal coloring* shows the best upper bound for $\omega(G)$ considering both the Dsatur and the IC coloring heuristics. The IC coloring is the obtained after 1,000 iterations, taking the Dsatur coloring as a starting point.

Our main goal in this section is to divide a given k-clique search problem into smaller instances. To achieve this goal, in the following section we analyze different known theoretical upper bounds for the clique number of a graph, which will then drive problem separation. All studied bounds have the capability of being tighter than the chromatic number and will be computed heuristically with a time limit of 24 h. Note, that the exact computation of such bounds is normally impractical inside a k-clique search. We consider the well known bounds in the literature: fractional coloring—χ_f, the Lovasz' theta number—$\vartheta(\bar{G})$ and vector coloring—$\chi_v(G)$, which relate to the chromatic number and clique number as follows, see [415,416]:

$$\omega(G) \leq \chi_v(G) \leq \vartheta(\bar{G}) \leq \chi_f(G) \leq \chi(G) \tag{6.37}$$

We further consider two more upper bounds for $\omega(G)$: a special version of edge coloring and the infra-chromatic bound based on a PMAX-SAT reformulation of a legal coloring. These last two bounds still require a deeper theoretical study, and their relation to (6.37) is still open to the best of our knowledge. On the other hand, a number of interesting facts are known for specific graphs. For example, the simplest graph where the clique and the chromatic number differ is the 5-cycle graph C_5. This graph has a clique number $\omega(C_5) = 2$ and chromatic number $\chi(C_5) = 3$. The bounds $\chi_v(G), \vartheta(\bar{G})$, and $\chi_f(G)$ on $\omega(G)$ are all real numbers between 2 and 3, the clique and the chromatic number, respectively. Namely, the fractional coloring number is equal to 5/2 and the other bounds are equal to $\sqrt{5}$ (see [417]). However, with edge coloring, we get the optimal bound 2.

From a computational perspective, some of the proposed bounds can be extremely hard to compute in the average case, as they are proven NP-hard problems, so we are interested in approximation algorithms. For example, state-of-the-art clique solvers use greedy coloring instead of $\chi(G)$ in every subproblem [418–421]. Table 6.13 at the end of Section 6.4.2 summarizes our results. Moreover, the Table also reports the values of coloring heuristics Dsatur (column *Dsatur coloring*) and IC (column *Iterated coloring*) for comparison purposes.

---

[3] http://iridia.ulb.ac.be/ fmascia/maximum_clique/DIMACS-benchmark
[4] http://mathworld.wolfram.com/MonotonicMatrix.html
[5] http://clique.ttk.pte.hu/evil

6.4.2   Subchromatic upper bounds

Fractional and b-fold coloring. Any legal k-coloring of the nodes of a graph $G = (V, E)$ assigns the same color number $i = 1, \ldots, k$ to the nodes of each independent set C_i that determines a partition of V. On the other hand, *fractional coloring* assigns one real number as the weight of a color to *every* independent set [416, pp. 135–138]. More formally, let $I(G, u)$ denote the independent sets of G that contain the node u. A fractional coloring of the nodes of G is a nonnegative real function f such that, for any node $u \in V$,

$$\sum_{S \in I(G,u)} f(S) \geq 1.$$

The sum of the values of f for every node is called the *weight* of the fractional coloring, and the minimum possible weight of every fractional coloring of the nodes of G is called the *fractional chromatic number* $\chi_f(G)$.

A simpler variation of the fractional coloring, the *b-fold coloring* of the nodes of G, is an assignment of a set of b colors to every one of its vertices such that adjacent vertices receive disjoint sets. An *a:b-coloring* is a b-fold coloring out of a available colors. Finally, the b-fold chromatic number $\chi_b(G)$ is the smallest a such that an $a:b$-coloring exists. The special case of $b = 1$, the 1-fold coloring, reduces to finding a legal node coloring, so consequently finding the b-fold chromatic number is NP-hard. The connection between fractional and b-fold chromatic number is the following:

$$\chi_f(G) = \lim_{b \to \infty} \frac{\chi_b(G)}{b} \tag{6.38}$$

A b-fold coloring of the nodes of a graph G also bounds the clique number from above. Clearly, each k-clique must receive $b \times k$ colors, thus $\omega(G) \leq \frac{\chi_b(G)}{b}$. Since computing the fractional chromatic number is NP-hard, we consider the heuristic b-fold coloring as substitute problem. To further reduce computation resources we consider only small values of b, in particular b has been set to 5 in our experiments.

Our choice of b-fold coloring is motivated by the fact that this coloring can be easily reformulated as a legal node coloring of a graph [422]. This is done by using an auxiliary graph $\Gamma = (W, F)$ constructed from the given $G = (V, E)$ graph. The nodes of Γ are ordered pairs $(v_i, k) \in W$, $v_i \in V$, $1 \leq k \leq b$. The edges are defined as follows:

$$F = \begin{cases} \{(v_i, k), (v_i, l)\} & \text{if } k \neq l \quad 1 \leq k, l \leq b \\ \{(v_i, k), (v_j, l)\} & \text{if } \{v_i, v_j\} \in E \quad 1 \leq k, l \leq b \end{cases} \tag{6.39}$$

It is easy to see from (6.39) that any legal node coloring of the graph Γ represents a b-fold coloring of the nodes of the graph G and vice versa. The key idea is that the different color numbers assigned to the nodes (v_i, k) in Γ become the set of colors assigned to v_i in the corresponding b-fold coloring of the nodes of G. Figure 6.20 shows Γ in a 5:2-fold coloring of the nodes of C_5 cycle, that is, a 2-fold coloring using 5 colors.

Since computing the chromatic number of the graph Γ is NP-hard, we resort to heuristic algorithms to compute a bound for $\omega(G)$. Specifically, we consider Brélaz's

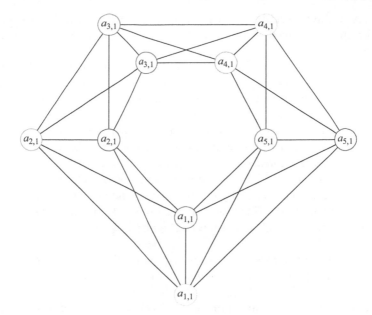

Figure 6.20   The Γ auxiliary graph for 2-fold coloring of C_5 and its node coloring with five colors

Dsatur and the iterative coloring scheme of Culberson, in the following IC (see Section 6.4.1.) We then compute the upper bound as follows:

1.   Construct auxiliary graph Γ_b for $b = 5$.
2.   Determine a greedy node coloring for Γ_b using Dsatur.
3.   Using the previous coloring as a starting point run Culberson's iterative recoloring (IC) 1,000 times to obtain a better coloring.
4.   The final upper bound is calculated by dividing the number of colors by b.

Table 6.13 reports these upper bounds for our graph data set, under the column header 5-*fold coloring*. The running times for all instances were below 5 minutes.

The partial MaxSAT bound. Recently, an interesting upper bound for the clique number of a graph G, $\omega(G)$, has attracted the attention of researchers. We will refer to it as UB_{SAT}. It was first described in [419] in terms of a reduction of the maximum clique problem (MCP) for a k-colored graph G to a partial maximum satisfiability problem, and employs typical Boolean constraint propagation techniques to prove that no k-cliques exist in G. The bound ranges between the clique number and the size of the input coloring ($\omega(G) \leq UB_{SAT} \leq k$). Moreover, it has been successfully applied as bounding function to determine the clique number of a graph in the algorithms MaxCLQ [423] and IncMaxCLQ [420].

UB_{SAT} receives as input an independent set partition $C_1, C_2, \ldots, C_k$ of the vertices of the G. It then greedily finds r *conflicting* subsets of independent sets $I = \{I_1, I_2, \ldots, I_r\}$ to reduce the upper bound for the clique number from the original

k to $k - r$. A conflicting subset I_j in I is such that $\omega(G[I_j]) < |I_j|, (1 \leq j \leq r)$, where $G[I_j]$ is the graph induced by the vertices in I_j, and $|I_j|$ denotes the number of independent sets.

To find a conflict, the heuristic uses *unit clause propagation* (UP for short) employed in SAT: after storing all unit independent sets in a queue Q, UP repeatedly dequeues each one and assumes that its single node v is part of a new clique. In the remaining independent sets, all vertices that do not belong to v's neighbor set $N(v)$ are removed, which, in turn, may lead to fresh independent sets added to Q. The procedure ends when either Q is empty, or an independent set becomes empty.

A node v is called *failed* if the application of UP driven by $Q = \{v\}$ leads to an empty independent set. If this is the case, and v belongs to a unit independent set f, a *conflict* I_v is determined by the set of independent sets that participated in the UP chain (including the final one that became empty) together with f. Another possible conflict derives from a non-unit f set with all its vertices failed. In this case, $I_f = \bigcup_{v \in f} I_v$.

Moreover, it is also possible to find disjoint conflicts with overlapping independent sets by using the *clause relaxation* method employed in maximum Boolean satisfiability (MAX-SAT) [424]. Once a conflicting set of cardinality s is found, a fresh node $w_i, (1 \leq i \leq s)$ is added to each independent set in the conflict such that it is connected to all the other vertices in G with two exceptions: those vertices that belong to its same independent set, and the other fresh vertices $w_j, (j \neq i)$. Each added node and its enlarged independent set are denoted *relaxed*. It is easy to see that for a given conflict I_l, the set of $|I_l|$ relaxed vertices thus defined cover all possible cliques of size $|I_l|$ in I_l. Once a relaxed independent set $C_j, (1 \leq j \leq k)$ from I_l becomes unit and is inserted into the UP queue Q, the remaining sets in $I_l \setminus C_j$ can take part in future disjoint conflicts.

For the experiments concerning UB_{SAT}, in this section, we used coloring obtained from IC as starting point. Results for this bound are summarized in Table 6.13, under the header *PMaxSAT*. In the tests, times taken to compute the PMAX-SAT bound were much lower than a second for all instances.

Edge coloring. Edge coloring can also provide a good upper bound for the clique number. We consider an *edge coloring* of a graph G with k colors an assignment of color numbers to the edges of G such that:

1. Each edge of G receives exactly one color.
2. If x, y, z are distinct nodes of a 3-clique in G, then the edges $\{x, y\}, \{y, z\}, \{x, z\}$ must receive three distinct colors.
3. If x, y, u, v are distinct nodes of a 4-clique in G, then the edges $\{x, y\}, \{x, u\}, \{x, v\}, \{y, u\}, \{y, v\}, \{u, v\}$ must receive six distinct colors.

Note that this edge coloring *differs* from the one usually found in the graph literature. Comparable to node coloring, edge coloring can also be used as an upper bound for the clique number of G, base on the following property:

Property 1. Let Δ be a maximum clique of size l in a graph G, and let G be edge-colorable with k colors. Then $l(l - 1)/2 \leq k$ holds.

Proof. A legal edge coloring of the nodes od G must also provide a legal edge coloring of Δ. Since any legal edge coloring of Δ must contain at least $l(l-1)/2$ colors, then $l(l-1)/2 \leq k$, as required. □

The procedure to color the edges of a graph G is to use an auxiliary graph $\Gamma = (W, F)$. Each edge of G is represented by a node in Γ. We connect the nodes of Γ according to the rules above, that is two nodes in Γ should be connected if the corresponding edges in G forming a 3- or a 4-clique. It is easy to see that any legal coloring of the nodes of Γ represents a legal edge coloring of the nodes of G. The auxiliary graph Γ can be quite large, but greedy coloring procedure like the Brélaz' Dsatur can still be used. We constructed the auxiliary graph Γ from all our test graphs and tried to run first the Brélaz' Dsatur coloring procedure, then using its output the Culberson's iterative coloring algorithm on these auxiliary graphs.

Table 6.13 shows the results obtained for the edge-coloring bound under the column header *Edge coloring*. Some of the instances reported had too many edges for G, that is too many nodes for Γ to fit into the memory of our computer. These cases are reported as "*." The time limit was set to 24 h, so some of the results did not finish the 1,000 iterations. In these cases we indicate the best upper bound calculated from the number of colors obtained by limit time.

Lovász number. The last bound considered is the *Lovász number* of a graph, a real number that is an upper bound on the Shannon capacity of the graph [415,425]. It is also known as *Lovász theta function* and is commonly denoted by $\vartheta(G)$. Lovász theta is actually an upper bound for the maximum independent set, so we compute it on the complement of the input graph. We used the CSDP program from Brian Borchers [426,427] for calculating the value of $\vartheta(\bar{G})$. The results are listed in Table 6.13, under the header $\vartheta(\bar{G})$. For calculations, we used 8 cores and 32 GB of memory.

A "*" in any cell refers to a bound that could not be computed due to memory or time limitations. Table 6.13 also reports some previous results for some problems using a supercomputer. These results are also indicated by a "*" and the bound is given in parenthesis. Those calculations used up to several hundred cores, up to half terabyte of memory, and they run sometimes for weeks.

To wrap this subsection, we briefly present some conclusions from the reported experiments. We run six different families of algorithms to estimate the maximum clique size of our 35 graph data set. The hardware used was a Xeon E5-2620 v2 at 2.10 GHz clock speed and 64 GB of RAM. The short summary of the results is listed in Table 6.13. Specifically, Table 6.13 reports the clique bound provided by Dsatur, and the best bound obtained by the iterative Culberson's method for legal coloring, the Lovasz' theta function over the complement graph, the partial MaxSAT bound, the Culberson's iterative method for the auxiliary edge graph and the 5-fold node coloring. From the table, the best results were always provided by the Lovasz' theta function. The second best bound came from different algorithms, but mostly from the 5-fold coloring.

To note, there are clearly two sets of running times in our measurements, which depend on whether the algorithm complexity depends on the number of nodes or edges. The size of the auxiliary graph for edge coloring is clearly the number of edges of the given graph. The heuristic coloring algorithm itself is polynomial. The CSDP program calculating the Lovasz' theta function is a polynomial method depending on the number of *non*-edges in the graph. These two methods were the only ones which went over the 24 h time limit in some of the instances. In contrast, the set of algorithms with complexity depending on the number of nodes took a couple of minutes, at most, to compute. This is negligible compared with the clique size solving time of the graphs.

6.4.3 Disturbing structures

One of the most convenient ways to divide a k-clique search problem into subproblems is to partition the node set V of the graph G into two subsets: A and $B = V \setminus A$. Let G_A be the graph that is spanned by the set of nodes A. The goal of our division is to prove that $\omega(G_A) < k$, and we shall find such an A for which this problem can be easier or trivially solved. That is, if we remove the nodes of B from the graph G, the remaining graph will admit to have no k-clique in it and this information is easier to determine than in the original problem. In the original Carraghan–Pardalos algorithm [428], this separation is made according to the number of nodes. Trivially, if we take out $(k - 1)$ nodes from V, the induced subgraph on these nodes cannot contain a k-clique. Thus, we need to remove, also eliminate, the remaining $|V| - (k - 1)$ nodes in order to solve the problem. Moreover, this elimination can be done one node at a time, producing an easier problem each time.

More formally, let $V = \{v_1, v_2, \ldots, v_n\}$. We then consider the following subproblems: $V_1 = V, V_2 = V_1 \setminus v_1, V_3 = V_2 \setminus v_2, \ldots, V_{n-k+1} = V_{n-k} \setminus v_{n-k}$. Clearly, solving the k-clique problem in G is equivalent to determining the existence of a $(k - 1)$-clique in the induced subgraphs defined by the node sets: $N(v_1) \cap V_1, N(v_2) \cap V_2, \ldots, N(v_{n-k+1}) \cap V_{n-k+1}$, where $N(v_i)$ denotes the neighbor set of v_i. Note that all these subproblems are independent and can be solved in parallel.

Instead of the size of the graph, tighter bounds for $\omega(G)$ may be employed. The most frequently used bound is some form of greedy coloring algorithm, as in [409,410], since computing the chromatic number is impractical for large problems. Given any legal coloring of the nodes, the graph spanned by the subset of nodes determined by any $(k - 1)$ color class cannot have a k-clique. Consequently, the separation is done in exactly the same way as before, but considering now the nodes of any partial $k - 1$ coloring of the nodes. This method was first described, with a number of minor modifications, in [429]. In this section, we shall analyze the described division of the problem into subproblems and propose some simple algorithms to assist this goal.

We start the discussion with the search for a *k-clique covering node set*. The separation method described above can be generalized as follows. Let $G = (V, E)$ be a finite simple graph and let k be a positive integer. Let $W \subseteq V$. If each k-clique in G has at least one node in W, then we call W a k-clique covering node set of G (see Figure 6.21).

Let $W = \{w_1, w_2, \ldots, w_n\}$ be a k-clique covering node set in G. Consider the subgraph H_i of G denote the graph induced by the neighbor set $N(w_i)$ in G for each i,

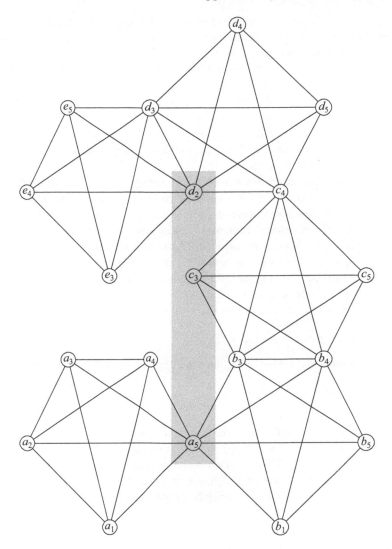

Figure 6.21 A 5-clique covering node set—$\{d_2, c_3, a_5\}$

$1 \leq i \leq n$. Let Δ be a k-clique in G. The definition of W states that w_i must be a node of Δ for some i, $1 \leq i \leq n$. Consequently, the subgraph H_i contains exactly $k - 1$ nodes of the clique Δ. This observation has a clear intuitive meaning: the problem of determining the existence of a k-clique in G can be reduced to a list of smaller problems of determining the existence of a $(k - 1)$-clique in the subgraphs H_i for each i, $1 \leq i \leq n$.

Moreover, the smaller the n, the fewer the subproblems to be analysed become. In other words, starting with a k-clique covering node set with a minimum number of nodes could save computational resources. However, finding an optimal k-clique covering node set is again an NP-hard problem. Clearly it is as hard as the k-clique decision Problem 1: a "yes" in the latter results in a non-empty k-clique covering node set; a "no" gives an empty cover.

As explained previously, by computing a legal coloring of the nodes of the graph we can partition the nodes of the graph into two sets: a first set consisting of nodes from the biggest $(k-1)$ color classes, and a second set with the remaining nodes. It is easy to see that the latter set must be a k-clique covering set, as any k-clique in the graph must have at least one node in this set. Thus we arrive to the partitioning method described in the previous section. Obviously, any other k-clique covering set can be used in the same manner.

Next, discuss the search for a *k-clique covering s-clique set*. More specifically, we are interested in searching for a *k-clique covering edge set*. This is an extension of the node cover described previously to other structures, such as s-cliques. Let $G = (V, E)$ be a finite simple graph and let k be a positive integer. Let F be a subset of all s-cliques in G. If each k-clique in G has at least one s-clique in F, then we call F a *k-clique covering s-clique set* of G. In particular, when $s = 2$, then F is an *k-clique covering edge set*. Figure 6.22 depicts an example of an edge covering of all the 5-cliques in a graph, that is, $s = 2$ and $k = 5$.

Let F be an s-clique cover of all the k-cliques in G, and let

$$c_i = \{u_{i,1}, u_{i,2}, \ldots, u_{i,s}\}, 1 \le i \le |F|$$

be all the s-cliques in F. Also, let H_i be the subgraphs spanned by the sets of nodes

$$H_i = \bigcap_j N(u_{i,j}) \quad 1 \le j \le s \tag{6.40}$$

and let Δ be a k-clique in G. According to the definition of F, there must be a c_i that is an s-clique of Δ for some i, $1 \le i \le |F|$. Consequently, the subgraph H_i contains exactly $k - s$ nodes of Δ. This observation has a clear intuitive meaning: the problem of determining the existence of a k-clique in G can be reduced to determining the existence of a $(k-s)$-clique in a series of graphs spanned by each of the subgraphs H_i, $1 \le i \le |F|$.

Rather than determining if a $(k-s)$-clique exists in each of the H_i subproblems, it would be preferable to examine the subproblems of finding a $(k-s)$-clique in $G'_i(H'_i, E'_i)$ graphs derived from the previously described general methodology. Specifically, we consider subproblems on the node set $H'_i = \bigcap_j N(u_{i,j})$ with some suitable E'_i edge set that takes into account the sequence of eliminated (examined) problems. For $s = 2$, when s-cliques are edges of the graph, we can easily construct these E_i subsets as follows. Let

$$E_1 = E, E_2 = E_1 \setminus \{u_{1,1}, u_{1,2}\}, E_3 = E_2 \setminus \{u_{2,1}, u_{2,2}\}, \ldots$$

Then let E'_i be E_i on the node set of H'_i. That is we consider only those edges, that have endpoints in this node set. However, for higher values of s we cannot subtract each s-clique from its corresponding V_i or E_i set in the same way. We will return to this issue in Section 6.4.4.

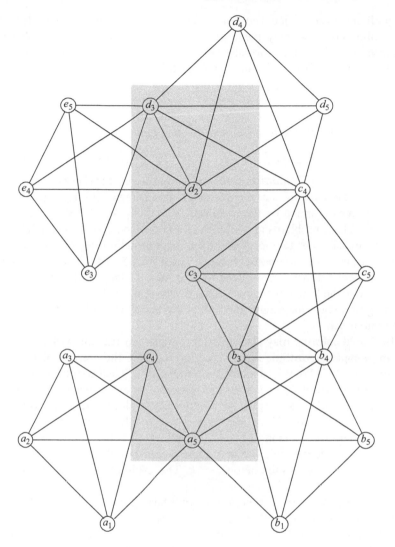

Figure 6.22   A 5-clique covering edge set—$\{\{d_3, d_2\}, \{c_3, b_3\}, \{b_3, a_5\}, \{a_4, a_5\}\}$

In what follows, we will refer to the k-clique covering node, edge and s-clique sets as *disturbing structures*, because we need to eliminate them to obtain simplified subproblems and to solve the original problem in the end.

6.4.4   Partitioning the k-clique problem for parallel architectures

In order to design a well-balanced parallel algorithm we now retake the discussion started in Section 6.4.3 concerning disturbing structures. We are interested in finding a set of such structures so as to partition the k-clique problem into several subproblems.

Recall that given any legal coloring of the nodes of a graph, it is possible to choose $(k-1)$ color classes (namely, the largest ones) and divide the k-clique problem using the *remaining* nodes. More formally, let $C_1, C_2, \ldots, C_r, (r \geq k)$ be the color classes of a legal coloring of the nodes of $G = (V, E)$. Let

$$V' = C_1 \cup C_2 \cup \cdots \cup C_{k-1} \qquad \text{and} \qquad V'' = C_k \cup C_{k+1} \cup \cdots \cup C_r$$

Also let $p = |V''|$ and $V'' = \{v_1, v_2, \ldots, v_p\}$. The set V'' is a k-clique covering node set. To partition the problem space, it suffices to define the subsets of nodes

$$V_1 = V, V_2 = V_1 \setminus v_1, V_3 = V_2 \setminus v_2, \ldots, V_p = V_{p-1} \setminus v_{p-1}$$

which incrementally *eliminate* the nodes of V'' and decrease in size as i increases. With the help of V_i, the k-clique can be partitioned into finding a $(k-1)$-clique in each one of the subgraphs spanned by the node sets $N(v_1) \cap V_1, N(v_2) \cap V_2, \ldots, N(v_p) \cap V_p$, respectively. These problems are independent and can be solved in parallel.

It can be easily seen that some of the proposed bounding methods can also be used for the same purpose, with minor changes. The PMAX-SAT method can be employed in a straightforward manner: we need to determine the largest possible color classes in V', such that the bound is below k. This can be achieved by solving a small integer linear program. The remaining nodes will be the branching set V'', which is a k-clique covering node set.

The b-fold coloring may also be used for such construction with the help of the following simple algorithm. First we count and store the number of nodes inside each color class C_i. We will denote this number by l_i. Then we place the nodes that belong to the smallest C_i in V''. By definition of b-fold coloring, these nodes can be in other color classes as well, so we subtract 1 from the total number of nodes count in each color class C_j, $i \neq j$, that is $l_j = l_j - 1$, for each node shared with C_i. We next choose the smallest color class in $V \setminus C_i$, that is the smallest l_j, and proceed in the same manner. The process is repeated until the number of remaining non-empty color classes falls below $b \times k$. The resulting V'' is a k-clique covering node set.

Using the Lovasz' theta function for partitioning the k-clique problem is more computationally demanding than in the previous case, because we need to calculate several theta functions. We start from a subgraph $S \subset G$ which does not contain a k-clique, for example because a legal $k-1$ coloring of the nodes exists for S. Then, at each step of the process, we add a new node $v \in V \setminus S$ and compute the theta bound of the complement of the graph spanned by the node set $S \cup \{v\}$. If this bound is still under k, the node is *accepted* and the partitioning algorithm takes as reference set $S \leftarrow S \cup \{v\}$ in future iterations; else v is not added to S. The procedure ends when all vertices have been examined. The set $V'' = V \setminus S$ is a suitable k-clique covering set.

As shown in Section 6.4.3, edges, instead of nodes, can also be used as disturbing structures. The edge coloring method described in Section 6.4.2 is a straightforward way to determine these edges. We choose the largest $(k(k-1)/2) - 1$ color classes, as the graph spanned by the union of the edges in these color classes by themselves cannot form a k-clique. We denote the set of edges inside these color classes by E'. The edges in $E'' = E \setminus E'$, form a k-clique covering edge set. From E'' we can construct the subproblems as described in Section 6.4.3.

Moreover, finding such disturbing edges is not restricted to edge coloring. For example, starting from a legal node coloring we can take the largest $(k-1)$ color classes and then move all the nodes from the other color classes at will into these color classes. We will then arrive to an improper node coloring in the general case, because some nodes in a color class will be adjacent. These *disturbing* edges will form a k-clique covering edge set and can be used to produce subproblems as described above (see [430]).

To achieve an even load in large-scale parallelization, more subproblems than the number of available processing cores are required. A reasonable ratio ranges between 3 and 10× more subproblems than processing units. The proposed k-clique covering node set will not meet this constraint in the general case: their size frequently range between 30 and 100 nodes, while a modern supercomputer may contain between 1,000 and 100,000 cores. Note that the k-clique covering edge set is more appropriate in this case, as it typically generates from 500 to 2,000 subproblems.

To overcome this limitation, we propose the following strategy. Let v, u be the first two nodes of one such k-clique covering set, such that $u \in N(v)$, that is $\{u, v\}$ an edge. The corresponding two subproblems following the general partition methodology are searching for a $(k-1)$-clique in each of the two subgraphs spanned by the node sets $N(v) \cap V$ and $N(u) \cap (V \setminus v)$. We propose to construct new subproblems using the edge $\{v, u\}$. Namely, we search for a $(k-2)$-clique in the graph spanned by node set $N(\{v, u\}) \cap V$, and search for a $(k-1)$-clique in each of the subgraphs spanned by node sets $N(v) \cap (V \setminus u)$ and $N(u) \cap (V \setminus v)$, respectively. Clearly solving these latter subproblems is equivalent to solving the former ones. This method may be trivially extended to all the other edges in the k-clique covering node set, and thus increment the number of subproblems by an order of magnitude.

We further discuss a problem that concerns the elimination of disturbing structures, once the corresponding subproblem has been examined, for the k-clique covering s-clique set strategy, where $s > 2$. In this case, it is not possible to directly remove the *disturbing* s-cliques from the node sets $V_i \subseteq V$, or edge sets $E_i \subseteq E$, where each i corresponds to an s-clique element of the cover. A possible solution is to consider additional edge subproblems instead of s-cliques. For $s = 3$ it works as follows. Let Δ be a 3-clique in the given k-clique covering 3-clique set, with nodes x, y, z and edges $e = \{x, y\}, f = \{y, z\}, g = \{x, z\}$. After failing to find a $(k-3)$-clique in the graph spanned by the node set $N(\Delta)$, we cannot delete it from the graph directly. The situation changes if it is possible to prove that there are no $(k-2)$-cliques in the graphs spanned by the node sets $N(e) \cap (V \setminus z), N(f) \cap (V \setminus x)$, and $N(g) \cap (V \setminus y)$, respectively. It is easy to see that by examining these additional subproblems, the nodes in Δ can be removed in all ensuing subproblems without losing completeness. If all the s-cliques of the cover are divided in this way, the general elimination methodology can be extended to these edge-based structures (see Section 6.4.3).

6.5 Summary

In this chapter, some topics related to applications in UCS have been presented. However, we still foresee near-term research topics and challenges in ultrascale applications, as shown below:

Multilevel methods: Performance engineering of current codes aimed at multicore architectures; multilevel heterogeneous methods and algorithms and their efficient mapping on the graph representation of heterogeneous ultrascale computing systems; multilevel multiscale methods and algorithms for multiphysics applications in strongly heterogeneous media and uncertain data. We will need a plethora of new algorithms, possibly implemented on novel architectures (such as dataflow).

Parallelism: Use of domain-specific languages for specific application areas with specialized compilers to generate efficient code for different HPC architectures; automatic inclusion of self-adaptivity features in existing algorithms, methods and implementations; self-healing and self-repairing methods and algorithms.

Data science methods: Machine learning and deep learning; advanced techniques and algorithms to parameterize deep neural network structures.

Simulation: Complex socio-technical environments and systems; functional resonance analysis in hazard identification; simulations in cognitive science, behavioral science, psychology, neuro-science, simulation of social behavior.

To cope with this challenges, we should be able to develop novel architecture-aware methods and algorithms that expose as much parallelism as possible, exploiting heterogeneity, avoiding communication bottlenecks, responding to escalating fault rates, and helping to meet emerging power constraints. But first, we should alleviate the effort needed to redesign applications by developing DSL with specialized compilers to generate efficient codes for different ultrascale computing architectures enabling self-adaptivity, deep machine learning, and complex socio-technical environments and systems.

Chapter 7

Conclusion

Emmanuel Jeannot[1] and Jesus Carretero[2]

As we have seen in the former chapters, facilitating the adoption and usage of sustainable ultrascale computing systems (UCSs) will need providing innovative solutions to advance the knowledge of designing sustainable ultrascale software and systems, which will be the basic facilities for new discoveries in science and technology and will have a direct impact on economic growth, society, and environmental aspects.

The main conclusion is that it is important to **enable ultrascale computing** by supporting the evolution of ultrascale systems towards on-demand computing across highly diverse environments by providing domain specific, but interoperable tools to enable high productivity of human–computer interaction, leading toward robust solutions through multi-domain cooperative approaches using energy efficient hardware–software co-design principles. However, there are still important points to be addressed, as pointed out in this book.

One of the key points will be the availability of programming abstractions for the different fields of Exascale such as data analysis, machine learning, scientific computing, Big Data management, and smart cities that will be based on asynchronous algorithms for overlapping communication and computation. To reach this overlap, parallel applications (such as the MPI-based one) will need to be optimized using platform topology and performance information. One crucial research topic will be programmability of UCS as applications will run millions of parallel execution flows. New workflow programming for very large plate forms will be needed. But interoperability and sustainability will only be reached when code will be prevented to be platform specific and still efficient on different platforms. From a broader point of view, the scale of UCS will lead to supercomputing on demand leading to a better use of the vast amount of available resources. The efficiency will be linked to researches on performance evaluation, modeling, and optimization of data parallel applications on heterogeneous HPC platforms. Management of such large distributed systems will be based on future researches on complex systems modeling, self-organizing systems, and cellular automata.

In addition, the characterization of hardware and software faults is essential for making the informed choice about research needs for the resilience of ultrascale

[1]INRIA Bourdeaux Sud-Ouest, LaBRI, Universite de Bourdeaux, France
[2]Department of Computer Science and Engineering, University Carlos III of Madrid, Spain

systems and for developing a standardized fault-handling model to provide guidance to application and system software developers about how they will be notified about a fault, what types of faults they may be notified about, and what mechanisms the system provides to assist recovery from the fault. This should pave the way toward improved fault prediction, containment, detection, notification, and recovery, which is needed to cope with scale.

This book has also studied the close relationship between HPC and data analysis in the scientific computing area and possible procedures to achieve the desired unification, including the appearance of new storage device technologies that carry a lot of potential for addressing issues in these areas, but also introduce numerous challenges and will imply changes in the way data is organized.

Models and simulation of energy consumption have been proposed for ultrascale systems, including metrics, models of energy consumption of heterogeneous hardware, and energy simulators. They have been complemented with the valuation of renewable energy usage for an Exascale computer, which can help to significantly reduce energy costs and carbon footprint of ultrascale systems, a review of cooling techniques in data centers, and full-cost model for estimating the energy consumption of computing infrastructures

Finally, the book has addressed the need for reformulation of algorithms and applications from different areas of research toward their usage for ultrascale systems, creating scalable parallel algorithms for several application areas, such as numerical solution of problems and to cope with the computational complexity of super-diffusion problems and 3D relaxation gravity, or massive parallelization of the maximum clique problem. Moreover, how to provide application-specific analytical energy models has been presented

As a result of the work made in the book chapters, and the research associated in the NESUS COST Action, it is clear that there are still challenges to be solved to arrive at UCSs. Achieving these challenges would require to:

Improve the programmability of complex systems. New programming paradigms are needed to help the programmer. These paradigms will solve the impossibility to have a global view of the whole system as the complexity of software workflow and hardware explodes and reach millions of heterogeneous entities.

Break the wall between runtime and programming frameworks. There is a need to adapt the generic high-level code to the underlying infrastructure by giving feedback to the programmers during development. This feedback will help programmer to have insight on the performance and capabilities of the targeted platform and to make informed decisions.

Enabling behavioral sensitive runtime. The ability to provide behavioral information along with applications will help runtime to take the most relevant decisions in function of its context such as other applications or characteristics of the execution platform. Runtime will be informed and will be able to allocate the right amount of resources at the right time but also will be able to reconfigure the application in the most relevant way.

Developing new programming abstractions for resilience and standardized evaluation of fault-tolerant approaches. Efficient tools and methods for characterization of both hardware and software faults are needed. Comprehensive and standardized fault-handling models for analysis of resilience of systems to improve fault prediction, containment, detection, notification, recovery mechanisms, and strategy for ultrascale systems is crucial in their operation.

To enforce the convergence of HPC, ultrascale, and Big Data worlds. Storage, interconnection networks, and data management in both HPC and Cloud needs to cope with technology trends and evolving application requirements while hiding the increasing complexity at the architectural, systems software, and application levels. Future work needs to examine these challenges under the prism of both HPC and Cloud approaches and to consider solutions that break away from current boundaries.

To design and develop intelligent data access mechanisms. Future applications will need more sophisticated interfaces for addressing the challenges of future UCSs. These novel interfaces should be able to abstract architectural and operational issues from requirements for both storage and data. This will allow applications and services to easier manipulate storage and data, while providing the system with flexibility to optimize operation over a complex set of architectural and technological constraints.

Adoption of intelligent methods for modeling and improving energy efficiency. We envision the wide use of machine learning techniques not only for understanding, but also for managing ultrascale systems. A methodology for modeling the whole system based on its subset must be created to allow for extrapolating the overall energy efficiency. A multi-layered approach allows feeding the models and management software with fine-grained measurements for the selected part of the system when needed without deterioration of the whole system performance.

Increasing awareness and focus on energy efficiency. To achieve significant impact on the energy efficiency of large systems in real life, appropriate incentives must be provided for all stakeholders including users, developers, and providers. Relevant metrics, going beyond Flops/W, focusing on ultrascale systems energy must be proposed and widely adopted. We recommend to put efforts into innovative usage and business models to provide incentives for energy-efficient use of resources, e.g. by methods to increase awareness, appropriate metrics, pricing models, energy-related SLAs, etc. These efforts must also include means (e.g. interfaces, APIs) to allow effective exchange of energy-related data and incentives within large collections of heterogeneous services that will be common application of ultrascale systems.

Designing software taking the advantage of heterogeneous hardware and infrastructure. Without careful integration of new hardware and infrastructure solutions, including optimization of software, significant reduction of energy consumption will not be possible. Therefore, energy-aware software development techniques must be developed (including autotuning, co-design, etc.). New methods of resource management for heterogeneous systems are needed in order to find the best hardware configuration for specific applications. Finally, we propose to put more efforts into achieving energy savings from the synergy of IT and infrastructure, including integration of IT management with cooling and heat re-use systems (and environmental data), the use of renewable energy sources, energy markets (e.g. applying demand response programs for IT), and other external systems.

Enabling complex ultrascale computing applications. Develop complex applications based on complementary utilization of numerical and non-numerical, deterministic, stochastic and hybrid, multiscale and multiphysics, direct and iterative methods, and algorithms. Support sustainable storage of Big Data and Big Data analytics including real-time multi-stream processing, processing of insecure, uncertain, incomplete and unreliable data. Integrate software tools providing fault-tolerance and resilience, self-correcting, automatic adaptation, and generation of codes for heterogeneous architectures including accelerators.

Towards total efficiency of ultrascale computing applications. Develop novel architecture-aware methods and algorithms that expose as much parallelism as possible, exploit heterogeneity, avoid communication bottlenecks, respond to escalating fault rates, and help meet emerging power constraints. Use domain-specific languages with specialized compilers to generate efficient codes for different ultrascale computing architectures enabling self-adaptivity, deep machine learning, and complex socio-technical environments and systems. Integrate the complex chain of modeling, simulation, optimization, Big Data analytics, and decision making. Develop integral measures of global efficiency including the scalability issues related to total solution of the problems.

References

[1] Janetschek M, Prodan R, Benedict S. A workflow runtime environment for manycore parallel architectures. Future Generation Computer Systems. 2017;75:330–347.

[2] van der Linde A, Fouto P, Leitão J, *et al*. Legion: Enriching internet services with peer-to-peer interactions. In: Proceedings of the 26th International Conference on World Wide Web. Republic and Canton of Geneva, Switzerland: International World Wide Web Conferences Steering Committee; 2017. p. 283–292. Available from: https://doi.org/10.1145/3038912.3052673.

[3] Bagein M, Barbosa J, Blanco V, *et al*. Energy efficiency for ultrascale systems: Challenges and trends from Nesus project. International Journal on Supercomputing Frontiers and Innovations. 2015;2(2):105–131. Available from: http://superfri.org/superfri/article/view/48.

[4] RTE. eCO2mix: energy mix for RTE, the French transmission system operator; 2018. Available from: https://www.rte-france.com/en/eco2mix/eco2mix-mix-energetique-en.

[5] Memorandum of understanding for the implementation of a European Concerted Research Action designated as COST Action IC1305: Network for Sustainable Ultrascale Computing (NESUS); 2014. Available from: https://e-services.cost.eu/files/domain_files/ICT/Action_IC1305/mou/IC1305-e.pdf, November 2013.

[6] Sousa L, Kropf P, Kuonene P, *et al*. A roadmap for research in sustainable ultrascale systems. University Carlos III of Madrid; 2017. Available from: https://www.irit.fr/~Georges.Da-Costa/NESUS-research_roadmap.pdf.

[7] Da Costa G, Fahringer T, Gallego JAR, *et al*. Exascale machines require new programming paradigms and runtimes. Supercomputing Frontiers and Innovations. 2015;2(2):6–27.

[8] Fortune S, Wyllie J. Parallelism in random access machines. In: Proceedings of the Tenth Annual ACM Symposium on Theory of Computing. STOC'78. New York, NY, USA: ACM; 1978. p. 114–118. Available from: http://doi.acm.org/10.1145/800133.804339.

[9] Valiant LG. A Bridging Model for Parallel Computation. Commun ACM. 1990 Aug;33(8):103–111. Available from: http://doi.acm.org/10.1145/79173.79181.

[10] Culler D, Karp R, Patterson D, *et al*. LogP: Towards a realistic model of parallel computation. In: Proceedings of the Fourth ACM SIGPLAN Symposium on Principles and Practice of Parallel Programming. PPOPP'93. New York, NY, USA: ACM; 1993. p. 1–12.

[11] Gautier T, Besseron X, Pigeon L. KAAPI: A thread scheduling runtime system for data flow computations on cluster of multi-processors. In: Proceedings of the 2007 International Workshop on Parallel Symbolic Computation. PASCO'07. ACM; 2007. p. 15–23.

[12] Augonnet C, Thibault S, Namyst R, *et al.* StarPU: A unified platform for task scheduling on heterogeneous multicore architectures. Concurrency and Computation: Practice and Experience 2011 Feb;23(2):187–198.

[13] Bosilca G, Bouteiller A, Danalis A, *et al.* DAGuE: A generic distributed DAG engine for high performance computing. In: 2011 IEEE International Symposium on Parallel and Distributed Processing Workshops and Phd Forum; 2011. p. 1151–1158.

[14] Bui TN, Jones C. A heuristic for reducing fill-in in sparse matrix factorization. In: Proceedings of the 6th SIAM Conference on Parallel Processing for Scientific Computing. SIAM; 1993.

[15] Hendrickson B, Leland R. A multilevel algorithm for partitioning graphs. In: Proceedings of the 1995 ACM/IEEE Conference on Supercomputing. Supercomputing'95. ACM; 1995. Available from: http://doi.acm.org/10.1145/224170.224228.

[16] Catalyurek U, Aykanat C. Decomposing Irregularly sparse matrices for parallel matrix-vector multiplication. In: Proceedings of the Third International Workshop on Parallel Algorithms for Irregularly Structured Problems. IRREGULAR'96. Springer-Verlag; 1996. p. 75–86.

[17] Hendrickson B, Kolda TG. Partitioning rectangular and structurally unsymmetric sparse matrices for parallel processing. SIAM Journal on Scientific Computing. 2000;21(6):2048–2072.

[18] Cierniak M, Zaki MJ, Li W. Compile-time scheduling algorithms for a heterogeneous network of workstations. Computer Journal. 1997;40(6): 356–372.

[19] Beaumont O, Boudet V, Rastello F, *et al.* Matrix multiplication on heterogeneous platforms. IEEE Transactions on Parallel and Distributed Systems. 2001;12(10):1033–1051.

[20] Kalinov A, Lastovetsky A. Heterogeneous distribution of computations solving linear algebra problems on networks of heterogeneous computers. Journal of Parallel and Distributed Computing. 2001;61:520–535.

[21] Lastovetsky AL, Reddy R. Data partitioning with a realistic performance model of networks of heterogeneous computers. In: 18th International Parallel and Distributed Processing Symposium. IEEE; 2004. p. 104.

[22] Lastovetsky A, Twamley J. Towards a realistic performance model for networks of heterogeneous computers. In: High Performance Computational Science and Engineering. Springer; 2005. p. 39–57.

[23] Lastovetsky A, Reddy R. Data partitioning with a functional performance model of heterogeneous processors. International Journal of High Performance Computing Applications. 2007;21(1):76–90.

[24] Lastovetsky A, Reddy R. Data distribution for dense factorization on computers with memory heterogeneity. Parallel Computing. 2007;33(12).

[25] Lastovetsky A, Szustak L, Wyrzykowski R. Model-based optimization of EULAG kernel on Intel Xeon Phi through load imbalancing. IEEE Transactions on Parallel and Distributed Systems. 2017;28(3):787–797.

[26] Lastovetsky A, Reddy R. New model-based methods and algorithms for performance and energy optimization of data parallel applications on homogeneous multicore clusters. IEEE Transactions on Parallel and Distributed Systems. 2017;28(4):1119–1133.

[27] Alexandrov A, Ionescu MF, Schauser KE, et al. LogGP: Incorporating long messages into the LogP model–one step closer towards a realistic model for parallel computation. In: Proceedings of the Seventh Annual ACM Symposium on Parallel Algorithms and Architectures. SPAA'95. NY, USA; 1995. p. 95–105.

[28] Kielmann T, Bal HE, Verstoep K. Fast measurement of LogP parameters for message passing platforms. In: Proceedings of the 15 IPDPS 2000 Workshops on Parallel and Distributed Processing. IPDPS'00. London, UK: Springer-Verlag; 2000. p. 1176–1183.

[29] Bosque JL, Perez LP. HLogGP: A new parallel computational model for heterogeneous clusters. In: IEEE International Symposium on Cluster Computing and the Grid, 2004 (CCGrid); 2004. p. 403–410.

[30] Lastovetsky A, Mkwawa IH, O'Flynn M. An accurate communication model of a heterogeneous cluster based on a switch-enabled Ethernet network. In: 12th International Conference on Parallel and Distributed Systems, 2006. ICPADS 2006. vol. 2; 2006. p. 6.

[31] Cameron KW, Ge R, Sun XH. $\log_m P$ and $\log_3 P$: Accurate analytical models of point-to-point communication in distributed systems. IEEE Transactions on Computers. 2007;56(3):314–327.

[32] Rico-Gallego JA, Díaz-Martín JC, Lastovetsky AL. Extending τ-Lop to model concurrent MPI communications in multicore clusters. Future Generation Computer Systems. 2016;61:66–82.

[33] Rico-Gallego JA, Lastovetsky AL, Díaz-Martín JC. Model-based estimation of the communication cost of hybrid data-parallel applications on heterogeneous clusters. IEEE Transactions on Parallel and Distributed Systems. 2017;28(11):3215–3228.

[34] Clarke D, Zhong Z, Rychkov V, et al. FuPerMod: A software tool for the optimization of data-parallel applications on heterogeneous platforms. Journal of Supercomputing. 2014;69:61–69.

[35] Beaumont O, Boudet V, Rastello F, et al. Matrix multiplication on heterogeneous platforms. IEEE Transactions on Parallel Distrib System. 2001;12(10):1033–1051. Available from: http://dx.doi.org/10.1109/71.963416.

[36] Malik T, Rychkov V, Lastovetsky A. Network-aware optimization of communications for parallel matrix multiplication on hierarchical HPC platforms. Concurrency and Computation: Practice and Experience. 2016;28(3):802–821.

[37] Bellosa F. The benefits of event: Driven energy accounting in power-sensitive systems. In: Proceedings of the 9th workshop on ACM SIGOPS European

Workshop: Beyond the PC: New Challenges for the Operating System. ACM; 2000.

[38]   Isci C, Martonosi M. Runtime power monitoring in high-end processors: Methodology and empirical data. In: 36th Annual IEEE/ACM International Symposium on Microarchitecture. IEEE Computer Society; 2003. p. 93.

[39]   Economou D, Rivoire S, Kozyrakis C, *et al.* Full-system power analysis and modeling for server environments. In: Proceedings of Workshop on Modeling, Benchmarking, and Simulation; 2006. p. 70–77.

[40]   Basmadjian R, Ali N, Niedermeier F, *et al.* A methodology to predict the power consumption of servers in data centres. In: 2nd International Conference on Energy-Efficient Computing and Networking. ACM; 2011.

[41]   Bircher WL, John LK. Complete system power estimation using processor performance events. IEEE Transactions on Computers. 2012;61(4):563–577.

[42]   Hong H Sunpyand Kim. An integrated GPU power and performance model. SIGARCH Computer Architecture News. 2010;38(3):280–289.

[43]   Song S, Su C, Rountree B, *et al.* A simplified and accurate model of power-performance efficiency on emergent GPU architectures. In: 27th IEEE International Parallel & Distributed Processing Symposium (IPDPS). IEEE Computer Society; 2013. p. 673–686.

[44]   CUPTI. CUDA Profiling Tools Interface; 2018. Available from: https://developer.nvidia.com/cuda-profiling-tools-interface.

[45]   Wang H, Cao Y. Predicting power consumption of GPUs with fuzzy wavelet neural networks. Parallel Computing. 2015;44:18–36.

[46]   Top500. Top 500. The List – November 2017; 2018. Available from: https://www.top500.org/lists/2017/11/.

[47]   Shao YS, Brooks D. Energy characterization and instruction-level energy model of Intel's Xeon Phi processor. In: Proceedings of the 2013 International Symposium on Low Power Electronics and Design. ISLPED'13. IEEE Press; 2013.

[48]   Ou J, Prasanna VK. Rapid energy estimation of computations on FPGA based soft processors. In: SOC Conference, 2004. IEEE International; 2004.

[49]   Wang X, Ziavras SG, Hu J. System-level energy modeling for heterogeneous reconfigurable chip multiprocessors. In: 2006 International Conference on Computer Design; 2006.

[50]   Al-Khatib Z, Abdi S. Operand-value-based modeling of dynamic energy consumption of soft processors in FPGA. In: International Symposium on Applied Reconfigurable Computing. Springer; 2015. p. 65–76.

[51]   Lively C, Wu X, Taylor V, *et al.* Power-aware predictive models of hybrid (MPI/OpenMP) scientific applications on multicore systems. Computer Science-Research and Development. 2012;27(4):245–253.

[52]   PAPI. Performance Application Programming Interface 5.6.0; 2018. Available from: http://icl.cs.utk.edu/papi/.

[53]   Bosilca G, Ltaief H, Dongarra J. Power profiling of Cholesky and QR factorizations on distributed memory systems. Computer Science-Research and Development. 2014;29(2):139–147.

[54] Witkowski M, Oleksiak A, Piontek T, *et al.* Practical Power Consumption Estimation for Real Life HPC Applications. Future Generation Computer Systems. 2013;29(1):208–217.

[55] Jarus M, Oleksiak A, Piontek T, *et al.* Runtime power usage estimation of HPC servers for various classes of real-life applications. Future Generation Computer Systems. 2014;36:299–310.

[56] Lastovetsky A, Manumachu RR. New model-based methods and algorithms for performance and energy optimization of data parallel applications on homogeneous multicore clusters. IEEE Transactions on Parallel and Distributed Systems. 2017;28(4):1119–1133.

[57] McCullough JC, Agarwal Y, Chandrashekar J, *et al.* Evaluating the effectiveness of model-based power characterization. In: Proceedings of the 2011 USENIX Conference on USENIX Annual Technical Conference. USENIXATC'11. USENIX Association; 2011.

[58] Hackenberg D, Ilsche T, Schöne R, *et al.* Power measurement techniques on standard compute nodes: A quantitative comparison. In: 2013 IEEE International Symposium on Performance Analysis of Systems and Software (ISPASS). IEEE; 2013. p. 194–204.

[59] Rotem E, Naveh A, Ananthakrishnan A, *et al.* Power-Management Architecture of the Intel Microarchitecture Code-Named Sandy Bridge. IEEE Micro. 2012 March;32(2):20–27.

[60] O'Brien K, Pietri I, Reddy R, *et al.* A survey of power and energy predictive models in HPC systems and applications. ACM Computing Surveys. 2017;50(3). Available from: http://doi.org/10.1145/3078811.

[61] Shahid A, Fahad M, Reddy R, *et al.* Additivity: A selection criterion for performance events for reliable energy predictive modeling. Supercomputing Frontiers and Innovations. 2017;4(4).

[62] Treibig J, Hager G, Wellein G. Likwid: A lightweight performance-oriented tool suite for x86 multicore environments. In: 2010 39th International Conference on Parallel Processing Workshops (ICPPW). IEEE; 2010. p. 207–216.

[63] Mobius C, Dargie W, Schill A. Power consumption estimation models for processors, virtual machines, and servers. IEEE Transactions on Parallel and Distributed Systems. 2014;25(6):1600–1614.

[64] Inacio EC, Dantas MAR. A survey into performance and energy efficiency in HPC, cloud and big data environments. International Journal on Networking and Virtual Organisations. 2014;14(4):299–318.

[65] Tan L, Kothapalli S, Chen L, *et al.* A survey of power and energy efficient techniques for high performance numerical linear algebra operations. Parallel Computing. 2014;40(10):559–573.

[66] Dayarathna M, Wen Y, Fan R. Data center energy consumption modeling: A survey. IEEE Communications Surveys & Tutorials. 2016;18(1):732–794.

[67] Mezmaz M, Melab N, Kessaci Y, *et al.* A parallel bi-objective hybrid metaheuristic for energy-aware scheduling for cloud computing systems. Journal of Parallel and Distributed Computing. 2011;71(11):1497–1508.

[68]   Fard HM, Prodan R, Barrionuevo JJD, *et al.* A multi-objective approach
       for workflow scheduling in heterogeneous environments. In: Proceedings of
       the 2012 12th IEEE/ACM International Symposium on Cluster, Cloud and
       Grid Computing (Ccgrid 2012). CCGRID'12. IEEE Computer Society; 2012.
       p. 300–309.

[69]   Beloglazov A, Abawajy J, Buyya R. Energy-aware resource allocation
       heuristics for efficient management of data centers for Cloud computing.
       Future Generation Computer Systems. 2012;28(5):755–768. Special Section:
       Energy efficiency in large-scale distributed systems.

[70]   Kessaci Y, Melab N, Talbi EG. A pareto-based metaheuristic for scheduling
       HPC applications on a geographically distributed cloud federation. Cluster
       Computing. 2013;16(3):451–468.

[71]   Durillo JJ, Nae V, Prodan R. Multi-objective energy-efficient workflow
       scheduling using list-based heuristics. Future Generation Computer Systems.
       2014;36:221–236.

[72]   Freeh VW, Lowenthal DK, Pan F, *et al.* Analyzing the energy-time trade-off
       in high-performance computing applications. IEEE Transactions on Parallel
       and Distributed Systems. 2007;18(6):835–848.

[73]   Ahmad I, Ranka S, Khan SU. Using game theory for scheduling tasks on multi-
       core processors for simultaneous optimization of performance and energy. In:
       IEEE International Symposium on Parallel and Distributed Processing, 2008.
       IPDPS 2008; 2008. p. 1–6.

[74]   Balaprakash P, Tiwari A, Wild SM. In: Jarvis AS, Wright AS, Ham-
       mond DS, editors. Multi-objective Optimization of HPC Kernels for Per-
       formance, Power, and Energy. Springer International Publishing; 2014.
       p. 239–260.

[75]   Drozdowski M, Marszalkowski JM, Marszalkowski J. Energy trade-offs
       analysis using equal-energy maps. Future Generation Computer Systems.
       2014;36:311–321.

[76]   Marszalkowski JM, Drozdowski M, Marszalkowski J. Time and energy per-
       formance of parallel systems with hierarchical memory. Journal of Grid
       Computing. 2016;14(1):153–170.

[77]   Reddy R, Lastovetsky A. Bi-objective optimization of data-parallel applica-
       tions on homogeneous multicore clusters for performance and energy. IEEE
       Transactions on Computers. 2018;64(2):160–177.

[78]   Juve G, Chervenak A, Deelman E, *et al.* Characterizing and profiling scien-
       tific workflows. Future Generation Computer Systems. 2013;29(3):682–692.

[79]   Fahringer T, Prodan R, Duan R, *et al.* ASKALON: A development and
       grid computing environment for scientific workflows. In: Taylor IJ, Deel-
       man E, Gannon DB, *et al.*, editors. Workflows for e-Science. Springer; 2007.
       p. 450–471.

[80]   Altintas I, Berkley C, Jaeger E, *et al.* Kepler: An extensible system for design
       and execution of scientific workflows. In: 16th International Conference on
       Scientific and Statistical Database Management; 2004. p. 423–424.

[81] Tristan Glatard DLXP Johan Montagnat. Flexible and efficient workflow deployment of data-intensive applications on grids with MOTEUR. International Journal of High Performance Computing Applications. 2008;22(3):347–360.

[82] Taylor I, Shields M, Wang I, *et al*. Triana applications within grid computing and peer to peer environments. Journal of Grid Computing. 2003 Jun;1(2):199–217.

[83] Kacsuk P. P-GRADE portal family for grid infrastructures. Concurrency and Computation: Practice and Experience. 2011;23(3):235–245.

[84] Deelman E, Vahi K, Juve G, *et al*. Pegasus, a workflow management system for science automation. Future Generation Computer Systems. 2015;46:17–35.

[85] Durillo JJ, Prodan R, Barbosa JG. Pareto tradeoff scheduling of workflows on federated commercial clouds. Simulation Modelling Practice and Theory. 2015;58:95–111.

[86] Arabnejad H, Barbosa JG. Budget constrained scheduling strategies for online workflow applications. In: International Conference on Computational Science and Its Applications. Springer; 2014. p. 532–545.

[87] Ullman JD. NP-complete scheduling problems. Journal of Computer and System sciences. 1975;10(3):384–393.

[88] Topcuoglu H, Hariri S, Wu MY. Performance-effective and low-complexity task scheduling for heterogeneous computing. IEEE Transactions on Parallel and Distributed Systems. 2002 3;13(3):260–274.

[89] Wieczorek M, Hoheisel A, Prodan R. Towards a general model of the multi-criteria workflow scheduling on the grid. Future Generations Computer Systems. 2009;25(3):237–256.

[90] Maheswaran M, Ali S, Siegel HJ, *et al*. Dynamic mapping of a class of independent tasks onto heterogeneous computing systems. Journal of Parallel and Distributed Computing. 1999;59(2):107–131.

[91] Arabnejad H, Barbosa JG. List scheduling algorithm for heterogeneous systems by an optimistic cost table. IEEE Transactions on Parallel and Distributed Systems. 2014;25(3):682–694.

[92] Bittencourt LF, Sakellariou R, Madeira ER. DAG scheduling using a lookahead variant of the heterogeneous earliest finish time algorithm. In: 2010 18th Euromicro International Conference on Parallel, Distributed and Network-Based Processing (PDP). IEEE; 2010. p. 27–34.

[93] Armbrust M, Fox A, Griffith R, *et al*. A view of cloud computing. Communications of the ACM. 2010;53(4):50–58.

[94] Leitão J, Pereira J, Rodrigues L. Epidemic broadcast trees. In: Proceedings of SRDS 2007; 2007. p. 301–310.

[95] Leitão J, Pereira J, Rodrigues L. HyParView: A membership protocol for reliable gossip-based broadcast. In: 37th Annual IEEE/IFIP International Conference on Dependable Systems and Networks, 2007. DSN'07. 2007. p. 419–429.

[96]   Shapiro M, Preguiça N, Baquero C, *et al*. Conflict-free replicated data types. INRIA; 2011. RR-7687.

[97]   Almeida PS, Shoker A, Baquero C. Efficient state-based crdts by delta-mutation. In: International Conference on Networked Systems. Springer; 2015. p. 62–76.

[98]   Carlos Baquero PSA, Shoker A. Making operation-based CRDTs operation-based. In: Distributed Applications and Interoperable Systems – 14th IFIP WG 6.1 International Conference, DAIS 2014, Held as Part of the 9th International Federated Conference on Distributed Computing Techniques, DisCoTec 2014, Berlin, Germany, June 3–5, 2014; 2014. p. 126–140. Available from: http://dx.doi.org/10.1007/978-3-662-43352-2_11.

[99]   Bonomi F, Milito R, Zhu J, *et al*. Fog computing and its role in the internet of things. Proceedings of the First Edition of the MCC Workshop on Mobile Cloud Computing. 2012;p. 13–16. Available from: http://doi.acm.org/10.1145/2342509.2342513\npapers2://publication/doi/10.1145/2342509.2342513.

[100]   Yi S, Li C, Li Q. A survey of fog computing: Concepts, applications and issues. In: Proceedings of the 2015 Workshop on Mobile Big Data. Mobidata'15. New York, NY, USA: ACM; 2015. p. 37–42. Available from: http://doi.acm.org/10.1145/2757384.2757397.

[101]   Verbelen T, Simoens P, De Turck F, *et al*. Cloudlets: Bringing the cloud to the mobile user. In: Proceedings of the Third ACM Workshop on Mobile Cloud Computing and Services. ACM; 2012. p. 29–36.

[102]   Fernando N, Loke SW, Rahayu W. Mobile cloud computing: A survey. Future Generation Computer Systems. 2013;29(1):84–106.

[103]   Hu YC, Patel M, Sabella D, *et al*. Mobile edge computing – A key technology towards 5G. ETSI White Paper. 2015;11(11):1–16.

[104]   Cisco. Cisco IOx Data Sheet; 2016. Available from: http://www.cisco.com/c/en/us/products/collateral/cloud-systems-management/iox/datasheet-c78-736767.html.

[105]   Dell. Dell Edge Gateway 5000; 2016. Available from: http://www.dell.com/us/business/p/dell-edge-gateway-5000/pd?oc=xctoi5000us.

[106]   Milojicic DS, Kalogeraki V, Lukose R, *et al*. Peer-to-Peer Computing. 2002. Available from: http://www.hpl.hp.com/techreports/2002/HPL-2002-57R1.pdf.

[107]   Jelasity M, Montresor A, Babaoglu O. Gossip-based aggregation in large dynamic networks. ACM Transactions on Computer Systems (TOCS). 2005;23(3):219–252.

[108]   Akyildiz IF, Su W, Sankarasubramaniam Y, *et al*. Wireless sensor networks: A survey. Computer Networks. 2002;38(4):393–422.

[109]   Gilbert S, Lynch N. Brewer's conjecture and the feasibility of consistent. Available, Partition-tolerant Web Services. SIGACT News. 2002;33(2): 51–59.

[110]   Meiklejohn C, Van Roy P. Lasp: A language for distributed, coordination-free programming. In: Proceedings of the 17th International Symposium on

Principles and Practice of Declarative Programming (PPDP 2015). ACM; 2015. p. 184–195.

[111] Carvalho N, Pereira J, Oliveira R, *et al.* Emergent structure in unstructured epidemic multicast. In: Proceedings of the 37th Annual IEEE/IFIP International Conference on Dependable Systems and Networks (DSN'07). Edinburgh, Scotland, UK; 2007. p. 481–490.

[112] Balegas V, Serra D, Duarte S, *et al.* Extending eventually consistent cloud databases for enforcing numeric invariants. In: Proceedings of SRDS 2015. Montréal, Canada: IEEE Computer Society; 2015. p. 31–36. Available from: http://lip6.fr/Marc.Shapiro/papers/numeric-invariants-SRDS-2015.pdf.

[113] Najafzadeh M, Shapiro M, Balegas V, *et al.* Improving the scalability of geo-replication with reservations. In: ACM SIGCOMM – Distributed Cloud Computing (DCC). Dresden, Germany; 2013. Available from: http://lip6.fr/Marc.Shapiro//papers/escrow-DCC-2013.pdf.

[114] Gotsman A, Yang H, Ferreira C, *et al.* 'Cause I'M strong enough: Reasoning about consistency choices in distributed systems. In: Proceedings of the 43rd Annual ACM SIGPLAN-SIGACT Symposium on Principles of Programming Languages. New York, NY, USA: ACM; 2016. p. 371–384. Available from: http://doi.acm.org/10.1145/2837614.2837625.

[115] Akkoorath DD, Tomsic A, Bravo M, *et al.* Cure: Strong semantics meets high availability and low latency. INRIA; 2016. RR-8858.

[116] Lasp: The Missing Part of Erlang Distribution. Accessed: 2018-04-27. http://www.lasp-lang.org.

[117] Meiklejohn C, Enes V, Yoo J, *et al.* Practical evaluation of the Lasp programming model at large scale. In: Proceedings of the 19th International Symposium on Principles and Practice of Declarative Programming (PPDP 2017). ACM; 2017. p. 109–114.

[118] Bichot CE, Siarry P. Graph Partitioning. John Wiley & Sons; 2013.

[119] Shewchuk JR. Allow Me to Introduce Spectral and Isoperimetric Graph Partitioning; 2016. Available from: http://www.cs.berkeley.edu/~jrs/papers/partnotes.pdf.

[120] Bellman R. Introduction to Matrix Analysis. Society for Industrial and Applied Mathematics; 1997.

[121] Chung FR. Laplacians of graphs and Cheeger's inequalities. Combinatorics, Paul Erdos is Eighty. 1996;2(157–172):13–2.

[122] Spielman DA, Teng SH. Spectral partitioning works: Planar graphs and finite element meshes. Linear Algebra and Its Applications. 2007;421(2): 284–305.

[123] Gantmakher FR. The Theory of Matrices. Vol. 131. American Mathematical Society; 1998.

[124] Berman A, Plemmons RJ. Nonnegative Matrices. Vol. 9. SIAM; 1979.

[125] Fiedler M. Algebraic connectivity of graphs. Czechoslovak Mathematical Journal. 1973;23(2):298–305.

[126] Mohar B. Isoperimetric numbers of graphs. Journal of Combinatorial Theory, Series B. 1989;47(3):274–291.

[127] Van Driessche R, Roose D. An improved spectral bisection algorithm and its application to dynamic load balancing. Parallel Computing. 1995;21(1): 29–48.

[128] Hendrickson B, Leland R. An improved spectral graph partitioning algorithm for mapping parallel computations. SIAM Journal on Scientific Computing. 1995;16(2):452–469.

[129] Lancaster P, Tismenetsky M. The Theory of Matrices: With Applications. Elsevier; 1985.

[130] Chevalier C, Pellegrini F. PT-Scotch: A tool for efficient parallel graph ordering. Parallel Computing. 2008;34(6):318–331.

[131] Anderson E, Bai Z, Bischof C, *et al.* LAPACK Users' Guide (Software, Environments and Tools). 3rd Edition. Society for Industrial and Applied Mathematics; 1997.

[132] Bergamaschi L, Bozzo E. Computing the smallest eigenpairs of the graph Laplacian. SeMA Journal. 2018;75(1):1–16.

[133] Soper AJ, Walshaw C, Cross M. A combined evolutionary search and multilevel optimisation approach to graph-partitioning. Journal of Global Optimization. 2004;29(2):225–241.

[134] Zheng A, Labrinidis A, Pisciuneri PH, *et al.* PARAGON: Parallel Architecture-Aware Graph Partition Refinement Algorithm. In: EDBT; 2016. p. 365–376.

[135] Fiduccia CM, Mattheyses RM. A linear-time heuristic for improving network partitions. In: Papers on Twenty-five years of electronic design automation. ACM; 1988. p. 241–247.

[136] Wasim MU, Ibrahim AAZA, Bouvry P, *et al.* Law as a service (LaaS): Enabling legal protection over a blockchain network. In: 2017 14th International Conference on Smart Cities: Improving Quality of Life Using ICT IoT (HONET-ICT); 2017. p. 110–114.

[137] Siewiorek DP, Swarz RS. Reliable Computer Systems (3rd Ed.): Design and Evaluation. Natick, MA, USA: A. K. Peters, Ltd.; 1998.

[138] Snir M, Wisniewski RW, Abraham JA, *et al.* Addressing failures in exascale computing. IJHPCA. 2014;28(2):129–173. Available from: http://dx.doi.org/10.1177/1094342014522573.

[139] Cappello F, Geist A, Gropp B, *et al.* Toward exascale resilience. IJHPCA. 2009;23(4):374–388. Available from: http://dx.doi.org/10.1177/1094342009347767.

[140] Cappello F. Fault tolerance in petascale/ exascale systems: Current knowledge, challenges and research opportunities. IJHPCA. 2009;23(3):212–226. Available from: http://dx.doi.org/10.1177/1094342009106189.

[141] Avizienis A, Laprie JC, Randell B, *et al.* Basic Concepts and Taxonomy of Dependable and Secure Computing. IEEE Transactions on Dependable and Secure Computing. 2004;1:11–33.

[142] Elnozahy ENM, Alvisi L, Wang YM, *et al.* A survey of rollback-recovery protocols in message-passing systems. ACM Computing Survey. 2002;34(3): 375–408. Available from: http://doi.acm.org/10.1145/568522.568525.

[143] Chen Z, Fagg GE, Gabriel E, *et al.* Fault tolerant high performance computing by a coding approach. In: Proceedings of the Tenth ACM SIG-PLAN Symposium on Principles and Practice of Parallel Programming. PPoPP'05. New York, NY, USA: ACM; 2005. p. 213–223. Available from: http://doi.acm.org/10.1145/1065944.1065973.

[144] Vosoughi A, Bilal K, Khan SU, *et al.* A multidimensional robust greedy algorithm for resource path finding in large-scale distributed networks. In: Proceedings of the 8th International Conference on Frontiers of Information Technology. FIT'10. New York, NY, USA: ACM; 2010. p. 16:1–16:6. Available from: http://doi.acm.org/10.1145/1943628.1943644.

[145] Dumas JG, Roch JL, Tannier E, *et al.* Foundations of Coding: Compression, Encryption, Error-Correction. Wiley & Sons; 2015. 376 p.

[146] Mazumder P. Design of a fault-tolerant DRAM with new on-chip ECC. In: Koren I, editor. Defect and Fault Tolerance in VLSI Systems. Springer US; 1989. p. 85–92. Available from: http://dx.doi.org/10.1007/978-1-4615-6799-8_8.

[147] Choi M, Park NJ, George KM, *et al.* Fault tolerant memory design for HW/SW co-reliability in massively parallel computing systems. In: 2nd International Symposium on Network Computing and Applications, 2003. NCA 2003; 2003. p. 341–348.

[148] Ernst D, Das S, Lee S, *et al.* Razor: Circuit-level correction of timing errors for low-power operation. IEEE Micro. 2004;24(6):10–20.

[149] Benini L, De Michelli G. Networks on chips: Technology and tools. The Morgan Kaufmann Series in Systems on Silicon. Amsterdam, Boston, Paris: Elsevier Morgan Kaufmann Publishers; 2006. Available from: http://opac.inria.fr/record=b1123186.

[150] Radetzki M, Feng C, Zhao X, *et al.* Methods for fault tolerance in networks-on-chip. ACM Computing Survey. 2013;46(1):8:1–8:38. Available from: http://doi.acm.org/10.1145/2522968.2522976.

[151] Park D, Nicopoulos C, Kim J, *et al.* Exploring fault-tolerant network-on-chip architectures. In: International Conference on Dependable Systems and Networks, 2006. DSN 2006; 2006. p. 93–104.

[152] Muszyński J, Varrette S, Bouvry P. Reducing efficiency of connectivity-splitting attack on newscast via limited gossip. In: Proceedings of the 19th European Event on Bio-Inspired Computation, EvoCOMNET 2016. LNCS. Porto, Portugal: Springer Verlag; 2016.

[153] Jelasity M, Voulgaris S, Guerraoui R, *et al.* Gossip-based Peer Sampling. ACM Transactions on Computer Systems. 2007;25(3). Available from: http://doi.acm.org/10.1145/1275517.1275520.

[154] MPI: A Message-Passing Interface Standard, Version 3.1. MPI forum; 2015. [online] see http://mpi-forum.org/docs/mpi-3.1/mpi31-report.pdf.

[155] Gropp W, Lusk E. Fault tolerance in message passing interface programs. International Journal of High Performance Computing Applications. 2004;18(3):363–372. Available from: https://doi.org/10.1177/1094342004046045.

[156]   Yaga D, Mell P, Roby N, *et al.* Draft NISTIR 8202: Blockchain Technology Overview. NIST; 2018. https://csrc.nist.gov/publications/detail/ nistir/8202/draft.

[157]   Dumas JG, Lafourcade P, Tichit A, *et al.* Les blockchains en 50 questions: comprendre le fonctionnement et les enjeux de cette technologie innovante (1st ed.). Collection Sciences Sup. Dunod; 2018. (french).

[158]   Wasim MU, Ibrahim A, Bouvry P, *et al.* Self-Regulated multi-criteria decision analysis: An autonomous brokerage-based approach for service provider ranking in the cloud. In: Proceedings of the 8th IEEE International Conference on Cloud Computing Technology and Science (CloudCom 2017). Hong Kong; 2017. p. 33–40.

[159]   Christidis K, Devetsikiotis M. Blockchains and smart contracts for the internet of things. IEEE Access. 2016;4:2292–2303.

[160]   Savelyev A. Contract law 2.0: «Smart» contracts as the beginning of the end of classic contract law. Information & Communications Technology Law. 2017;26(2):116–134.

[161]   Verbeek M. A Guide to Modern Econometrics. John Wiley & Sons; 2008.

[162]   Rummel R. Applied Factor Analysis. Evanston, IL: Northwestern University Press. Google Scholar; 1970.

[163]   Rencher AC. Methods of Multivariate Analysis. Vol. 492. John Wiley & Sons; 2003.

[164]   Taylor HM, Karlin S. An Introduction to Stochastic Modeling. Academic Press; 2014.

[165]   Cooper BF, Silberstein A, Tam E, *et al.* Benchmarking Cloud Serving Systems with YCSB. In: SoCC' 10 ACM; 2010.

[166]   Papagiannis A, Saloustros G, González-Férez P, *et al.* Tucana: Design and implementation of a fast and efficient scale-up key-value store. In: Proceedings of the 2016 USENIX Annual Technical Conference (USENIX ATC 16); 2016. p. 537–550.

[167]   Apache. HBase. Accessed: December 3, 2018. https://hbase.apache.org/.

[168]   O'Neil P, Cheng E, Gawlick D, *et al.* The log-structured merge-tree (LSM-tree). Acta Informatica. 1996;33(4):351–385.

[169]   Brodal GS, Fagerberg R. Lower bounds for external memory dictionaries. In: Proceedings of the Fourteenth Annual ACM-SIAM Symposium on Discrete Algorithms. SODA'03. Philadelphia, PA, USA: Society for Industrial and Applied Mathematics; 2003. p. 546–554. Available from: http://dl.acm.org/citation.cfm?id=644108.644201.

[170]   Cooper BF, Silberstein A, Tam E, *et al.* Benchmarking cloud serving systems with YCSB. In: Proceedings of the 1st ACM Symposium on Cloud Computing. SoCC'10. New York, NY, USA: ACM; 2010. p. 143–154. Available from: http://doi.acm.org/10.1145/1807128.1807152.

[171]   Oliker L, Biswas R, Van der Wijngaart R, *et al.* Performance evaluation and modeling of ultra-scale systems. Parallel Processing for Scientific Computing. SIAM; 2006. p. 77–93.

[172] Da Costa G, Fahringer T, Rico-Gallego JA, *et al.* Exascale machines require new programming paradigms and runtimes. Supercomputing Frontiers and Innovations. 2015;2(2):6–27.

[173] Marozzo F, Rodrigo Duro F, Garcia Blas J, *et al.* A data-aware scheduling strategy for workflow execution in clouds. Concurrency and Computation: Practice and Experience. 2017;29(24):e4229.

[174] Marozzo F, Talia D, Trunfio P. A workflow management system for scalable data mining on clouds. IEEE Transactions on Services Computing. 2018;11(3):480–492.

[175] Duro FR, Blas JG, Carretero J. A hierarchical parallel storage system based on distributed memory for large scale systems. In: Proceedings of the 20th European MPI Users' Group Meeting. EuroMPI'13. New York, NY, USA: ACM; 2013. p. 139–140.

[176] Thain D, Moretti C, Hemmes J. Chirp: A practical global filesystem for cluster and Grid computing. Journal of Grid Computing. 2009;7(1):51–72.

[177] Marozzo F, Talia D, Trunfio P. JS4Cloud: Script-based workflow programming for scalable data analysis on cloud platforms. Concurrency and Computation: Practice and Experience. 2015;27(17):5214–5237.

[178] Duro FR, Marozzo F, Blas JG, *et al.* Exploiting in-memory storage for improving workflow executions in cloud platforms. Journal of Supercomputing. 2016:1–20.

[179] Wu X, Kumar V, Ross Quinlan J, *et al.* Top 10 algorithms in data mining. Knowledge and Information Systems. 2007;14(1):1–37.

[180] Gilbert S, Lynch N. Brewer's conjecture and the feasibility of consistent, available, partition-tolerant web services. Acm SIGACT News. 2002;33(2):51–59.

[181] Shapiro M, Preguiça N, Baquero C, *et al.* A comprehensive study of convergent and commutative replicated data types. INRIA–Centre Paris-Rocquencourt; INRIA; 2011.

[182] Almeida PS, Shoker A, Baquero C. Delta state replicated data types. Journal of Parallel and Distributed Computing. 2018;111:162–173.

[183] Baquero C, Almeida PS, Shoker A. Pure Operation-based Replicated Data Types. preprint arXiv:171004469. 2017.

[184] Martí Fraiz J. dataClay: Next generation object storage. Universitat Politècnica de Catalunya; 2017. PhD dissertation.

[185] Martí J, Queralt A, Gasull D, *et al.* Dataclay: A distributed data store for effective inter-player data sharing. Journal of Systems and Software. 2017;131:129–145.

[186] Terry D. Replicated data consistency explained through baseball. ACM Communications. 2013;56(12):82–89. Available from: http://doi.acm.org/10.1145/2500500.

[187] Goodman JR. Cache Consistency and Sequential Consistency. University of Wisconsin-Madison, Computer Sciences Department; 1991.

[188] Lamport L, *et al.* Paxos made simple. ACM SIGACT News. 2001;32(4):18–25.

[189]   Abadi D. Consistency tradeoffs in modern distributed database system design: CAP is only part of the story. IEEE Computer. 2012;45(2):37–42. Available from: https://doi.org/10.1109/MC.2012.33.

[190]   Vogels W. Eventually consistent. Communications of the ACM. 2009;52(1):40–44.

[191]   Lamport L. Time, clocks, and the ordering of events in a distributed system. Communications of the ACM. 1978;21(7):558–565.

[192]   DeCandia G, Hastorun D, Jampani M, *et al.* Dynamo: Amazon's highly available key-value store. In: ACM SIGOPS Operating Systems Review. Vol. 41. ACM; 2007. p. 205–220.

[193]   Davey BA, Priestley HA. Introduction to lattices and order. Cambridge University Press; 2002.

[194]   Vitor Enes, Carlos Baquero, Paulo Sergio Almeida, and Ali Shoker. Join decompositions for efficient synchronization of CRDTs after a network partition. In: Proceedings of the ECOOP Programming Models and Languages for Distributed Computing Workshop. PMLDC'16. ACM; 2016.

[195]   Bailis P, Fekete A, Franklin MJ, *et al.* Coordination avoidance in database systems. PVLDB. 2014;8(3):185–196. Available from: http://www.vldb.org/pvldb/vol8/p185-bailis.pdf.

[196]   Careglio D, Costa GD, Ricciardi S. 2. In: Hardware Leverages for Energy Reduction in Large-Scale Distributed Systems. Wiley-Blackwell; 2015. p. 17–40. Available from: https://onlinelibrary.wiley.com/doi/abs/10.1002/9781118981122.ch2.

[197]   Chen Y, Das A, Qin W, *et al.* Managing server energy and operational costs in hosting centers. SIGMETRICS Performance Evaluation Review. 2005;33(1):303–314.

[198]   Gschwandtner P, Knobloch M, Mohr B, *et al.* Modeling CPU energy consumption of HPC applications on the IBM POWER7. In: 2014 22nd Euromicro International Conference on Parallel, Distributed and Network-Based Processing (PDP); 2014. p. 536–543.

[199]   Hamilton J. Internet-scale service infrastructure efficiency. SIGARCH Computer Architecture News. 2009;37(3):232–232.

[200]   Rivoire S, Ranganathan P, Kozyrakis C. A comparison of high-level full-system power models. In: Proceedings of the 2008 Conference on Power Aware Computing and Systems. HotPower'08. Berkeley, CA, USA: USENIX Association; 2008. p. 3–3.

[201]   Orgerie AC, Lefevre L, Gelas JP. Demystifying energy consumption in Grids and Clouds. In: 2010 International Green Computing Conference; 2010. p. 335–342.

[202]   Wang D, Ganesh B, Tuaycharoen N, *et al.* DRAMsim: A memory system simulator. SIGARCH Computer Architecture News. 2005;33(4):100–107.

[203]   Kim Y, Yang W, Mutlu O. Ramulator: A fast and extensible DRAM simulator. Computer Architecture Letters. 2016;15(1):45–49.

[204]   Waldspurger CA. Memory resource management in VMware ESX server. SIGOPS Operating System Review. 2002;36(SI):181–194. Available from: http://doi.acm.org/10.1145/844128.844146.

[205] Zhang G, Wang H, Hongwu LV, *et al.* A dynamic memory management model on Xen virtual machine. In: Proceedings 2013 International Conference on Mechatronic Sciences, Electric Engineering and Computer (MEC); 2013. p. 1609–1613.

[206] Habib I. Virtualization with KVM. Linux J. 2008;2008(166). Available from: http://dl.acm.org/citation.cfm?id=1344209.1344217.

[207] Zhu Q, David FM, Devaraj CF, *et al.* Reducing energy consumption of disk storage using power-aware cache management. In: The 10th International Conference on High-Performance Computer Architecture (HPCA-10); 2004. p. 118–129.

[208] Helmbold DP, Long DDE, Sherrod B. A Dynamic Disk Spin-down Technique for Mobile Computing. In: Proceedings of the 2nd Annual International Conference on Mobile Computing and Networking. MobiCom'96. New York, NY, USA: ACM; 1996. p. 130–142.

[209] Colarelli D, Grunwald D. Massive arrays of idle disks for storage archives. In: ACM/IEEE 2002 Conference on Supercomputing; 2002. p. 47–47.

[210] Greenawalt PM. Modeling power management for hard disks. In: Proceedings of the Second International Workshop on Modeling, Analysis, and Simulation of Computer and Telecommunication Systems, 1994. MASCOTS'94. 1994. p. 62–66.

[211] Alshahrani R, Peyravi H. Modeling and simulation of data center networks. In: Proceedings of the 2Nd ACM SIGSIM Conference on Principles of Advanced Discrete Simulation. SIGSIM PADS'14. New York, NY, USA: ACM; 2014. p. 75–82.

[212] Hu N, Fu B, Sui X, *et al.* DCNSim: A unified and cross-layer computer architecture simulation framework for data center network research. In: Proceedings of the ACM International Conference on Computing Frontiers. CF'13. New York, NY, USA: ACM; 2013. p. 19:1–19:9.

[213] Shirayanagi H, Yamada H, Kono K. Honeyguide: A VM migration-aware network topology for saving energy consumption in data center networks. 2014 IEEE Symposium on Computers and Communications (ISCC). 2012;000460–000467.

[214] Zhang Y, Su AJ, Jiang G. Evaluating the impact of data center network architectures on application performance in virtualized environments. In: 2010 18th International Workshop on Quality of Service (IWQoS); 2010. p. 1–5.

[215] De Maio V, Nae V, Prodan R. Evaluating energy efficiency of gigabit ethernet and infiniband software stacks in data centres. In: Proceedings of the 7th IEEE/ACM International Conference on Utility and Cloud Computing (UCC 2014). IEEE Computer Society; 2014. pp. 21–28.

[216] Orgerie AC, Lefevre L, Guerin-Lassous I, *et al.* ECOFEN: An end-to-end energy cost model and simulator for evaluating power consumption in large-scale Networks. In: 2011 IEEE International Symposium on World of Wireless, Mobile and Multimedia Networks (WoWMoM); 2011. p. 1–6.

[217] Pelley S, Meisner D, Wenisch TF, *et al.* Understanding and abstracting total data center power. Workshop on Energy-Efficient Design; 2009.

[218]   Mastelic T, Oleksiak A, Claussen H, *et al.* Cloud computing: Survey on energy efficiency. ACM Computing Survey. 2014;47(2):33:1–33:36.

[219]   Kansal A, Zhao F, Liu J, *et al.* Virtual machine power metering and provisioning. In: Proceedings of the 1st ACM Symposium on Cloud Computing. SoCC'10. New York, NY, USA: ACM; 2010. p. 39–50.

[220]   Rong H, Zhang H, Xiao S, *et al.* Optimizing energy consumption for data centers. Renewable and Sustainable Energy Reviews. 2016;58:674–691.

[221]   Ben-Itzhak Y, Cidon I, Kolodny A. Performance and power aware CMP thread allocation modeling. In: Proceedings of the 5th International Conference on High Performance Embedded Architectures and Compilers. HiPEAC'10. Springer-Verlag; 2010. p. 232–246.

[222]   Lewis AW, Tzeng NF, Ghosh S. Runtime energy consumption estimation for server workloads based on chaotic time-series approximation. ACM Transactions on Architecture and Code Optimization. 2012;9(3):15:1–15:26.

[223]   Beltrame G, Palermo G, Sciuto D, *et al.* Plug-in of power models in the stepnp exploration platform: Analysis of power/performance trade-offs. In: Proceedings of the 2004 International Conference on Compilers, Architecture, and Synthesis for Embedded Systems. CASES'04. New York, NY, USA: ACM; 2004. p. 85–92.

[224]   Itoh K, Sasaki K, Nakagome Y. Trends in low-power RAM circuit technologies. Proceedings of the IEEE. 1995;83(4):524–543.

[225]   Maio VD, Kecskemeti G, Prodan R. An improved model for live migration in data centre simulators. In: 2016 IEEE/ACM 9th International Conference on Utility and Cloud Computing (UCC); 2016. p. 108–117.

[226]   Sun H, Stolf P, Pierson JM. Spatio-temporal thermal-aware scheduling for homogeneous high-performance computing datacenters. Future Generation Computer Systems. 2017;71:157–170. Available from: http://doi.org/10.1016/j.future.2017.02.005 - http://oatao.univ-toulouse.fr/18918/.

[227]   Capozzoli A, Primiceri G. Cooling systems in data centers: State of art and emerging technologies. Energy Procedia. 2015;83:484–493. Sustainability in Energy and Buildings: Proceedings of the 7th International Conference SEB-15.

[228]   Song Z, Zhang X, Eriksson C. Data Center Energy and Cost Saving Evaluation. Energy Procedia. 2015;75:1255–1260. Clean, Efficient and Affordable Energy for a Sustainable Future: The 7th International Conference on Applied Energy (ICAE2015).

[229]   Ham SW, Kim MH, Choi BN, *et al.* Simplified server model to simulate data center cooling energy consumption. Energy and Buildings. 2015;86:328–339.

[230]   Feitelson DG. Workload modeling for computer systems performance evaluation. Cambridge University Press; 2015.

[231]   Costa GD, Grange L, de Courchelle I. Modeling, classifying and generating large-scale Google-like workload. Sustainable Computing: Informatics and Systems. 2018;19:305–314. Available from: http://www.sciencedirect.com/science/article/pii/S2210537917301634.

[232]   Feitelson DG. Resampling with feedback – A new paradigm of using work-load data for performance evaluation. In: European Conference on Parallel Processing. Springer; 2016. p. 3–21.

[233]   Casanova H, Legrand A, Quinson M. SimGrid: A generic framework for large-scale distributed experiments. In: Proceedings of the Tenth International Conference on Computer Modeling and Simulation. UKSIM'08. Washington, DC, USA: IEEE Computer Society; 2008. p. 126–131.

[234]   Kliazovich D, Bouvry P, Khan S. GreenCloud: A packet-level simulator of energy-aware cloud computing data centers. Journal of Supercomputing. 2012;62(3):1263–1283.

[235]   Casanova H. Simgrid: A toolkit for the simulation of application scheduling. In: CCGRID. IEEE Computer Society; 2001. p. 430–441.

[236]   Calheiros RN, Ranjan R, Beloglazov A, *et al.* CloudSim: A toolkit for modeling and simulation of cloud computing environments and evaluation of resource provisioning algorithms. Software: Practice and Experience. 2011;41(1):23–50.

[237]   Ostermann S, Plankensteiner K, Prodan R, *et al.* GroudSim: An event-based simulation framework for computational grids and clouds. In: Guarracino MR, Vivien F, Träff JL, *et al.*, editors. Euro-Par 2010 Parallel Processing Workshops. Berlin, Heidelberg: Springer Berlin Heidelberg; 2011. p. 305–313.

[238]   Kecskemeti G. DISSECT-CF: A simulator to foster energy-aware scheduling in infrastructure clouds. Simulation Modelling Practice and Theory. 2015;58:188–218. Special issue on Cloud Simulation.

[239]   Piątek W, Oleksiak A, Costa GD. Energy and thermal models for simulation of workload and resource management in computing systems. Simulation Modelling Practice and Theory. 2015;58:40–54. Special Issue on Techniques and Applications for Sustainable Ultrascale Computing Systems. Available from: http://www.sciencedirect.com/science/article/ pii/S1569190X15000684.

[240]   Meisner D, Wenisch TF. Stochastic queuing simulation for data center workloads. In: Exascale Evaluation and Research Techniques Workshop; 2010. p. 9.

[241]   Liu N, Carothers C, Cope J, *et al.* Model and simulation of exascale communication networks. Journal of Simulation. 2012;6(4):227–236.

[242]   Heinrich FC, Cornebize T, Degomme A, *et al.* Predicting the energy-consumption of MPI applications at scale using only a single node. In: 2017 IEEE International Conference on Cluster Computing (CLUSTER); 2017. p. 92–102.

[243]   Guérout T, Monteil T, Da Costa G, *et al.* Energy-aware simulation with DVFS. Simulation Modelling Practice and Theory. 2013;39:76–91.

[244]   Caux S, *et al.* datazero: Deliverable D2.4 Sources and Material profiling. IRIT; 2017.

[245]   Caux S, Rostirolla G, Stolf P. Smart datacenter electrical load model for renewable sources management (regular paper). In: International Conference on Renewable Energies and Power Quality (ICREPQ), Salamanca, Spain,

21/03/18-23/03/18. Vol. 16. http://www.icrepq.com: European Association for the Development of Renewable Energies, Environment and Power Quality; 2018. p. 127–132. Available from: https://doi.org/10.24084/repqj16.231.

[246]   Grange L, Da Costa G, Stolf P. Green IT scheduling for data center powered with renewable energy. Future Generation Computer Systems; 2018;86:99–120. Available from: https://doi.org/10.1016/j.future.2018.03.049.

[247]   Solar Radiation on a Tilted Surface. PVeducation; 2018. Available from: http://www.pveducation.org/pvcdrom/properties-of-sunlight/solar-radiation-on-a-tilted-surface.

[248]   Sheme E, Holmbacka S, Lafond S, *et al.* Feasibility of Using Renewable Energy to Supply Data Centers in 60 Degrees North Latitude. Sustainable Computing: Informatics and Systems. 2017;17:96–106.

[249]   Holmbacka S, Sheme E, Lafond S, *et al.* Geographical competitiveness for powering datacenters with renewable energy. In: Third International Workshop on Sustainable Ultrascale Computing Systems, NESUS 2016. Sofia, Bulgaria; October 2016. p. 15–22.

[250]   Sheme E, Lafond S, Minarolli D, *et al.* Battery Size Impact in Green Coverage of Datacenters Powered by Renewable Energy: A Latitude Comparison. In: Barolli L, Xhafa F, Javaid N, *et al.*, editors. Advances in Internet, Data & Web Technologies. Cham: Springer International Publishing; 2018. p. 548–559.

[251]   Tesla Powerwall. Wikipedia; 2017. Available from: https://en.wikipedia.org/wiki/Tesla_Powerwall.

[252]   The Green500 list. Available from: https://www.top500.org [cited 27.04.2018].

[253]   Koomey J, Berard S, Sanchez M, *et al.* Implications of historical trends in the electrical efficiency of computing. IEEE Annals of the History of Computing. 2011;33(3):46–54.

[254]   Klingert S, Basmadjian R, Bunse C, *et al.* Fit4green-energy aware ict optimization policies. IRIT; Proceedings of the COST Action IC0804; 2010.

[255]   Bertoncini M, Pernici B, Salomie I, *et al.* Games: Green active management of energy in it service centres. In: Forum at the Conference on Advanced Information Systems Engineering (CAiSE). Springer; 2010. p. 238–252.

[256]   Basmadjian R, Lovasz G, Beck M, *et al.* A generic architecture for demand response: The ALL4Green approach. In: 2013 Third International Conference on Cloud and Green Computing (CGC). IEEE; 2013. p. 464–471.

[257]   vor dem Berge M, Christmann W, Volk E, *et al.* CoolEmAll-Models and tools for optimization of data center energy-efficiency. In: Sustainable Internet and ICT for Sustainability (SustainIT), 2012. IEEE; 2012. p. 1–5.

[258]   Wajid U, Pernici B, Francis G. Energy efficient and CO2 aware cloud computing: Requirements and case study. In: 2013 IEEE International Conference on Systems, Man, and Cybernetics (SMC). IEEE; 2013. p. 121–126.

[259]   Pierson JM, al. datazero: DATAcenter with Zero Emission and RObust management using renewable energy. IRIT; 2018.

[260] Delaval G, Gueye SMK, Rutten E, *et al.* Modular coordination of multiple autonomic managers. In: Proceedings of the 17th International ACM Sigsoft Symposium on Component-based Software Engineering. ACM; 2014. p. 3–12.

[261] Zhang Y, Wang Y, Wang X. GreenWare: Greening cloud-scale data centers to maximize the use of renewable energy. In: Kon F, Kermarrec AM, editors. Middleware 2011. Berlin, Heidelberg: Springer Berlin Heidelberg; 2011. p. 143–164.

[262] Andre JC, Antoniu G, Asch M, *et al.* Big data and extreme-scale computing: Pathways to convergence. University of Tennesse; 2018. Available from: http://www.exascale.org/bdec/sites/www.exascale.org.bdec/files/whitepaper s/bdec2017pathways.pdf.

[263] Acton M, Bertoldi P, Booth J, *et al.* 2018 Best Practice Guidelines for the EU Code of Conduct on Data Centre Energy Efficiency. Joint Research Centre; 2018. Available from: http://publications.jrc.ec.europa. eu/repository/bitstream/JRC110666/kjna29103enn.pdf.

[264] Committee AT. Data Center Design and Operation. ASHRAE Datacom Series; 2014.

[265] Sartor D. Best Practices for Data Center Energy Efficiency; 2017. Available from: https://datacenters.lbl.gov/sites/default/files/Shanghai%20Data %20Center%20Dynamics%20Workshop%20060917%20%281%29.pdf.

[266] Open Data Center; 2018. Available from: http://www.opendatacenter.cn.

[267] Open Compute Project; 2018. Available from: http://www.opencompute.org/.

[268] Barrass H, Belady C, Berard S, *et al.* PUE: A comprehensive examination of the metric. The Green Grid; 2012. Available from: https://datacenters.lbl.gov/sites/default/files/WP49-PUE%20A%20Compreh hensive%20Examination%20of%20the%20Metric_v6.pdf.

[269] Barroso LA, Clidaras J, Hölzle U. The datacenter as a computer: An introduction to the design of warehouse-scale machines (2nd ed.). Vol. 24 of Synthesis Lectures on Computer Architecture; 2013.

[270] Fu RH, He ZG, Zhang X. Life cycle cost based optimization design method for an integrated cooling system with multi-operating modes. Applied Thermal Engineering. 2018;140:432–441. Available from: https://www.sciencedirect.com/ science/article/pii/S1359431118309049.

[271] Chen H, Cheng WL, Zhang WW, *et al.* Energy saving evaluation of a novel energy system based on spray cooling for supercomputer center. Energy. 2017;141:304–315. Available from: http://www.sciencedirect.com/ science/article/pii/S0360544217316080.

[272] Ndukaife TA, Nnanna AGA. Optimization of water consumption in hybrid evaporative cooling air conditioning systems for data center cooling applications. Heat Transfer Engineering. 2018; p. 1–15. Available from: https://doi.org/10.1080/01457632.2018.1436418.

[273] Li Z, Kandlikar SG. Current status and future trends in data-center cooling technologies. Heat Transfer Engineering. 2015;36(6):523–538. Available from: https://doi.org/10.1080/01457632.2014.939032.

[274]   vor dem Berge M, Costa GD, Kopecki A, *et al.* Modeling and simulation of data center energy-efficiency in CoolEmAll. In: Energy Efficient Data Centers (E2DC 2012); 2012. p. 25–36.

[275]   Oleksiak A, Piatek W, Kuczynski K, *et al.* Reducing energy costs in data centres using renewable energy sources and energy storage. In: Proceedings of the 5th International Workshop on Energy Efficient Data Centres. E2DC'16. New York, NY, USA: ACM; 2016. p. 5:1–5:8. Available from: http://doi.acm.org/10.1145/2940679.2940684.

[276]   Center for Expertise in Energy Efficient Data Centers; 2018. Available from: https://datacenters.lbl.gov/.

[277]   The Green Grid; 2018. Available from: https://www.thegreengrid.org.

[278]   Asetek; 2018. Available from: https://www.asetek.com/.

[279]   Aquaris^{TM} Water Cooled Cooling Solutions; 2018. Available from: https://www.aquilagroup.com/aquarius/.

[280]   CoolIT; 2018. Available from: https://www.coolitsystems.com.

[281]   Green Revolution Cooling; 2018. Available from: https://www.grcooling.com/.

[282]   Eiland R, Fernandes JE, Vallejo M, *et al.* Thermal performance and efficiency of a mineral oil immersed server over varied environmental operating conditions. Journal of Electronic Packaging. 2017;139:041005. Available from: https://doi.org/10.1007/s00450-016-0328-1.

[283]   Rugged POD; 2018. Available from: http://www.horizon-computing.com/?page_id=172.

[284]   Tuma PE. Evaporator/boiler design for thermosyphons utilizing segregated hydrofluoroether working fluids. In: Twenty-Second Annual IEEE Semiconductor Thermal Measurement And Management Symposium; 2006. p. 69–77.

[285]   Tuma PE. Fluoroketone C2F5C(O)CF(CF3)2 as a Heat Transfer Fluid for Passive and Pumped 2-Phase Applications. In: 2008 Twenty-fourth Annual IEEE Semiconductor Thermal Measurement and Management Symposium; 2008. p. 173–179.

[286]   Tuma PE. Design considerations relating to non-thermal aspects of passive 2-phase immersion cooling. In: 2011 27th Annual IEEE Semiconductor Thermal Measurement and Management Symposium; 2011. p. 1–9.

[287]   Campbell L, Tuma P. Numerical prediction of the junction-to-fluid thermal resistance of a 2-phase immersion-cooled IBM dual core POWER6 processor. In: 2012 28th Annual IEEE Semiconductor Thermal Measurement and Management Symposium (SEMI-THERM); 2012. p. 36–44.

[288]   Coles H, Ellsworth M, Martinez DJ. "Hot" for Warm Water Cooling. In: State of the Practice Reports. SC'11. New York, NY, USA: ACM; 2011. p. 17:1–17:10. Available from: http://doi.acm.org/10.1145/2063348.2063371.

[289]   Smoyer JL, Norris PM. Brief historical perspective in thermal management and the shift toward management at the nanoscale. Heat Transfer Engineering. 2018; p. 1–14. Available from: https://doi.org/10.1080/01457632.2018.1426265.

[290] Qouneh A, Li C, Li T. A Quantitative analysis of cooling power in container-based data centers. In: Proceedings of the 2011 IEEE International Symposium on Workload Characterization. IISWC'11. Washington, DC, USA: IEEE Computer Society; 2011. p. 61–71. Available from: http://dx.doi.org/10.1109/IISWC.2011.6114197.

[291] Flucker S, Tozer R. Data centre energy efficiency analysis to minimize total cost of ownership. Building Services Engineering Research and Technology. 2013;34(1):103–117. Available from: https://doi.org/10.1177/0143624412467196.

[292] Hardware Labs; 2018. Available from: http://hardwarelabs.com/.

[293] Svensson G, Södberg J. A heat re-use system for the Cray XE6 and future systems at PDC, KTH. In: Proceedings of Cray User Group. Stuttgart, Germany: Cray User Group; 2012. .

[294] Romero M, Hasselqvist H, Svensson G. Supercomputers Keeping People Warm in the Winter. In: Proceedings of the 2014 conference ICT for Sustainability. Advances in Computer Science Research. Paris, France: Atlantis Press; 2014. p. 324–332. Available from: https://www.atlantis-press.com/proceedings/ict4s-14/13458.

[295] Ovaska SJ, Dragseth RE, Hanssen SA. Direct-to-chip liquid cooling for reducing power consumption in a subarctic supercomputer centre. International Journal of High Performance Computing Network. 2016;9(3):242–249. Available from: http://dx.doi.org/10.1504/IJHPCN.2016.076269.

[296] Shoji F, Tanaka K, Matsushita S, *et al.* Improving the energy efficiencies of power supply and cooling facilities for 10 peta-scale supercomputer. Computer Science – Research and Development. 2016;31(4):235–243. Available from: https://doi.org/10.1007/s00450-016-0328-1.

[297] Coles H, Herrlin M. Immersion Cooling of Electronics in DoD Installations. Lawrence Berkeley National Laboratory; 2016. LBNL-1005666. Available from: https://datacenters.lbl.gov/sites/default/files/ImmersionCooling2016.pdf.

[298] Volk E, Rathgeb D, Oleksiak A. CoolEmAll–optimising cooling efficiency in data centres. Computer Science – Research and Development. 2014;29(3–4):253–261. Available from: https://doi.org/10.1007/s00450-013-0246-4.

[299] Kurowski K, Oleksiak A, Piatek W, *et al.* DCworms – A tool for simulation of energy efficiency in distributed computing infrastructures. Simulation Modelling Practice and Theory. 2013;39:135–151. Available from: https://doi.org/10.1016/j.simpat.2013.08.007.

[300] OpenFOAM; 2018. Available from: https://openfoam.org/.

[301] OpenLB; 2018. Available from: http://optilb.org/.

[302] Palabos; 2018. Available from: https://palabos.org/.

[303] Fluent; 2018. Available from: https://www.ansys.com/Products/Fluids/ANSYS-Fluent.

[304] CoolSim; 2018. Available from: http://coolsimsoftware.com.

[305] Comsol Multiphysics; 2018. Available from: https://comsol.com/.

[306]   Star-CCM+; 2018. Available from: https://mdx.plm.automation.siemens. com/star-ccm-plus.

[307]   6SigmaRoom; 2018. Available from: https://www.futurefacilities.com/produ cts/6sigmaroom/.

[308]   FlowTherm; 2018. Available from: https://www.mentor.com/products/ mechanical/flotherm/.

[309]   TileFlow; 2018. Available from: http://inres.com/Products/TileFlow/ tile-flow.html.

[310]   Dakota; 2018. Available from: https://dakota.sandia.gov/.

[311]   Kunkel J. Virtual Institute for I/O; 2018. Available from: https://www. vi4io.org/.

[312]   Bates N. Energy Efficiency Working Group; 2018. Available from: https:// eehpcwg.llnl.gov.

[313]   Varrette S, Bouvry P, Cartiaux H, *et al.* Management of an Academic HPC Cluster: The UL Experience. In: Proceedings of the 2014 International Conference on High Performance Computing & Simulation (HPCS 2014). Bologna, Italy: IEEE; 2014. p. 959–967.

[314]   Emeras J, Varrette S, Bouvry P. Amazon Elastic Compute Cloud (EC2) vs. in-House HPC Platform: A Cost Analysis. In: Proceedings of the 9th IEEE International Conference on on Cloud Computing (CLOUD 2016). San Francisco, USA: IEEE Computer Society; 2016. p. 284–293.

[315]   Jiang W, Liu F, Tang G, *et al.* Virtual machine power accounting with Shapley value. In: IEEE International Conference on Distributed Computing Systems (ICDCS); 2017. p. 1683–1693.

[316]   Kurpicz M, Orgerie AC, Sobe A, *et al.* Energy-proportional profiling and accounting in heterogeneous virtualized environments. Sustainable Computing: Informatics and Systems. 2017;18:175–185.

[317]   Margery D, Guyon D, Orgerie AC, *et al.* A CO_2 emissions accounting framework with market-based incentives for cloud infrastructures. In: International Conference on Smart Cities and Green ICT Systems (SMARTGREENS); 2017. p. 299–304.

[318]   Cappello F, Caron E, Dayde M, *et al.* Grid'5000: A large scale and highly reconfigurable grid experimental testbed. In: The 6th IEEE/ACM International Workshop on Grid Computing, 2005; 2005. p. 8.

[319]   O'Loughlin J, Gillam L. Towards Performance Prediction for Public Infrastructure Clouds: An EC2 Case Study. In: CloudCom 2013 IEEE. vol. 1; 2013. p. 475–480.

[320]   Ostermann S, Iosup A, Yigitbasi N, *et al.* A Performance analysis of EC2 cloud computing services for scientific computing. In: Avresky D, Diaz M, Bode A, *et al.*, editors. Cloud Computing. vol. 34. Springer Berlin; 2010. p. 115–131.

[321]   Jiang C, Wang Y, Ou D, *et al.* Energy proportional servers: Where are we in 2016? In: IEEE International Conference on Distributed Computing Systems (ICDCS); 2017. p. 1649–1660.

[322] Statista. Global electricity prices by select countries in 2017; 2017. urlhttps://www.statista.com/statistics/263492/electricity-prices-in-selected-countries/.

[323] Guyon D, Orgerie AC, Morin C. GLENDA: Green Label Towards Energy proportioNality for IaaS DAta Centers. In: International Conference on Future Energy Systems (e-Energy) Workshops; 2017. p. 302–308.

[324] Sastre J, Ibáñez JJ, Defez E, *et al.* Efficient scaling-squaring Taylor method for computing matrix exponential. SIAM Journal on Scientific Computing. 2015;37(1):A439–455.

[325] Hochbruck M, Lubich C, Selhofer H. Exponential integrators for large systems of differential equations. The SIAM Journal on Scientific Computing. 1998 Sep;19(5):1552–1574.

[326] Higham NJ. Functions of Matrices: Theory and Computation. Philadelphia, PA, USA: SIAM; 2008.

[327] Williams DF, Hayden LA, Marks RB. A complete multimode equivalent-circuit theory for electrical design. Journal of Research of the National Institute of Standards and Technology. 1997;102(4):405–423.

[328] Cox SM, Matthews PC. Exponential time differencing for stiff systems. Journal of Computing Physics. 2002;176:430–455.

[329] Kassam AK, Trefethen LN. Fourth-order time-stepping for stiff PDEs. SIAM Journal on Scientific Computing. 2005;26(4):1214–1233.

[330] Sastre J, Ibáñez JJ, Defez E, *et al.* Computing matrix functions arising in engineering models with orthogonal matrix polynomials. Mathematical and Computer Modelling. 2013;57:1738–1743.

[331] Sastre J, Ibáñez JJ, Defez E, *et al.* Accurate matrix exponential computation to solve coupled differential. Mathematical and Computer Modelling. 2011;54:1835–1840.

[332] Alonso P, Ibáñez J, Sastre J, *et al.* Efficient and accurate algorithms for computing matrix trigonometric functions. Journal of Computational and Applied Mathematics. 2017;309:325–332.

[333] Alonso P, Peinado J, Ibáñez J, *et al.* Computing matrix trigonometric functions with GPUs through Matlab. Journal of Supercomputing. 2018. p. 1–14.

[334] Beaumont O, Boudet V, Legrand A, *et al.* Heterogeneous matrix-matrix multiplication, or partitioning a square into rectangles: NP-completeness and approximation algorithms. In: EuroMicro Workshop on Parallel and Distributed Computing (EuroMicro'2001). IEEE Computer Society Press; 2001. p. 298–305.

[335] DeFlumere A, Lastovetsky A, Becker B, *et al.* Partitioning for parallel matrix-matrix multiplication with heterogeneous processors: The optimal solution. In: Parallel and Distributed Processing Symposium Workshops & PhD Forum (IPDPSW), IEEE 26th International. IEEE; 2012. p. 125–139.

[336] Tomov S, Dongarra J, Baboulin M. Towards dense linear algebra for hybrid GPU accelerated manycore systems. Parallel Computing. 2010;36(5–6): 232–240.

[337]   Haidar A, Dongarra J, Kabir K, *et al.* HPC Programming on Intel Many-Integrated-Core Hardware with MAGMA Port to Xeon Phi. Scientific Programming. 2015. Article ID 502593, p. 1–11.

[338]   Lawson CL, Hanson RJ, Kincaid DR, *et al.* Basic linear algebra subprograms for Fortran Usage. ACM Transactions on Mathematical Software. 1979;5(3):308–323.

[339]   Intel Corporation. Intel Math Kernel Library (MKL). Accessed: 2016-04-12. Available from: http://software.intel.com/en-us/intel-mkl.

[340]   OpenBLAS: An optimized BLAS library. Accessed: 2016-04-12. http://www.openblas.net.

[341]   Van Zee FG, van de Geijn RA. BLIS: A framework for rapidly instantiating BLAS functionality. ACM Transactions on Mathematical Software. 2015;41(3):14:1–14:33. Available from: https://github.com/flame/blis.

[342]   NVIDIA. NVIDIA CUDA Basic Linear Algebra Subroutines (cuBLAS) library; 2016. https://developer.nvidia.com/cublas.

[343]   The Open MPI Team. Open Message Passing Iterface: Open Source High Performance Computing; 2016. Accessed: 2016-04-12. https://www.open-mpi.org.

[344]   Ravi Reddy Manumachu. `powerrun`: A tool to measure energy.

[345]   NVIDIA. NVML Reference Manual; 2013. https://developer.nvidia.com/nvidia-management-library-nvml.

[346]   Intel Corporation. Intel Manycore Platform Software Stack (Intel MPSS); 2016. Available from: https://software.intel.com/en-us/articles/intel-manycore-platform-software-stack-mpss.

[347]   Zhuo J, Chakrabarti C. Energy-efficient dynamic task scheduling algorithms for DVS systems. ACM Transactions on Embedded Computing Systems 2008;7(2):1–25.

[348]   Rauber T, Rünger G, Stachowski M. Model-based Optimization of the Energy Efficiency of Multi-threaded Applications. In: Proceedings of the 8th International Green and Sustainable Computing Conference (IGSC'17); 2017. p. 1–6.

[349]   Choi J, Bedard D, Fowler RJ, *et al.* A Roofline Model of Energy. In: 27th IEEE International Symposium on Parallel and Distributed Processing, IPDPS 2013, Cambridge, MA, USA, May 20-24, 2013. IEEE Computer Society; 2013. p. 661–672. Available from: https://doi.org/10.1109/IPDPS.2013.77.

[350]   Rauber T, Rünger G. How do loop transformations affect the energy consumption of multi-threaded Runge-Kutta methods? In: Proceedings of the 26th Euromicro International Conference on Parallel, Distributed and Network-Based Processing; 2018. p. 499–507.

[351]   Cabrera A, Almeida F, Blanco V, *et al.* Analytical modeling of the energy consumption for the high performance Linpack. In: 2013 21st Euromicro International Conference on Parallel, Distributed, and Network-Based Processing; 2013. p. 343–350.

[352]   Cabrera A, Almeida F, Arteaga J, *et al.* Measuring energy consumption using EML (energy measurement library). Computer Science – Research and Development. 2015;30(2):135–143. Available from: https://doi.org/10.1007/s00450-014-0269-5.

[353]   Zaslavsky GM. Chaos, fractional kinetics, and anomalous transport. Physics Reports. 2002;371(6):461–580.

[354]   EringenBates AC. Nonlocal Continuum Field Theories. Springer; 2002.

[355]   Silling SA. Reformulation of elasticity theory for discontinuities and long-range forces. Journal of the Mechanics and Physics of Solids. 2000;48(1):175–209.

[356]   Bakunin OG. Turbulence and Diffusion: Scaling Versus Equations. Springer; 2008.

[357]   McCay BM, Narasimhan MNL. Theory of nonlocal electromagnetic fluids. Archives of Mechanics. 1981;33(3):365–384.

[358]   Ainsworth M, Glusa C. Aspects of an adaptive finite element method for the fractional Laplacian: A priori and a posteriori error estimates, efficient implementation and multigrid solver. Computer Methods in Applied Mechanics and Engineering. 2017;327:4–35.

[359]   Bear J, Cheng AHD. Modeling Groundwater Flow and Contaminant Transport. Springer; 2010.

[360]   Bates PW. On some nonlocal evolution equations arising in materials science. Nonlinear Dynamics and Evolution Equations. 2006;48:13–52.

[361]   Zijlstra ES, Kalitsov A, Zier T, *et al.* Fractional diffusion in silicon. Advanced Materials. 2013;25(39):5605–5608.

[362]   Bueno-Orovio A, Kay D, Grau V, *et al.* Fractional diffusion models of cardiac electrical propagation: Role of structural heterogeneity in dispersion of repolarization. Journal of the Royal Society Interface. 2014;11(97). Available from: https://doi.org/10.1098/rsif.2014.0352.

[363]   Harizanov S, Margenov S, Marinov P, *et al.* Volume constrained 2-phase segmentation method for utilizing a linear system solver based on the best uniform polynomial approximation of $x^{-1/2}$. Journal of Computational and Applied Mathematics. 2017;310:115–128.

[364]   Gilboa G, Osher S. Nonlocal operators with applications to image processing. Multiscale Modeling & Simulation. 2008;7(3):1005–1028.

[365]   Abirami A, Prakash P, Thangavel K. Fractional diffusion equation-based image denoising model using CN–GL scheme. International Journal of Computer Mathematics. 2017;p. 1–18.

[366]   Kilbas AA, Srivastava HM, Trujillo JJ. Theory and Applications of Fractional Differential Equations. Elsevier; 2006.

[367]   Pozrikidis C. The Fractional Laplacian. Chapman and Hall/CRC; 2016.

[368]   Čiegis R, Starikovičius V, Margenov S. On parallel numerical algorithms for fractional diffusion problems. In: Proceedings of the Third International Workshop on Sustainable Ultrascale Computing Systems (NESUS 2016). IICT-BAS, Sofia, Bulgaria; October 6–7, 2016. p. 85–90. NESUS, ICT COST Action IC1305.

[369] Čiegis R, Starikovičius V, Margenov S, *et al.* Parallel solvers for frac-
       tional power diffusion problems. Concurrency and Computation: Practice
       and Experience. 2017;25(24):e4216.

[370] Čiegis R, Starikovičius V, Margenov S, *et al.* A comparison of accuracy and
       efficiency of parallel solvers for fractional power diffusion problems. In:
       Parallel Processing and Applied Mathematics, (PPAM2017, Lublin, Poland,
       September 9–13, 2017) Proceedings, part I. vol. 10777 of Lecture Notes in
       Computer Science. Berlin, Heidelberg: Springer; 2018. p. 79–89.

[371] Nochetto RH, Otárola E, Salgado AJ. A PDE approach to fractional diffusion
       in general domains: A priori error analysis. Foundations of Computational
       Mathematics. 2015;15(3):733–791.

[372] Vabishchevich P. Numerical solving unsteady space-fractional problems with
       the square root of an elliptic operator. Mathematical Modelling and Analysis.
       2016;21(2):220–238.

[373] Bonito A, Pasciak JE. Numerical approximation of fractional powers of
       elliptic operators. Mathematics of Computation. 2015;84(295):2083–2110.

[374] Harizanov S, Lazarov R, Marinov P, *et al.* Optimal solvers for linear systems
       with fractional powers of sparse SPD matrices. Numerical Linear Algebra
       with Applications. 2018.

[375] Napov A, Notay Y. An algebraic multigrid method with guaranteed
       convergence rate. SIAM Journal on Scientific Computing. 2012;34(2):
       A1079–A1109.

[376] Falgout R, Yang U. Hypre: A library of high performance preconditioners. In:
       Computational Science 2002. International Conference (ICCS, Amsterdam,
       The Netherlands, April 21–24, 2002) Proceedings, part III. vol. 2331 of
       Lecture Notes in Computer Science. Berlin, Heidelberg: Springer; 2002.
       p. 632–641.

[377] Falgout R, Jones J, Yang U. The design and implementation of Hypre, a
       library of parallel high performance preconditioners. In: Numerical Solution
       of Partial Differential Equations on Parallel Computers, part III. Vol. 51 of
       Lecture Notes in Computational Science and Engineering. Springer, Berlin,
       Heidelberg; 2006. p. 264–294.

[378] Bonito A, Lei W, Pasciak JE. The approximation of parabolic equations involv-
       ing fractional powers of elliptic operators. Journal of Computational and
       Applied Mathematics. 2017;315:32–48.

[379] Bonito A, Borthagaray J, Nochetto RH, *et al.* Numerical methods for fractional
       diffusion. Computing and Visualization in Science. 2017. p. 1–28.

[380] Lazarov R, Vabishchevich P. A numerical study of the homogeneous elliptic
       equation with fractional order boundary conditions. Fractional Calculus and
       Applied Analysis. 2017;20(2):337–351.

[381] Acosta G, Borthagaray J. A fractional Laplace equation: Regularity of
       solutions and finite element approximations. SIAM Journal on Numerical
       Analysis. 2017;55(2):472–495.

[382] Vabishchevich PN. Numerically solving an equation for fractional powers of elliptic operators. Journal of Computational Physics. 2015;282: 189–302.

[383] Čiegis R, Starikovičius V, Tumanova N, *et al.* Application of distributed parallel computing for dynamic visual cryptography. Journal of Supercomputing. 2016;72(11):4204–4220.

[384] Nochetto R, Otárola E, Salgado A. A PDE approach to numerical fractional diffusion. In: Proceedings of the 8th ICIAM, Beijing, China; 2015. p. 211–236.

[385] Quarteroni A, Valli A. Domain decomposition methods for partial differential equations. Oxford Science Publications; 1999.

[386] Čiegis R, Tumanova N. On construction and analysis of finite difference schemes for pseudoparabolic problems with nonlocal boundary conditions. Mathematical Modelling and Analysis. 2014;19(2):281–297.

[387] Varga RS, Carpenter AJ. Some numerical results on best uniform rational approxiumation of x^α on [0, 1]. Numerical Algorithms. 1992;2(2):171–185.

[388] Amiranashvili S, Čiegis R, Radziunas M. Numerical methods for a class of generalized nonlinear Schrödinger equations. Kinetic and Related Models. 2015;8(2):215–234.

[389] Hadamard J. Sur les Problemes aux Derivees Partielles et leur Signification Physique. Bull Princeton University; 1902.

[390] Lowrie W. Fundamentals of Geophysics. Cambridge University Press; 2007.

[391] Sen M, Stoffa P. Global Optimization Methods in Geophysical Inversion. Elsevier Science B.V.; 1995.

[392] Xiaobing Z. Analytic solution of the gravity anomaly of irregular 2D masses with density contrast varying as a 2D polynomial function. Geophysics. 2010;75(2):I11–I19.

[393] Xiaobing Z. 3D vector gravity potential and line integrals for the gravity anomaly of a rectangular prism with 3D variable density contrast. Geophysics. 2009;74(6):I43–I53.

[394] Silva J, Medeiros WE, Barbosa VCF. Gravity inversion using convexity constraint. Geophysics. 2000;65(1):102–112.

[395] 3D stochastic inversion of borehole and surface gravity data using geostatistics. In: EGM International Workshop on Adding new Value to Electromagnetic, Gravity and Magnetic Methods for Exploration, Capri, Italy, April 11–14; 2010.

[396] Wellmann FJ, Horowitz FG, Schill E, *et al.* Towards incorporating uncertainty of structural data in 3D geological inversion. Elsevier Tectonophysics TECTO-124902; 2010;490(3–4):141–151.

[397] Zhdanov MS, Wilson GA, Xiaojun L. 3D imaging of subsurface structures using migration and regularized focusing inversion of gravity and gravity gradiometry data. Airborne Gravity - Abstracts from the ASEG-PESA Airborne Gravity Workshop, Geoscience Australia Record. 2010;23.

[398]   Kiflu H, Kruse S, Loke MH, *et al.* Improving resistivity survey resolution at sites with limited spatial extent using buried electrode arrays. Journal of Applied Geophysics. 2016;135:338–355.

[399]   Rickwood P, Sambridge M. Efficient parallel inversion using the neighborhood algorithm. Geochemistry Geophysics Geosystems – Electronic Journal of the Earth Sciences. 2006;7(11):1–16.

[400]   Loke MH, Wilkinson P. Rapid parallel computation of optimized arrays for electrical imaging surveys. In: Near Surface 2009 – 15th European Meeting of Environmental and Engineering Geophysics, Dublin, Ireland, 7–9 September 2009. p. B11.

[401]   Zuzhi H, Zhanxiang H, Yongtao W, *et al.* Constrained inversion of magnetotelluric data using parallel simulated annealing algorithm and its application. In: EM P4 Modeling and Inversion, v.29. SEG Denver Annual Meeting – SEG Expanded Abstracts; 2010. p. 895–899.

[402]   Wilson G, Čuma M, Zhdanov MS. Massively parallel 3D inversion of gravity and gravity gradiometry data. Magazine of the Australian Society of Exploration Geophysicists (Preview). 2011; p. 29–34. Available from: http://www.cemi.utah.edu/PDF_70_10/2011c.pdf.

[403]   Högbom JA. Aperture synthesis with a non-regular distribution of interferometer baselines. Astronomy and Astrophysics, Supplement. 1974;15:417.

[404]   Frasheri N, Bushati S. An algorithm for gravity anomaly inversion in HPC. SCPE: Scalable Computing: Practice and Experience. 2012;13(2):51–69.

[405]   Frasheri N, Cico B. Analysis of the convergence of iterative gravity inversion in parallel systems. In: Kocarev L, editor. Springer Advances in Intelligent and Soft Computing 150: ICT Innovations 2011. Springer-Verlag; 2012. p. 219–222.

[406]   Frasheri N, Cico B. Scalability of geophysical inversion with OpenMP and MPI in parallel processing. In: Markovski S, Gusev M, editors. Springer Advances in Intelligent Systems and Computing 207: ICT Innovations 2012: Secure and Intelligent Systems. Springer-Verlag; 2013. p. 345–352.

[407]   A parallel processing algorithm for gravity inversion. European Geosciences Union General Assembly EGU'2013 Vienna 7-12 April; 2013. Available from: https://meetingorganizer.copernicus.org/EGU2013/EGU2013-8739-1.pdf.

[408]   Brélaz D. New methods to color the vertices of a graph. Communications of the ACM. 1979;22(4):251–256.

[409]   Culberson J. Iterated greedy graph coloring and the difficulty landscape. University of Alberta; 1992.

[410]   Sloane N. Challenge problems: Independent sets in graphs. Information Sciences Research Center, http://neilsloane com/doc/graphs html. 2005.

[411]   Hasselberg J, Pardalos PM, Vairaktarakis G. Test case generators and computational results for the maximum clique problem. Journal of Global Optimization. 1993;3(4):463–482.

[412]   Szabó S. Monotonic matrices and clique search in graphs. Annales Universitatis Scientiarium Budapestinensis, Sect Comp. 2013;41:307–322.

[413] Szabó S, Zaválnij B. Benchmark problems for exhaustive exact maximum clique search algorithms. In: Middle-European Conference on Applied Theoretical Computer Science (MATCOS 2016): Proceedings of the 19th International Multiconference. Information Society – IS; 2016. p. 65–67.

[414] Karger D, Motwani R, Sudan M. Approximate graph coloring by semidefinite programming. Journal of the ACM (JACM). 1998;45(2):246–265.

[415] Godsil C, Royle GF. Algebraic graph theory. vol. 207. Springer Science & Business Media; 2013.

[416] Elphick C, Wocjan P. An inertial lower bound for the chromatic number of a graph. The Electronic Journal of Combinatorics. 2017;24(1):1–9.

[417] Östergård PR. A fast algorithm for the maximum clique problem. Discrete Applied Mathematics. 2002;120(1–3):197–207.

[418] Li CM, Quan Z. An efficient branch-and-bound algorithm based on MaxSAT for the maximum clique problem. In: Proc. of American Associations for Artificial Intelligence. Vol. 10; 2010. p. 128–133.

[419] Li CM, Fang Z, Xu K. Combining MaxSAT reasoning and incremental upper bound for the maximum clique problem. In: Tools with Artificial Intelligence (ICTAI), 2013 IEEE 25th International Conference on. IEEE; 2013. p. 939–946.

[420] San Segundo P, Nikolaev A, Batsyn M. Infra-chromatic bound for exact maximum clique search. Computers & Operations Research. 2015;64:293–303.

[421] Szabó S, Zaválnij B. Reducing graph coloring to clique search. Asia Pacific Journal of Mathematics. 2016;3(1):64–85.

[422] Li CM, Quan Z. Combining graph structure exploitation and propositional reasoning for the maximum clique problem. In: 2010 22nd IEEE International Conference on Tools with Artificial Intelligence (ICTAI). vol. 1. IEEE; 2010. p. 344–351.

[423] Fu Z, Malik S. On solving the partial MAX-SAT problem. In: International Conference on Theory and Applications of Satisfiability Testing – SAT2006. Lecture Notes in Computer Science; 2006. p. 252–265.

[424] Lovász L. On the Shannon capacity of a graph. IEEE Transactions on Information Theory. 1979;25(1):1–7.

[425] Borchers B. CSDP, A C library for semidefinite programming. Optimization methods and Software. 1999;11(1–4):613–623.

[426] Borchers B, Young JG. Implementation of a primal–dual method for SDP on a shared memory parallel architecture. Computational Optimization and Applications. 2007;37(3):355–369.

[427] Carraghan R, Pardalos PM. An exact algorithm for the maximum clique problem. Operations Research Letters. 1990;9(6):375–382.

[428] Balas E, Yu CS. Finding a maximum clique in an arbitrary graph. SIAM Journal on Computing. 1986;15(4):1054–1068.

[429] Zavalnij B. Speeding up Parallel Combinatorial Optimization Algorithms with Las Vegas Method. In: 10th International Conference on Large-Scale Scientific Computing. Lecture Notes in Computer Science; 2015. p. 258–266.

[430]   Tanenbaum AS, Van Steen M. Distributed Systems: Principles and Paradigms. 2nd edition. Prentice-Hall, Inc.; 2006.

[431]   Coulouris G, Dollimore J, Kindberg T, et al. Distributed Systems: Concepts and Design. 5th edition. Addison-Wesley Publishing Company; 2011.

[432]   Hwang K, Dongarra J, Fox GC. Distributed and Cloud Computing: From Parallel Processing to the Internet of Things. 1st edition. Morgan Kaufmann Publishers Inc.; 2011.

Index